P9-DDF-815

Swingin' the Dream

BIG BAND JAZZ
AND THE REBIRTH
OF AMERICAN
CULTURE

LEWIS A. ERENBERG

The University of Chicago Press   Chicago & London

LEWIS A. ERENBERG is professor of history and director of graduate programs at Loyola University.

The University of Chicago Press, Chicago 60637
The University of Chicago Press, Ltd., London
© 1998 by The University of Chicago
All rights reserved. Published 1998
Printed in the United States of America
07 06 05 04 03 02 01 00 99 98   1 2 3 4 5

ISBN: 0-226-21516-4

Title page photograph courtesy Frank Driggs Collection.

Library of Congress Cataloging-in-Publication Data

Erenberg, Lewis A., 1944–
    Swingin' the dream : big band jazz and the rebirth of
American culture / Lewis A. Erenberg.
        p.   cm.
    Includes index.
    ISBN 0-226-21516-4 (alk. paper)
    1. Big band music—History and criticism.   2. Jazz—History
and criticism.   3. Popular culture—United States.   I. Title.
ML3518.E74   1998
781.65'4'0973—dc21   97-39135
                                                          CIP

♾ The paper used in this publication meets the minimum
requirements of the American National Standard for Information
Sciences—Permanence of Paper for Printed Library Materials,
ANSI Z39.48-1992.

For Sue

"AS TIME GOES BY"

Contents

Illustrations

Preface

In 1943, when *Metronome* magazine celebrated sixty years of covering American popular music, its editors took advantage of the occasion to express their great pride in the accomplishments of contemporary musicians. "Some day, when their music has been established for many years as the magnificent thing it is, Americans will look back to Benny Goodman and Duke Ellington, to the Dorseys and Count Basie, Benny Carter and Coleman Hawkins, and all their associates, as the heroes of a Golden Age." Writing during World War II, the editors allowed their patriotic rhetoric to soar. As they examined the slow emergence of popular music in the United States from under Europe's long shadow, they maintained that American national musical culture had reached a pinnacle, "for the final stage of this evolution finds America with the most brilliant group of musicians of our time." Unlike classical musicians, these "musical giants" were unconstrained by the "clumsy and narrow and twisted conventions which have straight-jacketed classical music in the twentieth century." Indeed, these big band leaders and musicians were part of a cultural rebirth that reached deep into the popular arts and American democratic culture to create "an era as important to American music as the time of Emerson and Thoreau and Whitman and Hawthorne and Melville was to American literature."[1]

This book is a cultural and social history of that "golden age," more conventionally known as the swing era, when from 1935 to 1948 big jazz bands defined and dominated popular music. Despite the soaring hopes exhibited by participants, by most accounts the music of the swing era offered only harmless fun or escapist release from the economic failures of the Great Depression. In particular, studies of big band jazz treat this musical expression as the commercial exploitation of black music and the delusions of white middle- and working-class youth in an era that called for greater radicalism. Musicologists continue to examine the era through the lens of commercialism, arguing that most of the big bands lacked jazz artistry and were influenced too much by commercial considerations. For some analysts, the popularity of big bands represents the culture industries' imposition of false values on unsuspecting youth. The best studies of big bands in general and swing in particular have been written from the perspective of bebop, which succeeded swing as the major innovative jazz form of the 1940s. As a result, they assume that little worthwhile occurred before the great bop explosion of the late 1940s.

There is no denying the tremendous commercial appeal of swing or the economic dominance of white bands, but the paradigms of commercialism and cultural hegemony offer little insight into the music's appeal to a mass youth audience. Nor do these models tell us how big bands evolved from the 1920s—when they were only one of several competing forms of popular music—to become the dominant paradigm in the music scene of the 1930s and 1940s. In general scholars have not fully grasped the forces that produced this musical culture and encouraged its national diffusion, nor the intense hopes that went into swinging the American Dream. Equally important, they have not examined the links between cultural expression and the politics and culture of the 1920s through the late 1940s and early 1950s. How do we explain the renaissance of democratic cultural forms, which *Metronome* noted, in the middle of the Great Depression? Or, as Eric Hobsbawm puts it, how did music of such quality emerge in a commercial music system in a time of such massive economic and political crisis? On a larger level, how do we take jazz out of the scholarly ghetto to which it has been consigned by historians to trace some of the deepest issues of American culture?[2]

To explore some of these questions, this study traces the development of big band jazz from the 1920s through the early 1950s as a vehicle for understanding the history of American culture and society during these years. By moving forward from the 1920s rather than backward from the 1940s, when swing seemed musically conventional, we can trace subtle but important shifts in American music and culture. Starting with Paul Whiteman's attempts to "civilize" African American music and Duke Ellington's efforts to claim European technique for black jazz, this book reveals how African American music became more central and visible in the bands of the 1930s and 1940s. I have situated this national musical culture in its commercial and creative capital, New York City, not to isolate big bands in the Big Apple but to explore how this urban form came to influence the rest of the country.

In the 1920s, between the poles of Harlem and Broadway, black and white jazz musicians from across the nation created what Ann Douglas calls a "mongrel," interracial musical vocabulary. Forged by blacks and children of immigrants, the new music of the 1920s gained wide national acceptance in the 1930s. Unmediated by moralist and governmental desires to uplift the music, black music and musicians gained new prominence in the national mass media of the swing era. A new mixed culture, formed by diverse populations in the vernacular arts, came to the fore. No longer despised as un-American music, swing symbolized a major reorientation in American national culture. For many of its most devoted fans, the music expressed a new model of pluralist democracy capable of challenging classical music for the mantle of cultural legitimacy and American national identity.[3]

Of course, swing bands, like the dance bands that preceded them and the bop combos that followed, had deep roots in youth culture. Like big band jazz, youth culture was not "invented" in the 1930s, and its association with music, fashion, and dating displays continuities with the peer culture of the 1920s. But by moving forward from the 1920s, we begin to discern subtle differences in the youth culture of depression and war. Fired by economic collapse, youth behavior and popular music registered the cultural and gender crisis of the day. Not only did bands change, with their particular representation of all-male musicians and female singers, to convey new models of gender interaction, but music institutions evolved differently as well. What did the decline of the nightclub and the rise of the ballroom, radio, or five-cent jukebox signify for depression youth? Why did these more inclusive musical institutions abandon jazz in the late 1940s?

Most studies of popular music focus heavily on music and musicians and pay little attention to audiences. A major stream of analysis suggests that the content of popular music is and was determined by those who own the means of musical production. A more recent school argues that audiences are not passive, but reinterpret music at the point of reception to suit their own purposes. My view is that at key points in the history of musical creativity and excitement, such as swing, the audience interacts with the creators of music and the musical promoters to determine the music's form and content.[4]

There are numerous descriptions of crowd behavior in the 1930s, in part because many people in and out of the music business were intensely concerned about whether mass culture was a harbinger of fascism, and in part because fans behaved in such noticeable ways. To determine audience response, I have examined several college newspapers (the Columbia *Spectator,* the UCLA *Bruin,* and the *Daily Illini*), and distributed questionnaires at fifty-year high school reunions of the class of 1939. I have also systematically read the music press—*Down Beat* and *Metronome,* especially—and the Communist and African American newspapers for the years 1934 to 1955. My most rewarding mode of inquiry has been the letter I placed in approximately two hundred newspapers nationwide seeking the experiences of fans of swing and bop. I received more than three hundred responses, many of them quite lengthy. From these sources it became clear to me that young people were part of a populist youth culture that treated the music as particularly theirs. As John Gennari notes, swing youth culture helped democratize connoisseurship and challenge the last vestiges of patrician, genteel cultural authority that had resided in the arts. If nothing else, this book should alert readers to a "missing era" of youth culture, which did not just emerge in the 1920s and then disappear in the depression, only to resurface in the prosperous 1950s.[5]

Most studies overlook music critics as well. This is unfortunate, for the writings of the 1930s critics shed much light on the political meanings of swing. During the 1920s jazz criticism was irregular, sporadic, and mostly negative. In the early 1930s, however, American jazz magazines appeared, thus placing the defense and definition of jazz in the hands of its friends. These young writers (primarily men) were intellectuals—often allied with the radical currents of the Popular Front and the New Deal. They not only appreciated the music's African American roots but also furthered its definition as a pluralist art form. For those who wanted to transform American society, swing represented a cultural phenomenon that bridged the significant gap between races and classes. The influence of the critics was not limited to the printed word, either, for as impresarios, talent scouts, and recording supervisors they pushed the music industry to include black artists. In the world of swing critics and the music press, politics and culture were often intertwined.

A key feature of big band swing was its synthesis of African American musical and dance styles for a white and black market. LeRoi Jones's *Blues People,* the most sophisticated study of modern black music, holds that in white hands *swing* went from verb to noun, becoming a commodity to be bought and sold for profit—primarily by whites. Yet, although black bands suffered commercial and racial disadvantages in the 1930s, it was then that black and white musicians first broke the color line in music, fraternized across the racial divide on a regular basis, and began the gradual, but for its day radical, integration of big bands. These challenges to white supremacy occurred a good decade before such changes took place in major league baseball or the armed forces.[6]

As David Stowe's *Swing Changes* argues, what stands out in the 1930s and 1940s is how the populist impulses of the day furthered appreciation of African American music and dance as the basis of a new American culture. An American identity based on whiteness was first questioned during the swing era. Many saw the music as an opening wedge for greater equality, although they might differ over how or what that meant. At the same time a number of businessmen in the mass media tried to keep the music white in order to ensure the largest possible "mass" market. These competing forces helped shape the limits of swing and set the stage for the bop revolt that followed.[7]

Equally important, race was "in play" because black bands imbued the entire popular music scene with greater populist energy. Historians and musicologists operating from the perspective of bebop have emphasized the conservatism of black bands. Jones, for example, dismisses most black big bands as too middle class, "white," and assimilationist. This interpretation makes light of the efforts of bandleaders and musicians who aspired to recognition as professional musicians and American artists. Moreover, this view provides little guidance in understanding the meanings the music had for its fans or the ways in which both blacks and whites exchanged culture and values through popular music. As Albert Murray and Ralph Ellison point out, black swing bands played powerful roles in black communities, and musicians served as popular heroes for African American youth. The music world underwent a populist regeneration during the middle years of the depression, as the swinging Kansas City blues of Count Basie attracted fans on a national and interracial level. In their own way, swing musicians served as models for racial pride and represented an assault on racial restrictions; they created a national black music that announced that African Americans had a rightful place in American life and culture.[8]

All of these contesting forces helped pave the way for a musical renaissance that appealed to young people, had interracial roots, and expressed in cultural form many of the themes of the depression—and the New Deal. At first glance, it might seem perverse to argue that a culture affirming personal experimentation, affluence, and ethnic and racial pluralism came to fruition within the context of the depression and the war. In fact, most historians assume that the depression signaled the decline of cultural values forged in big cities during the 1920s. Yet while many elements of urban culture did collapse, by the mid-1930s a regeneration of popular culture and music occurred in which New York City's influence reached a peak. In the guise of swing, jazz became the foundation of American popular music. An exploration of the national appeal of urban music allows us to see that amid the crises of depression and war, there emerged a new vision of American life. Swing music mirrored a new optimism about democratic culture, an appreciation of ethnic and racial pluralism, and a delight in the utopian promise of urban life. For a variety of fans in the 1930s and 1940s, dreams of new sexual relationships and new American identities came together in the throes of jitterbug dance.

As a key part of the growing consumer culture and as an expression of cultural pluralism, swing also played an important role in the American campaign against Nazism and racial supremacy during World War II. The war heightened and then exhausted the hopes engendered by swing as it brought the central musical and cultural tensions of the 1930s to a head. Swing musicians served the war effort in a variety of ways, from entertaining troops to enlisting in the military. But even while bands were promoted as the representatives of American democracy in action, deep-seated conflicts arose. Would swing promote democratic culture as racial pluralism, or would it perpetuate images of a home front that was increasingly depicted as white and private? Why were singers singled out as individuals rather than as part of the larger group? How did black bands and musicians react to themes of racial inclusion as they endured increased incidence of segregation? How did the racial achievements and racial tensions of the war interact with fears over gender to blunt the advance of swing and its successors, bebop and modern jazz?

The war was a turning point, as the musical culture that made up swing fragmented. By the late 1940s, new musical expressions appeared: bebop, which sought to reorder generational and racial power in jazz, and traditional jazz, which sought to resurrect the music of the first two decades of the century. Bop was new, to be sure, but it was not just a rebellion against swing. Instead, it emerged from and against the culture of swing and embodied both continuities and conflicts with its predecessor. Coming out of the war, music expressed many of the soaring hopes and fierce conflicts that embroiled American culture.[9]

As a cultural and social history of big bands, this study enters territory long claimed by musicologists and music critics, from whom I have learned an enormous amount. While not ignoring the contributions of individual musical giants, this work is part of a new jazz history that analyzes the music's historical and cultural context, exploring the ways in which the music was performed and presented to the public and the meanings that audiences and musicians attached to it. The history of the big band helps illuminate the sexual, racial, and political values in a youth and music culture that developed in the prosperity of the 1920s and reached fruition despite the traumas of depression, world war, and cold war.[10]

In studying music's role in the larger culture, I have sought to examine the many ways musicians, impresarios, critics, and audiences interacted to create meanings in the music. This dialogical or interactional approach differs from the more impositional models of culture, which posit a hegemonic control of mass communications industries over the musical product. In my view, the meaning of the music is contained not only in particular musical styles or song lyrics but also in the performance of that music before particular audiences. It is for this reason that I have actively pursued audience responses.[11]

While my book draws on the many excellent studies that portray the era as a distinct cultural moment, I depart from the view of the 1930s and 1940s as a conservative era of shame and insecurity in which Americans sought the reassurances of a homogeneous culture from an older, Protestant, small-town past. Such a view leaves little room for those creators of popular music from black and recent immigrant backgrounds who produced a different sound for modern America, one bound up with both the rural folk and the city. The white, Protestant model of the era overlooks the likes of Duke Ellington, Count Basie, and Benny Goodman, who carried the excitement, freedom, and diversity of the big city jazz age into the 1930s and 1940s. For the major black and white big bands of the era, the city remained the realm of modern hopes of freedom, and New York City stood as the capital of those aspirations. Some studies show a split between radical intellectuals and popular culture, but in music a group of swing intellectuals initially supported swing as the herald of a new national culture. At several levels, the swing band explosion suggests that the preoccupation with democratic cultural forms that marked the New Deal years was wider and deeper than we have previously realized.[12]

Acknowledgments

Over the course of researching and writing this book I have piled up more debts than I can ever hope to repay. First and foremost, I wish to thank the more than three hundred people who wrote to me of their fan experiences and the many others who sat for interviews. My good friend Elaine Tyler May graciously showed me the ropes of audience response research and gave me copies of the model letters she used in *Homeward Bound.* My research assistant, Scott Newman, helped me handle the flow of correspondence and keep track of the most interesting responses. Many other people made my task so much easier: the staffs of the Institute of Jazz Studies, Rutgers University; the Yale Music Library; the New York Library of the Performing Arts, Lincoln Center; Special Collections, Harold Washington Branch of the Chicago Public Library; and the Duke Ellington Scrapbook Project, Smithsonian Institution. Alan Cass at the Glenn Miller Archives, University of Colorado, Boulder, deserves a special mention for his generosity. Without Lorna Newman and her Interlibrary Loan staff at Loyola University's Cudahy Library it would have been impossible to complete this book. J. Fred MacDonald placed his enormous Archives of Popular Culture at my disposal, loaned me books and materials without question, and shared some of his own research data with me. The staff of the FBI made reams of material available to me. Erika Doss and Geof Thrumston housed me in Boulder, while Peter Hobbes ably duplicated materials at the Institute of Jazz Studies. Bill Adler arranged for me to interview members of the Evanston, Illinois, High School class of 1939. I also wish to thank the Fulbright Committee for making possible a delightful year in Munich and the National Endowment for the Humanities Summer Fellowship that enabled me to launch this study.

I am also grateful to several publishers for permission to reprint a number of materials. An earlier version of chapter 3 appeared as "Things to Come," in *Recasting America: Culture and Politics in the Age of Cold War,* ed. Lary May (University of Chicago Press, 1989); an earlier version of chapter 4 appeared as "News from the Great Wide World: Duke Ellington, Count Basie, and Black Popular Music, 1927–1943," *Prospects* 18 (1993), reprinted with the permission of Cambridge University Press; portions of chapter 6 appeared in "From New York to Middletown," *American Quarterly* 38 (winter 1986), reprinted by permission of Johns Hopkins University Press; and an earlier version of chapter 7 appeared as "Swing Goes to War," in *The War in American Culture: Society and Consciousness during World War II,* ed. Lewis A. Erenberg and Susan Hirsch (University of Chicago Press, 1996).

Loyola University has supported my work generously in the form of research leaves, travel grants, and research support. Members of the Department of History, particularly chairperson Joseph Gagliano, gave me teaching schedules that made research and writing possible. They also provided me with excellent research assistants, who helped with many different aspects of data collection and without whom I could not have completed this book: Lilia Kulak, Donna Neary, Lori Witt, Tae Ok, Julia Foulkes, Greg DeBenedictis, Katherine Dishman, Timothy Neary, Ariel Orlov, and Adam Stewart. Sylvia Rdzak, the department secretary, proved invaluable in many ways, as did Wanda Sala, the late graduate programs secretary.

Many others have contributed to this book. My dear friend Lary May encouraged me to develop my ideas when they were still young and continued over the years to read each draft and provide firm support. Our many discussions and arguments, in and out of academic settings, will always remain a high point of my scholarly life. Many other friends and colleagues read and commented on various drafts and pieces of the manuscript. Anthony Cardoza, John Cumbler, David Dennis, John Higham, Susan Hirsch, William Kenney, George Lipsitz, Donald Meyer, Sheldon Meyer, the late Russell B. Nye, Adam Stewart, and the late Warren Susman all offered support and different points of view. That I did not always heed their wisdom makes me alone responsible for the errors that lie within. Bruce Tyler graciously sent me a copy of an unpublished chapter, while Margaret McFadden took time away from her work to discuss the role of gender in the 1930s. Steve Rosswurm helped me through the Freedom of Information process. I owe a special debt to Harold Platt, Carol Woodworth, and Clarke Halker for friendship and musical good times. Sam Warner encouraged me to take piano lessons; my piano teachers, Deborah Sobol and Carol Lems-Dworkin, might not be as thankful as I am for his suggestion. Berndt Ostendorf of the Amerika-Institut, Universität München, urged me to apply for a Fulbright, and with his wife, Jutta, and their colleagues at the Amerika-Institut made 1990–91 a memorable year for my family and me. Robert Lewis and Joseph Zitomersky arranged for me to present my work at Birmingham University and the University of Paris, respectively. Steven Kern did the same for me at Northern Illinois University. Jill Jonnes provided delightful historical conversation in Munich. William R. Taylor and the New York Institute for the Humanities offered me a forum for presenting related aspects of my work. Douglas Mitchell, Matt Howard, and Leslie Keros of the University of Chicago Press, and copyeditor Jane Zanichkowsky, were patient and supportive. Dan Barnes and Rudy Schneider helped me keep my work in perspective.

My parents, Elie and Shirley Erenberg, provided continuous support and encouragement, as did my brothers, Ira and Stan, and my mother-in-law, Margaret Hirsch. I'm only sorry that my father did not live to see this book. My children, Jesse and Joanna, have had to share their father with a project that is nearly as old as they, but they took me away to better and more interesting things that have enriched my life. Finally, this book is dedicated to Susan Hirsch, who, besides carefully reading every draft, assured me more than a measure of happiness by agreeing to spend her life with me.

Abbreviations

AN *Amsterdam News*

BB *Billboard*

BG Benny Goodman Archives, Music School, Yale University

CD *Chicago Defender*

COHP Columbia University Oral History Project

DB *Down Beat*

DE Duke Ellington Scrapbook Project, Smithsonian Institution

DW *Daily Worker*

GM Glenn Miller Archives, University of Colorado, Boulder

IJS Institute of Jazz Studies, Rutgers University, Newark

JOHP Jazz Oral History Project, IJS

KOS Benny Goodman with Irving Kolodin, *Kingdom of Swing* (New York, 1939)

LPA Library for the Performing Arts, Lincoln Center

M *Metronome*

MM *Melody Maker*

MPAS Library of the Academy of Motion Picture Arts and Sciences, Los Angeles

M&R *Music & Rhythm*

NM *New Masses*

NYT *New York Times*

PC *Pittsburgh Courier*

V *Variety*

PART ONE

From Jazz to Swing, 1929–1935

1930s, continued to dominate ballrooms and radio shows. Bookers everywhere hesitated to gamble on jazz. In fact, when Goodman's leery agency, Music Corporation of America, reluctantly scheduled the national tour after the twenty-six-week radio show ended, music insiders predicted disaster. The first stop proved them right. The Hotel Roosevelt, home to sweet band king Guy Lombardo, fired them because their loud playing disturbed the patrons. At a "tacky ballroom in Michigan," only thirty people, "most of them musicians," even bothered to show up, recalled pianist and band member Jess Stacy. The low point occurred near Denver at Elitch Gardens ballroom, when patrons, disappointed at not hearing waltzes and other ballroom music, demanded their money back. Goodman called it "the most humiliating experience of my life." Only the urging of Stacy and Goodman's agent, Willard Alexander, convinced him to finish the tour.[1]

After some success in Oakland at Sweet's Ballroom and more failure in Pismo Beach, the band traveled south to the Palomar to meet its fate. Expecting the worst, the orchestra opened with its more conventionally melodic numbers. When the crowd failed to react, Goodman figured the end of his jazz band experiment had arrived. It was at that point, however, that trumpeter Bunny Berigan yelled, "let's cut this shit," and Goodman decided that if they were going to fail, the band would go down swinging. As they reeled off one hot Fletcher Henderson arrangement after another, a roar rose from the crowd, which stopped its desultory dancing and surged around the stand to watch and listen. Goodman and his musicians were elated. "That was the moment that decided things for me. After traveling three thousand miles, we finally found people who were up on what we were trying to do, prepared to take our music the way we wanted to play it." The swing era, one of the defining moments in American popular music, was born.[2]

After eight months at the Urban Room of Chicago's Congress Hotel, where the band played nightly for dancing, performed several special jazz concerts, and pioneered a racially integrated trio with Teddy Wilson on piano, Goodman returned triumphant to New York and the Hotel Pennsylvania's Madhattan Room in fall 1936 as the "King of Swing." A raucous engagement at Broadway's Paramount Theater set the tone for the intense youth culture that grew up around swing. Even before sunrise, thousands of high school boys and girls "multiplying by the minute, pouring out of the Times Square subway exits like bees from a smoked hive," played hooky in order to secure a good place in line. As the band slowly made its appearance, the crowd went wild, dancing in the aisles and even on the stage. In only two years, noted *Billboard*, the band became "one of the top drawing cards in show business." Popular with college and high school youth in person and on his radio show, Goodman brought swing to its pinnacle and stood at its center as "The Alligator's Idol," a hero to modern youth.[3]

Goodman's success demonstrated that New York was once more the capital of the dance band industry and that its arranged jazz band style was now appreciated across the nation as American music. Although Fletcher Henderson, Don Redman, Benny Carter, Duke Ellington, and other top New York black musicians had created the big band swing style in the late 1920s and early 1930s, in the hands of Benny Goodman jazz moved from the margins to the center of American culture. As popular music, it excited an adolescent generation with its liberating charge and dazzled the music industry with dreams of renewed creativity and profits. Although racial tensions would intensify over the advantages enjoyed by the many white bands who followed on Goodman's heels, Goodman and Henderson's breakthrough made popular music exciting again and rooted it in the vital and democratic soil of jazz. After six years of bitter depression, during which sweet bands and crooners reigned, jazz came back. According to Willard Alexander, "a whole series of new musical" swing bands, as opposed to "strictly commercial bands," formed in Goodman's wake to compete for a mass youth audience with the already established bands of Ellington, Chick Webb, and Jimmie Lunceford. Tommy and Jimmy Dorsey, Artie Shaw, Count Basie, Charlie Barnet, Bob Crosby, Andy Kirk, Glenn Miller, Woody Herman, Harry James, Teddy Wilson, Lionel Hampton, Gene Krupa, and scores of others started new orchestras. To everyone's surprise, American popular music, mass youth culture, and the democratic arts in general were reborn in the depression.[4]

Biting the Apple

The crash had dashed much more than the stock market. As unemployment shot up to record levels, the depression quickly took on the magnitude of a crisis. The first wave of layoffs hit African Americans and women, then spread throughout the blue-collar workforce. By 1932–33, the nadir of the depression, middle-class families were forced to scale back their standard of living and their expectations for the future. The entire entertainment industry—movie studios, the record industry, the theater, ballrooms, and even radio—felt the severe sting of the depression as well. Among these forms of cultural expression, jazz was particularly hard hit. In part, this economic and cultural crisis arose from the marginality of popular entertainments in American culture.

Modern popular culture, including popular music, emerged in the early years of the twentieth century. Until this time, American culture had been divided by class, race, and ethnicity. Protestant middle-class values dominated cultural life. Most middle-class Americans felt removed from the more vibrant lives of the lower classes and plebeian amusements. But out of Victorian values, an organized, rationalized society and family emerged that produced a crisis for the middle classes. In the search for vitality, the white middle classes turned to modern popular entertainments. Movies, Tin Pan Alley music, cabarets, dance bands, and personal sexual and moral experimentation became the loci of individualism. As older Anglo-Saxon values eroded, the cultural capital shifted from New England to "mongrel Manhattan," where blacks, Jews, and other outsiders created a cultural modernism that broke the old restraints and liberated the individual. In the 1920s a divide still existed, however, between Chicago and New York's streetwise, secular vernacular arts and the prosaic world of organized society and the workplace. Prohibition played a major role in the separation of play from social values, for it rendered illegal the search for a moral revolution in the cabarets and nightclubs of the big cities. The result was that although urban popular culture was a vibrant part of American life, the culture and its capital, New York, were perceived as not fully American. The secretiveness and the African jungle atmosphere of low-down and upper-class speakeasy-nightclubs and the exotic designs of movie palaces and ballrooms in cities like Chicago and New York were anathema in the heartland. Modern popular culture and official values were at odds.[5]

It was in this context that jazz rose from the position of a music produced and consumed primarily by African Americans to one patronized also by urban whites. As the middle classes turned away from the more organized realms of work and civic life to new forms of leisure, they were attracted to the formerly forbidden music of American blacks. Yet, when whites first encountered jazz in the 1920s, it had a dangerous as well as liberating aura. The new music that emerged in black urban areas in the early twentieth century had an enormous vitality and spontaneity. On the segregated South Side of Chicago and even more in New York's Harlem, blacks created their own cultural expressiveness in the area that was least policed—their music and dance. Jazz bore the spontaneous, improvisatory energy of this one realm of freedom and expressed the body as a natural and divine feature of human existence. Attracted to the personal freedom, cultural possibility, and economic opportunity of the black migration, musicians like King Oliver and Louis Armstrong moved to Chicago while Fletcher Henderson, Fats Waller, and Duke Ellington went to Harlem. There they created a modern black music that held out the hope for individual and group liberation. They also sought to blend the African past and the European classical tradition to enrich African American culture. In black jazz, as in black churches, the individual soloist interacted with the community in an organic connection of call and response, improvisation, and polyrhythm. By the middle of the 1920s, the soloist, in the personage of Louis Armstrong, came to occupy the central role in jazz as he or she (blues singers like Bessie Smith functioned similarly) played out deeply personal inner feelings in accord with the arranged, organized framework of the modern band and the modern world.[6]

The enormous vitality of black music in New York was part of the Harlem Renaissance. Jazz bands and commercial entertainment expressed the hopes and ambitions of the black migration and helped form a bridge to the larger New York cultural world. As Ann Douglas argues, the unique development of Harlem as a black community made it particularly cosmopolitan. In Chicago, black migrants were forced to settle in areas already inhabited by whites, and the intense competition over space and housing helped produce the race riot of 1919. This cataclysm permanently scarred Chicago's racial and cultural relations. Because Harlem was a new community at the northern edge of the city that whites had refused to settle, it developed as a full-scale, segregated community without a riot. As a result, racial, cultural, and musical relations were much less hostile in New York and much more open to the exploration of black heritage and identity in a wider American context. Black musicians were free to create a jazz style that drew confidently on black folk traditions and European techniques as equal parts of their own identity and the mixed heritage that all Americans shared. In this atmosphere, black and white artists found it easier than ever before to exchange and appropriate aspects of each other's cultural traditions.[7]

Despite the popular belief that jazz was a primitive "jungle" music, black jazzmen were in the process of developing a professional band style that incorporated the blues polyphony of the New Orleans small group format into the larger, arranged dance orchestra. New York musicians led the way. As the theatrical and musical capital of the country, New York attracted many middle-class musicians bent on making a profession out of music. Without a strong indigenous music tradition to limit them, New York jazz players forged a new synthesis of black regional musical styles. The city's cosmopolitanism also led to greater interaction between black and white bands. Black bands competed for jobs with Paul Whiteman, Jean Goldkette, and Sam Lanin, exponents of the arranged dance band of ten to twelve players. Whether at Harlem's Cotton Club, Connie's Inn and Plantation, or downtown at the Roseland Ballroom, black bands who could play for white dancers were at a premium. It was in downtown white venues in 1923 that Fletcher Henderson created the jazz dance band from an amalgam of black music and white orchestral traditions.[8]

Although they started out with the familiar waltzes, tangos, and fox trots that white orchestras played at the Roseland Ballroom, Henderson and his arranger, Don Redman, quickly moved beyond imitation to experiment with a variety of traditions. The arrival of Louis Armstrong in 1924 pushed them toward greater innovation, and Redman re-created the band to display the driving, pyrotechnic solo trumpeter, rooted in New Orleans and blues polyphony. While Armstrong built sweeping improvisations on traditional rhythmic, harmonic, and melodic patterns, quoting other tunes, exaggerating a song's distinctive features, or using a phrase for the whole, Redman and Henderson made the brass and reeds—organized into legitimate orchestral sections—emulate the improvising soloist. Written arrangements integrated them into a unified musical statement. By drawing on African American call and response, Redman and Henderson also set the reed and brass sections against each other to increase the harmonic complexity of the music, heighten the rhythmic intensity of the band, and expand the role of the soloist in an arranged jazz orchestra. The Redman-Henderson innovations took place mostly on so-called race records—aimed at the black audience—where improvisation was prized rather than at Roseland, where dancers demanded melodic playing. Their style spread rapidly, however, on records and through the playing and jamming that occurred after-hours in Harlem cafes. By 1930, the use of three trombones, four reeds, four rhythm instruments, and hot soloists linked by complex written arrangements requiring musically literate sidemen and arrangers had become standard for New York black jazz bands.[9]

Although Henderson led the first big "name" black jazz band, he was soon eclipsed by Duke Ellington. Born into a middle-class Washington, D.C., family, Duke came to New York in 1923 to take part in the flourishing African-American show business. After playing small clubs around town, his small band was hired in 1927 at the Cotton Club, the "aristocrat of Harlem" for wealthy whites. There his small cabaret band grew to a ten-piece orchestra. Responsible for writing production and dance numbers for the Cotton Club revues, Ellington rapidly mastered composition and began creating music that attracted listeners as well as dancers. Because of the club's radio broadcasts and Ellington's many recordings and theater tours, he achieved fame and a measure of fortune. Sophisticated and urbane in bearing, dress, and musical ambition, Ellington testified to the dream of an African American big-city culture.[10]

Fletcher Henderson's pathbreaking Roseland Orchestra, 1924. Henderson is seated center, fifth from left, Coleman Hawkins is second from left, and Louis Armstrong is third from left. Don Redman, the brilliant alto saxist and arranger, is at the far right. Note how the early band photos show musicians as a collection of individuals and instruments. Frank Driggs Collection.

The extended engagement at Harlem's top club gave Ellington the stability to create one of the world's most innovative orchestras. He was the only jazz band leader who was at once composer, arranger, and leader of an orchestra shaped by his own hand. As the elegant musical representative of the Harlem Renaissance, he fashioned a rich and complex modern music rooted in African American communal creativity. Ellington achieved superb symphonic and tonal effects, but he was less a composer in the classical mold and more one whose compositions emerged from the unique body of musicians he assembled through the late 1920s and early 1930s. Writing for particular players in the band, he allowed the musicians to collaborate on the creation of a finished musical product. After playing out an idea on the piano, for example, he would encourage the musicians to make suggestions. As trumpeter Cootie Williams later noted, "Everyone in the band would pitch in and help write songs, everything that, almost, Duke did in those days." Then the sections would work out the harmonies, usually on chords he provided. As the music grew out of the group's individual and communal strong points, Ellington blended black communal creation and improvisation with European art composition. Writing for individual musicians, he used the entire orchestra as a jazz instrument and stamped every facet of the music with his personality. Ellington's orchestra demonstrated the Harlem Renaissance goal of producing great art out of folk experience and thereby dethroned the white European tradition's dominance in music and culture. From the late 1920s onward, Ellington used European techniques effectively to extend the vernacular tradition and place it on an equal level with "superior" white culture.[11]

Almost from the start, this great flowering of black music attracted many white artists who saw it not just as a new music but also as a means to reorient their own lives. All during the era, the music drew young, white Chicago musicians like Eddie Condon, Dave Tough, Bud Freeman, Jimmy McPartland, Mezz Mezzrow, Jess Stacy, Benny Goodman, and young men from elsewhere, like Bix Beiderbecke, Hoagy Carmichael, Artie Shaw, Glenn Miller, and Jimmy and Tommy Dorsey. Jazz offered them a personal and emotionally authentic expression, and these white artists often romanticized the black community as a spontaneous, unrepressed community through which they might find their own free selves. Mezzrow eventually considered himself black because of the sense of freedom he witnessed on the south side of Chicago and in Harlem, and he and Tough married black women. More important, these young white musicians were the first to idolize black musicians—especially Louis Armstrong—and to look up to them as mentors and models of modern playing. Because of Chicago's segregated music scene, however, the Chicagoans had few places to play jazz in their home town. Unable to play in black bands, in which they might have been more comfortable, they found little jazz work in white areas. Some, like Goodman, joined traveling white jazz bands, while others, like Condon, Mezzrow, and Art Hodes, pursued a hard-drinking, spontaneous style of music and life but had trouble making a living. The former group went on from the dance bands of the 1920s to lead swing orchestras; the latter rejected dance bands and arrangements for small combos where they could improvise at will. Nearly all of them migrated to New York at the end of the decade to avail themselves of the many opportunities in radio, recording, nightclubs, and theater in the jazz capital of the world.[12]

White audiences, however, were ambivalent about jazz. They often considered the new music a racial and ethnic attack on middle-class, Protestant values of self-discipline, sexual propriety, and self-advancement. As John Philip Sousa declared, jazz was popular, but it "does not truly represent America to the world" because "it employs primitive rhythms which excite the basic human impulses." Many moralists feared that the sensual music of African America—and its adaptation and promotion by Jewish singers like Al Jolson and Sophie Tucker, impresarios like Irving Mills, and songwriters like Irving Berlin, George Gershwin, and Harold Arlen, all from the other major outsider group undergoing a cultural awakening in New York—threatened to lower the morals of American womanhood and mongrelize American national identity. For many hostile observers, New York culture was an "asphalt jungle," created by Harlem blacks and Broadway Jews. Although critics and moralists failed to outlaw jazz, they succeeded in driving it into speakeasies, with their criminal ties and outlaw status.[13]

Consequently, while white audiences found "hot" music an exciting, exotic means of personal expression, they preferred Paul Whiteman's refined, symphonic jazz. Having ascended to the heights of New York's nightclub world through his ability to please upper-class patrons with exciting arrangements of black rhythms in the early 1920s, Whiteman was besieged by internal doubts of jazz's worth, fueled by the preachers and "club lady uplifters who put on sheets and pillow cases to go jazz-klanning." He responded by attempting to bridge the gap between civilized public values and the new music by making "a lady of jazz." According to the *New Yorker,* the result was "a sweet jazz . . . with his violins, muted brasses, and soft symphonic effects." His large society orchestra adapted polyrhythms and syncopation, "but improvisation was held in check and the hot stuff was dispensed only in teaspoonfuls." He also hired white jazz players in the 1920s, notably Bix Beiderbecke, but to their disappointment the opportunities for solos virtually disappeared in the orchestra's refined arrangements and elaborate section playing. Only Whiteman, the showman-conductor, stood out as the star. At the same time, the black originators were kept segregated in their own units. Refusing to hire African American musicians, Whiteman never acknowledged the racial origin of his music in his autobiography, and even eliminated blacks from the musical melting pot scene at the climax of his lavish film, *King of Jazz* (1930). In a culture still fearful of jazz as an inducement to sexual promiscuity and national anarchy, Whiteman legitimated the big-name professional white orchestra that drew on jazz but linked it to ordered white civilization and European refinement.[14]

After the Jazz Age

The crash and the depression brought an abrupt end to the jazz age's cultural outpouring among whites and dramatically transformed the music business both in New York and in the nation as a whole. Even Whiteman felt the sting. In 1930, after the long-delayed and wastefully expensive *King*

Paul Whiteman's Symphonic Jazz Orchestra, at the height of its fame during the late 1920s. Note the string section to Whiteman's right. By this time, Whiteman had given up his violin for full-time leading. Institute of Jazz Studies, Rutgers University.

of Jazz movie flopped, he found himself in economic distress when his studio failed to pick up his option. In the 1920s, he had cut an extravagant figure as the primary exponent of refined jazz and as an important embodiment of the new consumer culture. He had delighted in luxury race cars, expensive champagne, and glamorous show girls, and his orchestra was as gargantuan as his girth. By 1930, however, the leader of the best-paid and best-known symphonic jazz orchestra in the country found himself and his music out of favor. When record sales plunged, Columbia Records dropped him, Old Gold Cigarettes canceled his radio show, and his wife filed for divorce. As a result of these setbacks, Whiteman was forced to fire ten jazzmen and arrangers from his thirty-man orchestra and had to ask the rest of his musicians to take a 15 percent pay cut. The King of Jazz had lost his crown.[15]

Whiteman eventually recovered by playing more sedate music, but the music business did not. At the end of 1933, noted the *Nation,* there were 15,000 members of the American Federation of Musicians in New York—and 12,000 of them were unemployed. Across the nation as well, at least two-thirds of the union's membership remained out of work. "Today an average musical performer is not only a drag on the market but an absolute dead weight."[16]

As the nervous energy of the 1920s gave way to shock and despair, the new pleasure institutions of the first two decades of the century—movies, cabarets, ballrooms, records, bands—collapsed. "Show business, as the current year closes out," noted *Variety* in 1931, "is in the most chaotic condition it has ever known." Massive unemployment and shrinking income meant iess money for going out. Live entertainment everywhere plunged into an abyss. Emblematic of twenties nightlife and amusement, Times Square came to resemble a frontier town of honky tonks, cheap dance halls, and bars. By 1931, 45 percent of Broadway theaters either closed or became movie houses. The movie houses, meanwhile, fired their pit bands. Having competed unfavorably with the new "talkies," vaudeville now completely disappeared. The lavish Broadway Follies and Vanities' revues, built around elaborate sexual titillation and conspicuous consumption, went out of favor. In 1932 Florenz Ziegfeld, the man most closely associated with the revue, died after suffering big stock market losses. As the Great White Way blew a fuse, the orchestra jobs that had sustained generations of musicians vanished. The decline of ballrooms across the country also hurt musicians. The New York City License Bureau estimated that between 1929 and 1930, 105 dance halls went out of business. The remainder hired unemployed chorus girls to lure male customers. Well-known bands found some work in halls, but now their salaries depended on the number of people in the house. Dance halls acquired seedy reputations as desperate managers turned to the marathons and walkathons that created spectacles of endurance and pain in the dog-eat-dog world of the depression.[17]

Aimed at a richer clientele, nightclubs took longer to feel the pinch, but by 1932, *Variety* noted, "the average layman and moderate spender up to and including the wealthier sport and wine-buying spender" had vanished. As business fell, many cafes became cheap dance halls. Exclusive East Side speakeasies that catered to society remained open, but even they were forced to lower prices to lure patrons. Only Harlem nightlife lingered, but huge black unemployment made rent parties more popular. Whites went uptown, but now more frequently to small, cheap speakeasies featuring singers and small bands. Nationally, the majority of nightclubs closed in Chicago, Minneapolis, Detroit, and Los Angeles. Only Kansas City, protected by the Pendergast machine, ran unchecked. Symbolically, the nightclub era ended in New York in 1932 when "Queen of Broadway" Texas Guinan departed the Great White Way and died a year later. Larry Fay, her former partner in Broadway speakeasies, was gunned down in front of his

Club Napoleon. The power behind Harlem's Cotton Club, mobster Owney Madden, left town to escape the uptown liquor wars, first to prison and then to Hot Springs, Arkansas.[18]

While the decline of live entertainment adversely affected musicians, the depression also crippled the music business. By 1932 sheet music and record sales had plummeted. Sales of radios fell, too, at least until manufacturers learned to make cheaper models. The phonograph industry suffered severely. Record player purchases fell 90 percent a year after the crash, but record sales took longer to drop. Purchases went from 104 million in 1927 to 6 million in 1932. With unsold surpluses piling up in warehouses, record executives worried that they "seemed to be experiencing not a slump but a final collapse." Even when record companies lowered prices from 75 to 35 cents, radio offered a free alternative. Columbia Records went bankrupt, kept alive only by orders from abroad. Smaller and independent record companies consolidated into three major labels: RCA Victor, Decca, and Columbia. None was thriving.[19]

As the crisis deepened, record companies cut back in other ways. By the end of 1930 firms eliminated race records. Foreign language sales dropped off soon after. When contracts expired in 1931, Victor, Columbia, and Brunswick dropped their most expensive artists. Victor's biggest hit of the year, "Little White Lies," sung by Johnny Marvin, sold only 40,000 copies, far below the 350,000 copies a hit registered a few years earlier. When Marvin's contract came due, he was offered a flat fee for each record session rather than royalties on sales. Record companies discovered that old vocal and band stars, "once big on discs," were "now fading out." Facing bankruptcy and loss of artistic direction, the industry, noted *Variety*, "showed every sign of being in its last throes." The stage was set for new bands and singers.[20]

The situation was particularly frustrating for the many jazz musicians in New York. The jazz capital had shifted from Chicago to Broadway and Harlem in the late 1920s when the election of a reform administration in the Windy City ushered in Prohibition enforcement. With a clampdown on clubs, Chicago's black and white jazz musicians headed for New York's thriving music scene. During the early 1930s, however, few jobs existed for jazzmen of any color in New York—or anywhere else. When Mezz Mezzrow arrived in New York at the decade's end, he found his pals scrounging for work. Max Kaminsky, a Boston trumpeter inspired by Armstrong and the white Chicagoans, followed his many black and white idols to New York in 1929, only to find that jazz had taken "a nosedive along with the blithe spirit of the twenties." Kaminsky retreated to Boston in 1931 to wait out the storm and wonder "if I had dreamed the wonderful times in Chicago and Harlem." Unemployed like any working stiff, he was now "just a little guy."[21]

When freelance recording dried up in 1932, the pick of the white jazzmen sought refuge in radio orchestras or commercial bands, but they chafed at the lack of personal and artistic freedom. Better off than the many black musicians barred from such work, Artie Shaw still found the experience galling. Moreover, since there were a hundred musicians for each position, there was "a lot of politics around the radio studios." When a job failed to come through at CBS, Shaw felt lost. "It seemed to me at the ripe old age of nineteen, that I had reaped nothing more from it than a crop of weariness, loneliness and insecurity." Forced to "suck up to the people who had power," he "felt trapped, helpless, bitter, desperate."[22]

Radio also stifled creative independence. "On most of the programs I did," noted Shaw, "there was little or no room for any sort of individual musical expression." When Kaminsky was hired to perform for Leo Reisman on NBC he was supposed to play only six bars of growling trumpet. Bored, he would try to sneak in a few more bars with the band, but Reisman would "shake his finger ferociously and hiss, 'You're *playing!*'" Radio, Shaw observed, was "run by a stop watch. Musical phrases [were] metered out in terms of minutes and seconds, rather than in terms of musical feeling." The work was lucrative but it "had a lot more to do with selling soap than with music." Radio players, he observed, "were some of the most cynical people I have ever known anywhere." Benny Goodman also resented the lack of room for individual freedom. Forced to play what conductors and sponsors demanded, he lost his artistic direction and contemplated playing society music to get out of the studios. He had reached his emotional and artistic nadir. For white players, the jazz age appeared over.[23]

Mood Indigo

Goodman's and Shaw's experience paralleled the entrapment and insecurity faced by the nation's youth during the worst years of the depression. Of the ten million young people who reached employable age during 1929–34, half remained unemployed in 1935. Young people were hardest hit by the depression; many lost or never found jobs. Only one-third of black New York youth lived in homes where fathers worked regularly; in 1935 they were two and a half times more likely to be on relief than white youth of the same age. While working-class children were hardest hit, even the most secure New York youth faced the possibility of unemployment. In 1935, only 41.6 percent of high school graduates had a job, and young men age 20–24 earned median wages of only $629 a year, half the rate of older men. Because of the scarcity of employment, historian John Modell notes, high school attendance rose, and more young people lived at home for longer periods before reaching independence.[24]

The growing numbers of high school students laid the basis for a more extensive youth culture in the latter part of the 1930s, but the dreams of the 1920s seemed a distant memory. When even well-off families were forced to cut back, they did so in areas of great importance to the new adolescent lifestyles: recreation, autos, clothing, and entertainment. Young women and men may not have felt conscious antagonism toward their parents, but they certainly felt constrained by their environment. Limited financial resources, moreover, delayed marriages, normally the mark of maturity for young women and men. In "Middletown," for example, the small Indiana city made famous by sociologists Robert and Helen Lynd, the marriage rate dropped 37 percent from 1929 to 1932. Postponement of marriage and longer engagements became a common pattern among "the wide middle band of incomes, the less secure business-class families and the more secure working-class families." Clearly, growing up was fraught with insecurity.[25]

Until 1932 middle-class college students had been insulated from the depression by their families' wealth and their immersion in college life. They had continued to buy records, dance to jazz bands, and go to places of amusement on dates. Indeed, while most of the country voted for Roosevelt in the presidential election of 1932, collegians supported Republican Herbert Hoover. That year, however, American college life began to show signs of change. Part-time jobs disappeared on campuses, one-quarter to one-third of students suffered losses in income, and corporate recruiting ended. Male graduates could not get jobs, while women's office positions fell by half. College enrollment dropped in 1932 by 4.5 percent and continued to fall in 1933. College traditions such as football games, proms, and fraternity and sorority functions came under criticism as students challenged the idea that college was geared toward personal pleasure and social conformity. Campus radicalism enjoyed a major upsurge, and by 1936, formerly solid Republican campuses turned Democratic and supported Franklin Delano Roosevelt.[26]

The depression also had an effect on dating. The 1920s ideal of the companionate couple linked to an exciting life of consumption became all but impossible to achieve. "Dutch dating"—women and men each paying their own way—achieved a brief vogue, and deans and student committees worked hard to make college proms and socials less expensive. At the Uni-

of the 1920s. Especially prominent was the sense that modern society had reduced the power of the once-masterful individual male. Overwhelmed by feelings of personal failure, young people's musical tastes showed uncertainty, a destabilization of gender roles, and a desire for security.[29]

Popular music registered the deflation of expectations. Large, commercial, white dance bands such as Paul Whiteman's became much more rhythmically conservative and less open to jazz. As hotter jazz groups disbanded and live entertainment shrank drastically, sweet (melodic) bands took over the commercial radio airwaves, content to comply with radio's insistence on inoffensiveness and the audience's desire for soothing sounds. Such bands also controlled the best remaining "location jobs" in hotels and cafes. Despite an interest in jazz, for example, future swing band leader Charlie Barnet led bands in New York hotels but "hadn't the guts to go 'way out' on the jazz thing for fear we wouldn't be able to work." Rather, Guy Lombardo's Royal Canadians enjoyed long-term success at New York's Hotel Roosevelt for years after 1929, while Emil Coleman, Eddie Duchin, and Leo Reisman played New York's major ritzy East Side hotels and clubs. Less interested in expanding the range of dance music, these bands relied on personality leaders and "successful formulas" to soothe audiences with romantic ballads set to muted trumpets, sweet saxophones, and subdued drums. Duchin delighted society crowds with his handsome profile and flashy piano runs. As a former sideman put it, "he was the only musician I've ever known who could play a thirty-two bar solo with thirty-two mistakes and get an ovation for it afterward."[30]

It was Guy Lombardo who set the tone for sweet bands. Born Gaetario Lombardo in London, Ontario, in 1902, he and his brothers built their quartet into an orchestral institution. The Royal Canadians earned their initial success at Cleveland's Claremont Hotel in 1924 and Chicago's Grenada Cafe in 1927. They played their first New York job at the Hotel Roosevelt in 1929, reaching a national audience just as the depression hit. Skillfully employing radio, the only truly effective means of musical promotion left, to build the band's name, Lombardo's band, broadcast over CBS, soon found an audience along the entire East Coast. He discovered that few could afford a night out at a club or hotel, so they turned to radio and made it "the dominant force in the entertainment business." Playing "The Sweetest Music This Side of Heaven," the band featured its sax section, muted brass, and a soft pulse to play a steady diet of romantic ballads. While the music required little concentration, the band played melodies expertly at a tempo that was easy on dancers. As Victor Greene notes, nearly every major white bandleader of the time imitated the Lombardo style: Art Krueger, Dick Jurgens, Glen Gray, Ozzie Nelson, Freddy Martin, Phil Spitalny, Art Kassel, Jan Garber, Sammy Kaye, and Blue Barron. Even Duke Ellington included sweet music in his repertoire. Sweet bands worked through the worst of the depression by playing calming music for dinner and dancing at plush hotels. Society support, the prevalence of commercial radio, and the dreary times ensured the dominance of low-key music to replace the jaunty, extroverted strains of the 1920s.[31]

Radio and the depression combined to create a dramatic shift in popular singing. The bombastic shouters of the 1920s gave way in popularity to the male crooners and female torch singers, described by Constant Lambert as the "first popularization of that well-known modern vice, the inferiority complex." The increasing role of the electronic microphone in recording and radio placed less weight on the big voices of Al Jolson, Sophie Tucker, and Bessie Smith, who had learned their craft in the fast-disappearing live venues. Filled with optimism and life, the shouters had challenged Victorian sentiment and stormed barriers to the self with the sheer force of their exuberance and the bawdy power of their bodies. As live entertainment gave way to radio, however, they failed to adapt. Brimming with energy, Jolson could not stand still in front of a mike. As he announced on his last Chevrolet Hour in 1932, "this radio business is not for Jolie," unlike the "weak-voiced singers that would fall down if they didn't have a mike to hold onto." Tucker and Smith proved too bawdy for radio's family audience. On the other hand, using the mike skillfully, noted Henry Pleasants, "crooners could *speak* to you without raising their voices, wherever you were. It is here that the story of the modern popular singer, in one vital aspect, begins."[32]

Yet technology alone does not explain the shift. In the ruin of dreams, torch singers and crooners expressed the spiritual letdown and insecurity of the era. The anguished and languid voice conveyed a loss of faith in individual power and male potency in a hostile world. The modern crooners seemed disembodied upper-class holdovers, romantic figures without punch. They understood the difficulties young people faced but could offer no plan of action other than the acceptance of fate. The first crooner, Rudy Vallee, for example, rose to stardom in 1929 using a megaphone and then a microphone during his broadcasts from New York's upper-class Heigh Ho Club. Two days after the crash, he had his own national *Fleischmann Hour* on NBC. His appeal lay in his collegiate image, evoked by his Yale sweater and a penchant for college songs. His voice "spoke in the nasal manner of a Calvin Coolidge," and was "simple and direct," while his "Connecticut Yankees" played uncomplicated melodies devoid of blaring brass. Like pop-

ular bandleaders of the day, Vallee discovered that the public was not interested in hot jazz. Most people "come home at night from a hard day's toil,"
he declared in 1930, "and seek comfort and rest in music of a sweet,
smooth, quiet nature." A consoling force, Vallee tried to keep listeners "up
in the clouds of sentiment and feeling," lulling them "into a feeling of
happiness, contentment and enjoyment." By 1932, however, youth felt the
depression's full weight, and turned to the likes of Bing Crosby, who was
less a comic figure and more a former collegian tempered by the times and
able to sing the pain of ordinary Americans.[33]

The most famous crooner of the era, Crosby rose to prominence on the
electronic media, reaching the height of his success in a national CBS radio
show broadcast from New York in 1932. His average American image and
self-assurance offered reassurance to a generation faced with adversity and
uncertainty. Not upper-class and supercilious like Vallee, and not a playboy
like Russ Columbo, Crosby was the ordinary-looking American male devoid
of social power. In fact, he found that audiences liked him because "I'm just
like the Mr. Averages in the audience who watch the glamour boys on the
screen and listen to the little woman at their side sighing like a furnace."
His "average" voice was the key to his appeal. Crosby attracted both male
and female fans because, he noted, every man "believes firmly that he sings
as well as I do, especially when he's in the bathroom shower." His unassum-
ing style emphasized jazz phrasing and avoided superficial effects. "I'm not
a singer; I'm a phraser," he said, who did not "think of a song in terms of
notes; I try to think of what it purports to say lyrically. That way it sounds
more natural." On radio his intimate tone made it seem that his problems
were everyone's. With a half-sob in his voice, and a relaxed scat style, he
gave vent to a common pathos and blamed himself for his woes. Expressing male pain, he also offered women masculine intimacy free of sexual
threat.[34]

Crosby's vocal style reflected his repudiation of the life he used to lead
as a jazz artist. He had sung with Paul Whiteman's Rhythm Boys, a trio that
performed a string of hot numbers, including "'Tain't So" and "My Baby
Don't Mean Maybe Now." As his friend Hoagy Carmichael noted of those
days, "he already had the high forehead, the easy lazy way, a capacity for
drink, and an interest in female company." This behavior, however, served
him ill in the depression. After a short prison term for drunk driving while
filming *King of Jazz* in Hollywood in 1929, he and the other Rhythm Boys
left Whiteman for an independent career. Finding nothing in movies, the
trio latched on at Los Angeles's ritzy Coconut Grove as part of a two-hour
radio show with Gus Arnheim's Orchestra that attracted the movie and col-

WHERE
THE BLUE OF THE NIGHT
MEETS THE GOLD OF THE DAY

WORDS & MUSIC BY
ROY TURK
BING CROSBY
AND
FRED E. AHLERT

FEATURED BY
BING CROSBY

Crooner Bing Crosby, looking sad and dispirited. This sheet music cover from his 1932 theme song was colored blue. Author's collection.

lege set. Crosby's drunken sprees, however, got the band fired, and the trio broke up. His irresponsibility and infidelity also threatened his romance with young actress Dixie Lee, whose father called him a "useless-good-for-nothing type." Crosby agreed. "I hadn't put out too much in the way of work. I'd played golf and had a good time. I couldn't seem to be serious about anything." When Dixie threatened to drop him, he felt like a "nobody going no place," while she was a somebody whom he needed. Only after Crosby vowed to change his ways did she agree to marry him. These rebuffs and failures informed a new Crosby style as he blamed himself and vowed reform. "I Apologize," "I Surrender Dear," "I'm Sorry," and "Just One More Chance," all detailed his guilt and sense of repentance, while "Just a Gigolo" pointed out the sad fate of the playboy. This cry of pathos won Dixie Lee, turned Crosby from his jazz age ways, and made him a star. Lee quit her job to become a supportive wife, and Crosby soon won an award for Catholic Father of the Year.[35]

Raising the interpretation of song lyrics to an art form, Crosby and the other languid-voiced singers exemplified the loss of power of the individual, and especially the man, to affect his fate. Young men unable to foresee themselves as good providers were unable to fulfill the demands of masculinity; in many songs the traditional male appears rudderless and on the verge of extinction. In "Brother Can You Spare a Dime?" Crosby gave vent to the masculine impotence that could no longer build skyscrapers or make trains run at high speed. The machine age had ground to a halt, and with it masculine power. This deflation of phallic power is made clear in "Life Is Just a Bowl of Cherries" (1931), in which Vallee laments that even "the strongest oak must fall."

In response, songwriters composed lyrics that turned to a misty past for security and peace of mind—as in Crosby's theme song, "Where the Blue of the Night," where the singer "live[s] in dreams of days I used to know." Rustic songs like "Old Spinning Wheel" enjoyed a vogue as they expressed longing for a womb-like security within a complex, modern world. Many songs tried to assure listeners that all was well or exhorted them to be strong in the face of disaster, but the singer's tone and the song's lyrics conveyed a fatalistic belief that little could be done. In "Life Is Just a Bowl of Cherries," Vallee counsels his listeners not to take life too serious because it was "too mysterious." Work and struggle produce only worry, and besides, "You can't take your dough when you go." Perhaps in such a world, it was best to "Wrap Your Troubles in Dreams." If work and love led nowhere, one could retire from the rat race, as in Hoagy Carmichael's "Bidin' My Time" (1930), "Lazy Bones" (1933), and "Up a Lazy River" (1933). As the pipe-smoking, golf-playing crooner, Crosby symbolized the deflation of individual male power.[36]

With male earning power diminished and marriage harder to come by, the crooners also spoke of the romantic difficulties of both sexes. Indeed, love shifted from imagery of wedded bliss or a good time to a desperate search for emotional security. Both men and women worried that the dream of home and marriage had become impossible to reach. In "How Deep Is the Ocean?" Crosby is at the ocean's depths yet his love is as far away as a star. Reaching out for someone, he finds no one there. When the young did marry they looked for emotional stability. In "Dancing in the Dark," Bing clings to his partner wondering "why we're here." Darkness is at hand, and in a world where he is alone, she is his last hope. Without love, men and women are, in the words of "Black Moonlight," "lost in the city, bewildered, betrayed . . . I have come to the bridge, to the line that divides." Suicide and death await in "Gloomy Sunday" and "Deep Purple." To be alone is to be weak and anchorless. Love came to be less an adventure than the basis for security.

At the same time that crooners evoked male weakness, torch singers expressed the corresponding fears and anxieties of women. The torch song, although not new, became dominant in the early 1930s as the "Big Mama" shouters and baby-doll singers of the 1920s receded from view. Ethel Merman belted out female power on stage, as did Mae West in films, but they acted as counterpoint to the scores of world-weary women who had tasted the high life of cabarets and sex—the promise of the 1920s—but now realized their falsehood and atoned for their sins. Sex in the songs of the 1920s could be playful and witty, reflecting the confidence of a prosperous age, but, according to Timothy Scheuer, in the music of the early 1930s sex reflected "the cynicism born of confronting the hangover" of the jazz age. Sexually experienced and wised-up, the torch singers sang of the spoiled idealism of "America's preoccupation with love and romance."[37]

The depiction of ruined love took root in the unhappy lives that these women led. One torch singer in the early 1930s had a life as depressing as her songs. "I made the same mistake over and over," she told her friend, singer Anita O'Day. "I thought if a man wanted to have sex with me, he loved me, instead of the other way around." Lacking self-confidence, she abased herself with mean mistreaters. Like other torchers, however, she saw no way out. Each of the famous torch singers followed the pattern. Fannie Brice pined for gambler Nicky Arnstein, who constantly cheated on her. Despite her belief in traditional Catholic morality and marriage, Helen Morgan had an affair with a married man. World-weary as she sat atop a piano, drink in hand, she conveyed by example that the price for sexual indulgence had to be paid, that sexual "looseness" was a sin. Libby Holman, of "Body and Soul" fame, was accused of shooting her wealthy husband. Ruth Etting lived with gangster Gimp Snyder, who never let her out of his sight. Each of these women invested everything in relationships that turned bitter. Yet love was their only subject. The romantic dream was exhausted, and they were dependent on male whim. That they were all connected to nightclubs symbolized a continuing disillusionment with the urban high life of the 1920s.[38]

The torch song describes women's dependence on mean men who were financially or emotionally unreliable, as in Helen Morgan's "Mean to Me." Like the crooner, the torch singer is powerless to affect her fate, because essentially she "Can't Help Lovin' That Man." Love and sex lead not to a happy marriage and emotional fulfillment but to emotional destruction and lifelong disappointment. Torch singers expressed the torment that many women felt in the early 1930s: they were emotionally involved with men who could not provide or who did not see marriage in their future. In the depths of the depression, however, women found it difficult to leave these abusive situations since they had few resources. Once they moved outside the secure role of wife and mother to work, they were only one step removed from sexual exploitation and prostitution.

These fears surface in Ruth Etting's rendition of "Ten Cents a Dance" (1931). As a taxi–dance hall hostess trying to support herself, her body was her only resource. Instead of dance leading to romance, however, it is here portrayed, as Scheuer observes, "as rock bottom economic necessity." She works "at the Palace Ballroom, but gee that Palace is cheap," Etting sings, undercutting the dream of mobility and status ironically represented by the word *palace*. "Sometimes I think / I've found my hero / But it's a queer romance / All you need is a ticket / Come on, big boy, ten cents a dance." Charging "exactly a dime a throw," she substitutes a work-related function for the hope of a normal love relationship. Like the crooners, the torch singers felt trapped in a world beyond their control. Their dreams dashed, they waited listlessly for the stormy weather to pass.[39]

If It Ain't Got That Swing

The energy and creativity of the musical awakening to come derived from a number of important black bands who were able to synthesize the modern swing sound despite the depression's devastating effects on their livelihood. By 1933, things looked bleak in the former jazz capital of Chicago; the city's entire old musical establishment, which had once warred with the blues playing New Orleans jazz men for preeminence, had fallen apart. King Oliver, the most prominent exponent of New Orleans jazz in Chicago, attempted to strike up a following in New York but to no avail, and his career began to decline. The refined orchestras of Dave Peyton, Doc Cooke, Sammy Stewart, Charles Elgar, and Erskine Tate were forced to disband because of the lack of work. Stable jobs for black musicians were so scarce that

Ruth Etting, torch singer, 1932. Frank Driggs Collection.

the segregated Local 208 of the American Federation of Musicians (AFM) decided to hold dances every Thursday night so that musicians could pay their union dues. Trumpeters William Samuels and George Mitchell, arranger Zilner Randolph, and other musicians joined the Works Progress Administration's local musical organizations. In New York, meanwhile, Sam Wooding, Elmer Snowden, and Fess Williams lost their prominence, while in the Southwest, the dance bands of Alphonso Trent, Jap Allen, T. Holder, and Troy Floyd broke up. The AFM's level C pay scale for Harlem dropped to only $35 a week for band members and $70 for leaders; many were more than willing to work for less. Clarinetist Sidney Bechet and trumpeter Tommy Ladnier opened a dry cleaning store to make ends meet.[40]

While New York's commercial music world provided a refuge for many white players, studio doors remained shut to black musicians. Duke Ellington, Fats Waller, and Art Tatum had short programs on the air, but the radio studios, which employed many staff musicians, were completely segregated. Black artists, no matter their popularity with live audiences, rarely found radio a reliable, long-term outlet for their talents. In 1931, for instance, Ellington's band broadcast in Chicago but not nationally, since sponsors did not want their products linked to black performers, especially in the South. Opportunities for black musicians to record, moreover, fell off as the depression wiped out the race record market. In 1931 Okeh and Columbia cut back the number of new releases for the black market, and Paramount, which had been prominent in the race field, folded entirely. As promoter and critic John Hammond noted, "Blues records, even by an artist of Bessie's [Smith] stature, were at the bottom of any list of record sales, and what records were being made for the almost nonexistent Negro market were washboard bands" that were paid substantially below scale. Although Ellington was one of RCA Victor's five most successful bandleaders, the company cut back his releases sharply. According to Hammond, "most Negro band leaders were discouraged, if not defeated, by the Depression."[41]

Yet for a few New York black bands, according to Thomas J. Hennessey, the depression opened new avenues to national prominence. While Harlem's smaller "black and tan clubs" lost clientele, the Savoy Ballroom, Connie's Inn, the Cotton Club, and Smalls' Paradise continued to offer a stable base for big name black bands until the Riot of 1935 discouraged upper-class white patrons from venturing uptown. At the same time, the depression tilted the balance away from local, "territory" bands working in a variety of styles toward national outfits based in New York. To save money, for instance, theaters, dance halls, and clubs across the nation fired their house orchestras in favor of touring big-name black groups, often organized in and promoted from New York. Ellington and Cab Calloway at the Cotton Club or Fletcher Henderson at Roseland had the advantage of national exposure on late-night nonsponsored radio remote broadcasts. Given the decline of white jazz bands, most work went to a few black orchestras, such as those headed by Ellington, Calloway, Henderson, and Claude Hopkins, as well as the Mills Blue Rhythm Band. These groups also began to tap the college prom market for hot music, while white bands played dates calling for a sweeter romantic style. New York black bands went on the road as amusement promoters in local areas sought to spice up attendance with new acts. Perhaps black bands were in demand for the jazz market because they remained stereotyped in white minds as impulsive and passionate—hot—and hence less a threat to the new seriousness demanded by the depression. One could watch Cab Calloway "heigh-de-hoing," throwing his hair and his body around, convinced that this impulsive behavior could never be white and sober.[42]

Name bands of Ellington's stature set the pace with their first national tours in 1931. In a period of intense competition, the best jobs went to national touring groups, run by white managers and booked by New York agencies, such as Irving Mills in New York. Indeed, as conditions worsened substantially after 1932, it was important for black bands to minimize disruption and loss of income by having a white representative of a national booking agency arrange engagements with movie chains, corporate radio, and ballroom circuits. While Ellington, Calloway, the Mills Blue Rhythm Band, and other orchestras understood the benefits of national booking offices, it was Fletcher Henderson's misfortune that he continued to arrange the bookings for his band personally. The result was a series of confused engagements, loss of pay, and, by November 1934, a dispirited group of musicians who tired of being stranded on the road. His star tenor saxophone soloist, Coleman Hawkins, was so discouraged that he left the country for the greener fields of Europe. Like other black bandleaders, Henderson finally signed with the Mills office, but by then Ellington had gotten the bread and Henderson was left with the crumbs. Henderson's carefree business style, moreover, left him unprepared for the intense competitive climate of the modern band business. By late 1934 he was bankrupt.[43]

In this period of national consolidation, the territory bands—those organized and working in outlying regions—were the major losers. As the entertainment business centralized in New York, younger black musicians in territory bands looked to national outfits as sources of employment, higher salaries, and greater prestige. The younger players in many regional bands heard the New York orchestras over radio or on records and sought to assimilate their style. Regional variations increasingly diminished, and players in local bands tried to latch on with national outfits. To hold onto one's top musicians, local groups had to get national exposure by going to New York. Otherwise, local bands would fall to the level of a farm team as national orchestras hired away their best men. Memphis high school teacher Jimmie Lunceford, for example, started an orchestra with students and friends from his alma mater, Fisk University. From the beginning, the band aimed for New York as the only way to survive as a unit. After local tours, they moved

The 1939 edition of the Jimmie Lunceford Orchestra. One of several important black bands to survive the depression, migrate to New York, and elaborate the swing sound in the early 1930s. Here the band plays to both blacks and whites at the Paramount Theater. From left to right: Paul Webster, trumpet; Russel Bowles, trumpet; Gerald Wilson, trumpet; Trummy Young, trombone; Eddie Tompkins, trumpet; Elmer Crumbley, trombone; Jimmy Crawford, drums; Dan Grissom, alto sax and vocals; Willie Smith, alto sax and clarinet; Lunceford; Al Norris, guitar; Teddy Buckner, alto sax; Moses Allen, bass; Joe Thomas, tenor sax; Earl Carruthers, baritone sax; Ed Wilcox, pianist and arranger. Frank Driggs Collection.

to Buffalo, honed their style, attracted better musicians, and looked to the big time. In 1934 they signed with Mills, recorded on Victor, and played at the Cotton Club. The competition to join a national band in the emerging pyramid structure placed even greater pressure on sidemen to adopt the middle-class ideals of professionalism, musical literacy, self-discipline, and reliability that had been hallmarks of the original New York approach. No one symbolized these ideals better than Lunceford, a solid, sober, and efficient musical taskmaster.[44]

The opportunity for top black bands to dominate the jazz scene in the early 1930s enabled them to continue their exploration of the arranged big band format. Long used to hard times and setbacks, African Americans were less prone to blame themselves or jazz for systemic breakdown. Those who continued to work in public or in more private jam sessions were able to extend and consolidate previous developments and create a new form, swing, based on a 4/4 beat rooted in a restructured rhythm section. The key was the switch from the clumsy 2/4 beat that originated with the tuba and banjo to the more supple 4/4 beat appropriate to string bass and guitar. Worked out by 1932–33, the new style stripped away the vertical harmonic elements to emphasize horizontal, flowing rhythm, with greater room for soloists to improvise. Having wrestled with the dynamic solo power of Louis Armstrong in the 1920s and then Coleman Hawkins in the early 1930s, Henderson created well-organized but still free arrangements that let the sections and soloists have their say. During the same period, Ellington was able to transform the dissonant harmonics of his "Jungle Band" from a gimmick into a standard feature of his unique sound. These advancements in the arranged style laid the foundation for the swing era that emerged after 1935.[45]

Yet plying their trade in the pit of the depression, black bands also had to appeal to disillusioned audiences—white and black. Henderson and Hopkins hired crooners who conveyed the introspective mood; Ellington not only hired Ivie Anderson as a singer, he wrote a whole series of mood pieces that captured the "down" side of the early 1930s. Duke toured extensively after 1931 across the South and in Europe, and he and other musicians were forced to deal with racial prejudice in its rawest forms. The general climate of defeat and poverty in Harlem, capped by the Riot of 1935, seemed to spell the end to the wildest hopes of the Harlem Renaissance. Ellington and other musicians pondered what role their music was to play in American life. He let his manager add popular lyrics to his songs and turned out a number of mood pieces that conveyed black America's own subdued tone and his diminished outlook. He wrote pieces on pastel blue themes like "Blue Mood," "Blue Tune," "Clouds in My Heart," "Solitude," "Sophisticated Lady," and, of course, "Mood Indigo." He also recorded "Stormy Weather," Ethel Waters's signature tune and an anthem of the era. These make less use of hot plungers and jungle sounds and more of quiet section work. The dissonant harmonies convey a sense of pervasive drift and a contemplation of fate.[46]

The Road Is Open Again

Although the depression continued, popular music underwent a powerful renaissance after 1935. Central to that resurgence were New Deal programs that stimulated the economy and brought back a measure of prosperity. Among the nation's youth, student work programs (Civilian Conservation

Corps, National Youth Administration) permitted a tempered optimism about the future. In addition, unprecedented numbers of young people remained in high school. Given the absence of jobs, a broad cross section of youth nationwide was in position to take advantage of new forms of entertainment. Of more immediate importance to musicians and entertainers was the repeal of Prohibition, the first act of the Democratic administration elected in 1932. Responding to organized lobbying groups and urban political machines, Democrats enunciated a platform of repeal and local option that enabled them to overcome the cultural battles over alcohol that had racked their party in the 1920s and made them the party of big-city Catholics and Jews. By the 1930s, Democrats argued that increased taxes on alcohol might stimulate the economy and that ending Prohibition might mitigate the lawlessness it had spawned. Through the mechanism of local option, repeal diffused Dry forces into innumerable local battles, especially since the major problem now was, according to Will Rogers, "food, not drink." Repeal thus decreased the power of those opposed to drink and increased the power of urban culture and amusements to expand and grow nationwide.[47]

The entertainment world quickly saw the potential of repeal and threw its support behind the New Deal. The election of 1932 signaled a shift of power in entertainment from prominent Republicans like Louis B. Mayer and Will Hays to New Deal supporters such as Harry Warner, president of Warner Brothers studios, vaudeville's Eddie Dowling, and Joseph Weber, president of the American Federation of Musicians. In fact, the AFM, "cognizant of the advantages that would accrue to musicians thru repeal of the prohibition amendment," urged its locals to support what it called "this vital social reform." Repeal would create "employment opportunities for hundreds of members" and divert "the huge profits now going to racketeers into legitimate business channels." Hollywood agreed, producing shorts endorsing repeal as a harbinger of a new day. Paramount's "New Deal Rhythm" showed congressmen enthusiastically demanding life, liberty, drink, and fun, while Warner's "The Road Is Open" depicted a blocked songwriter who came up with a new tune only when repeal and the New Deal allowed his creativity to flourish.[48]

When repeal passed in December 1933 and took full effect a year later, entertainment entrepreneurs, encouraged by new liquor revenues, expressed their optimism by reopening hotel dance rooms, ballrooms, and nightclubs. Billy Rose expressed entertainment's debt to repeal in the show "Here's to Broadway" at his Manhattan Music Hall. After reprising Broadway's grand past and attacking Prohibition's blight on amusements, the show forecast a "New Deal" for Broadway, with help from repeal and FDR. In some ways Rose was right. As a result of repeal, nightlife revived across the country. As *Variety* declared, "there are more niteries, pubs, taverns, roadside inns, large and small cafes, hotels and nite spots offering entertainment today than there were speakeasies during the Great Drought." Moreover, repeal allowed legitimate entrepreneurs into the industry. Ballrooms now were allowed to serve liquor, and dance hall owners soon had the revenue to hire touring big bands.[49]

New York musicians viewed this as their chance to leave the radio studios where they had been languishing to start their own bands and play creative music once again. Benny Goodman and the Dorsey Brothers followed the example of Glen Gray's Casa Loma Orchestra and began playing the new venues. Bankrupt and desperate for ready cash, Fletcher Henderson agreed to write a host of arrangements for Benny Goodman's *Let's Dance* radio program. In Goodman's hands, the arrangements would turn swing into a mass phenomenon equivalent to rock and roll, as the younger generation asserted its place in the sun through music and dance. The trends of the 1920s and 1930s would have another chance, but in light of the economic and cultural crises of the early 1930s, they would be linked less to crime and aristocratic decadence and more to central American values. Once they heard this new and exciting music, young people were prepared to go wild.[50]

PART TWO

Now They Call It Swing, 1935–1942

2

The Crowd Goes Wild

The Youth Culture of Swing

The melting pot boils over, and now we have the hoarse and jitterbuggy days. No longer prim, we've all gone primitive.—*Chicago Daily Tribune*, 26 August 1938

Swing is the voice of youth striving to be heard in this fast-moving world of ours. Swing is the tempo of our time. Swing is real. Swing is alive.—*New York Times*, 26 February 1939

Intent on giving the city's young people a rare opportunity to hear their music live, the New Century Committee of Chicago staged a free Swing Jamboree at Soldier Field on the evening of 24 August 1938. Drawing a racially mixed audience, the concert presented twenty white and black big-name orchestras, amateur band and dance contests, and "free public truckin'" on three dance stages. Before the gates closed, 100,000 fans streamed into the cavernous football stadium; outside almost as many gathered. Then, "with a deafening groan, the gates caved in, and the boys and girls poured in." The result "was a barrelhouse, boogie-woogie, bacchanal worthy of 18-year-old ecstasy, as it seemed the whole younger generation of the city—a generation born since the World War and scarred by the depression—let down its hair, lost its hat and danced wherever there was room to dance to the hot lick rhythms of gutbucket gorillas."[1]

Despite the crush, the Jamboree proved "the most hysterical orgy of joyous emotions by multitudes ever witnessed on the American continent." As Jimmy Dorsey's band went into "Flat Foot Floogie," one of the major anthems of the swing era, "men climbed over each other, girls perched on their partners' shoulders, babies were held aloft, the younger generation scrambled up on the stands, car tops and construction work at the north end . . . and swing really broke loose." Surging through police lines, the crowd overran the three dance platforms, "drove the white-coated dance bands to cover," and knocked out the microphones. When Jamboree officials finally managed to restore order, no time remained for the amateur contests. Before the professional bands resumed, however, young black men and women, stimulated by the Earl "Fatha" Hines Band, snake-danced through the crowd while other impatient fans played their own instruments, beat time on their bodies, and went wild over two seventeen-year-old amateur dancers who trucked, shagged, and pecked to "the off beat and wild rhythm of swing. The crowd loved 'em."[2]

Shocked reactions greeted this outpouring of "jitterbug ecstasy." Struck by such an unfettered emotional display, observers pondered the unprecedented crowd behavior. The *Daily News,* noting "the world's largest crowd . . . for a musical event," called the concert "the strangest manifestation of youthful exuberance perhaps ever witnessed since the Middle Ages' ill-fated Children's Crusade." Some psychologists warned of "mass hysteria" linked to "unrest, insecurity, repression . . . and . . . sex," but others dismissed the behavior as merely "simple, uncomplicated childishness." Instead of coupling, young people "came out in the circle . . . and danced in a mass."[3]

Whatever their views, all agreed with *Metronome* that "this is a perfect example of the powerful hold that swing has on its followers." For observer after observer who followed in the wake of Benny Goodman's surprising breakthrough in 1935, jazz had reached a mass audience by becoming the favorite music of American youth. Most historians, however, have tended to treat the swing audience as passive receivers of musical products rather than as active participants in creating a music vital to their own lives. In fact, black and white jitterbugs, like those at the Swing Jamboree, crashed the gates to express themselves through music despite parental objections and the restrictions on youthful lives and dreams created by the depression. More than ever before, the difficulties of earning a living and gaining independence through social mobility or marriage reduced the differences among young people. Increasingly part of the crowd, young people helped transform the whole concept of mass culture. When new voices of youth appeared in the 1930s, they forced dramatic changes in musical performance, democratized the consumption of music, and helped create what jazz critic Ralph Gleason calls a "whole way of life" around swing."[4]

Voices of Youth

Audience behavior sparked widespread debate over the nature of the most intense swing fan, the "jitterbug," and the dangers of mass musical culture. Worried about the nation's youth, critics attacked swing as a contagion spread by insidious rhythms that undermined self-control. One scientist maintained that the music caused sexual boldness, while classical violinist Fritz Kreisler claimed that jazz was "the expression of primeval instincts." Fears that black rhythms led to sexual barbarism underlay these concerns. James Moynahan traced swing's roots to "the rhythmic jungle chants of the descendants of Africans" and their "jungle discords." In the most extreme attack, Francis J. L. Beckman, the Catholic archbishop of Dubuque, denounced swing as "evil" and "communistic": "We permit jam sessions, jitterbug and cannibalistic rhythmic orgies," he declared, "to occupy a place in our social scheme of things, wooing our youth along the primrose path to hell."[5]

Even more prominent was the fear of a crowd psychology bordering on mass hysteria. Large public events, critics worried, would lead to youth riots and violence. Observers of the Swing Jamboree, for example, feared that the crowd's emotional intensity and interracial composition might have led to "real trouble." Some outbursts did occur, such as that at a Jimmie Lunceford concert at Los Angeles's Shrine Auditorium in March 1940, where white, black, Mexican, and Filipino jitterbugs rioted. The rise of fascism led to anxiety that jitterbugs represented the decline of rationality and the rise of a mass psychology that could produce what a Barnard College social scientist called "Musical Hitlerism."[6]

While many critics viewed the jitterbug as symbolic of mass culture's flaws, others defended swing as a positive expression of modern youth. Indeed, the negative reactions seem tame compared to those heard in the 1920s, when jazz was attacked in the name of defending white Protestant small-town values or the hierarchy of genteel American culture. In the 1930s, attacks rarely rose above the level of personal morality to that of national xenophobia. It became increasingly apparent that the country had indeed survived the jazz age. Even William Allan White, who considered swing "merely syncopated raw emotion," acknowledged that each generation created "its own rowdy modern music." Many parents shared this attitude. Some were hostile to what they considered "wild and strange" music and behavior, but this was tempered by the recollection of their own youthful musical foibles. Cultural relativism thus undercut the fears of critics and parents and permitted a modern youth culture to flower.[7]

Meanwhile, cultural commentators defended swing as a positive expression of modern youth. Irving Kolodin, for example, pointed out that "youngsters who have reached adolescence during its vogue recognize it as something of their own, an exciting and stimulating sound to which they react spontaneously." Similarly, a self-described jitterbug argued that one could not expect "a modern girl who drives a car, knows about planes and fast ships to monkey around with minuets. . . . Those dances go with horses and buggies." Music critic Cecelia Ager said that swing expressed "the immortal right of adolescence to assert itself" after the "darkest despair" of the depression. As a letter to the *New York Times* declared, "Swing is the voice of youth striving to be heard in this fast-moving world of ours."[8]

Defenders of swing further argued that it represented a democratic form of artistic expression. While deploring jitterbug excesses, Kolodin declared that swing contained "elements of a new art, the symbols of a significant musical renaissance." Gama Gilbert found it "the most widespread artistic medium of popular emotional expression." Another advocate noted that popular music "is the music of the cities" and "has a definite place in our musical expression." Agreeing, violinist Mischa Elman saw jitterbug dancing as "merely the social outlet for our city just as folk-dancing goes on in the country." Many music critics, writing in new jazz magazines, praised swing as a national art form created by blacks and adopted by a pluralistic society; jitterbugs, they said, only detracted from a true appreciation of the music's artistic potential. Avid defenses of swing and fervent attacks on fan behavior often issued from the same pens.[9]

Together, attackers and defenders viewed swing as the center of a national youth culture that transcended class, ethnicity, and race. Bandleader Larry Clinton called it "the most popular diversion in colleges," the "favorite sport of youngsters." In 1934 small groups of collegians kept jazz's flame alive by collecting records and forming "Hot Clubs" to sponsor jazz events, lobby for jazz recordings, and serve as listening groups. Many Ivy League newspapers, like Columbia University's *Spectator,* started swing record columns, which served as outlets for informed student opinion on popular music. Close to New York and Harlem and an early stop on the swing band circuit, New England colleges and cities strongly supported swing tours.[10]

Mass interest and a growing music industry quickly extended this musical youth culture beyond elite colleges. As bandleader Joe Reichman noted in 1942, everyone danced to the same numbers. With regional variations, "kids in Tennessee shag to the same music as the 'sharpies' in the Bronx." From the start, urban campuses and dancers asked for more jump tunes, while the more culturally conservative Midwest preferred ballads and novelties. Surveys in *Variety* and *Billboard* found that midwestern colleges lagged in swing interest, and then, as the editor of the University of Missouri's paper argued, "'It's gotta be smooth.'" The racially conservative South especially lagged behind other regions in appreciation for swing, but even there young people danced to black and white swing bands at proms and hops. Once Glenn Miller, the most popular dance band leader after 1939, moderated dance tempos, small-town youth across the nation also caught the bug. The eastern seaboard, the West Coast, and big midwestern cities, with numerous colleges and many blacks, Jews, and Italians, continued to lead the way.[11]

But it was high school students who composed the largest following for swing bands. Middle-class high schools had been important centers of youth culture in the 1920s, but in the 1930s lack of jobs forced even more working-class teens to stay in school. (From 1930 to 1940, high school enrollment rose from half to three-quarters of all fourteen- to eighteen-year-olds.) Often the attraction began in junior high, just as youth began to assert autonomy. Jack McNulty, the son of Irish working-class parents in Lawrence, Massachusetts, entered swing's subculture in 1937 at junior high hops. "Every aspect of my life and that of my friends, revolved around big bands, jazz, dancing, jitterbugging, in my formative teens." At that age "our heroes, our dress, look, styles, morals, sex lives" were based on immersion in bands and "the lives they showed us." The same year, fourteen-year-old Orin Stambaugh of York, Pennsylvania, was hooked by Harry James. "The freewheeling playing, the ad lib solos, the driving rhythms, all struck a very responsive chord. Although we did not articulate it then, we had found the music of our time."[12]

The utopian possibilities of swing attracted young people aspiring to establish their independence from their families and to affirm a more vigorous personal experience that cut across ethnic, class, and, at times, racial lines. More than ever before, popular music meant a new life for an expanding youth audience. Fans included prep school student Sidney Curran, whose father "detested [swing] so much so that I never played any in his hearing"; it was "an unconscious form of generation gap." In his quest for autonomy, McNulty found his parents less hostile, but his father despaired of his clothes and "ducktail haircut." For many, swing defined an American world of personal freedom different from their immigrant roots. Ted Karamanski came from a Polish working-class family in Chicago; his father worked half-time in the stockyards, his mother was a janitor. Going to high school gave Ted the chance to "do things like ordinary American children." His social club, the Jolly Jives—young men of Bohemian, Polish, and Irish descent—danced avidly but had little interest in their parents' polkas. In jitterbug dances, "for the first time [we] expressed [our] own ways," and created a new American identity built on personal experimentation, dating, and self-discovery. Small-town youth also sought new ways. Jean Lukhard's family left sharecropping to return to Marshall, Texas, in 1940 when her father got a part-time job. The Lukhards now had indoor plumbing, electricity, "and best of all: a RADIO!!" Her family loved Grand Ole Opry, but she chose "Glenn Miller and the others," who better expressed her "awakening hormones." In York, Pennsylvania, Louise Strayer's friends also saw Opry as "the worst kind of music," and she didn't want her friends to know that her parents listened to it.[13]

As they made this music their own, white youth from varied class and ethnic backgrounds identified less with traditional icons of wealth and more with a musical expression created by those who had been left out of the American success story. In fact, it was youth from racial groups outside white society who invested swing with an intense search for liberation from the racial and class restrictions of their lives. Black youth invented most of the new dances that accompanied the music, created swing's slang and clothing, and idolized black musicians as heroes. Urban black youth faced more unemployment than their white peers and had fewer leisure outlets. Living in rooming houses apart from families more than other groups did, young black men and women could more readily frequent dance halls and clubs. Sixteen-year-old Malcolm Little, for instance, a recent migrant to Boston from East Lansing, Michigan, was free to absorb the "neon lights, night clubs, poolhalls, bars" where juke boxes blared the music of "Erskine Hawkins, Duke Ellington, Cootie Williams, dozens of others." Mexican Americans also followed the music intensely. Together with her friends, Gloria Vargas, a poor girl in the Lincoln Heights section of Los Angeles, won playground dance contests and frequented ballrooms and theaters whenever her favorite bands played. She loved the challenge and recognition of the dance contests and "the high that I would get hearing the band playing." For a time she styled herself a Zoot Suit girl, and the music became more important to her than school.[14]

Youth of all races thus followed black and white bands as extensions of their own hopes and dreams. As they criss-crossed the nation, performing endless one-nighters for young people in small towns and cities, bands were as powerful as the railroad trains that chugged across the prairies, and the musicians seemed as glamorous as movie stars. "You must never forget that you're making rhythms for the kids," noted one bandleader. "You're . . . the only flesh-and-blood entertainment thousands of rural communities experience since minstrel shows and vaudeville disappeared." Dressed in sleek uniforms, playing behind streamlined music stands shimmering with the excitement of modern urban life, they heralded dynamic movement over fixity, inclusiveness over exclusivity. When bands swung the classics or folk tunes, as in Maxine Sullivan's treatment of "Loch Lomond," or created flagwavers like "In the Mood" or novelties like Ella Fitzgerald and Chick Webb's "A Tisket a Tasket," they challenged the authority of the past and provided a picture of a future open to new experience. That potential also gave boys and girls the chance to experiment with the opposite sex on their own terms. In a world of music, the swing bands and their young fans articulated a desire "to live 'in marble halls'—even though the plumbing be bad."[15]

Make Believe Ballroom

In creating a swing subculture, young people transformed the consumption of jazz. While movies and radio shows courted general audiences, young people forced music institutions to cater to their desires to form a world of their own in more inclusive spaces. By creating a national network of musical outlets, for instance, band agencies, radio stations, and jukeboxes brought urban culture to smaller towns, made musicians household names, and gave youth easy access to music of their choice. Without cost on radio or for the price of a nickel in a jukebox or twenty-five cents at a movie theater, young people could hear their favorite bands at will. A combination of ready access and the mechanical reproduction of music removed some of the sacredness surrounding works of art, enabling young fans to treat swing as particularly theirs. When they screamed at a concert or danced in the aisles to an exciting band, they were exercising their right to respond to music in their own ways—not as parents, bandleaders, or swing critics told them they must behave. At the same time, swing musicians operated nationally, in more open, democratic spaces. Those spaces now included greater interaction between whites and blacks than ever before. As aural media, radio and records removed some of the visual definitions of race, allowing music played by blacks or whites to reach the senses in direct, unrestricted ways. The swing era thus witnessed the possibility for mass personal liberation and the democratization of cultural connoisseurship.[16]

During the depression, radio "was our main source for big band music," recalls Elliot White of Graham, North Carolina. As the cheapest form of commercial amusement, radio grew steadily in popularity. "Few of us," noted Sidney Curran of New Britain, Connecticut, "could afford records, let alone record players." For firms hit hard by the economic crisis, radio offered direct access to mass audiences of youthful consumers. Eager to tap this economic potential, advertisers featured in prime time the type of music they thought would attract a large following. Yet sponsors could not always predict the type of music that would grab listeners. In 1935, for example, National Biscuit's *Let's Dance* program on NBC presented three types of music—melodic, Latin, and Benny Goodman's jazz, with the latter on from 12:30 to 1 A.M. After a single season sponsors dropped Goodman, but West Coast fans, who had heard him from 9:30 to 10 P.M., knew about the band and turned out to hear it several months later in Los Angeles. Because of his new popularity with youth, Camel Cigarettes and CBS decided to sign Goodman on to a nationally broadcast *Camel Caravan* show, and Camel sponsored Bob Crosby as well. Other cigarette and personal care firms dependent on a youth market soon joined them: Chesterfield sponsored Hal Kemp, Glenn Miller, and Harry James; Philip Morris backed Horace Heidt; and Raleigh offered Tommy Dorsey. Over the years, Old Golds sponsored Whiteman and Woody Herman, Coca-Cola had a *Spotlite* on various bands, and Wildroot Cream Oil presented Woody Herman.[17]

Late-night remote broadcasts, meanwhile, transported youth to nightclubs, ballrooms, and theaters where bands played live. After the New York and Chicago stations signed off, Milwaukeean Carl Smaida noted, West Coast programs were broadcast "until the wee hours of the morning. This was the usual fare for radio stations after the news ended at 10:30 P.M. until their sign-off time." As Chicagoan Howard Becker recalled, "I used to listen to earshots from night clubs and ballrooms . . . I would hear everything in the distance . . . from everywhere: Wichita, Pittsburgh, and Denver." In sum, "I had a whole geography in my head, of places where big bands played." For young people, according to critic John Wilson, radio created a mixture of places, names, and events that "were immediately and exhilaratingly real, but at the same time were part of the fabric of dream-world fantasy." Announcers fed the fantasy, describing the crowd at the dreary Essex House Hotel, for instance, as "a sea of happy faces dining and dancing here in this beautiful dining room overlooking lovely Central Park in New York." Hokum or not, fans at home could construct a world of excitement outside the everyday humdrum.[18]

While most sponsored radio was racially segregated, there were opportunities for youth of all races to hear black bands. On *Camel Caravan*, for example, Goodman regularly presented his integrated trio and quartets featuring "professors" Gene Krupa, Teddy Wilson, and Lionel Hampton as well as regular guests such as Ella Fitzgerald, Count Basie, and Billie Holiday. But Goodman was an exception; as the King of Swing, he had the leverage to get his way with reluctant sponsors and music business executives. As a consequence, it was the sustaining programs (known as "sustainers"), either remote broadcasts ("remotes") from various locations or local late-night programming, that offered greater chances to hear black bands than nationwide shows whose sponsors worried about losing the southern white market. Roy Porter, a poor black youth in Colorado, for example, had few luxuries other than his radio. During prime time he heard white bands, and afterward, "once in a while you could hear Jimmie Lunceford, Count Basie, and Erskine Hawkins' bands from the Savoy Ballroom in Harlem or Duke Ellington and Earl Hines from the Grand Terrace Ballroom in Chicago." At the same time, Count Basie rose to national fame through remotes from the Famous Door on Fifty-second Street in 1938. Late-night broadcasts not only added to a black band's allure, they also attracted white fans.[19]

In addition to remotes from Harlem's Cotton Club, Savoy Ballroom, and Apollo Theater, black bands received some exposure on local radio shows that featured the first disc jockeys spinning records and on unsponsored programs. Independent (local) radio stations around the country saw an opportunity to compete with the powerful networks by playing "an inexhaustible supply of recorded jazz" that included work by Louis Armstrong, Duke Ellington, and Benny Goodman. The more commercially valuable the airtime became, of course, the less attention was given to the music. Such was the case with WNEW's (New York) *Make Believe Ballroom*, which had a national audience. For years the show was, according to one listener, "a letter from home for jazzophiles," as disc jockey Martin Block played "the best new records." The highlight of the week was *Saturday Night in Harlem*, a two-hour version of the program featuring the finest black bands in New York. As the show attracted a larger following, however, it became commercially valuable, and an increasing number of ballads replaced jazz. Other network shows, responding to youth demand, presented a mix of black and white swing to the public. The fledgling CBS network, competing hard with the more established NBC, relied on popular music shows to attract young audiences. WABC in New York broadcast swing shows on morning and afternoon sustainers, reserving the Saturday slot for "Saturday Night Swing," the "hottest show ever put on." The Raymond Scott Quintet, an innovative and wacky swing unit, did the house band chores, with guest appearances by the top jazzmen in New York, including Benny Carter, Roy Eldridge, Fats Waller, and Jack Teagarden. The least "commercial" programs were usually the most innovative—both musically and racially.[20]

Teenage listeners recognized the link between music and personal identity, and their first declaration of independence was often an argument with parents over control of the radio. At fourteen, Leonard Pratt of Des Moines argued "with my dad, who wanted to hear *Amos 'n' Andy,* while I wanted to listen to the *Hit Parade.*" To avoid such battles, many teens simply went out and purchased their own radios. Jean Lukhard noted that "most of us had our own little radios at bedside (mine was a little white Philco named Oscar)." So popular were band shows that parents of high schoolers often prohibited radios in their childrens' rooms. As one parent put it, "It's not that I object to swing. But I don't think they should study to it or go to sleep to it." Yet many did. Every night, Elliot White fell asleep with "the radio tuned to late-night band broadcasts." If they could afford it, teens used car radios to define their world. Pratt saved his paper-route money to put a radio "in the family car as soon as I was allowed to drive it." Music "on the car radio while joy riding or parked in lovers lane" led to intimacy with the opposite sex. "Many times, the car battery was drained . . . while listening and necking in a secluded parking space." South Carolinian Sara Vann said, "If someone we dated had a car with a radio . . . we would park somewhere, maybe at the end of a dead-end street, and dance on the pavement."[21]

The young used radio in their dating culture in other ways. Teens had inexpensive dates at home, in which they danced to the radio, drank beverages, necked, and used the lyrics to communicate their feelings to the opposite sex. At another level, certain programs were generational rituals, with young fans as devoted listeners. "One of our almost religiously observed" activities at Prep School, notes Curran, was listening to *Make Believe Ballroom.* At Davidson College, White reports, "every radio on campus would be turned to the same station. No one cracked a book" until Miller's closing theme "faded from the airwaves." *Your Hit Parade* on Saturday nights was another icon, according to June Canter. She and her friends were glued to the radio "waiting to hear if [their] favorite song was number one." They rooted for their favorites as the songs climbed the charts and debated the worth of each tune. (And for ten cents, one could buy various *Hit Parade* books of popular song lyrics.) Others rooted for different reasons. During a parlor date, Lukhard's boyfriend asked, "If Amapola is number one, may I kiss you?" When it hit the top spot, "I got my first kiss."[22]

While radio linked the private home to the public world, the jukebox transformed public spaces into inexpensive arenas for youth dancing and dating removed from the parental eye. Young people could select their music for a nickel in soda fountains, candy shops, restaurants, and pool rooms. As a result, jukeboxes exploded in popularity, accounting for 44 percent of all popular records sold, or 30 million a year at swing's height. To attract patrons, for example, Orin Stambaugh reports that Sadie Stover installed a jukebox in her restaurant in Spring Grove, Pennsylvania, in 1939, "cleared the center area for dancing and invited the young adults to eat, dance, and enjoy the music." Seeking people her own age with her own tastes, Louise Strayer frequented a soda fountain "where in the middle of everything was that beautiful Juke Box with bright lights and for only a nickel we could listen to that great sound and forget all the troubles." Since no alcohol was served, parents were more willing to let their young go to dance and mix with members of the opposite sex. At the same time, jukeboxes let whites hear the music of black bands and singers. Given exposure on remotes from the Savoy Ballroom, Levaggi's in Boston, and Moe Gale's "Goodtime Society," Ella Fitzgerald and Chick Webb, for example, had several major jukebox hits. They started with "A Tisket a Tasket," followed by "Undecided," both on Decca, which specialized in records for jukeboxes. Similarly, while selections by black performers were often limited, Jack McNulty recalls frequenting a pool hall run by a Syrian American whose jukebox played only tunes by Count Basie and Jimmie Lunceford. He had thought that black bands were only "natural" swingers, incapable of fine ensemble work. But "I learned to be tolerant in that pool room." McNulty soon joined Al Kattar's "motor caravans, to see these black bands, whenever they played within 150 miles of Boston."[23]

Similarly, movie theaters featured swing bands at cut rates to draw youth. When the depression made it impossible for New York's Paramount Theater to fill its 3,664 seats, manager Bob Weitman turned to big-name bands, realizing that "at least half the public who patronized a boisterous young band in the fall of 1936 were as happy listening as they were dancing to it." *Metronome* found attendance up 100 percent at matinees, with teens the "foundation of box office receipts" during the day. Theaters across the country followed suit. "Early shows were the norm everywhere, because our music was the entertainment of youth," noted Woody Herman. "Kids would skip school to hear us before the prices changed [at] noon." Sitting through B movies was a small price to pay as the fans waited for the band to rise from the pit, creating magic with "their gleaming golden instruments flashing in the spotlights that bathed the whole scene." Unlike the 1920s, when bands were part of a longer program, now they were "a show in itself, as the current fashion has it." By putting bands on stages with special lighting and sets—and, at the Paramount, on stages that elevated the band over the pit—film houses promoted the concert status of swing bands, showcasing their artistry and power. Of Count Basie at Omaha's Orpheum in 1941, for instance, a listener noted, "the acoustics in the old, traditional movie houses captured the sounds of the great swing bands in a unique way. The cathedral-like height of the stage and back stage and the width and breadth of the seating auditorium gave the music a special resonance." "There was hardly time to catch your breath," another fan noted; "the band was already pulsating with life, the front sax section filling the hall with sweet notes, the brass setting your ears afire."[24]

In staging swing bands, movie houses became unexpected arenas of youthful audience participation, as formerly staid movie palaces featured Jitterbug Nights and dance contests. Radio City Music Hall presented amateur lindy hoppers from Harlem's Savoy Ballroom, where they competed for cash prizes. In fact, several Savoy groups traveled a circuit of theaters and clubs putting on shows and competing for prize money in front of audiences large and small, with audience applause determining the winners. In Philadelphia, one maestro drew his best house the night "bugs were turned loose on the stage." Jitterbug contests became a major attraction at Harlem's Apollo Theater, and on Wednesday night (amateur night) youngsters could display their talents backed by a top swing unit.[25]

Meanwhile, the young fans in the audience let go their emotions, challenging the rules of theater decorum and setting themselves on an equal footing with the band. Whenever a band would take off and play a killer-diller, as particularly loud and fast numbers such as Goodman's "Sing, Sing, Sing" or Basie's "One o'Clock Jump," were called, young people would go wild. Although Goodman was often annoyed by such behavior, he was forced to recognize something unique about swing fans: "We looked at them, I guess, [as if] they were the show and we were the audience." They clapped time, bounced in their seats, and screamed. They also danced in the aisles and onstage, a practice that began with Goodman's first Paramount stint in March 1937. Unlike the sedentary audience that most sweet bands observed, noted the *Los Angeles Times* about that climactic engagement, a polyglot group of kids would "jump out of their seats and actually hold a Carnival in the aisles." When "the band played a hot, fast one a . . . youth grabbed his best girl and proceeded to shag in the main aisle." Ushers rushed to stop them, according to the *San Francisco Chronicle,* but "theater history was made when . . . a few more of the enthusiastic swingdings tried to climb onto the stage, lured irresistibly forward by the Pied Piper of the clarinet," and took "to shagging *on the stage* with the audience beating out a vast rhythm with their palms." Dozens more jammed the pit, content to stand there and "soak in the throbbing rhythms." Ultimately the manager was forced to throw a cordon of ushers around "the plague spots."[26]

After this, audience response often bordered on the riotous. At the Stanley Theater in Pittsburgh in 1941, the management was forced to call the police to quell a commotion of young fans. Trombonist Lou McGarrity, who was in charge of the band while Benny Goodman was undergoing his army physical, said, "Go away man. We've got this place jumping." When Duke Ellington played the Palace in Fort Wayne, Indiana, noted Charles Travelbee, "there was pure pandemonium, dancing in the aisles, in the orchestra pit . . . we all went nuts." In Des Moines, Leonard Pratt said, "more than once we impulsively got out of our seats to swing in the aisles to the faster numbers, not hearing the ushers screaming 'Please sit down.'" It was the same at a Glenn Miller Bond Rally in St. Louis in 1944, according to Leonard Meenach. "The young people were dancing in the aisles and the lobby. This was a very exciting reminder of present day rock concerts and just as loud and wild. It took several policemen to control the crowd." Indeed, the Brandt Theatres in New York had house police patrol the aisles to "curb effervescent jitterbugs." Other forms of behavior reached extremes too. When Tommy Dorsey played the Paramount, Travelers' Aid agents grabbed a girl in the first row who had followed Dorsey to New York from Pittsburgh via Washington, D.C. Each day she entered the theater as it opened and stayed seated until the last performance of the night. She lasted through fifty-four successive shows before they sent her home.[27]

This carnival helped young people transcend the depressing outside world and the restraints of adult prescription. In reviewing Glenn Miller at a Cleveland theater, a critic showed how out of place adults felt when the young let go. The more rhythmic the music, "the louder the cheers and applause from the audience, and when the brasses and the drummer began to work on the emotion of the crowd, I began to question both its sanity and mine." Another wrote, "The frenzy and the ecstasy" Miller created "are as far beyond me as they always are when the boys and girls get into the groove." Swing's elemental nature, he added, was both "impolite and inconsiderate. It seems to be a case of every emotion for itself . . . it stirs other emotions as well as other individuals to be up and doing—and shouting." This expressiveness also transformed genteel concert halls. When Goodman's sextet played Rochester's Eastman Theater, for example, "one could almost feel the temperature of the audience rise as the session progressed, with the floor vibrating to the 'jitterbugging' of the enraptured audience, over whom an hypnotic rhythmic spell was so astonishingly exerted."[28]

Dance of the Jitterbugs

If the desire for release transformed theaters into impromptu ballrooms, dance halls assumed new importance as settings for mass self-expression in an era of scarcity. "It was not that places did not exist in the Twenties," a fan said, "but then there were more things to do and see, and there was more money for traveling." In fact, ballrooms replaced nightclubs as key jazz institutions because the former appealed to a mass rather than a class clientele. Ballrooms competed with clubs by adding a "nitery atmosphere with tables, liquors and foods." *Variety* noted that the "idea that dancing was dancing and clubbing was clubbing and the two could never meet has been dissipated." As a result, bands played music for dancing and put on shows with singers, small combos, and special arrangements.[29]

By adapting the cabaret to more modest circumstances, and by mixing dancing with performing, the ballroom of the 1930s helped democratize the nightclub. With its new aura of sophistication, the dance hall allowed young people to experiment with adulthood. To aid those on limited budgets, many halls abolished the "taxi dance" custom—charging men to dance with hostesses. Ballrooms also stopped charging a couple for each dance. Instead, halls now established a fixed entrance fee to encourage couple dancing. "The fact that they can dance whenever they want to without thinking of the money involved each time, encourages them," noted the manager of Broadway's Arcadia Ballroom. As part of the democratization process, halls also offered a variety of contests and special events to attract a diverse patronage. Harlem's Savoy Ballroom, for example, instituted Thursday Kitchen Mechanics Nights, bathing beauty contests, and Sunday Opportunity Days when dancers competed for cash prizes. Exciting and more inclusive than in the past, modern ballrooms took jazz outside the swanky club or low-class dive and made it accessible to ordinary young people.[30]

Like jukeboxes, ballrooms also made black bands more accessible to white audiences. While hotels, theaters, and sponsored radio programs rarely presented black bands, dance halls booked them for one-nighters. In general, the swing era witnessed an increase in dancing by whites to black bands and in listening and dancing by black audiences to white or mixed units. The Savoy attracted a sizable white patronage, and white units like those of Charlie Barnet, Goodman, and Miller played there or at the Apollo. A surprised *Metronome* noted "the great reception accorded white bands in Harlem recently" and the "near riot that broke out when Charlie Barnet shattered all precedent and opening day records as he brought the first white

Lindy hoppers take flight, Savoy Ballroom, New York City, early 1940s. Frank Driggs Collection.

band into the Apollo Theatre." When Goodman and his integrated quartet played the Paramount, black patronage jumped from 3 to 15 percent of the house.[31]

Black dancers may not have been welcome at white dance halls, but black bands regularly crossed racial lines to play white dances. As R. L. Larkin noted, "The swarms of jitterbugs of the 1937–39 period . . . knew no color lines, and to them Chick Webb and Count Basie were as fine to jig to as Goodman and Shaw." Fan accounts support this observation. Down South, black bands played for whites or for whites and blacks divided by a rope across the dance floor in elegant ballrooms or in huge cotton or tobacco warehouses. Despite segregation, white fans patronized black bands. Ruth Shapiro, a young white woman from Dallas, found herself uncomfortable listening to Count Basie in Harlem, but she eagerly went to hear black bands in whiter settings in Texas. Elliot White on several occasions drove or hitchhiked across North Carolina to attend dances played by Chick Webb and Basie. Once, he and several friends sat outside a tobacco warehouse for hours listening to Erskine Hawkins. "It was a black dance. So we couldn't go in. So much for segregation!"[32]

Whatever the setting, white jitterbugs crossed racial barriers by doing black dances. Not only did whites and blacks perform similar dances, whites acknowledged that the steps originated in black culture and that the best dancers were black. As the *New York Times* put it, "The white jitterbug is oftener than not uncouth to look at, but his Negro original is quite another matter. His movements are never so exaggerated that they lack control, and there is an unmistakable dignity about his most violent figures." A fan who was a junior high school girl in the Bronx notes wistfully that "we all wished we were old enough to go to the Savoy Ballroom, as that was where the really hip jitterbugs showed their stuff." Even in Bangor, Maine, and Holdenville, Oklahoma, it was clear that Harlem created the new dances. Newspaper headlines in both towns read, "Mad 'Suzy-Q' Is Harlem's New Gift to Swing." Uncouth or not, whites adopted black moves in their quest for greater personal freedom.[33]

The inventive new dance styles were sparked by black jitterbugs at Harlem's Savoy Ballroom. A "folk avant garde" created the lindy hop in 1927 while improvising variations on the Charleston. The lindy's simple open hold and the relaxed 4/4 beat of swing allowed dancers to invent the lindy's most unusual feature, the "breakaway." Encouraged by the underlying security of the beat, dancers engaged in flights of improvisational fancy. At the climactic moment partners let go of each other's hands, and then, noted the dancer Shorty Snowden, "anything you could dream up was okay for the breakaway, you tried all kinds of things." In 1936, a group of younger dancers added air steps. In moves such as the back flip, the over-the-head, and the snatch, men threw their partners in the air, between their legs, and over their backs and caught them on the beat as they came down. In swing, one could fly.[34]

As the new forms swept the swing subculture from the bottom up, according to Marshall and Jean Stearns, they caused "a general revolution in the popular dance in the United States." White youth took up the black vernacular variations on the lindy and delivered the death blow to the ballroom gentility that had linked dance to social manners and courtship rather than to individual freedom. The Charleston had opened up the traditional couple embrace in the 1920s, to be sure, but its movements usually were a momentary, jerky, and vertical diversion in the fox-trot. Even then most dancers had a standard step, "always dancing close to our partners," in the basic waltz and fox-trot. By grounding the movements of the dancers in a steady, 4/4 horizontal beat, however, swing let one "get with it and be carried away." And, when partners became separated, they would truck or strut "or maybe improvise something on their own." At first middle-class whites were shocked by the pelvic rotation necessary to keep one moving with the flow of swing rhythms. Pittsburgh dancer Ernie Smith turned to the working-class girls in nearby mill towns for with-it partners. Moving in authentic flowing style, they were the first white girls who "could really dance." With Glenn Miller's more relaxed tempos, introduced in 1939, the lindy achieved mass success. Still, Smith noted, it remained "a black dance even when whites were doing it" and became "the bread-and-butter style" of subsequent generations as it consolidated steps from the turkey trot to the Charleston into a full-fledged American form that *Life* called "a true national folk dance." Since "the Lindy revolution," notes dancer George Wendler, no "conservative style of dancing" has succeeded.[35]

With these decidedly improvisational steps, black and white dancers discarded "the sophisticated mask" of the ballroom. As Cecelia Ager put it, "After years of dancing in darkest despair, of straying about the dance floor as if they didn't care if they lived or died," young people now came "into their birthright" to enjoy themselves again. Earlier steps had been "very smooth, very uniform, very easy, very lifeless and very unrhythmic." Now kids "could try improvising with their feet and bodies, instead of just listening to somebody else do it with a horn." The new steps gave the young a great amount of personal freedom. "You don't see a whole ballroom moving sedately around in the same direction with the same steps—ice-skating style." Instead, noted music critic Mike Levin, "you see some very good and very bad stabs at really original styles."[36]

An important part of interaction between the sexes, these steps featured honest emotional expression more than overt sexuality or obsessive and sentimental love. Levin reported that "the way most of these kids dance, they are seldom less than four feet apart—which permits of far less jive than I remember in the dreamy Lombardo days." There was sexual suggestion, to be sure, as girls twirled with enough force to show legs and panties, but it was playful absorption in the moment. Rooted in the dance's earthy horizontal movements and the steady beat, both partners could be themselves rather than play the usual social and gender roles. According to Ager, both sexes "care less than nothing about how they look. They are dancing entirely for themselves, animated by high and supremely honest emotion." Letting "oneself go naturally," there was little room for social niceties: "People can't talk in a trance." Free improvisation let girls and boys break through sentimental facades and fixed roles to more independent selves.[37]

The lindy held out a model for the sexes. The dance depended on coordination between partners, which took practice. "Young people in those days took their dancing very seriously," says dancer Dean Collins. "They spent a lot of time with their partner." The Bronx fan notes that partners practiced

Jitterbug dancers, Hotel Pennsylvania, ca. 1937. Frank Driggs Collection.

all week to big band arrangements for the Friday afternoon school dances. Moreover, the dance's hand clasp engaged boys and girls in intimate communication, ensuring that the couple could survive the centrifugal force and the obstacles of the dance. At the same time, the rooted quality of the beat balanced flight. To let go, both sexes had to be down to earth. It was not that slow dancing and romance were not important, but rather that the lindy created a sense of liberating camaraderie and interplay. The males still led, but toward the freedom of both genders in an erotic relationship removed from the world. "He may improvise all sorts of fantastic figures and even try a touch of acrobatics, to all of which his partner will respond with calm and cooperative agility," noted the *New York Times*. Couples aimed for a spontaneous union. "During the faster numbers," notes Leonard Pratt, "there was the simultaneous sharing of the quicker steps, the twirls and turns which gave us a feeling inside of togetherness not achieved in any other activity."[38]

At any ballroom where a swing band played, the message was as clear as Harry James's or Roy Eldridge's trumpet: on the dance floor, amid a crowd of other people, ecstasy and personal freedom could be asserted against the depersonalized and restrictive modern world. In these dances both sexes expressed their individuality. In their improvisations, young men and women confidently carved out the space around them with their horizontal thrusts and recreated themselves through their unique movements. Without the aid of teachers, new popular dances spread quickly from black culture into the white working and middle classes. Joyful yet serious, swing dancing, as expressed by Jimmie Lunceford and Trummy Young's "'Taint What You Do (But the Way That Ya Do It)," elevated stylistic, relaxed movement as a form of grace under pressure and a way to withstand the chaos and uncertainty of the modern world.

Swing bands played more than fast lindys. When a good swing band focused its hot sound on love songs, it intensified the personal meanings of ballads. "We had fun dancing to swing," notes Kentuckian Susie Tucker. "We knew about romance from the love songs." Chummy MacGregor, Glenn Miller's pianist, writes that during the last hour of a dance, "we made a lot of friends with those long dreary dance sessions with the lights low, the tempo relaxed, those nice saxophones, and Ray Eberle stirring the imagination of all the 'jail bait' sub-debs in the hall." As he asserts, "more engagement rings" were "contracted for (on the installment plan)" at school dances or lakeside pavilions than anywhere else. Often, notes Leonard Pratt, "the initial romantic relationship began on the dance floor." As he and a girl danced, their cheeks touched and they drifted along to the "dreamy melody," and "whispers of the romantic lyrics in her ear soon followed."[39]

Unlike sweet music, however, swing fused love songs to a jazz style that gave ballads a lift and heightened their emotional power. Each band's use of individualized arrangements and versatile instrumentation helped make love songs seem more personal. Band singers performed a chorus of a song much as an instrumental soloist would, while the full band teased out the emotional nuances. At the end, no matter the sentiment, the band picked up the tempo as if to affirm that life goes on despite obstacles and that dreams come true. In "These Foolish Things," "It's All Yours," "I'll Never Smile Again," "Stardust," "Memories of You," "Green Eyes," "Darn That Dream," "Begin the Beguine," and "I Let a Song Go out of My Heart"—to cite only a few—love was an agent that would transport one from the everyday to the exalted. Yet these romantic songs lacked the self-pity, insecurity, and obsessive sentimentality of early '30s torch songs. Instead, they promised possibility, even in a depression. In "It's All Yours," Helen Forrest, who sang with Artie Shaw, Benny Goodman, and Harry James, offers "everything you see" to encourage her love to come out of his "cloister" and enjoy life. When singing "Imagination," Frank Sinatra mused that dreaming of his girl made "a cloudy day sunny." With her swing sensibility and her spectacular improvisational skills, Billie Holiday transformed even the most maudlin tune into a testament to the power of the human spirit.[40]

Many songs emphasized dreams of love that all listeners could share, rather than hopes of success or status, which the depression rendered much more difficult to achieve. In fact, the songs asserted the importance of dreams, as against the obstacles placed in the way of their realization, and still chose love over money. In Jimmie Lunceford's rendition of "Slumming on Park Avenue," the singer juxtaposes her modest social position to that of the "rich," while "Position's Everything in Life" holds up a basic truth. In "I Can't Afford to Dream," Tony Pastor, the singer for Artie Shaw, announces, "I dream but I shouldn't," because he lacks money to make the dreams come true. Martha Tilton, a vocalist with Benny Goodman, sang the depression standard "I Can't Give You Anything But Love," observing that "diamond bracelets Woolworth's doesn't sell." Although lack of money was a problem, the rich were too concerned with money to have any fun. In "The Honorable So and So," Helen Forrest portrays a woman kept by a socialite more interested in social position than in love. In the bitterest song of the era, "God Bless the Child," Billie Holiday notes that rich relations might give handouts, but it was better to be "the child that's got his own."

Despite obstacles of class and circumstance, the young followed Forrest in yearning, "I Want My Share of Love." They might be "rented dreams," but "rented or not, they help a lot." Comparing Wall Street to empty pockets, "I've Got a Pocketful of Dreams" held up the superior worth of ideals and hopes for the future. "I Can't Get Started," another standard of the era, moreover, has the singer traveling around the world in a plane, settling revolutions in Spain, but all his wealth and power do not satisfy him. While some songs were undeniably escapist, an indomitable spirit emerges in tunes such as "I've Got a Right to Dream." Despite the depression, these songs seemed to say, one had a right to feel good, find love, and enjoy life. Irene Daye, who sang with Gene Krupa's band, for instance, claimed that she "Never Had Less, Never Felt Better." As in the fast dances, moreover, the search was less for frivolity than for a mate who could love you for yourself. In "You're a Lucky Guy," the singer notes that "you've got a honey who wants no money / who'll take you just as you are." Similarly, Frank Sinatra and Tommy Dorsey essayed a better world where "There Are Such Things" as someone "not caring what you own / but just what you are." In a parallel, Ella Fitzgerald sang "I've Got a Guy" who "don't dress me in sable / He looks nothing like Gable / But he's mine." Although he is tough, "He's just a gem, in the rough."

The democratization process at work on the dance floor also influenced the fashion and the slang adopted by young jitterbugs. In the beginning, noted Helen Ward, girls "were all dressed up, but then when the lindy really caught on, the gals began wearing saddle shoes," the white "bobby sox," and the full skirts "necessary to do all those gyrations." Later in the decade, girls wore short skirts, and boys, sport coats without ties. Chicago high schooler Gloria Sadowski agreed. "You enter with your escort. He's dressed in a two-tone tweed suit, saddle shoes, bright rainbow socks, bow tie." The girl is "dressed almost the same," unlike the pretty girl who is "out of place" with her "high-heeled shoes, silk stockings, a pretty blue dress." The style expressed deeper concerns. In Leonard Pratt's experience, the "marriage-oriented, prestige girls" wanted guys with cars and money, but they were "not known to be fun-loving, were not in my circle of friends and were not in the majority. Rarely did I see them at a dance featuring a big band."[41]

In addition to a general informality, around 1940 specialized male attire emerged that was more decidedly working-class, black, and rebellious in origin—the zoot suit. The zoot suit achieved wide popularity among blacks in northern cities, especially Harlem, Chicago, and Boston, among Mexican Americans in Los Angeles, and among working-class white "sharpies," all of whom made a style out of their marginal social status in defiance of middle-class expectations of respectability. The zoot suit featured trousers that had tight cuffs and very wide knees, thus producing a "pegged" effect. The single-breasted jacket had wide artificial shoulders and a narrow waist and came to the thighs. Men might also adopt the porkpie hat and the long key chain. Malcolm X, who purchased his first zoot in 1940, noted, "That was just wild. The sky-blue pants thirty inches in the knee and angle-narrowed down to twelve inches at the bottom, and a long coat that pinched my waist and flared out below my knees." The hat was wild too. "Blue, with a feather in the four-inch brim." The store threw in a long, gold-plated chain "that swung down lower than my coat hem." His half sister Ella was dismayed by its impropriety. Because of its outrageousness, the zoot suit remained a "minority" style that took on greater importance as a result of the social dislocations of World War II. Yet, it emerged from the street, entered the music world, and affected hepcat dress. Its influence showed in the wide-shouldered jackets and broad-legged pants of the day.[42]

Along with new styles of dress, jive—a slang language code invented by blacks—circulated in the music world and influenced the language of swing-loving youth. Goodman noted that "a whole new crop of words has been created" by musicians "which describe what goes on in Swing." Many of these terms originated in black street and musical cultures, according to Cab Calloway's 1936 *Hepster's Dictionary,* and made their way to white swing fans. For example, the clothier Harold Fox took the name "zoot suit" from street slang. "It was cool in those days to talk in rhymes," he said. The highest compliment you could pay something was to say it was the end to end all ends. "I needed a word to rhyme with suit, so I used the letter of the alphabet that is the end to end all ends—Z—and came up with 'zoot.'" This rhythmic invention and manipulation of the world through language, so popular among lower-class blacks and jazz musicians, soon entered the larger society, often through swing songs such as Slam Stewart and Slim Gaillard's "Flat Foot Floogie with a Floy Floy" or through musicians themselves. Goodman explained to fans that improvisations were "licks, riffs, or get-offs," the improviser is called "the sender" or the "ride-man," and when he gets going he's "in the groove." For those who needed to know, "we swing musicians," he said, "are called cats." Swing dancers "are fondly termed alligators." While musicians soon rejected these overused terms, jive talk rooted black and white swing fans in the street and hence helped them keep their feet on the ground. Along with fashion, dance, and music, jive language bespoke a creolization of American youth culture.[43]

To Hell with the Jitterbugs

For many jitterbugs, the emotional experience of swing transcended romance. Eager fans transformed dance hall culture by crowding around bandstands to watch and listen; some listeners exhibited wild bodily exertions even without partners. Goodman described the first jitterbug he ever saw. At a Kansas City ballroom in 1934, a male dancer began to go "off his conk. His eyes rolled, his limbs began to spin like a windmill in a hurricane—his attention, riveted to the rhythm, transformed him into a whirling dervish." Releasing his partner, he "went into a little neo-African footwork." Members of the band thought he was drunk, but "it was just that the music did things to him." When not dancing he stood in front of Ziggy Elman's horn and "put on an emotional display of adoration that would have shamed a Father Divine fish fry." The next night "the worshipper" stood before the stand "growing more and more plastered by the music as the evening wore on." Male jitterbugs were soon joined by their female counterparts. Some observers described impresario John Hammond as a jitterbug. In response to the music, "he begins to move his head, his feet, and sometimes his whole body," said the *New Yorker.* "His eyebrows go up, his

The Alligator's Idol. Dancers and fans get close to the Benny Goodman band, New York World's Fair, 1939. Frank Driggs Collection.

mouth opens wide and reveals a set of even, gleaming teeth, and a long-drawn-out 'Yeah' slides out of his throat." But he does not "shag. He never dances at all."[44]

Described as "dervishes"—"violent," "nervous," and "plastered"—jitterbugs changed dance floor behavior. In the past, noted a band booker, "it was only a dozen or two hep musicians that crowded the floor space around a band shell." Now, of a thousand crowded into a ballroom, "only 100 or so are actually dancing, while the others jam the floor and render themselves hysterical by the gymnastics of the hot horns getting in a groove." To get in free and be first in front of the bandstand, Jack McNulty and his friends went to the ballrooms two hours early, waited for the band bus, and helped carry the equipment backstage. They would stay there all night "unless our girls dragged us away to dance, but we left them, and went back up front." Unexpected interactions with musicians often resulted. One night at a hall in Lynnfield, Massachusetts, bandleader Tony Pastor leaned over and asked Charles Hayden to dance with his vocalist to keep her warm. "There I was with that little darling in my arms and doing my best Fred Astaire."[45]

The close proximity of artistic idols in ballrooms and theaters and the important role that they played in expressing the yearnings of young men and women rendered musicians and singers accessible gods—often under the control of audiences who easily crossed stage barriers to interject themselves into the performance. Unlike rock stars, who often perform in huge stadiums, Helen Forrest noted, "when we were in a theater or at a ballroom we were really in reach and we loved it, we loved the adulation." Fans reached across footlights and bandstands or waited outside for autographs. At a Waltham, Massachusetts, hall, for example, "autograph hounds [were] pleading for something to show their grandchildren. Everything was used for signatures, from the back of a card advertising" to "huge placards." On another occasion, hundreds of black fans tore off Ella Fitzgerald's clothes in a scramble for her autograph as she left the bandstand at New Orleans's New Rhythm Club. Many kids collected autographs, and they often judged musicians by their willingness to meet their demands. A letter to *Down Beat*, for instance, complained that Charlie Barnet was not a "solid guy" because he "refused to sign autographs" or shake hands at a ballroom. Another letter writer praised Gene Krupa as "the finest guy there is," because he took him behind the stand and gave him five autographed pictures.[46]

Excited fans often became pests. Much to the dismay of musicians, they shouted for "killer-dillers" and disturbed performances by clapping and yelling during quiet passages, dancing in theater aisles, and climbing onto the stage. While singing with the Chico Marx Orchestra at Denver's Lakeside Ballroom in 1942, for example, Mel Torme felt a pain in his leg. Looking down, he found a young tough yelling "Sing 'Sweet Eloise.'" As he tried to go on, the boy "pinch[ed his] right calf so hard that [he saw] stars." When Torme kicked him in the mouth, two of the boy's pals tried "to climb onto the stage to kill [him]." Excited fans sometimes grabbed instruments too, or tried to beat Hampton's vibes or Krupa's drums at intermission, or, worse, tried to blow Goodman's clarinet. Others took instruments, "for what truer expression of worship could a jitterbug display than to take it home and worship it as a fetish?"[47]

These constant annoyances raised the ire of fans, critics, and bandleaders. *Down Beat* critic George Frazier charged that audience reaction to Goodman's Boston Symphony Hall concert "was damned distracting." The three thousand fans "behaved so bastardly that some magnificent jazz was completely drowned out." The crowd yelled for the killer-dillers, and "there was so much deafening noise from the audience that one had to strain to hear the subtle passages." Critic Dick Jacobs complained that the jitterbug "knows how to shag," and "he can whistle and hog call louder than three ordinary human beings," but "his clamor makes it impossible for a real fan to enjoy a band's playing" and retards "the appreciation of swing as a fine American art." Bandleaders agreed. Goodman yelled at "ickies"—the most exhibitionistic of the jitterbugs—to shut up. Artie Shaw found that kids demanded "hot licks" so that they could go "dance crazy," but their demands undermined his wish to evoke varied moods. "They won't even let me play without interrupting me. They scream when I play, they don't listen." Once he was so enraged that he called the fans "morons." In 1939, at the height of his fame, he quit to get away from the "hundreds and thousands of crazy people pushing and shoving and crowding and milling around in mobs, shrieking for your autograph, or your picture or something—or just plain shrieking for no reason."[48]

Vote for Mr. Rhythm

While critics and bandleaders decried the jitterbugs as symbols of mass culture excess, many fans claimed that real jitterbugs did not go "crazy every time they hear a lot of drums or trumpets and shout out loud at every climax whether it's good or bad." As one self-proclaimed "bug" argued, real jitterbugs distinguished good from bad swing, collected records according to their own taste, and listened seriously. In essence, many fans appreciated the artistic power of the music, producing in a variety of ways the democratization of artistic connoisseurship. According to historian Alice Goldfarb Marquis, the mass arts of the 1930s saw the last aristocracy, "the peerage of art, music, literature," give way "to the democratic impulse" as ordinary fans treated popular music with the devotion usually accorded to high culture. William Glackin, for example, notes that swing stimulated him "intellectually" as well as physically. Many fans sat entranced or crowded around bandstands to better hear the music. Jazz critic Nat Hentoff, for example, idolized the Duke Ellington Orchestra. At dances "[I] stood as close as I could to the band to gape as these necromancers conjured up mobile mosaics of sound . . . I was in awe." Ellington noted in 1937 that audiences "invariably crowd around the bandstand eager to grasp every solo note and orchestral trick, and certain to 'shush' down any rowdiness that may hamper the enjoyment of the music." Swing thus enlarged "the public's knowledge of music, mainly in the world of modern American jazz." Goodman agreed. "Jitterbugs helped us drag jazz out of the old saloon mechanical piano, and give it new life and dignity." Even at the Savoy Ballroom, known for its ecstatic dancing, listening often took precedence too. When Teddy Hill's men swung the last choruses of "Christopher Columbus," for example, "dancers forg[o]t about dancing and flock[ed] around the stand ten deep, to register the time merely with their bones and muscles, standing there in one place with their heads back and letting it flow over them like water."[49]

In fact, as discerning listeners, swing fans were called on to play active roles as critics and connoisseurs in popular plebiscites to decide the winners of the many battles of the bands held in the nation's ballrooms. As a regular part of the entertainment, for instance, Chick Webb battled Benny Goodman in June 1937 at the Savoy, Charlie Barnet fought Louis Armstrong in Washington D.C., Count Basie and Jimmie Lunceford sparred at the Larchmont Casino, and at the Savoy, Basie and Webb competed in a much-publicized event. Such bouts encouraged intense audience involvement. They were advertised for weeks and discussed in the press, and they drew huge audiences eager to cheer on their favorites. Often fans were asked to fill out ballots. At other times they chose their champions through applause or dancing fervor. However decided, the plebiscite lay with the fans. In one battle, Ella Fitzgerald, Chick Webb's singer, urged listeners in song "to vote for Mr. Rhythm," in this case Webb, because he was "the people's choice."[50]

Music publications and fans treated the battles as championship fights or other heroic male contests. Such was the case when Benny Goodman journeyed to the Savoy to battle Chick Webb, giving the contest an interracial dimension frequently seen during the swing era. As *Metronome* described it, "On the left platform was Benny Goodman, White King of Swing. On the right was Chick Webb, idol of Harlem." Police kept the crowd at bay as "Benny's boys fired the first shot. The crowd went wild. Its white idol was really shelling out." After the first barrage, Chick opened up on drums, and "from then on Chick fought Benny every inch of the way, and Benny fought Chick every inch of the same way." In sum, "it was really a torrid battle." The crowd of jitterbugs, black and white, proclaimed Webb the winner with its applause. In this plebiscite talent rather than color prevailed. On another occasion, in Madison Square Garden, Count Basie, the "Kansas City Killer," was voted the winner over "Barrelhouse Benny" by a largely white crowd.[51]

Hepcats took pride in their musical sophistication. To help them, specialized magazines emerged in the mid-1930s. *Down Beat,* the first American periodical devoted exclusively to jazz, debuted in 1934 as swing took off and grew to a circulation of more than 50,000. The tabloid featured sexy heartthrobs, record reviews, combative music critics, and coverage of black and white bands. Its lively slang, outrageous articles, screaming headlines, biting criticism, and screwball mix of serious commentary and offbeat humor gave the magazine, according to swing critic Dave Dexter, Jr., "the wild

Advertisement for Battle of Swing Bands, Chick Webb vs. Count Basie, Savoy Ballroom, 16 January 1938. Frank Driggs Collection.

approach and the unsophisticated and rowdy touch which made it so popular with musicians as a form of free expression comparable to swing itself." In 1935, *Metronome* turned its attention from standard dance orchestras to swing bands, while a host of other swing periodicals emerged to give fans direct and inside access to the band world. Howard Becker, an amateur musician and fan, read *Down Beat* for its updates on band personnel every two weeks; "we kept track of that the way people keep track of football or baseball." In North Carolina, Elliot White and his friends passed copies of *Metronome* around to find out "how each band was doing and what sideman was leaving one band to join another. It listed the latest releases on records, with a critical review." Indeed, critics were as outspoken and direct as swing solos. "George T. Simon's comments were read with anticipation. He spared no one!"[52]

Moreover, the magazines invited active critical participation through lively letters columns. In the contested terrain between critics and fans, critics often acted as glorified fans and fans as incisive critics. The combative style of critics such as George Frazier and John Hammond stimulated outspoken fan response. *Metronome,* for example, carried a constant stream of arguments over particular bands and performers. Simon graded bands on a scale of A to D in his "Simon Says" column and did the same for records in "DISCussions." The responses were heated as well as knowledgeable. Fans defended favorites or attacked other fans. In April 1943, for instance, Barbara Wright angrily wrote, "I, like many others who read this issue, am inclined to disagree" with a review of a hotel appearance by Johnny Long. Some issues caused hotter reactions than others, as in the responses to sweet music fans who wrote to protest that the critics were biased against sweet bands like Kay Kyser's and Harry James's. An outraged P. Biagini declared that "Kay couldn't even be a 'can pusher' for the Duke, and James wouldn't even be able to shine Cootie [William]'s shoes." Another angry fan wondered "how you gentlemen can rave about a lot of meaningless and out of tune tenors" like Bud Freeman, "just about the world's worst tenor man." In a combative era, swing fans pulled few punches.[53]

Readers' polls offered a more structured form of registering opinion. *Metronome* and *Downbeat* ran yearly polls in which musicians and fans voted for their favorite bandleaders, instrumentalists, and vocalists in a variety of categories. As an example of their democratic nature, the magazines advertised the polls well in advance, carried running accounts of the balloting, and gave full totals at the end. Winners were then assembled for special "All-Star" concerts and recording sessions that constituted meetings of the swing gods. Moreover, radio shows, college and high-school newspapers, general magazines, and other periodicals conducted fan polls. In Los Angeles, for example, Don Otis of KFAC's *Dance Time* polled listeners on whether they preferred Goodman to Guy Lombardo. In a 59–16 decision, the *Times* announced, "right prevailed." Martin Block's *Make Believe Ballroom* poll on WNEW New York also gave fans the opportunity to vote for their favorites. In 1936 and 1937 the poll ran for six weeks, with over 90,000 votes cast. Not to be outdone, *Radio Guide* exhorted its readers to vote for their favorites. "It's up to you to do your part!" they shouted, "Vote! and vote now!"[54]

Until the 1940s, poll winners were generally white, as black bands had fewer chances to be heard on a regular basis by white audiences. Black newspapers took up the slack, however, by giving black audiences an opportunity to be heard. In 1939 the *Pittsburgh Courier* began an "All-American Band Poll," followed by similar polls in the *Amsterdam News* and the *Chicago Defender*. As *Courier* columnist Frank E. Bolden declared, "A musician is a musician—so sez us, the people—regardless of the color of skin." A promo for the 1941 poll stressed the populist ethos of such polls. "YOUR VOTES DECIDE THE WINNER. No stuffed shirt, long haired judges will decide what band, YOU THE PUBLIC SHOULD HAVE AS KING OF SWING. . . . That makes the decision more democratic and void of partiality." The public should vote because "you spend your money to dance to your favorite band, buy your favorite wax recordings, play every juke box within nickel range and listen to them over the radio." Fans agreed. More than 100,000 readers took part in the *Defender's* first poll, and the winners played special dances in important swing cities.[55]

While battles of the bands, polls, and letters measured the bands' popularity, they also expanded the musical knowledge of a good portion of the swing audience. As Harry James put it, "Swing created a following of music-conscious kids such as jazz was never able to do." Radio and the jukebox, often viewed as encouraging passivity, actually helped expand musical sophistication to a mass audience. Albert Murray suggests that radio acted as a "concert hall without walls" as listeners "huddled around radios all over the nation." An integral part of youth culture, radio also fostered serious and active listening to and debate about swing. Leonard Pratt and his friends often discussed the music on the radio. "We had some knowledge of the members of various bands and we debated about who was the best trumpet player, drummer, pianist." Moreover, one had to be an expert. Elliot White and his friends spent a lot of time debating the worth of various bands. "Was Shaw better than Goodman on clarinet? . . . Could the Basie band outswing Lunceford's? . . . Each person had his own opinions and stoutly defended them." In Charles Hayden's Haverhill, Massachusetts, home the radio was always on, prompting the query, "what's the tune?" One had to know or "you were a dope and you only got a few seconds to answer." Miller Tucker and a friend at the University of Tennessee played a similar game. "We would twist the dial until we heard a song, then we would guess whose band it was. We prided ourselves that we could name the band after no more than eight bars." The jukebox expanded listening too. As Orin Stambaugh notes, he and his musician friends "would drop a nickel in the slot, stand in front of the juke box, and listen to our favorite tunes paying particular attention to any good solo work or comment on the fine arrangements. We were so enthralled by the music that we seldom danced."[56]

Radio also fostered musical knowledge by encouraging fans to play instruments. Amateur band contests abounded. Frank Mathias, a high school saxist in Carlisle, Kentucky, for instance, followed bands on radio, but, he says, "I yearned to play that music myself, to share the work of a sax section as it swung the lovely ballads and exciting jump tunes of the day." At state amateur contests he was criticized for "going astray," which he could not help, "for I imitated every great sax man I heard on the radio," from Coleman Hawkins to Jimmy Dorsey. After Leonard Pratt heard Goodman on the radio, moreover, he took up the clarinet, which he learned to play by ear. After school band practice, he and several bandmates "had jam sessions until the school janitor forced us [to] leave." Together, he and his friends formed a five-piece band to play lodges and taverns. "We listened closely to the big band programs on radio and desperately attempted to follow the various styles and arrangements of the day." The movies helped too. After Mel Torme saw Goodman and Krupa in *Hollywood Hotel*—"no less than five times"—he drove his parents crazy practicing to killer-dillers on the radio. So many amateur bands formed during the era that Goodman called them "the nicest compliment paid to Swing."[57]

Youth audiences were part of the process by which jazz crossed the barrier from dance music to the concert hall and the public festival. The mass culture of the 1930s did not destroy rational controls and cheapen art; rather, radio, jukeboxes, movie theaters, and dance halls included the mass audience in the artistic process. The jitterbug represented both the emotional loosening of American musical culture and its democratization. Emotional spontaneity and personal freedom on the part of the young were linked not to fascism, as some critics feared, but to a revitalization of mass democratic culture in which the boundaries—around the self, between various ethnic and racial groups, and around the concept of art—faded. The spread of popular musical appreciation and the rise in listening—as well as dancing—gave to swing the designation of art, but art rooted in popular knowledge and the desires of young men and women. It is no accident that, in this cultural environment, the concert hall and the public festival took on the flavor of the crowd, while the movie theater and the dance hall became "concert halls without walls." Listeners did not replace exhibitionist jitterbugs. Rather, they inhabited the same spaces and together made possible a popular art that crossed the boundary between the highbrow and the lowbrow. The growth of this mass youth audience made possible the many concerts, jam sessions, festivals, and swing jamborees that marked the era by merging listening and dancing. In swing, personal liberation and the revitalization of democratic culture went together.[58]

Big bands lay at the heart of this new youth culture. They expressed the hopes and feelings of young people, put them in touch with modern culture, and produced a new generation of popular heroes and heroines. No band embodied this revitalized democratic culture better than Benny Goodman's.

the hallowed home of classical music, a jazz band demonstrated that American popular music had broken from its vice-ridden past and its subordination to European forms to stand as the true American musical culture. In spectacular fashion, the concert demanded for American music the same attention and respect that was given the concert music of Europe. As the program declared, the Fletcher Henderson compositions, "which daily thrill fifty millions of Americans" and which centuries from now would be called "American folk-music," are as "indigenous to this life as a Bach passacaglia is to the eighteenth century."[1]

The audacious act of performing under this weighty mantle in "sedate, solid Carnegie Hall" made this group of dance band musicians extremely nervous. The fact that Paul Whiteman had performed there in 1925, or that Louis Armstrong and Duke Ellington had played concert engagements in Europe, could not ease Goodman's "cold feet." "Sure, I'm nervous," star soloist Harry James told *Down Beat.* "You know—Carnegie Hall—after all." As the curtain went up, he whispered, "I feel like a whore in church." According to reports, the nervousness affected the start of the first number, Edgar Sampson's "Don't Be That Way," but then Gene Krupa, another of the band's great stars, "emitted a tremendous break on drums," and the band started to roar. In response to one hot number after another, the crowd "cheered, yelled, howled. Gene's hair fell into his eyes. The band fell into a groove, and when it had finished . . . received tumultuous applause. Now the concert was in a groove too." After a powerful version of Count Basie's "One o'Clock Jump," the orchestra was "drowned out by applause and cat-calls. The cats were surely having their evening."[2]

In addition to achieving musical success, the "cats" presented a portrait of American culture that was racially and ethnically mixed. After a steady procession of high-powered big band numbers, the first set featured a version of Duke Ellington's "Blue Reverie" with several of Ellington's soloists—saxophonists Johnny Hodges and Harry Carney, and trumpeter Cootie Williams—with Goodman's rhythm section. After the full band played Harry James's "Life Goes to a Party," Goodman, James, Krupa, and trombonist Vernon Brown joined Carney, Count Basie, and several of his sidemen—saxophonist Lester Young, trumpeter Buck Clayton, bassist Walter Page, and guitarist Freddie Green—for a jam session. Although the jam session failed to sparkle, Goodman's racially integrated trio (Goodman, Teddy Wilson, and Krupa) and quartet (which added Lionel Hampton to the lineup) provided an exciting climax to the occasion's first half with some of the evening's most memorable music. Pianist Wilson, the first African American to play regularly with a white ensemble, contributed the lyricism to "Body

Benny Goodman Orchestra at Carnegie Hall, 16 January 1938. Note fans seated on the stage. Goodman is on clarinet, center; Gene Krupa at far left is on drums. As usual, Krupa's hair flies as he gets in the groove. Frank Driggs Collection.

and Soul," while black vibraphonist Hampton electrified Goodman and the audience with "Avalon," "The Man I Love," and "I Got Rhythm." After the intermission, the band displayed its urban ethnic roots. As Ziggy Elman "blasted like hell" with his *"fraylich"* trumpet, the band snuck into Sholem Secunda's Yiddish ditty "Bei Mir Bist Du Schoen." Originally a hit for the Andrews Sisters, but now featuring Martha Tilton's vocal in an arrangement by Jimmy Mundy (another African American), it proved, according to *Metronome*, "that New York isn't inhabited entirely by Irishmen." With this combination of musicians of various backgrounds, the Goodman orchestra struck a note for a new democratic American pluralism.[3]

This unvarnished program of swing, with only a slight detour into a section called "Twenty Years of Jazz," differed in nearly every major respect from Whiteman's Aeolian Hall concert. Bent on civilizing raucous and bawdy African American jazz, Whiteman had led his symphonic-sized orchestra through a program that emphasized the evolution of jazz from its "animalistic" origins to its politer, more symphonic forms. Starting with the Original Dixieland Jazz Band's "Livery Stable Blues," in which musicians replicated animal noises on their instruments, the program moved through semiclassical versions of popular songs and light operetta tunes and climaxed with George Gershwin's "Rhapsody in Blue." To legitimate jazz, Whiteman sought to demonstrate that it could be uplifted and transformed with the addition of European classical themes. In his zeal to purify jazz for a society frightened by the music's sexual and racial implications, Whiteman omitted black players and black music. Ironically, the audience of symphonygoers and classical music observers responded enthusiastically to the raucous jazz but found the overdone arrangements and baroque treatments of popular tunes only mildly stimulating.

Goodman's audience responded in decidedly different ways. Although a number of classical music fans attended, for the most part the band's usual fans—the college students who came to the Hotel Pennsylvania and the adolescents who went wild at the Paramount Theater—predominated. As *Down Beat* observed, the audience included "adolescent schoolboys attired like misprints in *Esquire* who applauded everything, including the klinkers" and "boggy-eyed pseudo sophisticates who applauded nothing." The night belonged to the young. "Responding as they might in a ballroom or theater," the audience acted with unbridled emotionality. Having no need for elaborate program notes to appreciate the music, young fans reacted as if the music was entirely theirs and not for music critics. They did far more than applaud. When the band went into the powerhouse finale "Sing, Sing, Sing," featuring Krupa's tom-tom duet with Goodman and Jess Stacy's churchlike piano, "one kid after another commenced to create a new dance: trucking and shagging while sitting down. Older, penguin-looking men in traditional boxes on the sides went them one better and proceeded to shag standing up." As the number reached its climax, the crowd "started to applaud, stamp, cheer, yell."[4]

That a straight swing presentation received such an uninhibited welcome in Carnegie Hall moved *Metronome* to declare that Goodman and "his veritable, virile vipers, had, in a record gate, cut to the core Jack Barbiroli and his Philharmonic Cats." Indeed, the concert announced the triumphant arrival of America's racially and ethnically pluralistic urban music as the equal of high culture in the mid-1930s. If anyone missed the point that this "concert music" was rooted in the American vernacular and vice versa, what happened afterward made the point explicit. As the final curtain fell, Count Basie and his musicians raced uptown to play a battle of the bands with Chick Webb's band at Harlem's Savoy Ballroom. Many fans and musicians in attendance at Carnegie Hall hurried after them as dancers eagerly awaited the start of the bout in the "Home of Happy Feet." Duke Ellington, Red Norvo, Mildred Bailey, Eddy Duchin, Gene Krupa, Lionel Hampton, and the Benny Goodman family, *Metronome* reported, "jammed into Harlem's Hottest Hot House" along with the "milling throng." In one momentous night, swing thus showed not only that it deserved careful listening and concert hall status, but also that the music was rooted in African American culture, vernacular dance, and the popular arts. The concert succeeded in establishing swing as "America's own urban folk music." Like the Marx Brothers playing baseball in the orchestra pit in *A Night at the Opera,* American vernacular culture demonstrated its potential to storm the citadels of high culture. "The short hair," declared George Simon, "had triumphed over the long."[5]

After the prolonged decline of jazz in the early 1930s, its resurgence to the heights of Carnegie Hall proved a remarkable event. Yet most historians dismiss swing as merely the music industry's commercialization of jazz. As a result, they miss how vital swing was, how much interaction between black and white musicians occurred, and most important, how swing's creators and performers viewed it as the real musical culture of a democratic society. Indeed, the industry only jumped on the bandwagon once swing proved popular. Three years earlier, after all, the Music Corporation of America had only reluctantly booked Goodman's band into dance halls and ballrooms, and venues such as the Roosevelt Grill preferred melodic orchestras; even NBC refused to pick up Goodman's option in 1935.[6]

From the perspective of 1934–35, in fact, swing was a revolt against the commercial sweet dance bands that dominated radio and the top band rooms. Goodman considered sweet music "a weak sister incapable of holding its own in any artistic encounter with the real music of America." Swing fans and musicians viewed sweet bands as impersonal and mechanical, symbolic of resignation in general and of male weakness and passivity in particular. George Simon, *Metronome*'s top critic, for example, called Sammy Kaye "Mickey Mouse," because his music "sounded as manufactured and mechanical" as Disney's character "and projected just about as much emotional depth!" He criticized forcing a musician "to play in one definite and very limiting style," like an "underling in an organization . . . who's permitted absolutely no leeway." Simon also charged that Shep Fields caused audiences to hop "daintily around the room on tip-toe, squeaking in a very high falsetto, 'o-o-o-h, lookie, don't you think I'm a cutey iddy biddy thing too.'" These images differed from those evoked by swing's emphasis on the soloist and the overall "masculine" power and assertiveness of the band. As one reviewer said, "To the average person, reared within the refined cloisters of the Whiteman-Kemp-Duchin cult," Jimmie Lunceford's band "carries a tremendous 'sock,' . . . the music parallel of Joe Louis' gloved fists."[7]

Behind that "sock" lay a renewed sense of physical vitality that enabled the new sound to challenge sweet music for audience loyalty. This renewal overlapped with the shift in public mood stimulated by the coming to power of Franklin Roosevelt and his New Deal programs. On material grounds there were reasons to stand up and cheer: the new administration's economic measures stimulated the band business, for by 1935 people had more money to spend on entertainment. It was the repeal of Prohibition, as we have seen, however, that had the most dramatic impact on the music business. Repeal played a major role in reviving entertainment, especially the band circuit, by making the sale of alcoholic beverages legal again. By the beginning of 1934, the owners of bars, restaurants, night clubs, and ballrooms had a secure revenue base that would permit them to present bands and musicians in open and legitimate settings. Moreover, in ending the reign of temperance, repeal also diffused the anti-urban, anti-Catholic, and anti-Jewish sentiment that lay at the core of the predominantly small-town Protestant prohibition movement into a wide variety of local temperance efforts. The first major act of the New Deal made it possible for bands to find larger audiences in the city and the countryside. The way was open for urban cultural figures like bandleaders and musicians to serve as models for a mass youth audience with music that had existed on the margins but that now could claim to be the central tradition of American culture.

In fact, the revival of hot music was part of a larger renewal of urban vernacular culture that held out strong promises of personal freedom, hope for a better life, and a measure of ethnic—and, more problematical—racial acceptance. An arranged form of jazz, swing represented trends from the 1920s reborn and reshaped in the 1930s. Swing bandleaders were convinced that the music was quintessentially American and expressed the best aspects of the nation rather than the worst. Growing "out of our brand of government," Goodman argued, swing "has the spirit of American Democracy in it" and hence was a truly national form of musical expression. It deserved to be played hot and free. The new bands presented images of urban freedom and possibility removed from jazz's links to decadence and the overly civilized adaptations of the 1920s. Because of its African American rhythmic origins, the music had a populist, expressive thrust and appealed strongly to young people, drawn to it regardless of class or background by its promise of spontaneous personal freedom and group cohesion in an indifferent and impersonal world. Led by jazzmen who had matured during the 1920s, swing bands emphasized a reawakened power and confidence capable of challenging the sticky sweet hold of passivity on the young.[8]

During the depression, once the older European hierarchical concepts of culture weakened and prospects for success and marriage became uncertain, formerly distinct elements of society rubbed against each other to reconfigure popular musical culture. In many ways, Benny Goodman demonstrates swing's power to cross boundaries. While black bands invented swing, Goodman commissioned Fletcher Henderson and other jazz arrangers, black as well as white, to write for his organization. Although he operated in a segregated music business, Goodman regularly employed black musicians, and both black and white swing bands interacted and fraternized publicly in ways that would have been impossible in an earlier era. The bands were all male but featured women singers, and thus gave unique expression to the relationship between the sexes. On another level, Goodman proved that bands could achieve commercial success in a youth market by playing good music and by attracting listeners to dance music. Finally, popular music could attain high-culture status as intellectuals and ordinary fans searched for an American national folk music. As the most notable figure in swing, Goodman became a hero not only to a mass white audience but also to black swing fans who acknowledged his racial innovations and to the Left, which believed him an ally of the Popular Front. Despite his protestations, Goodman melded popular music and popular political energies. That is why in the period from 1935 to 1948, what may look hopelessly commercialized to later generations expressed the optimism attendant on the rebirth of democratic culture.

Sometimes I'm Happy

It is not surprising that Goodman was instrumental in bringing jazz from the margins to the center of American culture. Unlike many white Chicago jazzmen, he had played jazz in commercial dance bands almost from the beginning of his career. Yet, his lower-class origins and "deviant" jazz interests placed him outside the traditional middle-class value system. His career paralleled the development of the new urban music. Born in 1909 into a desperately poor family of eleven children on Chicago's Jewish west side, Goodman saw music as an avenue to self-expression and self-improvement. His father, a tailor in a sweatshop and a socialist in his politics, nurtured his ambitions. "Pop was always trying to get us to study, so that we would get ahead in the world," Benny noted. "He always envied people with book-learning and education. Whatever any of us have amounted to may be pretty much traced to him." At his father's urging, Goodman began studying clarinet at age ten at the Kehelah Jacob Synagogue. In 1921 he played in the Hull House band, where he met Franz Schoepp, one of the nation's finest clarinet teachers, who taught him musical fundamentals. Schoepp also had him play duets with two older students, the black musicians Buster Bailey and Jimmie Noone. Goodman heard jazz on records, and while still in school, occasionally gigged with the Austin High Gang at pickup jobs for "kicks." When he quit school at fourteen to work full-time as a musician, the young prodigy had the time to visit Chicago's clubs, where he heard the era's black and white stars.[9]

Goodman found a relatively open path out of the poverty of his Jewish family to American success as a "hot soloist" in the commercial dance bands of the 1920s. Jazz offered the introverted young man, and the other Chicago players, an expressive outlet for their innermost feelings and their alienation from the Victorian sexual and social codes of their day. Like many other southern and eastern European Jews who gravitated to jazz— Artie Shaw, Mezz Mezzrow, Bud Freeman, Max Kaminsky—by religion and disposition Goodman stood outside America's racial divide. He was able to serve as a cultural bridge between the white and black worlds because he, like many other Jewish artists, was able to understand both. As a white man, he was more acceptable to the majority society than an African American man would be. As a member of a marginal group that throughout history had known persecution and enslavement, however, he could appreciate the tensions, anxieties, and oppression in African American music and culture. Both musical cultures, moreover, feature the blue note and the wail, as well as a delight in ecstatic release from the burdens of living. What's more, Jewish performers and entrepreneurs, oriented toward vernacular culture by the Yiddish renaissance at the turn of the century, were drawn to jazz as a way to enter mainstream American life. Mass culture became a bridge to assimilation, spanning ethnic and class barriers. In jazz, Goodman found a chance to express his tragic awareness of the world and his desire for personal freedom. "Even from the very start," he noted, "I always liked to play free." By the mid-1930s, he was able to bring that African American sense of freedom to the larger white world.[10]

Almost from the start, his poverty had led him to view jazz as a career. Because he could "read right from the start, and played correct clarinet," he fared better in dance bands than the west side mob, who "barrelhoused" everything. Indeed, from the age of sixteen he worked in professional dance bands to support himself and his family. In 1925 he joined the Art Kassel Midway Gardens Orchestra, and from there went to Ben Pollack's band, the hottest white orchestra in the country. Like other white jazzmen, he might have been happier in black orchestras, for he was restless and often rebelled. Even the Pollack band, "the only white band playing jazz," according to

Yank Lawson, compromised with entertainment when they hit New York. The musicians rebelled, and Goodman quit to freelance in the New York recording studios.[11]

As we have seen, the depression was not kind to hot players, including Goodman. When freelance recording and band work collapsed in 1932, he turned to radio. Although his pay remained high, he was now only one of many anonymous players in the studios, and in 1932 he hit bottom emotionally. After a series of run-ins with bandleaders, he lost touch with the jazz crowd and began to frequent the swanky Central Park Casino. In need of money to support his family, he saw no future for jazz and contemplated forming a society orchestra. "I guess I was in kind of a bad groove mentally at the time," he said, "with not much desire other than to make money, keep the place going for my mother and the kids, and have as much fun as possible." He found it difficult to follow the wishes of radio conductors who told him what and how to play, however, and by 1933 he was reduced to one radio job at $40 a week. Having lost his artistic independence and his only emotional outlet, Goodman felt trapped. He was, notes James Lincoln Collier, "depressed, surly, and generally hostile."[12]

Goodman's hope for musical and personal revival lay in renewed contact with black jazz and jazzmen in New York. "I first began to make records with colored musicians" in 1933, he noted. "For this the responsibility must be given almost entirely to John Hammond, who really put me back in touch with the kind of music they could play." A political radical and a jazz impresario, Hammond urged Goodman to record and play with black musicians to revive jazz and foster racial integration. Hammond's efforts reestablished the interracial jazz contacts of Goodman's youth that had been lost working in commercial bands and radio orchestras. As a result of making these recordings (including the last Bessie Smith session, Billie Holiday's first records, and several sessions with pianist Teddy Wilson), black and white players began playing together on a regular basis in the studios, and Goodman revived his enthusiasm for jazz at a critical juncture in the nation's musical history. As he sought greater creative freedom, he developed "a burning desire" to have a band that would "play the music that gave them satisfaction." As he put it, "I was only interested in jazz."[13]

Equally important, the Goodman band differed from white dance bands of the 1920s and early 1930s in that it based its approach on jazz band concepts that were being worked out by African American bandleaders and arrangers. With the Fletcher Henderson swing arrangements of jazz numbers, popular tunes, and standards, the band established its direction in a creative exchange between African American musical conceptions and Tin

Pan Alley. The result was a new sense of freedom in American popular music. The Goodman band's recording of "King Porter Stomp," arranged by Henderson, "is something of a landmark in white jazz circles," wrote Hammond. "It is the first time, to my knowledge, that a large white orchestra has succeeded in capturing the attack and freedom of the best coloured bands." The opportunity for white bands to work in a decidedly jazz vein would never have arisen, however, without the collapse of the record companies and the weakening of the sheet music publishers brought about by the depression. These former music business powers had influenced the material bands used and even how they performed it. "The stranglehold music publishers had on the performance of popular songs was broken," Hammond noted, and musicians could "take liberties with the melody." Further, "the union of Henderson and Goodman was the making of both of them, for without Smack's [Henderson's] arrangements Benny would probably not have made his great name." After success with Henderson, Goodman hired other top black arrangers, including Benny Carter, Jimmy Mundy, and Edgar Sampson, along with excellent white jazz writers such as Spud Murphy. Goodman's band cemented a union of black and white musical traditions as it tied jazz more firmly to the mainstream of American music and youth culture.[14]

Obviously, Goodman benefited the most from the relationship. The American pattern of segregation favored white entertainers, and Goodman was no exception. Benny Carter recalled the rigid segregation of New York's music world in 1933. Radio staff and studio orchestras, well-paid and secure positions, were closed to blacks. Better-paid white musicians came uptown to "listen to us and play with us. We welcomed them and enjoyed the jamming. But we couldn't go downtown and join them. We learned from each other and we didn't much blame the white musicians—we did envy them though." As he noted, "what was holding us back was not just the individual differences but a whole system of discrimination and segregation involving musicians, audiences, bookings, productions and so on." Henderson could have used a commercial radio engagement during the depression. He was well known on the air through remote broadcasts from ballrooms, but this was not the same as having a commercial sponsor. Goodman could get national radio exposure where Henderson could not. This is not to damn Goodman personally, for he hired Henderson to write charts when the latter was bankrupt, dispirited, and without a band, and he always acknowledged Smack as the originator of his musical style. Being an arranger had some advantages for Henderson. After a serious auto accident in 1928, he had difficulty holding bands together and attending closely to business, and he therefore lost the respect of his musicians. With Goodman, however, Henderson heard his arrangements played and recorded to perfection and saw his fame spread. He also earned the money to form another band under his own name and had a hit with "Christopher Columbus" in 1936. When that band failed, Goodman hired him as a regular pianist for the big band and the sextet. Together, the two brought African American music to national prominence, but in a segregated society, Goodman became the idol.[15]

Their new musical synthesis generated a greater sense of freedom and excitement for young audiences than earlier white bands had. To some extent black music with a white face, his brand of swing differed from Paul Whiteman's in that the musicians played in a jazz manner, with spontaneity and improvisation. No longer did they try to uplift or refine jazz according to the dictates of European tastes and the belief that black music was inferior to European music. Goodman brought to the music a firm respect for jazz and its creators, as well as the conviction that it was a form of American urban folk music. As he noted, swing was just "another word for jazz. But it means 'hot' jazz and 'improvised' jazz, as distinguished from the 'sweet' jazz and the 'symphonic' jazz so popular some years ago." His autobiographical collaborator, Irving Kolodin, called it an "inevitable reaction against the white man's jazz of the 1920s." Henry Busse, Whiteman's trumpeter, sensed Goodman's black influences. "Goodman," he complained, "has been successful principally because he essays a NEGRO MOTIF," which led dancers to "emote themselves into a terrific frenzy in which they are slaves to a savage rhythm," unlike Whiteman's "beautiful and modern dance music." Helen Ward, the Goodman band's first singer, saw the matter in a more positive way. "Maybe it was the pioneer spirit," she said, "the fact that they were playing a brand of music nobody else had attempted with a white band at that time."[16]

As in the best black bands, the new white bands that followed Goodman tried for a free, natural rhythmic feel. His band, for example, liberated the drummer from his former timekeeping role. As the top white drummer of the era and the star of the Goodman band, Gene Krupa typified the music's rhythmic power. He viewed swing as the "complete and inspired freedom of rhythmic interpretation," and he also embodied this idea. As one fan described it, "He hunched over his drums, chewing gum in vigorous tempo with the beat, a dangling lock of black hair waving back and forth in front of his eyes, which filled with an almost fiendish zest as he flailed away at his snare drum, tom-toms and cymbals." Building to a crashing climax, "perspiration dripping from him like a tropical rainfall, his arms and drumsticks became a blur of motion." His wild drum solos and his pounding

4/4 beat drove the band and electrified dancers. Like many white drummers, he had learned from the best black percussionists. It was "my good luck," he said, "to be weaned and raised on" the percussion technique of black Chicago drummers such as Baby Dodds, Zutty Singleton, and Tubby Hall, and he also studied African "tom toms." Other white drummers, such as Dave Tough and Buddy Rich, also learned from black models.[17]

A key to Goodman's success was the band's strong rhythmic foundation; the hard-driving beat loped along in a steady, flowing rhythm, making it superb for dancing. Another element in the band's success was the personnel, all of whom remained together through the band's early years, gaining a feel for one another impossible in hastily assembled units. As a hot player, moreover, Goodman's musical conception was rhythmic. He demanded that the entire band keep the beat. Trumpeter Jimmy Maxwell noted his admonition, "If you can't play without the rhythm section, you can't play." As Goodman noted, "To know what swing music" is, "you have to feel it inside." Once a unified rhythm section laid down the beat, musicians and dancers could feel the beat, get in a groove, and move with the power and punch of a modern locomotive.[18]

A firm rhythmic foundation allowed the other sections to play more freely and actually opened up more room for what Goodman called "sustained individual expression." Goodman's brass sections, composed of trumpets and trombones, opened up and blasted with confident power. In his most famous trumpet section, for example, Harry James, Ziggy Elman, and Chris Griffen achieved stardom playing variants of "Bugle Call Rag," "Sing, Sing, Sing," "Ridin' High," and other hot numbers. All three could read music as well as execute first-rate dynamic jazz solos. In fact, robust brass sections distinguished swing and served as a call to a new musical era. As the brass played powerfully and in unison, it worked against a more melodic sax section. Using Henderson-style arrangements, Goodman and his followers treated sections as solo voices, playing them off each other in an improvisational manner. Each section would play particular figures, comment on the general melody, and help propel the music. White bands also added the African American call-and-response pattern, which, together with simple riffs, helped these orchestras achieve a free musical style and a sense of drive.[19]

Cementing African American traditions and European style also accomplished what had seemed impossible in older musical forms: the creation of a highly organized group that provided the platform for both coordination and greater personal freedom for the soloists, most notably Goodman on clarinet. "The most important element is still improvisation, the liberty a soloist has to stand up and play a chorus in the way he feels," he noted, "as an expression of *himself*." As one fan declared, "To us, the song was not the thing. Often we knew the words, always we knew the melody. What we did not know and wanted to hear was what Harry James or Charlie Christian would do with it, and that, to us, was the difference." In fact, the big swing bands employed more hot jazzmen than "anyone in the old days would have dreamed possible," Benny noted. Soloists added surprise and adventure. Comparing swing to baseball, Goodman declared, "You may have a fair idea of what Joe DiMaggio is likely to do . . . but with a *swinging cat sending*, you can never tell where he's going—only that he is going 'out of the world.'"[20]

Swing bands also featured soloists as stars on theater marquees and on recordings. "The essential part of this trend," noted Goodman, "has been the interest of the public in following musicians as individual instrumentalists." Trade and fan magazine polls allowed fans to vote for their favorite instrumentalists, while record companies, in response to buyer demand, began listing personnel on labels. "People are more conscious than ever before," Goodman noted, "of the importance of each and every man in the dance band's organization." Soloists got higher pay and greater freedom of expression than ordinary section men, and many of Goodman's soloists became stars. Bunny Berigan, Gene Krupa, Harry James, Lionel Hampton, and Teddy Wilson eventually led their own bands, as did the great soloists in the top black bands—Roy Eldridge, Coleman Hawkins, Cootie Williams, and Lester Young. "Who knows the names of any of the men in Sammy Kaye's band," *Metronome* asked sarcastically, "or even if they are men?"[21]

Freedom of expression for individuals, however, came from inclusion in a larger collective entity. The improvising soloist had to strike a proper balance with the ensemble dynamic. Goodman disdained "just isolated exhibitions." According to one reviewer, good swing men avoided "barrel house," where "it's every man for himself." As the *New Yorker* noted, "Because it's likely to end up in a dog fight, it is frowned upon by good musicians." In contrast, swing leaders demanded coordination and symmetry: "the solo was treated as a consistent element of the entire performance, as the development of an idea that had gone before, as a preparation for something that was to follow." Goodman, for example, sought "consistency rather than genius," professionals eager to strive for perfection in his endless rehearsals.[22]

Finally, to create a recognizable group sound, the wide array of musical voices had to work together smoothly. Swing arrangements provided a logical structure on which to improvise. Goodman and Hammond defined swing as "collective improvisation, rhythmically integrated," combining freedom and order, adventure and security. These arrangements also gave the solos direction and gave the bands a "tight small band quality . . . a driving beat, a rhythmic brass section and a sax section that would be smooth but with lots of punch." When all the elements worked well, the bands' powerhouse performances overwhelmed listeners. Yet arrangements could not be imposed entirely from above. In an attempt to allow greater freedom and room for improvisation, arrangers built charts around a band's personnel, as Duke Ellington did in his superb charts, or else they were built up in rehearsal or during working hours, on the bandstand. Arrangements also merged individual contributions with group effort. Writing in the *New Republic,* the critic Otis Ferguson noted that "the feeling that the whole band is effortless and right will give the individual power to each man as he stands out to play alone." In turn, "each man who plays his few individual bars with inspiration will inspire all the rest as a unit, until they come as near to forgetting selfish pride and ego as any artist has come." Hence, the freedom and power of the soloist was based on a group dynamic. As Max Kaminsky observed, "having a big live band right behind you backing you up with those big fat solid chord-sounds so that you don't have to do it all yourself is a great spur musically."[23]

The Players Take Over

The first wave of swing bandleaders to follow on Goodman's success had been part of the "hot clique" of the 1920s, and they brought to the band business a sense of purpose and integrity. The "players took over," Goodman declared, ushering jazz, with its irreverence and honesty, into the mainstream of popular music. The top bands were led by improvising soloists who "established," Benny said, "personal styles on their horns," rather than nonplaying "baton wavers" like Whiteman and the sweet band leaders. Except for Jimmie Lunceford and Cab Calloway, the black swing bands, for instance, were led by top-flight musicians—Ellington, Henderson, and Basie, all on piano, Chick Webb on drums. Tommy Dorsey on trombone, Artie Shaw on clarinet, Jimmy Dorsey on alto sax, Charlie Barnet on tenor, and even Glenn Miller on trombone did the same with the white bands. As Gene Krupa put it, "Benny built himself a band playing musician's music, but it didn't shoot over the heads of the public." Younger musicians fought to play with him. "It allowed us to play how we honestly wanted to play, with good pay and before huge appreciative audiences." In their sense of purpose and commitment to musical ideas, swing bandleaders became male idols for a more serious age.[24]

According to agent Willard Alexander, Benny "was even different physically, contrary to what everybody expected in a band leader. No glamour. No sex appeal. But a well-grounded musician. Once he hit, in came the others in the same pattern. Tommy Dorsey, Glenn Miller. Like Goodman, they were not the typical Hollywood glamour boys. They wore glasses. They had musical experience." Similarly, Jimmie Lunceford and Benny Carter wore glasses and had professional demeanors, Teddy Wilson appeared dignified and reserved, Andy Kirk was a businesslike college man. Chick Webb, the mainstay at the Savoy, suffered from tuberculosis of the spine and barely reached four feet in height. Portly and taciturn, Count Basie let his piano do the talking. The *New Yorker* too noted that Goodman was different from the entertainer-leaders of the 1920s. He was "not a 'personality' lad." He was described as "sincere," genuine," "the perfect American Prince Charming." His life paralleled those of others who had suffered through the depression. Having lived poverty and failure, "people like Benny have had modesty practically whipped [into] them." Moreover, "he had an air about him that was like a college professor." Artie Shaw rebelled against glamour. When Hollywood demanded that he say, "'Hi-Ho, lads and lassies!' [he] refused. It [wasn't him]. It [was] a mixture of Rudy Vallee and Ben Bernie." Even today, he insists that his music has lasted because of "personal integrity. If I do what I firmly believe in—what my deepest inner voices tell me is right—then something good will come of it."[25]

Goodman and the other bandleaders created respect for jazz within a commercial framework. Having experienced unemployment or confinement in studio bands, musicians wanted the economic security that the bands offered, as well as the opportunity to play the adventurous jazz music of their youth on a more regular basis. The sense of individual weakness, entrapment, and emasculation that so many musicians had felt in the early 1930s was now compensated for by the opportunity to play a powerful, driving music with a full-bodied group sound. As Hammond surmised, public acceptance of swing reduced drunkenness and marijuana use among musicians and "brought back into their natural place in society countless numbers of defeated souls who had long since been given up as lost souls." In scorning sweet music, leaders and musicians reacted against their own experiences of weakness and loss of direction by fighting commercial pressures in order to play what they wanted. This aura of manly artistic struggle also emerged in the numerous "battles of the bands" in which fourteen-man units fought to win the plaudits of the crowd.[26]

The lore surrounding bands emphasized their willingness to risk security to fight for creative principles rather than for personal success alone. For example, the Goodman myth was that he fought against insuperable odds and survived failure and humiliation to become "an honest-to-goodness jive outfit." When other bands passed him by, Duke Ellington gained a reputation for holding out for "the development of an authentic Negro music, of which swing is only one element." Glenn Miller was credited with knowing exactly what he wanted to play and surviving failure with two bands and public humiliation before audiences caught on. Through it all, he maintained a belief in himself and followed his convictions. As Miller's friend and pianist Chummy MacGregor put it, arrangers worked all night after jobs "for an idea! For a belief in a guy and his talent. Certainly not for money." Goodman, moreover, fought the idea that musicians were merely entertainers. He emphasized instead the commitment of his players. "We knew we were doing something nobody else had done. We were all bound and determined to show the public that jazz was a healthy form of expression, not just a passing fancy on the part of some kids. We were dedicated." Reviewers agreed. "The men in Goodman's band perform with unusual dignity, for swingmen." They might stand and shake to the beat a bit, but there is "a minimum of hokum. They don't swing, dance, recite, clown or double on a variety of instruments." The result was powerful. "There were no cream-puff passages—no twittering, bubbling novelty effects. Benny's music is solid, meaty swing."[27]

To establish the style they wanted and survive in the organized band business, leaders emphasized discipline, professionalism, and decorum on the stand. As such, they tamed the 1920s' image of the errant jazz musician to create effective musical teamwork based on the older values of craft and hard work. To do so, they had to be tough. Having put their own personal rebellions behind them, swing bandleaders demanded that their men meet high standards of behavior. Goodman, Miller, Lunceford, Calloway, Shaw, and Tommy Dorsey were known as taskmasters who insisted that the music come first. Leaders who indulged in excess usually failed in this highly competitive business. Trumpeter Bunny Berigan, for instance, attempted to lead his own band, but his alcoholism proved a severe handicap and he failed miserably. Successful swing leaders avoided these pitfalls. Part of swing's appeal thus lay in its purging hot jazz of its decadent associations. According to Lionel Hampton, Goodman did not "fool around like most jazz artists. . . . No boozing or dope for Benny." Such habits "may go for fellows in a little ginmill or hole in the wall," Goodman asserted, "but it simply doesn't go for the musicians in the big bands, if for no other reason than they couldn't hit the stuff and still keep in shape to play seven hours a night, or do five shows a day in a theatre." Musicians continued to drink, smoke marijuana, and engage in anarchic behavior off the bandstand, but at work leaders frowned on these excesses and insisted on discipline, professionalism, and teamwork. Leaders' enforcement of these standards led audiences to treat musicians as professionals and even artists, but it could also lead eventually to alienation among creative players.[28]

At the same time, the fact that swing bands had a high percentage of jazzmen gave them a sense of adventure and linked them to the rougher excitements of big-city life. Like Goodman, few important swing musicians had college backgrounds—in contrast to the many college-trained sweet musicians. Only Miller had been to college, and only for two years. Rather, "the real sturdy stuff of jazz is produced by the men who have been gutter-cats in their time," noted Kolodin, "out on their own at seventeen, clubbing round in night spots, honky-tonks, and gin mills before they were old enough to vote." The results were in the music. "It is the smoother, relatively more cultivated boy . . . with four years in a State university who provides the more salable 'commercial' dance music."[29]

In fact, part of swing's appeal lay in bringing the egalitarian urban jazz world to the middle and working classes. What counted was how one played. As a result, swing bands were profoundly cosmopolitan, including Italians, Irishmen, Poles, Jews, Catholics, and Protestants. Goodman's urban Jewish roots and "Negroid" accent were a primary part of his appeal. Drawn to entertainment like many Jews before him, he did not have to adopt an upper-class image or perform in blackface to freely express himself. Instead, he was a city boy who learned English on the streets and in school and learned many of his values in the jazz world. Artie Shaw (born Arshawsky) sought big band success as an escape from both his parents' Jewish identity and the narrow bigotry and anti-Semitism of Christian America. Indeed, Shaw was eager to play black-inspired music because he saw blacks as the only group in the industrial age that still retained a sense of humanity and community. Other children of immigrants were prominent in the bands, including the Dorseys and Bunny Berigan, who were Irish, and Tony Pastor, Lee Castle, Vido Musso, and Jerry Gray, who were Italian. Charlie Barnet, heir to wealth, chose, as *Metronome* put it, "Basin Street instead of Easy Street," and modeled his bands on Duke Ellington's and Count Basie's. In bringing together Americans of such diverse origins, the big swing bands fostered what Frank Sinatra called "collaboration, brotherhood and sharing rough times." That he became the most popular singer of the 1940s as an "All-American" Italian, and that Helen O'Connell,

Jimmy Dorsey's "sweetheart" singer, wore a crucifix in films and public appearances, demonstrated that swing offered an urban model of cultural pluralism as a new national ideal.[30]

In making black music the basis of swing, white musicians and bandleaders—as well as audiences who accepted the music—expanded the definition of American culture. But could they accept black musicians as equal Americans to the same extent that they promoted swing as the true American music? Given the segregation of performance venues and the reluctance of agencies to book mixed bands, it is perhaps surprising that Goodman challenged the color line in music long before this occurred in other areas of American life. At a time when many states legally barred blacks and whites from appearing on the same stage, Goodman featured black musicians in racially mixed trios and quartets in first-class venues. His desire to play hot led him to hire the best black musicians. Although recently Goodman has been criticized for exploiting black talent for his own profit, Lionel Hampton declared that he "didn't have to hire Teddy or me; he hired us because we made his kind of music." Goodman often denied that he was a crusader for "colored musicians—just a crusader for music. I needed those people because they were great musicians." In featuring pianist Wilson and vibist Hampton in trios and quartets along with himself and Gene Krupa, Goodman paid them top dollar, made them stars, and insisted that they be treated with dignity wherever they played. The spotlight was on the Goodman Trio, Wilson noted, "because we were the first interracial organization in this country." As he said, "it was an asset, racial mixing," because jazz fans "were just hungry for this sort of thing."[31]

Pressure from his agency and from hotels and ballrooms initially led Goodman to present Wilson and Hampton in trios and quartets, but by the end of the 1930s several black artists (among them Henderson) were featured in his big band and in those of Shaw, Barnet, Krupa, and Jimmy Dorsey. In addition, by the early 1940s, Henderson and Benny Carter employed white players in otherwise all-black bands. Goodman also played a major role in promoting black bands such as those of Count Basie and Chick Webb as the "real swing bands," as part of his crusade for the music. Interviewers often learned "that most of his admiration and allegiance go to Negro performers." In fact, speaking to a reporter days before the Carnegie Hall concert, Goodman announced that "if a lot of the [symphonic] concert stars had Lionel Hampton's rhythm, they'd be even greater. And the arrangements I play of Fletcher Henderson's are classics, and Jimmy Mundy's too." As the predominant white employer of black musicians in the 1930s and early 1940s, Goodman was the most visible symbol of racial integration in

The Benny Goodman Trio in rehearsal, 1937. From left, Goodman on clarinet, Teddy Wilson on piano, and Gene Krupa on drums. The trio became a quartet with the addition of Lionel Hampton on vibraphone. The trios and quartets established the precedent for racially integrated bands. Frank Driggs Collection.

the music business. For him, jazz was "completely democratic," and "difference of race, creed or color has never been of the slightest importance in the best bands." Although there was extreme resistance to mixed groups from many quarters, by presenting such groups Goodman set an important precedent for jazz and for American society. Recalling the racial, religious, and ethnic backgrounds of the musicians, pianist Teddy Wilson declared, "The thing was as solid as a family, the Goodman thing. We were all there, just like brothers. Everybody was a dedicated musician, we believed in what we were doing, socially and musically."[32]

Girl Singers and Canaries

As aggregations of brothers, swing bands were nearly all-male teams of musicians who countered depression-era worries about masculine weakness. With trumpets blaring and hungry lions roaring, swing offered a feeling of freedom to both boys and girls. In terms of onstage representation, however, it is clear that democratic freedom applied overwhelmingly to men. Although there were many female swing fans—and a number of female

The Benny Goodman Sextet, Waldorf-Astoria Hotel, October 1939. Lionel Hampton is on vibes, a hidden Charlie Christian is on guitar, and to the right, on piano, is Fletcher Henderson, the key to Goodman's success. He played in the sextet and the full band in 1939. Artie Bernstein is on bass and Nick Fatool is on drums. Note that the audience is listening, not dancing. Frank Driggs Collection.

swing bands—the players accepted by the public and written up as worthy of attention were male. As exemplars of the values of work, creativity, and freedom, men were assumed to be the skillful producers of public culture. With work scarce and love and domesticity potentially entrapping for men, there was little interest on their part in integrating women musicians into swing or jazz bands before World War II. Men were the craftsmen, creative artists, money makers, and patriarchal leaders who showed that such traditionally masculine pursuits as adventure, creativity, and power were still possible. To achieve this freedom and opportunity, men had to immerse themselves in all-male families or teams who took pride in their work habits and musical abilities and who were led by patriarchal fathers. On the road, rootless for long periods of the year, younger male musicians often found in these bands a tighter feeling of family than anywhere else. The band was the musician's family and the bus his home. The imagery of all-male teams can be found in the "battles of bands," the swing-era equivalent of physical combat. The imagery also surfaced in the baseball games played by the all-male ensembles to while away the time on the road. Such bands offered a model of male group strength that avoided the entanglements of home, family, and women.

Yet every swing band had its lone female participant—the girl singer, or canary—who enacted a model of male-female relations during the 1930s and 1940s. While male musicians represented public values, women singers articulated private emotions. Many leaders would have been content to function without vocalists, but they needed singers of romantic songs and iconic models of femininity to appeal to a heterosexual youth culture. After Mildred Bailey joined Paul Whiteman and Ivie Anderson signed with Duke Ellington in the early 1930s, singers became integral but secondary parts of otherwise all-male bands. "Singers were a necessary evil to Benny," declared Goodman's first vocalist, Helen Ward. "Commercial music, you know. Benny was strictly the jazz hound. But he felt he had to have them." Helen Forrest described singers as accessories: "I sat on the bandstand and smiled a lot . . . I sang maybe a couple of songs a set . . . I never sang an entire song." In that era, "the band was the thing and the arrangements were written for the band, not the singer." The singers stood in front of the bands, rather than among their rank, and they dressed in glamorous gowns rather than in the uniform worn by the rest of the band. Most of all, their musicianship was masked by lyrics steeped in the emotions of private life. As the only emblems of femininity on stage, they offered sexual attractiveness and a heightened promise of love, and they balanced male aggression with womanly cooperation.[33]

The singers also showed how women were to make their way in a male-dominated universe. In a parallel to the upbeat lyrics of their songs, band vocalists no longer wept in resignation, as had the torch singers. Instead, they portrayed themselves as working girls and artists who were capable of taking care of themselves, come what may. Despite the obstacles, Ward set the tone for swing band singers with a good rhythmic drive that turned ballads into up-tempo, exuberant statements. In "Goody Goody," she humorously chides the lover who jilted her: "Well hooray and hallelujah / You had it coming to ya / goody goody for you." Her playful sophistication suggested that love was not everything; self-possession was also essential. Another Goodman singer, Peggy Lee, made that clear in 1942 with "Why Don't You Do Right?," a blues that wittily demanded that men live right. Singers thus conveyed personal integrity in a world where they had to make their own way.[34]

Most of the women singers were not remote love objects, sophisticated society singers, or "hot mamas." Rather, they were young, down-to-earth, and familiar people whom young women could emulate and young men could desire. As Louise Strayer noted, "many of the girls dreamed of being a big band singer. I would sing along with them as I listened to my radio," dreaming that she was the person being sung about. "Those dreams," she added, "transported us from our stark surroundings into romantic encounters." Yet, most of the singers conveyed a wised-up quality, a knowledge about life and suffering that gave these dreams a down-to-earth feeling. Ella Fitzgerald, Billie Holiday, Helen Forrest, and Anita O'Day came from impoverished, broken families but exuded confidence and dignity. On the other hand, Holiday, Fitzgerald, and O'Day were also known for up-tempo swing work that conveyed optimism about life's possibilities, and few could match Billie's ability to improvise with the band. Similarly, when Ella sang in her early cute-girl style (as on "A Tisket a Tasket"), she, like Marion Hutton, Helen O'Connell, and Martha Tilton, seemed like the girl next door. By creating a comic style for girl singers, Fitzgerald and O'Connell became love objects for boys and yet retained their autonomy since they were not overtly sexual. The comedic style also made these singers models of companionability. Edythe Wright, for example, liked "dresses that [were] unlike the usual nightclub spangles" so that "when she [got] up to sing, she look[ed] rather like a nice girl that any college boy in the audience would like to take dancing."[35]

Fan magazines, moreover, portrayed singers as independent career women and deemphasized their fashion and love tips. When Marion Hutton did talk about clothes, she advised aspiring singers that certain gowns were easier to maintain while working with a band. Martha Tilton's mother approved of her daughter's ambition because "she takes her job as seriously as others take theirs." Her two daughters earned more than secretaries did, "their work is less confining and more fun," and, most important, they learned "self-reliance from being on their own as they are and from being financially independent at such an early age." Aspiring singers had to know that it was more than fancy dresses, night life, and men. Rather, it was an occupation "like any other for which she must have real ability, real ambition, a lot of good sense, and a knowledge of how to conduct herself as any nice girl would." Fan magazines also made it clear that women's creative aspirations transcended the roles of wife and mother. Judy Starr, who sang with the Hal Kemp band, married a boy who wanted "a wife," not a band singer. They had a child, but she missed singing—"there was still the unquenchable urge"—so she left him to return to work.[36]

Still, the band world was overwhelmingly male, and it evinced much distrust of women singers as "poison" who might disrupt a band's fellow-

Helen Ward, Goodman's first singer, in 1937. The girl singer was a feature of the swing era, adding sex appeal for male fans and giving women a voice in the otherwise all-male bands. Frank Driggs Collection.

ship, teamwork, and sense of freedom. Moreover, while male musicians might work up to the role of leader—a father figure often called "Pops" or "the old man"—women found few leadership roles to emulate. They remained "canaries" or "chicks." Indeed, many were praised by the instrumentalists not only for their singing but also for their ability to act as band mothers, taking care of the boys on the road while they performed the most creative parts of the job. Helen Humes, Marion Hutton, Ella Fitzgerald, Helen Ward, and many others were known for handling some of the nurturing, cooking, and sewing chores.

Needed and resented, women walked a fine line, since they also had to support themselves during the depression. O'Connell noted that she began singing not for the glamour but for money when her father died and left the family destitute. "It was only a job." In a band, though, she had to learn to get along in a male world. "If I wanted to be a good member of the band I must forget that I was a girl," she told fans. Sexual relationships created resentments, so, for the "good of the band," she refused to let any musician "single me out for his personal property—no matter how innocently." She made a rule never to date a band member: "I'm just one of the gang, and nobody ever thinks of me as anything else." On the other hand, she advised against being too much the lady. One singer made that mistake, O'Connell wrote. She "wanted the best seat in the bus. . . . If somebody swore or in any other way forgot his company manners . . . she'd look shocked or reprimanding." The key to good relations, she felt, was "to be natural, friendly, hard working and self-respecting." On the stand, however, she must be alluring. But this "is only for display." Away from the stand, she had to minimize her femininity. "I must be one of the gang. I must be tough enough to stand the physical strain of working long hours, and look as if I'm so fragile a hard day's work would finish me off." Her stage persona as a comedienne brought these competing images together. Beneath her allure was a coolness that allowed her to be perceived as a person in her own right. Her "quiet dignity, contrasted to her playful delivery, [was] the appeal of young romance." Enmeshed in the male-ordered band world as secondary figures, the singers accepted the patriarchalism they found there and moderated their own desires for the sake of the group. While supporting the male creators, however, they conveyed the sense that women could not rely on men entirely. Women could look to greater equality in private relations with men, the subject of their songs, but they had to rely on themselves.[37]

Let's Dance

As swing bands brought jazz to radio, ballrooms, and theaters, they offered more than a democratic vision of American music and culture. They also expressed the intense hopes, dreams, and anxieties of middle- and working-class youth, who sought personal freedom and fulfillment in an organized and industrialized world. As Goodman noted, the power of swing offered dancers and listeners an "outlet for fear, inhibitions, dreams, hopes": "'Out of the world' . . . they are free from . . . the pressures of depression and war clouds, from nagging friends and duty-calling love." Indeed, much of swing's appeal was its power to push the young toward a sense of ecstatic release and individual freedom at a time of life when breaking free was a critical personal task. As the arrangements unified the solos, they used the interaction of the sections to push the tunes *Bolero*-like toward the climax. And as the bands revved up, they seemed to gain a "lift" from the powerful rhythm sections and to "take off" until, like the soaring strains of Goodman's clarinet, they were flying over the crowd, released from their earthly constraints and limitations. With all the power of a big band, boys and girls were propelled into an open universe, their innermost desires for personal identity and release confidently declared to the world, while at the same time they could revel in the driving power of a locomotive. In the ecstatic dancing that accompanied the music, young people took off into new realms of freedom.[38]

As we have seen, the utopian promise of swing found its primary audience among college- and high-school-age youth of varied class and ethnic backgrounds aspiring to break with the past and affirm a more vigorous urban experience. Middle- and upper-middle-class college students of largely Protestant backgrounds were the initial audience for swing. Although least touched by the depression and hence the freest to experiment with culture again, they were not totally unmarked by economic difficulties. More than ever before, many had to work. Their futures after graduation were uncertain, and they, too, often identified with democratic as opposed to aristocratic themes. Goodman's *Camel Caravan* radio show, with its campus motif and Goodman as the "Professor," appealed to this audience. The band might convert a European waltz to swing or convince an aristocratic Englishman that this rough American music was fine. "I may be English," comedian Pat O'Malley said in one skit, "but I'm crazy about the Yankee band."[39]

The appeal of swing was not limited to the middle class, however. There is a remarkable passage in John Okada's *No-No Boy,* a powerful novel of a Japanese American war resister, that suggests the attraction of swing. Having served a jail sentence during World War II for remaining true to his mother's Japanese nationalism, Ichiro summarizes his conflicts in a discussion of music. Before the war, he notes, his mother "would slip into his room where he was studying and listening to Glenn Miller or Tommy Dorsey and firmly switch off the set." When he learned to dance, "the phonograph was methodically smashed to bits. Nothing survived." Released from jail at the end of the war, deeply embittered, Ichiro blames his mother. "All she had wanted from America for her sons was an education, learning and knowledge which would make them better men in Japan. To believe that she expected that such a thing was possible for her sons without acquiring other American tastes and habits and feelings was hardly possible and, yet, that is how it was." Only when dancing to swing at a roadhouse with his girl does Ichiro accept his new American identity. "This is the way it ought to be, he thought to himself, to be able to dance with a girl you like and really get a kick out of it because everything is on an even keel and one's worries are only the usual ones of unpaid bills and sickness in the family." And he concludes, "There's a place for me and Emi and Freddie here on the dance floor and out there in the hustle of things if we'll let it be that way."[40]

This child of immigrants was not alone. By the mid-1930s swing defined a new, more inclusive vision of American culture that cut across ethnic and class lines. In the Southwest, Mexican American bands played their own versions of swing, while the western style of Bob Wills and his Texas Play-boys merged urban swing with more rural fiddle, guitar, and yodeling sounds. Young Chinese and Japanese Americans started their own swing bands too. "As a young bachelor," recalls jazz musician Steve Hashimoto, his father "was a member of Asian-American swing bands that played on the Chinatown circuit and in black-owned clubs," and even "in the reloca-tion centers during the war." In ballrooms, at open-air festivals, from radio and recordings, young people absorbed the new music. In "Bei Mir Bist Du Schoen" and Ziggy Elman's "And the Angels Sing," Jews of all ages found their traditional melodies and "frayliches" (lively dance tunes associated with celebratory events) performed with great sophistication by swing bands. In "Ciribiribin," Harry James performed the same function with an Italian folk melody. Vernon Jarrett, an African American newspaper colum-nist, recalls that listening to swing music as a youth in the rural South conjured up a new world of possibility. "When I used to listen at night, it was not only to hear Duke Ellington from the Cotton Club. You also heard the man say: 'Fatha Hines from the Grand Terrace in Chicago.' It seemed as though from the noise in there the people were just free. White and black people in there together." And the train songs, a staple in black culture, promoted a sense of mobility and promise, deliverance to a world different from the South. Indeed, young people committed themselves to swing be-cause it heralded a more optimistic view of the future, capable of uniting an organic rootedness with modern individuality.[41]

Short Hair Triumph

As a full-blown cultural phenomenon, swing's fascination went beyond young dancers and jitterbugs. "We were popular not only among the swing-crazy kids, but among the intelligentsia," too, Goodman declared. "The lit-erary set took us up." Book critic Clifton Fadiman wrote two scripts for Goodman's radio show, as did novelist Robert Paul Smith. Humorist Robert Benchley appeared on the program and introduced the band to writers at the *New Yorker,* including S. J. Perelman and E. B. White. Malcolm Cowley, literary critic and editor at the *New Republic,* recalled the great enjoyment he and his friends experienced listening to Goodman, Ellington, and Basie up and down Manhattan. A host of other intellectuals discoursed on the meaning of swing and on swing bands in journals of opinion, newspapers, the left-wing press, jazz histories, and, most regularly, in the new swing publications, such as *Down Beat* and *Metronome.* In part, they were drawn to the rambunctious, irreverent elements in the music. Leftist publications emphasized the music's black origins, Goodman's attempts at integration, and the democratic cultural renaissance both of these represented. Goodman contributed to this view with his constant refrain that "there's a sort of freedom about jazz, every man for himself, every man expressing himself, each man in the orchestra going his own way, doing his own thing." Unlike classical music, "It's very American really."[42]

Independent radical intellectuals such as John Hammond and the *New Republic* critic Otis Ferguson saw swing in much the same populist terms. As he listened to Goodman's trio, quartet, and orchestra at the Hotel Pennsylvania, for instance, Ferguson noted that swing was capable of uniting soul-satisfying and organic nature with modern civilization. Having brought jazz to the fore, swing's spontaneity, individual freedom, and group cooperation provided an antidote to urban, machine-driven, and success-obsessed New York. In the music, he said, "You will seem to hear this great rattling march of the hobos through the taxis, lights and people, ringing under the low sky over Manhattan as if it were a strange high thing after all (which it is), as if it came from the American *ground* under these buildings, roads and motorcars." This vernacular music was freer, more natural, and older than the modern world. "And if you leave the band and quartet and piano of the Goodman show and still are no more than slightly amused, you may be sure that in the smug absence of your attention a *native true spirit of music* has been and gone."[43]

In a variety of ways, then, swing held out the possibility that jazz, a vernacular music, was a higher form of American cultural expression. Americans seemed to agree. Having struggled to build a dance band, for instance, Goodman was startled when so many dancers at the Palomar and elsewhere stopped what they were doing to crowd around the stand to listen. In ballrooms and theaters, near radios and jukeboxes, ordinary fans often listened as much as they danced. As a result, the number of jazz *concerts* grew at a remarkable rate from 1935 to 1945. The Goodman band inadvertently performed one of the first when the audience at a Rhythm Club dance in Chicago in 1935 "positively preferred to listen and watch." The few brave souls who tried to dance were "instantly booed." Moreover, while Goodman set the precedent, other top swing bands soon were performing in concerts of their own, most notably Duke Ellington's, which gave annual concerts starting in 1943, Lionel Hampton's during the war, and Glenn Miller's in 1939. Other concerts, such as Hammond's 1938 and 1939 "Spiritual to Swing Concerts" and those staged by political groups on behalf of leftist causes, featured multiple bands. These performances, with the Carnegie Hall concert as their fountainhead, proved that the high hopes for swing as a democratic art form were not misplaced.[44]

Two days after the Carnegie Hall event, meanwhile, Goodman found other ways to challenge the boundary between classical music and swing. On his *Camel Caravan* radio program he performed the allegro movement of the Mozart Clarinet Quintet with the Coolidge String Quartet. Encouraged by this performance, he embarked on an ambitious program of playing and recording classical music. After a good deal of rehearsal, he recorded the Mozart Clarinet Quintet with the Budapest String Quartet in March 1938. The recording became a best-seller, and, on the whole, Otis Ferguson approved: "The Quintet is played the way the writing indicated, and for once perhaps the way it spun and lifted in the composer's head." Shortly thereafter, Goodman and the Budapest String Quartet engaged in a series of public concerts of Mozart's music at Town Hall. Olin Downes noted in the *New York Times* that "the alligators and jitterbugs . . . [who] were not present in overwhelming numbers . . . said that Benny would show them. And he did, in the most legitimate manner." All in all, the concerts were well-received by classical music reviewers, and two months later Goodman and Joseph Szigeti commissioned Béla Bartók to write a piece for classical and jazz clarinet. At the peak of the swing era, Goodman thus led a double musical life. While he underwent the rigors of playing nightly with his swing band and practicing between shows, he also took part in an extremely demanding classical repertoire. At the time, however, he said, "I suppose I just took it in my stride and said, 'Well, so I do another show in between.' It was like an extra performance." Aside from the individual accomplishment, by playing two repertoires Goodman established that swing musicians were artists equal to the greatest players of the legitimate canon.[45]

The Carnegie Hall concert also marked a high point in Goodman's career. Soon after, his biggest stars left to form their own bands, and in 1940, saddled with painful sciatica, he was forced to remove himself from the limelight. He came back in the early 1940s with several top-flight big bands that played arrangements by Eddie Sauter and Mel Powell. His sextet, featuring guitarist Charlie Christian, established new milestones for small-group collaborations. By the start of the war, however, the swing world had begun to change. Instead of Goodman setting the pace for white swing bands, it was the clean-cut crew of Glenn Miller who took white Americans into war. Still, Goodman remained a larger-than-life figure. He would forever be identified as the man who brought swing to national prominence at a time when Americans seemed defeated by the depression. Coming at the same time as the New Deal, his success demonstrated swing's power to garner a profitable youth audience and to achieve cultural, intellectual, and social importance. The music crossed the boundaries of race and energized youth culture with hopes of personal renewal, especially for young men, who roared back from the pit of the depression with a new self-confidence. In response to the depression, Goodman's bands emphasized traditional personal virtues. The bands also expanded the definition of American society, however, by having black and white musicians perform as equals on the same stage. If swing was American culture, its origins lay with the African Americans and urban immigrants who were beginning to make their mark on American life. Despite the depression, faith in American popular culture as a democratic force was higher than ever.

Black musicians, most notably Count Basie, benefited from the swing revival and the precedents for hard-hitting jazz established by the Goodman orchestra. The swing era represented new opportunities for black musicians to reach wider audiences, but they continued to function primarily in black bands and in the black community. In that capacity they were popular heroes who expressed the highest hopes of black youth to find a culture to sustain them in their search for a more equitable place in American life.

4

News from the Great Wide World

Count Basie, Duke Ellington, and Black Swing Bands

At its best, the Basie rhythm section was nothing less than a Cadillac with the force of a Mack truck.—Dicky Wells

They were news from the great wide world, an example and a goal; and I wish that all those who write so knowledgeably of Negro boys having no masculine figures with whom to identify would consider the long national and international career of Ellington and his band, the thousands of one-night stands played in the black communities of this nation. . . .
—Ralph Ellison, "Homage to Duke Ellington on His Birthday"

When the curtain came down on Benny Goodman's Carnegie Hall concert, the Count Basie band and many of the other musicians present raced uptown to the Savoy Ballroom in Harlem for the momentous battle of the bands with the Chick Webb Orchestra. "That was one hell of a battle," recalled Buck Clayton, Basie's trumpeter. "All concerned were putting down some heavy swing." *Metronome* declared that Basie's outfit, "a bluesplaying (with variations) band if ever there was one, devoted its attack to the body, to the heart, with a steady hammering of truly sending rhythm figures, behind truly sensational solos." On the other hand, Webb's orchestra, the house band at the Savoy all through the late 1930s and the winner of numerous battles against visiting hopefuls, aimed its "sensational, whirlwind barrage . . . chiefly at the ears and head with resounding arrangements." Adding to the intensity of the combat, Ella Fitzgerald and Billie Holiday, Webb's and Basie's vocalists, respectively, battled for vocal supremacy.[1]

Swing journals disagreed over who won this epic battle, but most commentators observed that Count Basie's Kansas City band posed a challenge to Chick Webb's New York style of swing. Basie's emergence on the New York scene at the end of 1936 suggests that significant changes were under way in black musical culture, changes that would affect the larger big band world in the late 1930s. Both black and white East Coast bands had developed the sophisticated hot orchestra pioneered by Don Redman, Fletcher Henderson, and Duke Ellington in the late 1920s and early 1930s. They had created a complex art by merging folk elements of the black experience with European classical forms and techniques. The style built on a black middle-class dream of the twenties to elevate the folk experience to grander, more elegant heights. The Basie style, conversely, had emerged from the isolated lower-class black ghetto of Kansas City and swung the blues with a drive and abandon that expressed the desires and hopes of ordinary black people. Using fewer formal arrangements, building the charts on a string of exciting, lengthy solos, the Basie band challenged the East Coast style and brought jazz's quintessential populism to the fore in the mid-1930s.[2]

As Basie's band gained in popularity and influence, the Count earned a place for himself in the pantheon of black bandleaders and musicians of the 1930s and 1940s. In numerous essays Ralph Ellison highlights the special role that big bandleaders and swing musicians played in defining a new future for black America. Led by sophisticated Dukes, hip Counts, elegant Luncefords, and swinging Chicks, big swing bands represented a flowering of black culture in the urban centers of the African American migration. With New York as their capital, these bands acted as the traveling representatives of the modern city as they toured the nation, performed on radio programs and recordings, and played for dancing at countless ballrooms and nightclubs. While they faced the indignities of segregation, they expressed heightened expectations for a people still bound by racial restraints and provided ecstatic communion to their many young followers in secular dance floor rituals. In the big band, folk culture and modern life were united in new ways to offer optimism—albeit tinged by hard reality—in the middle of the depression. In the process black entertainers emerged as heroes. The *Pittsburgh Courier* declared that Ellington was the "Joe Louis of Music." If so, Basie was its Henry Armstrong.[3]

The Chick Webb Orchestra with Ella Fitzgerald, Apollo Theater, New York City, June 1938. Webb is the drummer. Note the streamlined music stands and platform. Frank Driggs Collection.

Take the "A" Train

By the time Count Basie's band arrived in New York in late 1936, Harlem had solidified itself as the jazz capital of black America, and Duke Ellington was its king. As the glamorous musical representative of the Harlem Renaissance, Ellington saw the city as a place of freedom and recognition. Associated with the neighborhood since the late 1920s, he trumpeted Harlem as occupying a special place in black music and mythology. Along with Fletcher Henderson and other middle-class, professionally oriented bandleaders, Ellington had helped create a New York big band synthesis, made the Cotton Club symbolic of black jazz, and honed a sophisticated approach to writing for a large jazz orchestra. As a result of national theater tours, motion picture appearances, and music publishing contracts, by the time of the swing band craze Ellington had already achieved fame and some fortune. He lived in an elegant apartment in the Sugar Hill district of Harlem, mixed with the best of black society, and created superbly elegant music in a stable orchestra. As Henderson's orchestra declined in the early

1930s, Ellington's stood as a testament to the dream of a big-city African American culture. In the words of one admirer, "Ellington was the epitome of black urban sophistication—he was what men dreamed of becoming, and women dreamed of possessing."[4]

As the capital of black swing, New York continued to influence black music nationwide, but by the mid-1930s its musical style was undergoing a major change. Basie's rise to stardom owed a good deal to his powerful modernization of folk currents for a black population devastated by economic hardship, but still dreaming of a better life in the city. Mired in a prolonged depression that culminated in the Harlem Riot of 1935, New York's black youth—and the national black community—were losing faith in middle-class ideals of assimilation and upward mobility. They turned to the powerful riff-oriented blues bands of Kansas City or the more propulsive New York bands in order to work out collective rituals on the dance floor. As the Cotton Club and Connie's Inn moved downtown and as upper-class slumming in Harlem declined, black youths at the more democratic Apollo Theater and Savoy Ballroom turned to music to achieve solidarity. It was then that Count Basie and other major Kansas City bands began to make their mark in New York. Their regional style produced a regeneration in black music that also deeply affected white swing bands.[5]

Basie's move from the isolation and poverty of the southwestern city to the national prominence of Harlem also owed a good deal to the cultural and political energies of the larger swing world. Goodman's success, shaped by black music, in turn made black and white swing commercially viable. According to Buck Clayton, after Goodman's success, "They was [sic] looking for swing music, and we played more swing music than all the bands in New York." Equally important, the circle around Goodman was more directly involved. John Hammond, the musical impresario and political radical, had just launched the Goodman band when he heard Basie in early 1936 over a shortwave radio remote from the Reno Club in Kansas City. As a swing critic in New York with his own column in *Down Beat*, Hammond was in a unique position to promote Basie's orchestra. The young impresario's success with Goodman enabled him to prevail on his close friend at Music Corporation of America, Willard Alexander, who was also Goodman's agent, to take the unheard-of step of signing and promoting such a rough-hewn black band in prime locations. Alexander, in turn, had a freer hand at the conservative agency because his success with Goodman was still fresh. Fascinated by jazz as an antidote to America's failed, machine-driven civilization, Hammond was part of an interracial group of leftists and musicians who looked to Basie as a symbol of musical, emotional, and social freedom.

A modern, improvising, free-spirited band rooted in the blues, Basie's orchestra appeared a model of a more democratic America. Many in New York's swing world were "positive that this was going to be terrific," noted promoter and music critic Helen Oakley, "this breath of something real that swung," that did "not bother with being commercial or anything else." Unlike Ellington, Jimmie Lunceford, or Cab Calloway, whom Hammond saw as having lost touch with their folk roots, Basie represented a regional and cultural authenticity that deserved national recognition.[6]

Commercial forces also played an important role in Basie's rise to national fame. Swing was a moneymaker, and record companies and band agencies eagerly hoped to find popular orchestras capable of turning a profit. After Hammond's enthusiastic reviews, for instance, Joe Glaser, head of Associated Booking Corporation, signed away the band's trumpeter, Lips Page. At the same time, Dave Kapp of Decca Records turned up in Kansas City keen to add Basie's orchestra to his stable of black bands for the jukebox market; he signed the band to an exploitive recording contract that lacked royalty payments. For Basie, who was earning $15 a week at the Reno Club, $750 a year for twenty-four sides per year was a lot of money. "It was devastating," Hammond declared, "for both of us." During the period when Basie recorded his biggest hits, he made no money from record sales. The contract even fell below the American Federation of Musicians' minimum scale for recordings. Although Basie would have been much better off financially with a different record company, Decca's promotion of his recordings on jukeboxes helped spread his name among black and white swing fans.[7]

By late 1936, Basie was on his way to New York. Discovered and promoted by a leftist jazz critic, booked by New York's top band agency, and signed to an important record contract, the Count stood at the confluence of musical, economic, political, and racial currents at work in the swing world. Success in New York was crucial for national prominence. After an engagement at the Roseland Ballroom, where they played for white dancers, Willard Alexander booked the band into the Apollo Theater and the Savoy Ballroom to give Basie exposure to audiences in Harlem. Success there, noted Hammond, "guaranteed acceptance by blacks everywhere." At the same time, Goodman included members of the Basie band in his Carnegie Hall concert, while Hammond made the band a major part of his Spirituals to Swing Concerts in 1938 and 1939. Radio exposure at the Famous Door on Fifty-second Street, arranged by Alexander and Hammond, brought the band national attention. That "really did it for us," Basie noted. People would drive "through Central Park listening to us on their radios in their cars," and "those jitney cab drivers out in Chicago used to run up and down South Parkway digging us on their radios, too, and when we got back there, they used to tell us about it." Out on the road—Dayton, Cleveland, Cincinnati—"everywhere you went there were all those people who knew about you from those broadcasts and your records and were just waiting to see the band live." For better or worse, he was now "Count Basie, the bandleader out of Kansas City back in New York . . . *Count Basie* was now a name that had been put up in lights as a featured attraction on Broadway."[8]

Goin' to Kansas City

Bands of national repute working out of New York in the 1930s and 1940s played important roles in the lives of their audiences. As had their blues predecessors, black swing musicians functioned as heroes and heroines for a black population suffering the effects of the depression and segregation. Hot bands offered temporary relief from daily pressures, but they also provided a good deal more. As Albert Murray argues, black musicians created music that "stomped" away personal and social troubles. Traveling to black and white venues, these musicians created models of hope, played music of solidarity, showed people how to address their troubles, and put working- and middle-class blacks in touch with their roots. Whether in Ellington's sophisticated New York style or in Basie's earthier Kansas City blues, black swing bands kept alive the joy of life as they increased the "velocity of celebration" and helped listeners transcend the pain of daily life. They also helped create a black cultural unity around music.[9]

Rather than losing their "blackness" to sophisticated arrangements and precision playing, the big bands continued to play ceremonial roles in the black community. They presided as ministers of the Saturday night function in dance halls, theaters, and clubs nationwide. As George Lipsitz has succinctly put it, the intense nature of audience participation in black music made the music part of a larger process of building cultural solidarity. When Ellington, for example, built a band style on the "growling" or speaking nature of the instruments, he was including blacks in the tradition of "speaking" instrumentation that went back to Africa, whether blacks knew it or not. Count Basie's heavy use of call and response in powerhouse fashion resonated with the deepest elements of the black religious experience. Whatever their outward appearances, both Ellington and Basie represented a tradition of reveling—rooted in the blues tradition—that glorified the experience of blacks apart from the work-driven white world that often excluded them. In their many stomps, shouts, jumps, boogies, and other

The Duke Ellington Cotton Club Orchestra, 1932. Note the elegant attire of the musicians, the art deco appearance of the band, and the clear division of the brass from the reed section. Frank Driggs Collection.

dance tunes, these bands were both raising the roof and extending a sense of kinship. Most important, as Basie's Kansas City style came to the fore in front of black audiences—rather than the many white ones for whom Ellington played—working-class musicians and working-class audiences had a chance to exult, strut, and reclaim their sense of personhood and creative power from an impersonal, mechanized world.[10]

At the highest level, Duke had worked since the late 1920s to establish the equality of black music with European classical music. It was no accident that he achieved fame in Harlem in the 1920s playing for whites at the Cotton Club or that he continued to play for the segregated club after it moved downtown in 1936 and all through the late 1930s. He recognized the effects of segregation on black artists, but he continued to put his faith in black music and art, demonstrating the equality and even the superiority of black culture. As part of the Harlem Renaissance, he showed that black musicians and music effectively could utilize European techniques to extend the vernacular tradition. "Familiar beneath the stylized jungle sounds (the likes of which no African jungle had ever heard)," noted Ralph Ellison, "there sounded the blues." In extending the possibilities of black music—especially its tonal range and harmonic complexity—Ellington demonstrated its equality with classical traditions. To Ellington it was no longer just jazz, but rather "essentially Negro music, and the elaborations of self expression."[11]

His forays into advanced composition, starting with "East St. Louis Toodle-oo" and "Black and Tan Fantasy" in the late 1920s, continued in the 1930s with greater self-consciousness. This impulse, stimulated by European acclaim and the American Left's support for jazz as artistic music, culminated in his first theater musical, *Jump for Joy* (1941), his extended composition "Black, Brown and Beige" (1943), and his annual Carnegie Hall concerts during the 1940s. Ellington showed white and black America that black artists could meet white standards. His band played from behind music stands, in direct contrast to James Reese Europe's Orchestra, which in the first decade of the century had had to convey the impression of being composed of untrained natural musicians. As a result of his many accomplishments, "during the thirties and forties . . . many jazz composers, orchestrators, and arrangers were following the example of Ellington, attempting to make something uniquely their own out of the traditional elements of the blues and jazz." Ellington's success thus opened the door for many other black bands, which developed their own unique sounds—even the much more unpretentious orchestras, such as Basie's.[12]

While Ellington represented the elegant artistic possibilities of jazz and of the modern city, Basie in many ways expressed the quintessential populism of jazz as he sought to swing the blues. Unlike Ellington, who came from a middle-class family, graduated from high school, and held himself aloof from rougher musicians, Basie hailed from the working class, barely completed the ninth grade, and in his early days reveled in the fast life of whiskey and prostitutes. Born in 1904 into a Red Bank, New Jersey, family, he left home at an early age to find employment and liberation in the world of entertainment. Drawn to Harlem in the early 1920s by the growing theater and club scene, he apprenticed with New York stride piano greats such as Fats Waller for a year, and might have ended up a piano player and bandleader in the New York tradition. However, on the road with Gonzelle White and Her Jazz Band, he was stranded in Kansas City in 1927. He joined the Blue Devils and the Bennie Moten Orchestra and immersed himself in the clubs and dance halls of a wide-open river town under the tolerant tutelage of a corrupt political boss. When Bennie Moten died in 1935, Basie assembled elements of both bands into a nine-piece unit and brought the Kansas City style to full flower. Both Basie and his star singer, Jimmy Rushing, were initially strangers to the blues, but in Kansas City they learned the hard-driving southwestern blues style in order to please lower-class black audiences. Reared musically in a black ghetto environment to be less dependent on written arrangements, he was more firmly grounded than Ellington or the other New York bandleaders in the oral tradition of black culture, which emphasized collective, spontaneous musical creation.[13]

Basie differed from many of the other black bandleaders in his working-class origins. His band, rakish in the extreme, was not made up of the college men whom one might find in Jimmie Lunceford's orchestra. According to bassist Gene Ramey, Basie's players "didn't believe in going out with steady black people." Instead, "they'd head straight for the pimps and prostitutes and hang out with them. Those people were like a great advertisement for Basie." Indeed, at New York's Apollo, recalled trumpeter Buck Clayton, "it would seem sometimes that all of the first rows of the theater would be filled with guys smoking pot. It would drift up on the bandstand but nobody minded. They were all our pals and we were playing just for them." Andy Kirk, another Kansas City leader, was considered, Ramey noted, "too uppity," but the Count "was down there, lying in the gutter, getting drunk with them. . . . All of his band was like that." In those days, the Count was always looking for a "taste" of liquor or a dice game; his nickname stuck because Bennie Moten would call him "no 'count" for his habit of ignoring matters of business.[14]

Basie's demeanor—and his music—reflected the Kansas City milieu. Symbolized by the blues, Kansas City fostered and preserved more traditional elements of black preindustrial oral culture than did New York. Compared to those of New York and Chicago, its black middle class was small and its ideology of progress and assimilation negligible. Instead, its black population drew its cultural identity from employment in meat packing, the river trade, and construction. Proximity to the South and the absence of opportunities for social mobility maintained the strength of rural folk culture.[15]

Working the many clubs protected by the corrupt Pendergast machine, Basie immersed himself in the distinctive musical culture of the Southwest. As the depression forced the collapse of jazz in the surrounding territories, to the detriment of touring bands, Kansas City jazz flourished, attracting black musicians from the entire region to its nearly fifty mob-run night spots. Although pay was poor, work was plentiful. Yet the city and its music remained isolated from national jazz currents. The national media largely bypassed Kansas City, and as a result, jazz performances continued as informal events dominated by the rituals and interactions created by the musicians themselves. Isolation also shaped the music stylistically by deepening the influence of regional blues styles on the city's jazz bands and by favoring the jam session mode of performance, which served as the key element in the city's jazz culture. Without hope for national recognition, musicians played for themselves and for the black community, using the continuous sessions as a way to test their manhood and their instrumental proficiency. As Basie said, "I mean, the cats just played. . . . We'd go to one job we'd play on, then go jamming until seven, eight in the morning. I don't think money was all that important then. . . . We never really thought too much about bread." The jam session emphasized the sheer joy of playing with other musicians and kept alive the African American tradition of spontaneous collective creation.[16]

Despite an increase to fourteen musicians and the use of more written arrangements, required for national bookings, the band that Basie brought to New York conveyed the improvisational freedom and collective spirit of the Kansas City jam session. Equally important, the band set itself off from the eastern style with a powerful 4/4 rhythm based on extended riffs. Even in the highly arranged New York bands of Ellington and Lunceford, the rhythm sections set the pace. In fact, Ellington and Basie on piano, and Chick Webb on drums, led their bands from the rhythm section. The pulsating beat was rooted in the dance and had to propel the dancers. Basie, however, was neither composer nor arranger. Rather, he considered himself a member of the rhythm section. According to trumpeter Harry "Sweets" Edison, Basie "was and is the greatest for stomping off the tempo. He noodles around on the piano until he gets it just right . . . Freddie Green [guitar] and Jo Jones [drums] would follow him until he hit the right tempo and when he started it they *kept* it." In addition, Walter Page on bass helped make the Basie rhythm section the "all-American rhythm section," as it was commonly called. "What other rhythm section?" asked Jo Jones. Duke's was great, but "always for presentation." In fact, no other rhythm section could equal the drive of Basie's, with its propulsive, linear thrust, light yet strong, rooted in the earth yet floating above it at the same time. As trombonist Dicky Wells declared, "Basie's rhythm section was nothing less than a Cadillac with the force of a Mack truck."[17]

In Basie's band all the instruments helped build the rhythm. After he laid down the tempo, Basie "set a rhythm for the saxes first . . . then he'd set one for the bones and we'd pick that up. Now it's our rhythm against theirs," Wells noted. "The third rhythm would be for the trumpets. . . . The solos would fall in between the ensembles, but that's how the piece would begin." Piano, reeds, and brass all interacted to keep the beat alive. Moreover, the band relied on the riff style of Kansas City to set soloists and sections against each other. Favored in jam sessions, riffs, or short, repeated rhythmic phrases, were often created spontaneously; they were powerful waves of sound that set a rhythmic groove and built to a climax. The soloists played a key role, for they intensified the rhythm and took off from it. Basie maintained that he developed his ideas of how the solos and sections should sound at the Reno Club in Kansas City. He created his "own way of opening the door for them to let them come in and sit around awhile. Then [he] would exit them." All of it eventually climaxed in shouting brass choruses that kept the dancers moving and provided them with a sense of ecstatic release. As a result, everything "becomes goodtime music because they always maintain the velocity of celebration."[18]

The riff structure allowed Basie to unite unique individual contributions to a collective sound with a minimum of formal planning, a process at the heart of the African American improvisatory tradition. Ellington composed the talents of his musicians into miniature orchestral gems, while Henderson, Lunceford, and Webb relied on well-written arrangements. Basie, on the other hand, reduced the process to its essence, combining down-home blues with popular dance music and the arranged performance with the jam session. The simple riff structure gave soloists room to improvise that no formal arrangement could match. In the Basie band, Clayton noted, first one person would play a phrase, and "we all had to follow. If you could think of a riff quicker than anybody else, then we'd all follow you." Meanwhile, the soloist would be "blowing away." From this process emerged many of Basie's early "head" compositions, initially unwritten charts worked up on the stand by musicians jamming together and playing their own ideas. Basie's role was to select what people were playing and shape it. His theme song, "One o'Clock Jump," was created in this manner. The band needed a number to close the radio show, and Basie looked at the clock and said, "'One o'clock jump.' And we hit with the rhythm section and went into the riffs, and the riffs just stuck. We set the thing up in D-flat, and then we just went on playing in F."[19]

In a collective framework, the Count learned how to position individual players for longer solos. The string of solos set against tight ensemble backgrounds became a central feature of the band's identity and style once it hit New York. His superb trumpeters, Buck Clayton and Sweets Edison, transformed the Armstrong style into southwestern riff solos that intensified and varied the band's rhythmic groove. His unique tenor sax men, Lester Young and Herschel Evans, assumed center stage and battled, to the crowd's delight. Young had a light, relaxed sound and a horizontal melodic feel that seemed to float above the beat, while Evans had a big soulful tone heard to best advantage in "Blue and Sentimental." Unintended at first, their battles soon became "a set-up thing," so "people really thought there was a feud going on between them." If Herschel led off, "he really gave Lester something to shoot at, and Lester did the same thing." According to Basie, "It really was a special kind of battle," and each player had his own fans.[20]

The singers in the band were equally adept with solos. When, at Hammond's behest, he added Billie Holiday in 1937 to give the band more popular appeal, Basie found a superb singer with a unique jazz voice, a flawless sense of tempo, and a penchant for singing by ear. Although her stay was brief, she proved the perfect vocalist for this rhythm machine. As Edison said, Billie "had a fantastic conception of when to sing and how to place the words to make them swing . . . she could *swing anything*. . . . If she couldn't swing, she couldn't have been in Basie's band." On fast numbers, such as "Swing! Brother, Swing," she traded riffs with the other musicians, spurring them to greater heights, and on slow tunes, such as "They Can't Take That Away from Me," the lift in her voice sparked the band. Furthermore, her voice expressed the dualism of a blues sensibility: her exuberance conveyed undertones of the pain of life and love that the band transformed and exorcised.[21]

In essence, then, Basie encapsulated in musical performance the folk tradition of allowing both assertion of individuality and cooperation. He made his band a band of brothers in the image of the Blue Devils, his first inspiration. "Everybody seemed to be having so much fun just being up there playing together, and they looked and sounded good to boot. There was such a team spirit among those guys, and it came out in the music, and as you stood there looking and listening you just couldn't help wishing that you were a part of it." As drummer Jo Jones noted, the early Basie band perfected that style, giving its players "the feeling of a small band. The

The Count Basie Band, with Helen Humes, Brooklyn Paramount, 1941. Personnel, left to right: Trumpets, Harry Golson, Al Killian, Ed Lewis, Buck Clayton; Trombones, Ed Cuffee, Dicky Wells, Dan Minor; Saxes, Buddy Tate, Tab Smith, Earl Warren, Jack Washington, Don Byas. Lester Young had left, but the "all-American rhythm section" was still intact: Freddie Green, guitar; Walter Page, bass; Jo Jones, drums; and Basie, the master of swing piano. Frank Driggs Collection.

arrangements were almost all 'heads,' and no matter how many men we had at any one time, there was all the freedom and flexibility of a small unit. This was not true of the other large bands." It was this sense of personal assertion, group identity, and control over one's fate that came out in the supreme joy that the band expressed.[22]

In other ways, Basie promoted black cultural solidarity in the modern world (represented by the professional orchestra) by organizing his music around remembered folk traditions. One key was his use of the basic blues and boogie woogie forms, the AAB song format, and the chord progressions that this engendered. Moreover, Jimmy Rushing, who went back to the Blue Devils days, was one of the first authentic blues singers to perform in a big jazz band setting. Ironically, neither he nor Basie knew the blues until they migrated to Kansas City, where they were forced to immerse themselves in the blues to please working-class audiences. The whole band drew on the blues for tonality, and they bent notes, in contrast to the more technically precise players of the New York bands. Many Basie numbers, noted Jo Jones, "updated" blues songs of the 1920s, such as Pinetop Smith's "Boogie Woogie," Leroy Carr's "How Long Blues" and "When the Sun Goes Down," and

Speckled Red's "The Dirty Dozen." In fact, Basie told one interviewer that he wanted "to be the social interpreter of blues music, the language of all Negroes, high and low, upright and ornery, alley and avenue."[23]

Yet, this was a blues tradition of the southwest, not the deep South, Ralph Ellison reminds us. In his analysis of Jimmy Rushing's singing, he finds a different note than the despair often heard in delta blues. In part, the distinctive quality arose from Rushing's earlier ballad singing, which imposed "a romantic lyricism upon the blues tradition . . . a lyricism which is not of the Deep South, but of the Southwest: a romanticism native to the frontier." His voice contains an "optimism in it that echoes the spirit of those Negroes, who, like Rushing's father, had come to Oklahoma in search of a more human way of life." He was no shouter. Instead, he "maintained the lyricism which has always been his way with the blues." In "Take Me Back Baby," "Sent for You Yesterday," "Going to Chicago," "I Left My Baby," and "Good Morning Blues," he sang the hurts of family separation and the conflicts between men and women that were so much a part of black culture in general and so problematic in the 1930s. Yet in the language of the blues he still managed to convey "an assertion of the irrepressibly human over all the circumstances whether created by others or by one's own human failings." Recognizing human limits, Rushing encouraged in his listeners optimism about their future and their very humanity. As the band achieved national fame among white as well as black swing fans in the late 1930s and early 1940s, Rushing could spread "the appeal of the blues to a wider American audience after the Depression had made us a bit more circumspect about the human cost of living our 'American way of life.'"[24]

Rooted in the blues and in black working-class life, moreover, Basie provided other forms of recognition and cultural continuity for African Americans in the urban environment. The riff style originated in the call-and-response pattern of African music, which remained alive in the black churches. Basie recalled that even when playing Kansas City dives, he and Rushing occasionally attended church together. "Jimmy used to sing "Rose in the Bud" . . . and a couple of other church songs. Jimmy was at home with those church folks, and they just loved him in there." And since the Count played the organ, "they appreciated what both of us were doing. I guess it showed that we hadn't forgotten our upbringing in spite of all the joints we hung out in." Indeed, the two used to steal into church, open the organ, and play it. "We'd have it shouting in there. Nothing sacrilegious. We'd just have it shouting like when the whole congregation was feeling the Spirit." His "Ride On" actually functioned as a sermon, with the band doubling as a choir and chanting "ride on" in the background. In fact, Gene Ramey notes, "the Kansas City sound was like an old-time revival. . . . You hear the people shouting, you hear that in Basie's band."[25]

The shouting brass style embodied in the riffs of Basie's orchestra, as in "Shout and Feel It," however, aimed at this world's salvation, not the consolation of the next world. Moreover, other elements in the music expressed a sense of joy that was not to be found in the industrial, workaday white world that had rejected black people in general and black youth in particular. The band seemed to strut and exult, to recognize that pleasure and the expression of one's feelings were more important than the daily grind. The rooting of the music in the jam session meant that performance time—human time, emotional time—was more important than industrial demands. The music was less a commodity than a means to respond to the world. As E. J. Hobsbawm reminds us, for working-class black musicians jazz was "a continuous means of asserting oneself as a human being, an agent in the world and not the subject of others' actions, as a discipline of the soul, a daily testing, an expression of the value and sense of life, a way to perfection."[26]

That marvelous sense of "lived time," as opposed to industrial time, also expressed itself in the band's distinctive sound. Even as the band roared ahead with the increasing speed of the modern world, the players retained a relaxed, lag-behind-the-beat rhythm that preserved the dimension of personal integrity. Similarly, the band had a sensual quality. In its best numbers the band built to roaring climaxes in which musicians and audiences "got off." Playing off each other in call-and-response patterns over a tight rhythm section, the brass and the reeds wove sinuous lines that ended in release. Basie's female singers, Billie Holiday and later Helen Humes, were fleshy women singing of love and its pain while embodying the delights of passion. In her youth, Billie was a beauty whose enunciation of the word "baby" held out sensual offerings. In "One Hour with You," Humes breathed the delights she would bring to an hour of hoped-for passion. Rushing's blues numbers always implied sexual knowledge, as in "Nobody Knows (But My Baby and Me)."

Many of the band's numbers referred to black experience or to current jive. "Down for the Double" derived from gambling, while "It's Sand, Man" referred to a light shuffle-step dance. In jive language, however, if someone was "sanding you," it meant he was bowing and scraping like a servant, an Uncle Tom—which the song inveighed against. At the same time, one sanded to get to know a woman. In "Ain't It the Truth," the band made references to the old jive saying, which, like "honey, hush" and "well, all right," were well known by black people. The boogies ("Boogie Woogie," "House Rent Boogie," "Red Bank Boogie," "Basie Boogie") and the jumps ("One o'Clock Jump," "Jumpin' at the Woodside"), filled with folk references and shout licks and choruses, touched on the realities of the depression for blacks, solidified the group around them, yet pointed toward a better future.

Black bands displayed a fascination with trains, but none equaled the Basie orchestra's ability to transform itself into a powerful locomotive, with embellishments stripped away and human movement the central function. With its integrated rhythmic section as its foundation, the Basie band drove along in horizontal fashion, reproducing a fundamental American myth of improvement through geographic mobility. The appeal of this metaphor emerged from the bandleaders' delight in trains. Duke Ellington, for example, described himself as a minstrel who traveled by train and incorporated its rhythms into his music, while Basie declared that he was "crazy about trains. I love the way they sound, whether they are close up or far away. . . . I like the way the bell claps and also all the little ways they do things with the whistle. And I also like the way they feel when you are riding them and hearing them from the inside." As the band rambled from place to place, the sound of the train "was music" to him.[27]

Both leaders put their fascination with trains, travel, and movement into music. Ellington did "Take the 'A' Train," "Day Break Express," "Choo Choo," and "Happy Go Lucky Local," while Basie turned out his powerful "Super Chief" and "9:20 Special." Albert Murray notes that the bell-like piano chorus that Basie played against the steady 4/4 of the bass, guitar, and cymbals in "One o'Clock Jump" suggests "the arrival and departure bell of a train pulling into or out of a station." And, the tonal coloration of Basie's ensemble passages, as on "9:20 Special," sound like sophisticated extensions of the train whistle. The basic Kansas City rhythm almost seems to derive from that of locomotive pistons. In referring to "Super Chief," Basie made the connection explicit: it was "another one of those super express coast-to-coast trains that used to go streaking across those Kansas plains like greased lightning, going west to California and east to Chicago and New York."[28]

The locomotive quality of the bands' sound connoted a continuing belief in the future, albeit one grounded in reality. The propulsive movement had an urban destination as its locus of freedom. The train would take one to northern cities, the "promised land." According to newsman Vernon Jarrett, during the 1930s in his part of the country, Paris, Tennessee, "Chicago was our heaven. . . . We had a world of dreamers," for black people had "to substitute dreams of what you thought might be the real world one day." In general, the dreams centered "around the North," where "everybody [was] treated equal" and oppression was absent. For him, the city was a place of hope, and the ghetto "had a beat, it had a certain rhythm, it was all hope." When World War II began, he enlisted to get to Chicago.[29]

Part of that dream lay in personal freedom. Jarrett recalled, "Up here you could just let your hair down" and "reclaim yourself as a man or become a woman." And as the beat underlying the lyrics of many songs indicated, one could triumph over sexual distance and find romantic and sexual freedom. Rushing's high and clear voice combined romantic lyricism with the blues to form a double vision of love: the pains and partings combined with the continued hope of love and romance. Many of the other major voices of the day, such as Ella Fitzgerald, who sang with Chick Webb, also projected a romantic picture of love. Ellington's best love songs of the 1930s and 1940s conveyed the romantic potential of love ("I Got It Bad and That Ain't Good," "I Can't Believe That You're in Love with Me," "I Let a Song Go out of My Heart," "Prelude to a Kiss"), but his rhythm section often lacked the drive and the power to express building sexual tension. Over a steady rhythm, however, with Basie at the helm, the shining train shot home as dancers let loose their bodies, stomping in improvised flights of fancy.[30]

The train imagery struck some of the deepest chords in African American experience. For blacks, trains connoted freedom through geographic mobility, but they also had religious associations. Albert Murray says that it is sometimes difficult to distinguish between a secular and a religious impulse behind the bell and whistle sounds, for spirituals and other religious songs had urged life's passengers to get on board the glory train. The blues also utilized the "down home" imagery and beat of the train, while even earlier, the Underground Railroad had defined the road to freedom from slavery. Although the original cultural impulse may have been religious, however, in swing the implications were secular.[31]

Do You Want to Jump, Children?

During the swing era, black audiences participated in the music's sense of freedom and exultation through the communal ritual of the dance. At bottom, the bands had to move the dancers or else they were considered second-rate. This rhythmic emphasis underlay a band as complex as Ellington's, whose "It Don't Mean a Thing If It Ain't Got That Swing" set out this principle, although his show band style made him less effective than Basie for dancers during the height of the swing craze. Yet after he hired Kansas City saxophonist Ben Webster and bassist Jimmy Blanton (as well as the incomparable arranger Billy Strayhorn), Ellington caught up with the driving quality of other swing bands in his masterpieces of the late thirties and early forties, such as "Cottontail," "Take the 'A' Train," and "Ko Ko." Chick Webb, leader of the house band at the Savoy Ballroom, gloried in his ability to work the dancers into a frenzy with "Stompin' at the Savoy," "Don't Be That Way," "In the Groove at the Grove," "Undecided," and others. Yet, the most rhythmic bands came from the Southwest, where the 4/4 riff style served as the organizing framework in the hands of the Blue Devils and then Count Basie.[32]

It was through dance music, performed amid swirling bodies, that black bands performed their most important function—moving audiences to ecstatic release. In his hipster days in Boston and Harlem, the young Malcolm X participated enthusiastically in the dance rituals of the swing era. At Boston's Roseland State Ballroom and Harlem's Savoy Ballroom, Malcolm noted the "styling out" that the oppressed enjoyed on their nights out: "They'd jam-pack that ballroom, the black girls in way-out silk and satin dresses and shoes, their hair done in all kinds of styles, the men sharp in their zoot suits and crazy conks, and everybody grinning and greased and gassed." Liquor fueled the scene: "After Negro dances, we would have to throw out cartons full of empty fifth bottles—not rotgut, either, but the best brands, and especially Scotch."[33]

After the liquor and the band worked their influence, the dancers went into high gear. Dancing was a major source of cultural pride, and the swing era took black stepping to new heights. This was the appeal of playing the Savoy Ballroom for Basie: "All the top swing bands in the country really wanted to come in there and see how they could make out with those dancers and that audience." At New York's Roseland Ballroom, by comparison, a white dance hall, standard steps were routine, but at the Savoy, "people who came in there to dance were out to swing," and the management gave bands free reign. As Basie said, "you felt that you were really at home." Malcolm X noted that "nobody in the world could have choreographed the way they did whatever they felt—just grabbing partners, even the white chicks who came to Negro dances." This was a chance to let loose social and racial restraints. "Some couples were so abandoned—flinging high and wide, improvising steps and movements that you couldn't believe it. I could feel the beat in my bones, even though I had never danced." In fact, high on marijuana, "that wild music wailing away," Malcolm let go of his inhibitions: "My long-suppressed African instincts broke through and loose." This cultural heritage was women's too. At Boston's Roseland, as "the Count's band was wailing," he grabbed Mamie, an avid dancer. The "band was screaming when she kicked off her shoes and got barefooted and shouted, and shook herself as if she were in some African jungle frenzy, and then she let loose with some dancing, shouting with every step, until the guy that was out there with her nearly had to fight her to control her." Freedom in this instance was highly individual, enacted through the ecstasy of the body.[34]

The interaction between dancers and band reproduced the classic call and response of the music, especially during the last hour of the dance— "showtime." Then, Malcolm recalled, "a couple of dozen really wild couples would stay on the floor, the girls changing to low white sneakers." The band's playing increased in intensity as the dancers took off. Those not dancing formed "a clapping, *shouting circle* to watch that wild competition." Everyone was part of the ritual. "The band, the spectators and the dancers would be making the Roseland Ballroom feel like a big rocking ship. The spotlight would be turning, pink, yellow, green, and blue, picking up couples lindy-hopping as if they had gone mad." Onlookers helped whip up the frenzy: "'*Wail*, man, wail!' people *would* be shouting at the band, and it would be wailing, until first one and then another couple just ran out of strength and stumbled off toward the crowd, exhausted and soaked with sweat." Swing encouraged improvisatory moves. When a musician soloed, dancers might make up a new step, which in turn encouraged the player. As dancer Leon James recalled of trumpeter Dizzy Gillespie when he played with Teddy Hill in 1937, "We loved him. Every time he played a crazy lick, we cut a crazy step to go with it. And he dug us and blew even crazier stuff to see if we could dance to it, a kind of game, with the musicians and dancers challenging each other."[35]

News from the Great Wide World

Vernon Jarrett and Ralph Ellison linked big band swing to the promise of the city, as one headed for Chicago, the other for Harlem. Such fascination was not limited to aspiring middle-class intellectuals. As a student in East Lansing, Michigan, Malcolm X "had been hearing about how fabulous New York City was, especially *Harlem*." From his father he had heard about Marcus Garvey, and in Joe Louis fight films he had seen Harlem Negroes cheering in the streets. "Everything I'd ever heard about New York City was exciting—things like Broadway's bright lights and the Savoy Ballroom and the Apollo Theater in Harlem, where great bands played and famous songs and dance steps and Negro stars originated." As a shoeshine boy at the Roseland State Ballroom in Boston, he had the chance to meet his many idols. Basie's players would "be up there in my chair, and my shine rag was popping to the beat of all their records, spinning in my head." He declared, "Musicians never had, anywhere, a greater shoeshine boy fan than I was." Soon he was off to Harlem.[36]

In turn, big bandleaders carried the aura of urban freedom across the width and breadth of black America in their roles as mythic national romantic heroes. While devoted white swing fans gravitated toward black bands, these orchestras played crucial roles within the black community. African Americans created their own royalty, whose orchestras engaged in numerous "battles" to decide which was the best. At the top was the Duke, whose classic elegance conveyed the message that self-possession was the proper response to chaos and uncertainty. Dressed in tuxedos or evening clothes, he and his men showcased urban royalty wherever they toured. Blessed with a deep-seated sense of dignity, Ellington showed that he was beyond the humiliations of segregation. Ralph Ellison paints a vivid picture of the Ellington Orchestra's visit to Oklahoma City, one of the "thousands of one-night stands played in the black communities of the nation": the visitors, "with their uniforms, their sophistication, their skills; their golden horns, their flights of controlled and disciplined fantasy; came with their art, their special sound," to relieve the landlocked town from its torpor. "They were news from the great wide world, an example and a goal," models of success for black boys and girls. "Where in the white community," Ellison asked rhetorically, "could there have been found images, examples such as these? Who were so worldly, so elegant, who so mockingly creative? Who so skilled at their given trade and who treated the social limitations placed in their paths with greater disdain?"[37]

Ellington may have been the apogee, but all bands, from Basie to Webb, conveyed urban style and freedom through manner and dress. Pianist Horace Silver recalled wanting to be a musician after seeing the Jimmie Lunceford band in Norwalk, Connecticut, in 1938. Excluded from the dance pavilion because of his color, Silver peered through the slats at the impeccably attired musicians. "First of all, they were dressed nice. Immaculate. I think they had white suits, and ties, and shiny shoes." Similarly, bassist Milt Hinton felt that Cab Calloway's band "was really something to see." Hinton and other Calloway musicians were "the tops and we knew it and we acted it. Arrogant as all get out. The guys dressed to kill—all the time." This could be expensive. "The first thing I did was to take $600 and buy a whole closetful of suits. I had to. It was embarrassing traveling with those guys unless you were suited down." And many bands imposed penalties on those whose attire was not just so. "Perhaps," remarked Hinton, Calloway intended to show the black community "the sharp zoot suit, the hip styles, the new lingo, and this kinda thing to elevate 'em." His emphasis on proper behavior and dress would demonstrate "the dignity of black people." However, Calloway's disdain for the blues, his "Broadway" style, and the fact that he played primarily for white audiences, even in the South, often alienated southern working-class blacks. This problem did not beset Basie. He was more self-effacing, with "his usual unassuming manner," as the *Pittsburgh Courier* said. He brought to this exalted fraternity a "simplicity and modesty" that never set him above ordinary black people. As Dizzy Gillespie said at his funeral in 1984, even at the pinnacle of success, Basie "still sat in the background. . . . He was the world's greatest accompanist."[38]

Successful black bands also traveled in style—either by train or by streamlined Greyhound bus. Severely limited in where they could stay, how they could travel, and where they could eat, black bands in the South often had to devise strategies to outwit racial oppression. Cab Calloway and Duke Ellington traveled in private Pullman cars in the South as a means of safety and a symbol of success. "It was always Pullman wherever he could get a Pullman, and a baggage car next to the Pullman," Hinton said of Cab—"a huge baggage car where he had a great big, green Lincoln Continental, and he carried a chauffeur." The luxury railroad car also gave musicians a place to bring women they met without conflicts with southern whites or blacks. All in all, the elegance of the mode of travel of the top bands matched their dress and their station.[39]

North as well as South, black musicians were figures of success. As visiting royalty, Ellington and his cohorts represented what Ellison called "the power of man to define himself against the ravages of time through artistic style." In the black community, especially during the depression, music and its makers were harbingers of hope, "the stewards of our vaunted American optimism and guardians against the creeping irrationality which ever plagues our form of society." While the front pages of the black press were filled with dangers and horror during the 1930s and 1940s, the entertainment and sports pages detailed with pride the accomplishments of black heroes and heroines. As Isadora Smith observed in *The Pittsburgh Courier*, "Because of Joe Louis, Henry Armstrong, John Henry Lewis and a collection of track and other stars of the sports world, the race today excels all in that field. As they go in such endeavors, so they run in the world of entertainment." Her champions were many: Count Basie, Bill Robinson, Ethel Waters, Ella Fitzgerald, all of whom gave black people pride of place in entertainment. Many of the newspaper profiles recognized the entertainers as Horatio Alger figures. This was especially the case with Basie, who seemed much closer to the average black person than the elegant Ellington or Calloway. The *Amsterdam News* portrayed Count Basie as coming from poor stock, having suffered, but eager to get ahead, filled with ambition; his band was made up of "young, driving, conscientious and willing to learn" musicians. "Excluded mostly from politics, and suppressed in economics," noted the *Courier*, "the Negro leads the invention of music, dance and entertainments of other sorts." Such was Basie, who was "working hard now to have one of the bands at the top." Dispensers of pleasure, the top musicians also exhibited dedication, hard work, and sacrifice.[40]

The bandleaders were living proof that black people were eminently capable of achievement in the fields open to them. Here "none have reigned more nobly or as constantly as Duke Ellington. Where others have followed a set trend, he has created," according to Isadora Smith, "a new one setting a tradition for a world to follow." Moreover, like many of the black bandleaders, he was considered a "race man." Smith, for example, found him "truly a great man, great in deeds to a people and great in character to self." Part of his achievement was his "setting the musical mind of the race apart on the musical horizon" and "opening fields to his people that before his coming offered no outlet to a race of great entertainment talent, musical or otherwise."[41]

As representatives of their race, black bandleaders were considered community assets, and they contributed to numerous community endeavors and charities. Many bands appeared, for instance, in the Apollo Theater's benefits for the Riverdale Boys Foundation. Ellington, Basie, and Lunceford performed for a variety of youth services. When the Count won the *Pittsburgh Courier's* "All-American Band Poll" in 1941 and 1942, he toured the important swing cities playing "coronation dances" whose proceeds went to black charities. Basie declared, the tour "will leave me feeling like Joe Louis, who did the grandest American act in history, putting his million dollar title on the block for the Navy Relief Society."[42]

When black entertainers suffered discrimination, it was page one news, and when they succeeded their success was taken to heart by the community. Indeed, the southern system of segregation ensured that black entertainers and celebrities shared a large measure of identity with southern blacks. Incidents of violence and discrimination served to link black bands and their black fans but also gave the fans an awareness of the dignity of their heroes and heroines. Cab Calloway was beaten, for example, when he tried to enter the segregated Pla-Mor Ballroom in Kansas City at the invitation of Lionel Hampton, who was on the bandstand. This was front-page news, and so was Hampton's decision to renege on his contract in protest.

Black newspapers trumpeted the fact that Duke Ellington was denied accommodations in Moline, Illinois; that bandleader Don Albert was beaten badly in Georgia; or that closer to home, the radio, movie, and band businesses continued to treat blacks as second-class citizens. Racist incidents increased during World War II. The underlying motif of these reports was that black talent was being denied unfairly. The incidents served as a measuring stick for use against white institutions, especially in music and entertainment, where black achievements were clear.

On the other hand, every black "first" was an achievement for the race. When Ellington played Carnegie Hall for the first time in 1943, it was a major event, as was Basie's breaking racial barriers at the Lincoln Hotel in Manhattan that same year. "The Count's advent into the Lincoln Hotel will mark the first time that a colored band has ever appeared at the spot," noted the *Courier*. "Still another first is the fact that this is the Basie aggregation's first hotel job in New York." The black press also detailed Billie Holiday's stint with Artie Shaw in 1938 and Basie's breaking away from the Music Corporation of America to become "a free man." Indeed, starting in the late 1930s, black bandleaders and musicians began to display a new and increasing assertiveness. Basie, for example, refused to play Kansas City's Municipal Auditorium, "his second home," in protest over audience segregation. As he put it, "if you don't want my people, you don't want my music." Music had the power to overcome racial barriers and challenge restrictions because of the musicians' competence as artists. As Jack Gould declared of Basie, "If swing does nothing beyond lifting the Negro to his proper stature . . . it will have justified the agony it has caused the classicist."[43]

As topflight entertainers, moreover, black musicians garnered praise from national and international sources and further contributed to black pride. Indeed, the *Courier* reprinted a *New York Times* article by Gould praising Basie and "the race" because swing demands "a high degree of musicianship," and because improvisation "has been a distinct boon to the prestige of the Negro musician who, with his inherent sense of rhythm to boot, has long been considered by the honest jazzman as the superior in the field of popular music." Similarly, the paper noted Leopold Stokowski's favorable views of "unknown Negro jazz bands," as well as Hugues Panassiè's belief in the superiority of black musicians over their white counterparts. But while praise from outside sources was welcome, the black press—as an extension of the black community—believed in its musical contributions to America. Numerous articles confidently attributed Benny Goodman's success to the presence of Teddy Wilson and Lionel Hampton and the success of other white bands to arrangements by African Americans.[44]

Bandleaders and musicians were also cultural heroes on a par with the sports figures of the day. No one stood higher than heavyweight champion Joe Louis. A symbol of racial self-assertion and democratic values, he became an American national hero by defeating Nazi Germany's Max Schmeling. Lawrence Levine has shown how quickly he was elevated to the pantheon of black heroes in blues, folk songs, tales, and jokes. Less well known is his importance to swing and to black entertainers. As "a great patron of swing music," Louis served as a judge of the *Courier*'s Swing Poll. When he fought Primo Carnera in 1935, twenty thousand fans, at seventy-five cents a head, crowded into the Savoy Ballroom eager to greet him. When he ascended the boxing hierarchy he became a Harlemite and associated with musicians at the hotels where they lived and the clubs where they played. Mercer Ellington, Duke's son, noted the relationship of sports and show business: great black fighters like Louis "would always come wherever Duke Ellington was, especially to the Cotton Club."[45]

Musicians also idolized Louis as a symbol of their own aspirations. They gloried in his victories and suffered deeply when he lost to Schmeling. Lena Horne, who dated Louis, was devastated as she listened to the match over the radio. "I was near hysteria toward the end of the fight when he was being so badly beaten and some of the men in the band were crying." Milt Hinton had similar feelings when he heard the results. The band was playing at the Fort Worth, Texas, World's Fair. "They wouldn't even let us listen to it on the radio." For Hinton, it was a major loss. "'Cause [he] was an impetus to dignity, to manhood, to us. He was a symbol. It was a chance for us to say, 'Hey, man, look out. Don't do that. Here we are.'" Like band musicians, Louis was a hero to blacks. As Dizzy Gillespie put it, "To be a 'hero' in the black community, all you have to do is make the white folks look up to you and recognize the fact that you've contributed something worthwhile." In addition, "black people appreciate my playing in the same way I looked up to Paul Robeson or to Joe Louis. [When Joe knocked someone out,] I'd say, 'Hey . . . ! and felt like I'd scored a knockout. Just because of his prowess in the field and because he's black like me."[46]

Basie also worshipped Louis. He put his feelings on record. At the instigation of John Hammond, Basie recorded "King Joe" with lyrics by Richard Wright and Paul Robeson on vocals. Uniting black and white leftists with a black swinging blues band, the recording immortalized the connections between black sports and music heroes. According to Louis's biographer,

The "King Joe" session. In a tribute to Joe Louis, Richard Wright, Paul Robeson and Basie collaborated in a recording with John Hammond (not pictured), 1941. This Popular Front endeavor brought together white and black leftists and creative artists to promote black cultural pride. Frank Driggs Collection.

the song was a tribute to black culture: "Black eye peas ask corn bread / What makes you so strong? / Corn bread says I come from / Where Joe Louis was born." Each of the participants in the recording had an important role to play in the fight for racial advancement and solidarity. Each bore testament to the breaking of cultural barriers, and each was a hero to the race. In sports, politics, and the arts, a racial self-awareness was building to the political awakening that followed World War II. Duke Ellington, on one hand, expanded the range of black music, and in *Jump for Joy,* his 1941 musical, he challenged "Uncle Tom" racial stereotypes and looked to a new day for black Americans. Count Basie, on the other hand, extended vernacular music and expressed the dignity of the average black person. Together they touched a growing sense of pride and impatience.[47]

During the depression, black vernacular entertainment was revitalized. While many blacks suffered during the depression, entertainers held out hope that life was better in northern cities. Indeed, migration from the South continued throughout the decade and exploded with the war. This renewed optimism, however, increasingly was rooted in the reality of the blues and the dignity of the common black person. This was Basie's contribution to black culture in the late 1930s and the 1940s. Just as his music helped transform eastern swing into an earthier working-class blues sound befitting this era of the "common man," so too his dignified yet hip presence brought to the pantheon of national black bandleaders a figure with whom the average black person, northern or southern, could identify. Whether an Ellington who demonstrated the high art possibilities of the music or a Basie who showed vernacular music's artistic power, the black swing musician created cultural solidarity around music, asserted that the black community could survive adversity, and declared that it was an integral part of the American landscape. In these ways, black swing figured in the resurgent energies of the New Deal era.

Moreover, radicals in the jazz world willingly advanced the notion that black music was the American contribution to art. The growing awareness that swing was American music—and that its players, black and white, deserved to be heard by whites and blacks equally—was a part of the excitement of swing. For radicals the music acted as a standard by which to judge American society and a model for how it might become truly democratic. To understand the direct links between politics, race, and culture we need to swing left.

5

Swing Left

The Politics of Race and Culture in the Swing Era

The strongest motivation for my dissent was jazz. I heard no color line in the music. . . . To bring recognition to the Negro's supremacy in jazz was the most effective and constructive form of social protest I could think of. . . .—John Hammond

Clarinetist Benny Goodman, who is a strong People's Front partisan, will be on hand to pied-piper the swing proceedings at the American Youth Congress Dance.—*Daily Worker*

On December 23, 1938, From Spirituals to Swing shook "the stage, the rafters and the audience at Carnegie Hall." Organized by John Hammond and sponsored by *New Masses,* the Communist Party's journal of culture, the concert assembled "for the first time, before a musically sophisticated audience, Negro music from its raw beginnings to the latest jazz." In pursuit of his unique conception of the event, Hammond scoured the South and the Southwest for artists who represented "authentic Negro music" but "whose music had never been heard by most of the New York public." The program attempted to show the common themes that ran through black music from its African beginnings, through gospel, blues, and Dixieland jazz, to swing. Awareness of the African roots of black music may be widespread today, but in 1938 it was still uncommon. Boogie-woogie pianists Albert Ammons, Meade Lux Lewis, and Pete Johnson, along with blues shouter Big Joe

Turner, highlighted the evening. Count Basie's Orchestra dominated the second half of the concert with a demonstration of the ties between modern jazz and Negro folk music. Because of the evening's enormous success, Hammond staged a similar concert a year later consisting of blues, gospel, boogie-woogie, and swing, this time sponsored by the left-wing Theatre Arts Committee. For the second concert, however, white pianist Joe Sullivan sat in with Basie's orchestra, and Benny Goodman's integrated sextet closed the show. As the *New Masses* observed, Spirituals to Swing succeeded in marking "the close alliance between the music made in the everyday life of the Negro and the music which has come to be called swing."[1]

The lead article in the program book for the first concert reveals the ideology that lay behind both events. Titled "The Music Nobody Knows," by John Hammond and James Dugan, a jazz critic for Communist publications, the notes stressed that the music and its creators represented an authentic but long-unappreciated expression of folk culture. "Serious" audiences had neglected American Negro music so that it "thrived in an atmosphere of detraction, oppression, distortion, and unreflective enthusiasm." Hot music, however, deserved to "be considered as *music;* it is not, as ignorant people contend, a sort of anarchy in music." Good jazz had outlived its "highbrow detractors of the twenties" and could provide "the same qualities you expect in the classics: expert instrumentation, a musical structure . . . and a quality that we must call sincerity." The music was "uniquely American, the most important cultural exhibit we have given the world." This creation of oppressed lower-class blacks, "whose musical qualities have long been recognized in Europe and neglected at home," would be the basis for an American national music.[2]

Hammond and Dugan's ideological views distinguished them from other swing enthusiasts. Jitterbugs and record collectors scared away serious audiences, Hammond and Dugan asserted, while commercial radio used jazz to sell breakfast food. While validating scholarly research in music, the concert also acted as a political protest against segregation and economic exploitation: Hammond dedicated the first event to blues singer Bessie Smith, "perhaps the greatest and least appreciated artist in American jazz," who died as a result of segregation in medical facilities. "Most of the people you will hear are absurdly poor," the notes asserted. The program also attacked "Jim Crow unions and unscrupulous nightclub proprietors," as well as radio stations that barred Negro performers. The notes listed the performers and detailed the neglect and oppression each had endured. Despite poverty and racism, however, they had created a vibrant culture of protest and freedom. Moreover, the program argued, the presence of black music in Carnegie Hall signaled the dawning of a more democratic American culture. Hammond and Dugan urged the audience to relax and swing with "an atmosphere of informality and interest. May we ask that you forget you are in Carnegie Hall?"[3]

Spirituals to Swing exemplifies one of the most important features of the swing era: the many connections between the popular music industry and the Left. Hammond is a case in point. The "Number One Swing Man" of the 1930s symbolized the intersection in New York and the nation of swing critics, the big band industry, European jazz enthusiasts, and the political and cultural Left. An independent radical, he made common cause with Communists and civil rights groups, as well as with the Benny Goodman and Count Basie orchestras, to foster integration and social justice. In these endeavors he embodied the commitment to an American national culture that historian Warren Susman believes defined this generation. Yet Hammond and his cohorts were less interested in conserving the values of the past than in creating a pluralist and socially democratic American culture. Allied with the Popular Front on behalf of "the forgotten man," he linked swing, as E. J. Hobsbawm put it, to the "political and cultural milieu of the Roosevelt era, which shaped the development of jazz to a considerable extent, often in a concrete way." More important, Hammond acted as part of a much larger group of young jazz critics and impresarios who, disillusioned by the failures of modern capitalism, labored to give jazz a specific ideological content. As part of this effort, they reinterpreted the music as an organic, democratic art form rooted in black culture that would serve as an antidote to the commercial glibness of Tin Pan Alley. The rise of a broad left-democratic commitment to swing as part of an authentic "people's culture" placed the music at the forefront of challenges to the music industry and to American society. With the help of cutting-edge bandleaders such as Basie and Goodman, these forces produced significant racial breakthroughs in the band world of the 1930s and 1940s.[4]

Number One Swing Man

On the surface, Hammond's background seems an unlikely one for a crusader. A Vanderbilt on his maternal grandmother's side, a Sloane on his maternal grandfather's, Hammond was born in December 1910 and grew up in an eight-story Manhattan mansion as a pampered child of the wealthy Anglo-Saxon elite. His father, a banker, railroad executive, lawyer, and club man, had every expectation that his son would follow in his footsteps. Yet, like the hero of a 1930s screwball comedy, Hammond soon re-

John Hammond (second from left) in his element, probably in Chicago, ca. 1940. On the right, Benny Goodman and Count Basie, jazz critic Dave Dexter, Jr. (fourth from right), and singer Helen Humes, right corner, along with Earl Hines (fourth from left). Hammond promoted fraternization between black and white musicians, which became common in the jazz world during the swing era. Frank Driggs Collection.

jected this world to associate with people from more ordinary walks of life. Part of that dissent derived from his mother, a devout Christian Scientist who was "both fascinated and repelled by the high society which was her natural station." Imbibing her moral code, which frowned on the use of alcohol and tobacco and smiled on the obligations of wealth, Hammond "shared her religious fervor, her prejudices, and her saintly resolve to set an example for others."[5]

There were other influences, Hammond averred, starting "with my objection to the discrimination I saw everywhere around me." The upper-crust schools he attended and the social circles in which he moved excluded Jews or subjected them to rigid quotas. His sensitivity to discrimination was nurtured by the associations he inherited from his family and those he found at the Hotchkiss School. A radical family member, the Reverend Henry Sloane Coffin, had graduated from Hotchkiss, and as head of Union Theological Seminary fought to increase the number of black students and ministers in the 1920s. The headmaster of Hotchkiss taught Hammond independent socialism, while another former Hotchkiss student, Ernest Gruening, hired him for his Portland, Maine, newspaper and introduced him to "journalism, the civil rights movement, and trade unionism." By 1929 he was "a changed young man," possessed of an intellectual and political independence indispensable in a social reformer and a liberal-to-radical intellectual network that gave meaning to his entire life. In 1931, during the depths of the depression, he dropped out of Yale and moved to Greenwich Village, where he devoted himself to music and radical causes. "I did not revolt against the social system," he argued. "I simply refused to be a part of it."[6]

As was true for many young people in the 1920s, jazz opened up a new world for Hammond, one that gave shape to his growing radicalism. While a student at Hotchkiss he took viola lessons in upper Manhattan and had the freedom to frequent Harlem clubs and theaters to hear and see his favorite performers. He was so deeply impressed by the facility of the musicians and the emotional depth of the music that he would later claim that it was his love for jazz that led to his role as a dissenter. When he listened to the music, he heard no color line. The knowledge that the best jazz players barely made a living—and were barred from all well-paying jobs in radio and in most nightclubs—enraged him. In his view, jazz was a cry of social protest, "an authentic indigenous expression of the social injustice he already knew intellectually but could now feel emotionally." Like other young jazz critics of the 1930s, Hammond worked to transcend the view of the 1920s that black musicians were uninhibited exotics and attempted to turn his love of jazz into political action.[7]

While he immersed himself in black music and the struggle for black rights, Hammond's broader conception of America posed a challenge to the WASP hegemony of his youth. His musical and theatrical activities brought him in contact with many Jews; this also fostered in him a pluralist conception of American culture. His admiration for Jews sprang from his love of theater and burlesque, which he frequented despite the condemnation of the theater censorship society headed by his mother. Reading *Variety*, he realized the number of Jews prominent in show business. "I admired them as I admired the black artists on my favorite records. I wanted to be Jewish." He elected to remove his name from the Social Register because of its anti-Semitism, and in 1933 he began a long association with Benny Goodman, who married his sister Alice in 1942.[8]

Hammond's political and musical activities placed him at the cutting edge of social activism during the depression. According to music critic John McDonough, "jazz—especially racially integrated jazz—was on the front line of social change along with the causes of anti-fascism, the New Deal, the Popular Front, the labor movement and the Scottsboro case." During the 1930s Hammond often cooperated with Communists to challenge racial oppression. When covering the Scottsboro trial for the *Nation,* he saw that the International Labor Defense Committee (ILD) took a more activist stance than the National Association for the Advancement of Colored People (NAACP). As a result, he helped stage a benefit for the ILD at Harlem's Rockland Palace. His sympathies for labor were clear too. He joined a group of radical intellectuals and reporters to deliver food and supplies to striking mine workers in Harlan County, Kentucky, and he helped publicize their plight. As a reporter, he firmly supported the American Newspaper Guild and the Congress of Industrial Organizations (CIO). A committed anti-Fascist, he organized benefits for the Spanish Loyalists too. When the NAACP stopped excluding Communists in 1935 and became more militant he joined its national board. Looking back, he declared, "Next to jazz the NAACP became the means to fight for the social change I sought." He was drawn to the Communist Party but never joined because it advocated integration only in the North; in the South, it supported a separate black state. Hammond's major concern was racial progress, but it was part of a larger fight against social injustice.[9]

From the nadir of jazz in the early 1930s to its high point during World War II, Hammond led a committed life in music. As a talent scout, he shared the leftist agenda of unearthing the creators and performers—usually black—of an authentic American musical culture. He traveled incessantly in search of talent. "A pattern had developed in my life style, centered around jazz but also reflecting an urge I have always felt to be the first to hear a great player, see a new show, and find out what is going on in every town and city I can get to." Down South, over to Kansas City, out to Los Angeles, up to Harlem, he visited barrooms, nightclubs, variety shows, and burlesque theaters for the little-known piano or horn player about whom he had heard. By putting his money behind his discoveries, he sought to bring them to the attention of the general public. During his career he helped record and promote singers Bessie Smith, Mildred Bailey, and Billie Holiday. He found Holiday in 1933, on his Harlem rounds, at Monette Moore's small club. Her discovery was "the kind of accident I dreamed of, the sort of reward I received now and then by traveling to every place where anyone performed."[10]

He became legendary. "'Johnny' hears someone, and 'Johnny' tells someone," wrote Irving Kolodin. "Presently that someone is being discovered, analyzed, and canonized (or perhaps vilified) by the intelligentsia of dance music from coast to coast." Filled with a moral fervor that bordered on paternalistic self-righteousness, Hammond expressed strong opinions that angered many people—including black musicians—but he produced prodigious results. Like the other critics and impresarios of his generation, he went beyond the traditional critic's role of aesthetic appreciation. He immersed himself in the record business and worked to record and promote bandleaders Fletcher Henderson, Benny Carter, Count Basie, Red Norvo, and Benny Goodman. His "discovery" of Teddy Wilson, Lionel Hampton, and Charlie Christian—and his placement of them with Goodman—helped them achieve critical acclaim and national stardom. It is unlikely that the national boogie-woogie craze would have occurred without his promotion of pianists Meade Lux Lewis, Pete Johnson, and Albert Ammons. During the ferment of the 1960s and 1970s, his career hit another peak when he discovered Bob Dylan, Aretha Franklin, and Bruce Springsteen. As McDonough declared, "His ears respond to new music as soundings of social change. He understands instinctively the equations between politics and culture."[11]

As a crusading journalist, moreover, Hammond used music journals and the radical press as "platform[s] for constructive criticism" of the "everyday abuses and the shocking exploitation of recording artists." His primary targets were the owners of the means of musical production, whom racial militants and Communists also attacked. "A systematic policy of segregation started by the employers and encouraged by reactionary union officialdom," Hammond charged, oppressed black performers. When no music magazine would agree to print his exposés of the recording industry, *New Masses* stepped forward. Using the alias Henry Johnson, he attacked Decca for signing Count Basie to a below-scale contract and for failing to pay him royalties. He also exposed American Record, Columbia's parent company, for its plant's oppressive conditions. As chair of the Trade Union Service, a labor press bureau, he contacted the radical United Electrical and Radio Workers' Union, which fed him important information on its drive to organize the plant, "the hottest and dirtiest place I had ever seen." The plant was cleaned up and the union recognized. In 1942, Hammond, Dave Dexter, and Carl Cons bought the magazine *Music and Rhythm* in order to make it a forum for attacking discrimination in the music industry.[12]

It was as an advisor to Benny Goodman that Hammond made his first big splash. He put Goodman back in touch with black musicians, and as a record producer for British-owned (and later American-owned) Columbia in the early 1930s, he recorded Goodman with black players, put Billie Holiday on wax, and produced Bessie Smith's last sessions. He also encouraged

Goodman to buy arrangements from Fletcher Henderson, Edgar Sampson, and Jimmy Mundy and was instrumental in locating key players for the band. He persuaded a reluctant Gene Krupa to join as a drummer and found pianist Jess Stacy. Hammond also brought Krupa, Teddy Wilson, and Benny Goodman together in the studio for their famous trio recordings. When Goodman became the King of Swing, Hammond became "his Harry Hopkins, the man behind the throne. He became famous."[13]

Goodman's phenomenal success validated Hammond as a talent spotter, and music industry executives had to pay attention. As a jazz devotee and a cultural radical, however, Hammond was primarily interested in promoting Negro performers who "could not get a break because of their race." He was Teddy Wilson's major backer during the 1930s, but he also went out of his way to push the Basie band. After hearing Basie on his powerful car radio, Hammond drove to Kansas City to hear the band in person, and then publicized it endlessly in his *Down Beat* columns and among his many musical connections. It was the Basie band's "un-buttoned, never-too-disciplined" style that attracted Hammond. He interpreted it as an "authentic" black band, unlike Duke Ellington's "show band," which, he believed, had lost touch with its blues roots. The "inspired economy" of Basie's piano, the band's improvisational style, the drive of the rhythm section, and the inventiveness of the top soloists astonished him. Basie noted, "He liked what I liked. He liked the blues." Hammond introduced him to Willard Alexander, Goodman's agent at MCA and a jazz lover committed to promoting black talent. Basie's orchestra became MCA's first black band. Together Hammond, Alexander, and Goodman helped the Basie band assault segregated hotels and nightclubs; hence the band's recorded tribute: "John's Idea."[14]

In many ways, Hammond was well positioned to bring relatively "non-commercial" artists into the commercial spotlight during the 1930s. His financial independence allowed him to take jobs in the music industry to help his protégés. At crucial points he was hired by advertising agencies to oversee talent acquisition for Goodman's radio shows, and he used these positions to book black artists who were otherwise rarely heard on the air. Perhaps his most important role was as a record producer when the recording of jazz was infrequent and the field ripe for reshaping. As associate vice president for recording at Columbia in the late 1930s he was able to record his discoveries; this was especially beneficial once he convinced Basie and Goodman to switch to the label. Having arranged sessions for Goodman, Gene Krupa, Teddy Wilson, Billie Holiday, Basie, Harry James, Red Norvo, Mildred Bailey, and a host of others, he could say of many historic recordings, "I was in the studio when it was made."[15]

Hammond did not use his position in the industry simply to publicize his finds, however. He was also instrumental in the movement to integrate the band business. "I thought music was a wonderful means of eliminating the divisions of the races," he noted. Although racially mixed recording sessions had occurred before his time, Hammond's many such endeavors, especially Goodman's 1934 trio recordings, helped ensure that this became a regular procedure. The power of recordings soon produced results in other areas of the business. "Squirrel" Ashcraft and Helen Oakley of the Chicago Hot Club were so impressed by the trio records that they insisted that Teddy Wilson appear at a Hot Club concert with Goodman and Gene Krupa at the Congress Hotel in 1936. "It was the first public performance of the Trio, an historic occasion, for after that Teddy became a regular member of the Goodman organization." As a result, Wilson became the first black player to join an all-white band.[16]

Goodman's band, the outlet for Hammond's many "finds," achieved fame as the first integrated dance band. For example, the trio quickly expanded to a quartet when Hammond discovered Lionel Hampton playing vibraharp in a downtown Los Angeles club and brought him to Goodman's attention. In 1939 Hammond alerted Goodman to guitarist Charlie Christian, paving the way for the famous Goodman quintet and sextet. For the rest of the 1930s, Goodman used these integrated smaller units, although the full band remained all-white. This compromise proved necessary to circumvent the rules of segregated venues that might accept some black "guest" players but were uncomfortable with a large integrated band that symbolized permanent equality between the races. By 1939, however, Goodman hired pianist Fletcher Henderson and guitarist Christian for the big band; in 1941 he hired trumpeter Cootie Williams, drummer Big Sid Catlett, and bassist John Simmons. In backing Goodman, Hammond promoted integration in the band world.

Goodman in turn used his position as the King of Swing to further Hammond's efforts. Despite the compromises, his bands established the principle of racial equality in swing. Goodman played many integrated jam sessions and concerts, and in traveling the South and playing first-class hotels nationwide with black musicians the band broke racial taboos. "With Benny, touring with two black musicians was a pioneering effort," Lionel Hampton noted. "Nobody had ever traveled with an integrated band before, and even though Teddy Wilson and I were only part of the Benny Goodman Quartet . . . that was still too much for some white folks." Despite protests, "Benny wouldn't back down. He once bopped a guy in the head with his clarinet when the guy told him he should 'get those niggers off his show.'" He booked black singers and musicians on his radio shows, extolled their musicianship, and urged Boston's swanky Ritz-Carlton to hire Basie. Goodman often said, "I am selling music, not prejudice." When bookers objected to the black musicians touring the South, he declared, "We had it understood that this was our orchestra and we wouldn't deviate." If they objected, "we just said skip it and wouldn't take the date."[17]

Goodman maintained that he was no "crusader for colored musicians— just a crusader for music." Since the best musicians were black, hiring them enhanced his career. But there was more to it. He had played with black musicians as a youth and been inspired by so many black jazz greats in Chicago that he was predisposed against racial prejudice. He also grew up in a left-wing environment; his father supported socialist Eugene Debs and unionism, and his sister Ida became a Communist. If nothing else, his close friendship with Hammond shows an open mind about politics. In addition, he participated in many Popular Front causes. He donated $1,000 to the Committee to Aid Spanish Democracy in 1937, for example. "Now look," Goodman reportedly said, "this isn't going to feed anyone very long. Let's do something on a bigger scale. There are a lot of other people in the the-atre, in music, who'll help out." The result was Stars for Spain, a benefit that he headlined and helped organize. In response, pro-Franco sympathizers picketed his Carnegie Hall concert and deluged his radio sponsors with mail. He "has been subjected to a violent reactionary attack for his liberal popular front stand," declared the *Daily Worker*. His sponsors received more than four thousand letters demanding his "removal from the air waves be-cause of his pro-Loyalist stand." The *Worker* advised readers that "the only way to counteract the Fascist attack is to reply with a barrage of letters upholding the King of Swing." Hammond and Teddy Wilson, meanwhile, pursued similar activities as members of the Harlem Musical Committee to Aid Spain. Goodman supported numerous other causes too, playing bene-fits for the Congress of the American Youth for Democracy, the election of Harlem Communist Ben Davis, and numerous other Popular Front causes. Wilson himself was politically aware, took part in numerous Popular Front causes, and ultimately refused to fight in World War II because he did "not share" in American democracy. These Popular Front activities attracted the FBI, which described Goodman as "an ardent Communist sympathizer."[18]

The efforts of Hammond, Goodman, Wilson, and Hampton established the idea that racial mixing was central to swing. "Audiences don't draw color lines when they're listening to music," observed Wilson. "When we go out to play, nobody cares what colors or races are represented just so long as we play good music." Such sentiments made Goodman's groups symbols of interracial cooperation in black newspapers and the leftist press, and by the late 1930s other white—and then black—bands followed suit. Having played privately with blacks, white bandleaders such as Charlie Barnet, Gene Krupa, Jimmy Dorsey, Joe Sullivan, and Bobby Burnet found the climate of opinion more favorable to mixed bands. Formerly all-black bands did too. In 1943, Fletcher Henderson, Lucky Millinder, and Earl Hines hired white players.[19]

Such actions still created controversy, however. Artie Shaw had to fight police in the border states and amusement operators in New York when he hired Billie Holiday, Roy Eldridge, and Lips Page. When his agency, General Artists Corporation, insisted that he drop Page for a southern tour in 1941, he chose to cancel thirty-two southern dates. The *Worker* called him a "champion" in the fight against "Jim-Crow in popular music circles." When Gene Krupa hired Roy Eldridge to play with his band, he got into a fistfight with the manager of a York, Pennsylvania, diner who declined to serve Eldridge; in the process, Krupa went to jail. He told the *Pittsburgh Courier* that "he would undergo such embarrassment again and again in defense of the race's right in this our land where all men have been decreed equal." His fight won him the first annual Chu Berry memorial award, given by the *Courier,* for the "man who each year contributes the most to the profession in an unprejudiced manner." Thus, on the eve of World War II, racial mixing in big bands was considered "the best American tradition."[20]

Swing America

Hammond's many activities make it clear that the effort to integrate big bands and other musical institutions and to bring recognition to black artists drew on the support of the organized Left during the 1930s. Underlying their efforts was the shared conviction that jazz was America's true art and the expression of the democratic way of life. Much of this redefinition of jazz emerged from the Harlem branch of the Communist Party, with which Hammond had extensive contact during the early 1930s. Composed of younger blacks and Jews, the Harlem branch endorsed black art forms early in the decade, even as the party leadership rejected jazz as bourgeois. Supported by the student movement on campuses across New York City, the youthful members of the Harlem branch pursued their own early "popular front" strategy for attracting black support and ultimately convinced the party hierarchy to adopt a more conciliatory position.

In order to attract the black masses to an interracial party, black and white Communists in the Harlem branch began in the early 1930s to recog-

The Benny Goodman Band, Meadowbrook Ballroom, Cedar Grove, New Jersey, 1941. By the early 1940s, a number of African American soloists were playing in white bands. John Simmons is on bass, Sid Catlett, drums, and Cootie Williams, trumpet. Note how fans crowd around the bandstand and how the streamlined music stands blend the individual musicians into one group. Frank Driggs Collection.

nize black vernacular culture as an essential ingredient of a democratic American culture. They presented black performers at interracial functions and made jazz a central part of their benefits and political activities in Harlem. "A Day of Unemployment" in March 1930, for example, featured an interracial Rockland Ballroom party with music by Duke Ellington. These efforts were surpassed by the series of benefits held on behalf of the Scottsboro defendants. Recognizing a clear case of social injustice and an opportunity for interracial organizing, the Harlem branch in May 1932 presented an array of performers including Cab Calloway's band, the cast of *Porgy and Bess*, the Hall Johnson Choir, and the Martha Graham dancers. Hammond arranged another benefit for the legal defense team at the request of his friend William Patterson, a Harlem attorney and newly appointed national secretary of the ILD. As a result of his efforts the Rockland Ballroom rocked to the sounds of W. C. Handy, Fats Waller, Fletcher Henderson, Duke Ellington, the Mills Brothers, Ethel Waters, Benny Carter's Orchestra, Paul

Whiteman, and the entire revue from Smalls' Paradise. As part of their policy of interracial unity, these occasions were politically and racially nonsectarian.[21]

Their views on jazz and their desire for nonsectarian alliances involved younger members in a challenge to the party hierarchy's conception of jazz as a decadent remnant of bourgeois civilization. Mike Gold expressed the orthodox view in the *Daily Worker*. Although he did not object to jazz as dance music, Gold proclaimed it "fairly tawdry and cheap," lacking any "real depths of emotion." Not truly proletarian since it had "no roots in anything except the Broadway pavement," jazz also lacked the "high lofty imagination of a Bach or a Beethoven." Neither folk nor high culture, it was "a kind of commercial product, rootless, meaningless, adulterated," little more than "a source of bourgeois corruption." In "The Shame of Jazz," a poem he wrote for his column, he made his point lyrically: "Wah, wah! in shrieking dance halls / I hear that sad mean capitalist wah," which needed to be drowned out by "O Lenin Beethoven music." To take part in the larger worker's revolt, the black working class would need proper revolutionary music.[22]

Gold's editorials produced an impassioned response by younger Communists who maintained that jazz was an authentic folk and protest music. Dale Curran argued that "jazz is the main American contribution to folk art and proletarian art." Since it grew up in reaction to white chauvinism, jazz "expresses both Negro and white." Its exploitation by radio and movies was "only an incident in its growth." The creative spark lay in the "Black Belt" and cannot be condemned "just because soap peddlers, crooners and greasy-voiced announcers are grafting a living off it." Charles Edward Smith put the argument in Marxist terms. In "Class Content of Jazz Music," he pointed out that spirituals, blues, and jazz were the folk music of proletarian African Americans, while sweeter sounds were attempts to transform this authentic voice into middle-class dreams. Thus, "Hot jazz aims to be genuinely the folk expression of a people. It has its roots in the denial to the American Negro of 'the right of self-determination.'" The battle between sweet and hot jazz was part of the larger class war.[23]

When the party adopted its Popular Front position in 1936, the link between the Left and swing became official policy. According to Mark Naison, the shift to multiracial, multiclass struggle encouraged the party to endorse the activities under way in Harlem and among younger communists generally. In the fight against Fascism, the Harlem branch already had made common cause with numerous black organizations, attracted intellectuals, artists, and performers, and reevaluated black culture and popular entertainment in a more positive light. Much of this was urged by younger American-born Jews in the party who had grown up with popular music and felt the pull of the American dream. In search of an American identity, they pushed the party to take cognizance of political realities and popular culture. According to Naison, they "invested Americanization with a romantic aura." They also extolled black artists, "particularly musicians, as a democratizing force, the source of much within the nation's culture which was distinctively 'American.'" They wanted a national culture to which they could assimilate, but one that differed greatly from the nineteenth-century Anglo-Saxon one.[24]

Many African American artists and intellectuals supported the party because of its activism on their behalf and because the party acknowledged their national aspirations and their desire for inclusion in American life. This link between music and politics became more apparent in the late 1930s as party fund-raisers for the defense of Ethiopia and Loyalist Spain featured swing bands as exemplars of the democratic ideals being defended. A Carnegie Hall concert to benefit Spanish Loyalists, for example, was sponsored by the Harlem Musical Committee for Spanish Democracy and featured Cab Calloway, Fats Waller, and Count Basie. These efforts, coupled with the party's fight for the Scottsboro defendants, brought many black artists, writers, and musicians into the party's orbit. As black Communist George Streator recalled, "Spanish freedom and Negro freedom were made to be synonymous." Teddy Wilson, Claude Hopkins, Duke Ellington, and other black bandleaders, moreover, appeared at benefits for the Disabled Veterans Fund sponsored by the Friends and Veterans of the Abraham Lincoln Brigade, the interracial army of volunteers who fought the Fascists in Spain.[25]

Many other bandleaders, musicians, and singers joined Paul Robeson to support the successful bid of black Communist Ben Davis to become Harlem's councilman in 1943. Pianist Luckey Roberts declared that in supporting Davis, "I feel that I am fighting Jim Crow in much the same way that I fight it in my music." Using "all the instruments of democracy to establish racial equality," he believed in "the ballad and the ballot." Benny Goodman's quartet reunited to play for a Ben Davis election event at Harlem's Golden Gate ballroom, and pianist Teddy Wilson starred in a celebration of the twenty-fifth anniversary of the Communist movement at Madison Square Garden in 1944.[26]

During the late 1930s, the party also attempted to advance black music through a series of concerts and other musical events held in dignified settings to counter the tendency of "some persons, however 'friendly,'" to conceive of Negro musicians as exotic natural performers. As James Dugan put it, swing was "as much for listening as it [was] for jittering." Hammond's two Spirituals to Swing concerts were linked to the party through the sponsorship of the *New Masses* and the Theater Arts Committee, as was the American Music Festival benefit for Dorothy Parker's Spanish Children's Relief Fund on May 8, 1940. The festival's theme was "American music" that reflected "the traditions and culture of the people." After an evening including Woody Guthrie, Leadbelly, boogie woogie piano, and Earl Robinson doing "We the People," Teddy Wilson's quartet concluded with a rousing swing session.[27]

As the Popular Front and the student movement expanded the ranks of young party members, the momentum shifted to the youthful Americanizers. They used their access to the party press to identify the Left with black and racially integrated swing. Benefit dances for the *New Masses,* the Workers' School, the Young Communist League, American Youth for Democracy, and other leftist youth groups and unions invariably included swing bands. On December 17, 1938, for example, the Fur Floor Boys and Shipping Clerks Union presented a "Battle of Swing" featuring Charlie Barnet's orchestra against Lucky Millinder's to benefit the Friends of the Lincoln Brigade. The night before, the Hunt's Point Branch, American League for Peace and Democracy, welcomed home Spanish veterans with Alfredo Kyle and his Pampas Swingsters at the Bronx's Hunt's Point Palace. On Halloween, 1937, there were dance parties all over town. As the *Worker* put it, "you get another chance tonight to make hay while the dance bands play, and at the same time know that what you're doin' with your dough is to make the *Daily Worker* go." The Social Workers Educational League rented the Savoy Ballroom, where Chick Webb and the Savoy Sultans played for lindy hop contests. In May 1939, meanwhile, the Young Communist League held their ninth national convention at Madison Square Garden, where "the kids will be kicking out that evening with song and dance enough to turn every ickie into an alligator." The convention's central exhibition, "Swing America," galvanized the delegates. "Swing America / Hear that good progressive beat," went the theme song, "Swing the nation to its feet."[28]

Swing America may have been an artificial attempt to attract young adherents to the party, a manipulative feature of the Popular Front that Hammond criticized severely. But the young leftists' interest in swing was real. It also reflected their dissatisfaction with the WASP-dominated fraternity-sorority youth culture; they wanted to link political concerns to the popular music—jazz—that represented freedom for the downtrodden. For younger

Communists, especially but not exclusively Jews and blacks, the fight for racial integration in music was also a fight for an America that realized social justice. This explains the decidedly integrationist tone in their jazz writings. When the American Youth for Democracy staged "A Salute to Fats Waller" in 1944 with Duke Ellington, Billie Holiday, Jimmy Rushing, Count Basie, Art Hodes, and many others, the *Worker* emphasized that the concert "was a testimonial to a 'good guy' who made music so that all people could live in a world where there aren't black people and white people any more than there are black keys and white keys on the piano." In the world of "popular music, people's music," argued the reporter, "there has never been anything as shockingly un-American as Jim Crow. That was Fats Waller's world. It's the world that the AYD and all of its friends consider worth fighting for."[29]

By the late 1930s leftist dogma held that swing was an authentic American folk culture. Dale Curran put it best: "Swing is important and significant precisely because it has taken the submerged and little known masterpieces of American folk music and applied to them the technique and musical richness of world music. And if that American music happens to be predominantly Negro that is just too bad for us white folks." Swing would become the "American music of tomorrow, solidly rooted in the people's culture, enriched by the musical tradition of the past." As other party supporters believed, "Negro musicians . . . have been the decisive element behind the history, development and course" of American music. Disagreement remained over the "sexual" content of the music, as many party puritans objected to the explicit tone of the blues, but the momentum was with those like James Dugan, who declared, "Hot jazz comes from the least coaching or theory right out of the music of the American Negro, the oppressed Negro." Many jazz writers traced the origins of the music to black New Orleans, and they hailed Louis Armstrong, Buddy Bolden, Bunk Johnson, and Freddie Keppard as swing's true originators. The popularity of black music, moreover, was interpreted as "a key manifestation of a broad democratic tendency in American life." As Dugan put it, "Swing is as American as baseball and hot dogs. A good hot band can claim as many raucous rooters as the Dodgers. There is a good deal of audience participation in swing . . . a rough democratic air invading the sacred halls of music."[30]

In linking black music to politics, young party members envisioned a future America in which blacks would be recognized and appreciated as culturally distinctive, yet quintessentially American. Leftists maintained that segregation in music went against American democratic traditions because "the stream of the peoples fused in the music itself." *Worker* music critic Martin McCall noted that despite Benny Goodman's example, few mixed bands existed in 1938. He blamed band and hotel managers and publicity agencies who still considered the prospect of mixed bands a "gamble." But jazz audiences and the determined actions of the best musicians "grateful [for] opportunities of playing with their Negro colleagues" served as models of racial democracy. Hammond concurred. Swing musicians, he argued in the *Worker,* were "the least prejudiced group in the country. Just ask the boys with Gene Krupa, Benny Goodman, Artie Shaw, Charlie Barnet, or any other band which has mixed racial contingents, and you will find respect and admiration on both sides."[31]

Regardless of Race, Creed, or Color

While Hammond often made common cause with the Left, his importance as a music critic also symbolized the broader links between jazz criticism and leftist ideology. As a writer for Britain's *Melody Maker,* music critic for the Brooklyn *Eagle,* columnist for *New Masses* and New York correspondent for *Down Beat,* he was perhaps the best-known swing critic of the era. He was not alone, however. Ben Ali Haggin in the *Nation,* Otis Ferguson in the *New Republic,* and Charles Edward Smith in the *Daily Worker* covered swing regularly. In the black press, Billy Rowe wrote entertainment and swing criticism for the *Pittsburgh Courier, Chicago Defender,* and *Amsterdam News.* In fact, the swing era witnessed the inauguration of an American jazz press. Prior to 1934, most jazz criticism was journalistic, with longer articles in general opinion magazines. In the 1920s Carl Van Vechten wrote occasional pieces on blues singers and jazz musicians for *Vanity Fair.* Most jazz writing involved record reviews, such as R. D. Darrell's brief pieces in the *Phonograph Monthly Review.* Looking for outlets, some of the earliest American critics, including Hammond and Marshall Stearns, wrote for Britain's *Melody Maker* and *Hot News and Rhythm Record Review.* Recognizing that Europe already had several jazz magazines by the early 1930s, jazz fans in the United States wanted American journals to cover their national art form. In 1934, *Down Beat* began life as the first jazz publication in the United States, followed by *Metronome* in 1935 and later in the decade by specialized magazines such as *Jazz Information, H.R.S. Rag,* and numerous fan publications.[32]

As a platform for the first generation of jazz critics, the swing press embodied the populist cultural attitudes of the 1930s. Published in Chicago but featuring strong coverage of New York, *Down Beat* maintained a broad democratic outlook, with its cartoons, sexy photos of "girl" singers, slang-filled headlines, combative columnists, and a letters department that took those same critics to task. *Metronome,* its New York counterpart, was a staid classical music and society band journal until Harvard graduate and drummer George Simon transformed it into a swing magazine. As the first musician to cover dance bands, Simon brought a wealth of musical knowledge and interest to the task, and his record and orchestra reviews were fierce. He lacked the political commitment of Hammond and Helen Oakley, however, and as a consequence, so did *Metronome.* Only in the early 1940s when the new editors, Barry Ulanov and Leonard Feather, came aboard did *Metronome* focus on black bands and music as central elements in American culture. Yet, in its coverage of popular music as a cultural entity and in its vibrant reviews and letter columns there was an implicitly democratic tone. *Down Beat,* which came to the fore with swing, expressed the broad democratic sweep of the music and its culture explicitly.

Down Beat's critics expressed disdain for their own upper-class backgrounds and immersed themselves instead in the decidedly more democratic swing music. Like Hammond, the critics were part of a new nationalism that rescued a number of wealthy young people from irrelevance in the 1930s. The *'Beat's* critics sought to educate and persuade their public, but they often ended up in combat with their readers and each other. Many of them took their evangelical tone from the United Hot Clubs of America, with which they were associated in an attempt to rescue jazz from the doldrums in 1934 and give it the scholarly and critical apparatus that their European colleagues had pioneered. Marshall Stearns, a Yale English instructor, founded the organization in 1934 along with Hammond, who served as New York and international president, and Milt Gabler, who started Commodore Records in order to reissue classic jazz recordings. George Frazier, an Irish American Harvard graduate, headed the Boston chapter, and Helen Oakley and "Squirrel" Ashcraft ran the Chicago branch. Other chapters existed in Birmingham, Los Angeles, Washington, D.C., and Cleveland. As an organizing force for young well-to-do college students and intellectuals, the UHCA pushed for reissues of jazz classics, promoted jazz as American culture, and validated scholarly research into jazz's origins. As Stearns said in *Billboard,* jazz was one of the "few unique American contributions to the world of art. Like the poets, Walt Whitman and Edgar Allen Poe, the fact that it was first truly appreciated abroad, only adds to our obligation to study it generally and spread an understanding of its greatness at home."[33]

The critics infused *Down Beat* with a nonsectarian leftist populism that fit with the magazine's screwball democratic ethos. Walter Schaap, writer for *Jazz Information,* and treasurer for *Jazz Hot* in Europe, declared, "The

American jazz [critics] tended to be left wing. To appreciate black musicians meant that you weren't a hidebound conservative or bigot." The "sometimes pro-Communist and sometimes not" left-wing movement directed "people toward appreciating blacks and therefore their music." Hammond certainly fit this mold, but so did others. George Frazier lambasted both pretense and inherited status and urged Goodman to hire a black singer who could keep up with him. "What, then is to prevent Benny's hiring a colored girl?" He also attacked "the Jim Crow complex" as a result of which white trombonist Georg Brunis, a native of New Orleans, prevented African American drummer Zutty Singleton from playing with Bobby Hackett's band in Greenwich Village: "There is more racial prejudice within the profession than anyone would care to believe." In response he declared that "there is no room in art for prejudice. Talent alone should be the requirement and not the color of one's skin."[34]

That phrase summed up *Down Beat*'s central position. An early editorial praised the inclusion of Teddy Wilson in the Goodman Trio. In a world sick with hate, "ravished with fevers of race discrimination, and nauseated by dictatorships based on force and oppression," argued *Down Beat,* "it is refreshing as all hell to witness an example of fine sportsmanship in any line of endeavor." In music there were many cases "of talent suffering because of race and color, and plenty more because of unjust and disgusting exploitation." Thus they took pleasure in "a colored boy of great talent employed with a group of white musicians and playing to generous applause night after night on the sole merit as a musician." While the use of *boy* offends modern ears, swing musicians and critics used the term to apply to all band musicians, regardless of color. Certainly *Down Beat*'s credo appeared colorblind: "We still believe that regardless of race, creed or color we are all Americans, and that as Americans we are all free and equal, and deserving of the respect and admiration of our fellow men according to the extent of our abilities." Further, the editors argued that they did not "subscribe to racial prejudice" in their reporting or criticism but preferred "to judge musicians strictly on their ability and not on any basis of the complexion of their skin!" Responding to proposals for an all-Jewish symphony, they propounded a larger view of American culture. "Each group in withdrawing its youth from the democratic environment of their fellow Americans of EVERY RACIAL ANCESTRY, is thereby depriving them of one of the greatest blessings of this country—the stimulation of creative impulses that comes from the exchange of ideas and the intermingling of different racial stocks."[35]

In a variety of ways, *Down Beat* critics attempted to educate their readership about the central role of African Americans in jazz. Marshall Stearns, for example, wrote a fifteen-part history of swing that introduced readers to serious jazz scholarship. Attuned to historical origins, Stearns demonstrated that swing evolved from African musical culture, from the music of American blacks as they experienced slavery in the nineteenth century, and from the migration to the cities in the twentieth. Diverging from past views of black musicians as untutored primitives, Stearns discussed their artistic contributions to American culture. Periodically, moreover, black columnist Frank Marshall Davis challenged white writers who ignored the primacy of black musicians in the creation and development of swing. An instructor in jazz history at Chicago's Marxist-oriented Lincoln School, Davis argued that the "best white bands copy negroes." At the same time, he acknowledged Goodman, Joe Marsala, Red Norvo, and others "who close their eyes to color and judge by ability instead of race."[36]

In its many discussions of black music and musicians, *Down Beat* served as one of the few consistent "white" forums on the subject of racial equality. Except for Hammond, who crusaded for mixed bands, the editors maintained that equal opportunity for black bands and musicians would better serve their cause than would the integration of individual blacks in white orchestras. In discussing the failure of a swing band composed equally of black and white musicians, for example, they held that integration by itself was not the issue. Instead, they viewed real democracy for black musicians as "equality of opportunity, not the fact that a Negro can sit side by side with a white, BUT THAT HE CAN BUILD A BAND AS GOOD AS CASA LOMA OR BENNY GOODMAN," and that he had a right to earn the same amount of money by playing the musical outlets currently open only to white bands.[37]

They also worried that integration stole the focus from the music. "A mixed band today still arouses racial prejudice and focuses the public's attention on its social aspects—NOT ITS MUSICAL VALUES." Although it held to equality of opportunity as a standard, the magazine also discussed the issue of integration sympathetically. When Goodman went to Dallas with Wilson and Hampton, for instance, Hammond dispelled fears of a race riot. "There was not even the slightest hint of a protest during the entire eleven day stay." Only a few southern white musicians "said that Benny could never get away with it." Goodman's Dallas appearance raised the question of "WHETHER A MIXED BAND IS A GOOD IDEA OR NOT." Clearly his southern success was "another victory for sportsmanship and fine talent." Yet, most mixed bands had failed because the "equality of a colored man playing alongside a white man was resented," and this "resentment cast its shadow over the commercial success of the proposed organization." The article argued that Goodman's success and the many good recordings by mixed groups showed that "musically it makes no difference whether a colored artist is playing with members of his own race or white musicians. God knows there are not race lines in music and that no race has any monopoly on musical talent." *Down Beat* worried, however, that if social ideals took over, musicians could not relax and play their best.[38]

The periodical featured wide-ranging discussions of racial issues in music. When Goodman hired Fletcher Henderson and Charlie Christian for his big band in 1939, for example, the magazine encouraged musicians to air their views. The *'Beat* quoted several white musicians who saw the move as a threat to white employment, as well as white southerners who argued that the presence of Negroes would hurt the business of mixed bands in cafes where women were present. The editors quickly pointed out, however, that those opposed to integration only spoke anonymously, whereas those in favor stated their views openly. Claiming neutrality, the editors tried "to encourage musicians to *think* about it instead of *feeling* about it." They proposed "a square deal. And any American, no matter what his race, his color, or his creed, is entitled to that." They then featured those who approved, with headlines such as "Benny Should Be Congratulated for His Courage— Jimmy Dorsey." Dorsey and Woody Herman, however, argued that it was a matter of style and choice. Teddy Wilson, Ella Fitzgerald, Artie Shaw, Jack Jenney, Shep Fields, and Vido Musso saw mixed bands as progress toward "equality of races in the music field." Several leaders predicted that "within two more years, use of colored artists in white bands will be accepted everywhere in the States." Ella Fitzgerald said, "I believe the hiring of colored musicians in a white band is really mutually beneficial." Leaving the issue to free choice, *Down Beat* essentially sanctioned mixed bands as part of its square-deal philosophy and its expanded vision of social and racial equality.[39]

Although the magazine's critics explored the historical origins of swing, they focused primarily on the virtues of modern bands. Hammond and Stearns, after all, saw the commercial orchestras of Count Basie and Benny Goodman as the culmination of a cultural continuity that began in Africa and developed during slavery. Others among the first generation of radical critics, however, sought to discover in early jazz the pure, undiluted musical culture of the people. This stance often led them to be critical of swing. Until the middle of World War II, however, they operated as an important minor strain of jazz criticism within the swing world. These critics gravitated to the little jazz magazines, such as *Jazz Information, H.R.S. Rag,* and *The Jazz Record,* as well as serious books that treated jazz as part of folk culture. Concerned for those forgotten by the swing era, they helped resurrect and promote older, more traditional blues recordings and singers. As a result of this political thrust, they redefined musical culture in more democratic ways. For example, eager to find authentic representations of traditional black music, folklorist Alan Lomax captured the life of the forgotten Jelly Roll Morton in a series of oral interviews and engineered the recording of his music by the Library of Congress. As Lomax recently noted, "folklore is moving across the class line and interesting yourself in the art of ordinary people."[40]

The fascination with authentic jazz was part of the search for a cultural alternative to the dehumanization of society in the industrial world. Radical critics such as Hammond, Ralph Gleason, Rudi Blesh, Charles Edward Smith, and Edward Ramsey explored the "authentic" blues and jazz background of swing, which they saw as rooted in southern black communities where "life and art seemed naturally in tune with the rhythms of the universe." Interested in preindustrial musical products of organic communities, the purists departed from the emphasis of the 1920s on primitive sexuality in jazz but still held to the notion of the natural simplicity of folk music. Their emphasis on culture allowed them to explore early blues and jazz with anthropological fervor. A growing army of record collectors, stimulated by the Hot Record Clubs' advocacy of reissues and historical accuracy, intersected with radical jazz critics in their insistence on the superiority of the unadulterated sounds of New Orleans and Chicago jazz. Many collectors and critics displayed what Francis Newton calls "a Calvinist spirit" in their distaste for heresy. Undiluted jazz was like "the ideal blood of an aristocratic family in constant danger of pollution from the floods around it. 'What is jazz?' is the single question which crops up most frequently in the discussions of the aficionados." This group of collectors combed Salvation Army bins, attics, and junk stores, according to Neil Leonard, "in search of splinters of the True Cross."[41]

The first jazz history grew out of the interest in hot music engendered by swing, the leftist concern with authentic folk culture, and the collector's fascination with pure jazz. In 1939 Frederic Ramsey, Jr., and Charles Edward Smith edited *Jazzmen*, a collection of articles by critics, historians, and collectors that combined research with the romance of discovering preindustrial musicians and cultures. The championing of those "who made hot spots hotter in New Orleans" was the major accomplishment of the volume, since most of the musicians had been "forgotten and neglected" by the modern world. Adopting techniques that Smith had learned on various writer's projects of the Works Progress Administration, the book pioneered the use of oral history to give voice to the key blues players and to Chicago and New York jazzmen who had left few written records. As Ramsey and Smith pursued the artists of the past, they took "to the dives of Harlem, Chicago and New Orleans, to the rice fields of Louisiana, to Storyville, the now legendary red-light district of New Orleans, to reform schools, even to the last stopping place of at least two jazz pioneers, a hospital for the insane." As an oral history, however, *Jazzmen* had a number of problems. For example, the authors put words in King Oliver's mouth, and they enhanced a number of situations to raise the role of earlier jazzmen to mythic quality.[42]

Smith clarified the theoretical foundations of *Jazzmen* in the *New Republic*. Unlike swing, hot jazz had African roots and became a folk music through the simple, functional blues. "Utility, as exemplified by thimbles and washboard, whiskbrooms and suitcase," influenced instrumental technique in jazz and helped create a national folk culture "coincident with the urbanization and industrialization of the country itself." Swing, on the other hand, had the technical excellence of early jazz but was "devoid of any but a purely instrumental virtue." Most popular musicians, Smith claimed, had lost touch with their roots. Modern radio and record companies had been "flooding the land for years with the work of large popular 'name' bands—spineless and unoriginal." Disdaining modern techniques of arranging in favor of folk simplicity, the traditional critics maintained that only in the small jazz combo of New Orleans and Chicago past could community and spontaneity be found. Moreover, Ramsey and Smith held to a view common among purists: that the music was not just black in origin but had emerged out of a black working-class culture that appealed to other lower-class musicians, particularly Italians in New Orleans. Hence, jazz was an American democratic and people's music, open to those sympathetic to the lower classes. Although these critics often disdained swing, *Jazzmen* also discussed the worth of New York's swing bands. The complete divorce of traditional jazz from modern swing in the work of the most radical critics lay in the future. Besides, most critics, radical and otherwise, considered swing democratic music and hence positive. In their minds, the swing craze provided an opportunity to educate popular music audiences about the democratic and interracial nature of American musical culture.[43]

The dispute between swing partisans and advocates of a pure folk past that simmered beneath the surface until World War II was only one of many conflicts among jazz critics. Their verbal jousts often rivaled the musical battles of the bands they covered. While fans challenged critics at every turn, critics often acted like fans with their many enthusiasms and dislikes. In a notable example, George Frazier charged in print that Martha Tilton

"Stinks!" while others derided certain musicians for being "corny," the worst sin in the critical lexicon. The clash of combative critics gave the era its style and tone, but it also led to hurt feelings on the part of musicians and bandleaders and resentment that rich white boys had such power over musicians—black and white. On occasion this fractious relationship also led to threats of violence against critics such as Hammond and Leonard Feather, both of whom pulled no punches.

As a political crusader and a swing enthusiast and critic, Hammond made as many enemies as friends in the swing fraternity. Otis Ferguson, a working-class populist who wrote on the popular arts in *The New Republic* and in small jazz publications, found much to admire in Hammond but also much to deplore. According to Ferguson, Hammond was a rich young man born with a silver spoon in his mouth who lacked critical standards and consideration for those he attacked. Consequently, Ferguson argued, Hammond suffered from "a complete lack of temperance and caution. He hasn't established for himself the intervening marks on the scale of achievement between 'it's terrific' and 'it stinks.'" While musicians appreciated Hammond's ear for talent and his generosity, they resented his "belting down like God off the mountain with the Word, the one and only." They also resented his meddling with their bands on the assumption that he knew what was best for them. Despite Hammond's many contributions to swing, Ferguson declared that in his moral self-righteousness, "he simply won't even try to work like a critic, and his idea of giving a musician a hint is to hit him in the face with a shovel."[44]

Duke Ellington felt the shovel. In "The Tragedy of Duke Ellington," Hammond showed the dangers of mixing aesthetic and racial-political judgments. The essay, published in *Down Beat* in 1935, blamed the "complete sterility" of "Reminiscing in Tempo" on Duke's hiring of "un-negroid musicians" and his failure to protest the racial abuses faced by him and his people. "The real trouble with Duke's music," asserted Hammond, "is the fact that he has purposely kept himself from any contact with the troubles of his people or mankind in general." Among other things, he "keeps himself from thinking about such problems as those of the southern share croppers, the Scottsboro boys, intolerable working and relief conditions." Even worse, "he has never shown any desire of aligning himself with forces that are seeking to remove the causes of these disgraceful conditions." As a result, Hammond maintained, Ellington's music "has become vapid and without the slightest semblance of guts." In his autobiography, Hammond revealed that he and Ellington also disagreed over the integration of orchestras, which Duke believed only helped white bands. Hammond, on the other hand, felt that "jazz always has had a duty to promote racial understanding and interracial cooperation."[45]

Ellington responded in a series of articles that derided swing critics in general and Hammond in particular. In part, Ellington noted, swing musicians were not used to serious criticism of their work. On the other hand, many critics lacked critical standards and had little knowledge of music. They also failed to inform themselves of a musician's intentions, which led to judgments based solely on personal whim. In Ellington's eyes, Hammond was one of the worst on this score. He had done much for musicians, but he also "perhaps has stirred up the greatest resentment." Ellington blamed Hammond's fervent political beliefs for warping his musical understanding, calling him "an ardent propagandist and champion of the 'lost cause,'" who identified himself with "the interests of the minorities, the Negro peoples, to a lesser degree, the Jew, and to the underdog, in the form of the Communist party." The fever of battle, noted Duke, rendered "his enthusiasm and prejudices a little bit unwieldy." One detects an even deeper resentment. Ellington must have wondered how a rich white critic filled with a crusading, but almost overbearing, zealousness could tell him that he lacked the proper consciousness of being a Negro and that his music was not "black" enough.[46]

Jump for Joy

Despite the tensions between musicians and critics, the redefinition of swing by the Left as an authentic and democratic American culture brought together white patrician swing intellectuals, Jewish impresarios, and African American and white swing band leaders and musicians in new ways. The Popular Front found expression not only in numerous concerts, but also in Barney Josephson's Cafe Society. Opened in late 1938 in Greenwich Village, Cafe Society was the first racially integrated cabaret in white New York and the nation's first Popular Front nightclub. "The concert at Carnegie Hall and the opening of one of the most successful and controversial nightclubs in New York," Hammond recalled, "took place on the same night and were very much related." Josephson attended the rehearsals of Spirituals to Swing and drew his talent from its ranks. A former shoe salesman and a lover of black music, Josephson hailed from a family steeped in radical Jewish politics. His brother Leon, who worked in the club, was a Communist, a member of ILD, and part of a group that had tried to assassinate Adolph Hitler. Helen Lawrenson, upper-class rebel, public relations worker at the club, and a Popular Front member, maintains that the idea for the club originated with Earl Browder as a way to raise money for the Communist Party.[47]

Eager to blend jazz with political and social satire, Josephson turned to Hammond for musical advice: "Without John I don't think I would . . . have accomplished this successful operation, talent-wise." When Josephson ran out of money, Hammond, Willard Alexander, and Benny Goodman each put up $5,000. Hammond also built Josephson's first orchestra around black trumpeter Frankie Newton and booked the stars of Spirituals to Swing. Perhaps his most notable booking was Billie Holiday, who in a long engagement at the cafe became the darling of Popular Front intellectuals. In addition, Jewish leftist comedians such as Jack Gilford and Zero Mostel performed political satire. Cafe Society proved popular in the New Deal era, and Josephson became an influential figure in New York nightlife. In 1940 he opened an uptown branch. Cafe Society became a club for intelligent people with a social conscience who were concerned about political, social, and racial justice. In the case of Lawrenson and her friends, it drew upper-class rebels unhappy with east-side cafe society life—until the red scare forced Josephson out of business in 1949.[48]

The club's racial policy stemmed from Josephson's distaste for discrimination as well as his political commitments. "Cafe Society was very much a part of the New Deal era," he recalled. As a young Jew in Trenton who felt less than fully American, he befriended the only black boy in his class, argued against military training in schools, and was beaten up for his efforts. "So all those things were in my background, and New York in the mid-thirties echoed my feelings. It was the time of the labor organizers and the Ladies Garment Workers' show called 'Pins and Needles' and the W.P.A. art movement and 'The Cradle Will Rock.'" Cafe Society's programming had a political flavor. It "was used for [benefits for] the Lincoln Brigade because I was active and interested in these things. This was [sic] my interests. I was giving my money too."[49]

The club's name, suggested by Clare Booth, satirized its upper-class namesake and class pretensions. Josephson hired a group of Village WPA artists such as Adolf Dehn, William Gropper, Sam Berman, Gregor Duncan, Anton Refergaiz, and Abe Birnbaum to "rib the upper classes" in a series of wall murals. Dehn depicted a debutante surrounded by fifteen to twenty "full dress-suited little bald guys with pot bellies," while Refregaiz painted a stylish lady, her gown flowing in the air and her head a gramophone machine. "With her nose on a record playing the music—it represented a yak-yak, talk society girl." In back of the bar, Berman's mural portrayed cabaret types as "all animals, all kinds in a menagerie, dressed like humans. . . . And the mural was as if it were a mirror." Topping off the decor, a plaster cast monkey in "Hitler mustache and hair" hung from one of the pipes "with a noose." As Josephson noted, "it was the first time that a night-club attempted to put a painting, a picture of something, on the wall." The club's ads also built on social satire. Billing itself as the "Rendezvous of Celebs, Debs and Plebs," the club ran one ad showing a top-hatted gent ringing up money in the "Social [Cash] Register." The caption read, "The Wrong Place for the Right People."[50]

Cafe Society's political thrust highlighted interracial themes. "I wanted a club where blacks and whites worked together behind the footlights and sat together out front. There wasn't, so far as I know," Josephson recalled, "a place like it in New York or in the whole country." Onstage, black enter-tainers were presented on mixed bills and in dignified settings. The manage-ment also insisted that black guests be welcomed in the audience along with white patrons. Black intellectuals often dropped in, and when Lena Horne performed, Joe Louis was often in attendance. Paul Robeson was an-other regular, as was the black actor Canada Lee. The club also drew many prominent white patrons, among them Eleanor Roosevelt (in perhaps her only visit to a nightclub), as well as college students, readers of *New Masses,* and liberal Jews. The dramatic success of the club worked as a powerful agent to convince other jazz club owners, especially on Fifty-second Street, that jazz, politics, and integrated audiences existed in harmony and made money.[51]

In attempting to break down segregation in the music industry during the 1930s, many black performers also participated in changing the way their world operated. Whether they were sanguine or pessimistic about these developments, black performers could not ignore pressures for change. Indeed, the involvement of both the Communist and non-Communist Left in these activities made a muted leftism acceptable. Many black performers benefited from the creation of Cafe Society, and they took part in fundraisers for the Spanish Republic, antiwar groups, and antisegre-gation causes organized by the Left. Billie Holiday, for example, expressed delight with Cafe Society's policy of "no segregation, no racial prejudice. . . . This was what I'd been waiting for." Her appearances at the club made her a star because they brought her into contact with intellectuals drawn to her moving renditions of popular songs. Her most famous song, "Strange Fruit," grew directly out of her appearances at Cafe Society. The idea for the song came from a poem by a Jewish leftist, Lewis Allen, whom she met at the club. "When he showed me that poem, I dug it right off. It seemed to spell out all the things that had killed" her father. The "strange fruit" of the title refers to a black man hanging from a tree after a lynching. Because of its potent subject matter in a period when an antilynching bill was a prominent part of the activist agenda, "Strange Fruit" quickly became one of the major protest songs of the era. As Holiday turned it into her signature song, she became a symbol of the downtrodden and a heroine in the battle against racial oppression.[52]

Other black bands and performers were an integral part of Popular Front activities. Count Basie appeared in both of the Spirituals to Swing concerts and worked with Paul Robeson and Richard Wright on "King Joe," the tribute to Joe Louis arranged by Hammond. His band also played various engagements and benefits at Josephson's club. In 1939, moreover, Basie's band toured with a Popular Front revue, "Meet the People," which produced "It's the Same Old South," with lyrics by Joe Eliscu. Recorded by the band with Jimmy Rushing, the song condemned the South's segregation, persecution of the CIO, and undemocratic nature. Its strong sentiments met with resistance by Columbia Records, however, and it was never released.[53]

Duke Ellington also worked in the space opened up by the Popular Front, despite his ongoing dispute with Hammond. During the 1930s and early 1940s, for example, the Ellington orchestra appeared in the musical revue "Bourbons Got the Blues," a satire of southern segregation. He and his orchestra also performed numerous benefits for the Scottsboro defendants, the Lincoln Brigade, antiwar rallies, and the election campaigns of Ben Davis, a Communist. Ellington was no naive believer in integrated bands; nevertheless, his racial aspirations placed him in contact with the Popular Front world. Having struggled successfully to put together an orchestra that could serve as the instrument for his musical ideas, he was committed to interpreting black life and culture as he understood it. A man of tremendous personal and racial pride, he took umbrage at John Hammond's charge that his music had lost touch with his roots. Moreover, he feared that the inclusion of the best black players in white bands would weaken black orchestras and dilute a true Negro art form. "Our music is always intended to be definitely and purely racial," he argued. What he wanted was equal treatment and opportunities for black bands and the dignity that any American had a right to expect. This meant battling segregation. Increasingly from the early 1940s onward Ellington put his music at the service of his racial politics.[54]

In 1941 he composed his first musical comedy, *Jump for Joy*, a topical revue that challenged segregation and prevailing racial stereotypes. As his son Mercer noted, "When he wanted to deliver a message to the world, as he demonstrated in *Jump for Joy*, he wanted a subtle means of stating his case but one that would have impact." Through music "he might be able to provoke thought and even get people to act." In creating the musical, Duke noted, the band was involved with "a strong social-significance element, which was now entering everything we did in music." Premiered at the Mayan Theater in Los Angeles before an integrated audience, the musical, said Mercer, was part of an effort by Ellington and Hollywood liberals to "correct the race situation in the U.S.A. through a form of theatrical propaganda." The story line was the work of Sid Kuller, a screenwriter with leftist sympathies. Orson Welles offered numerous staging suggestions. The show ran for three months and was poised for a national tour when World War II forced it to close.[55]

Ellington and Kuller designed the musical revue to "take Uncle Tom out of the theatre, eliminate the stereotyped image that had been exploited by Hollywood and Broadway, and say things that would make the audience think." The show opened with a paean to black people, "The Suntanned Tenth of the Nation," which challenged Hollywood's minstrel images and called instead for "our place in the sun." The show included "I've Got a Passport from Georgia (and I'm Going to the U.S.A.)," which spoke of a "better day" when signs said "out to lunch, not out to lynch." When the local Ku Klux Klan chapter threatened violence, however, the producers dropped the song. But no one could have missed the significance of the moment when Uncle Tom lay on his deathbed surrounded by Hollywood and Broadway producers, who tried to keep him alive. Uncle Tom's children, meanwhile, surrounded the bed to sing, "He lived to a ripe old age. Let him go, God bless him!" Ellington insisted that the comedians appear without blackface. "The importance of [the show's] message," Duke noted, "caused a wave of enthusiasm throughout the cast, which was well aware of its controversial impact. All the sketches had a message for the world." Mercer concurred: "When he wrote it Ellington meant it absolutely and definitely as an indictment of the South, but not perhaps in a strictly geographical sense." The revue summed up all the negative experiences he had faced as a touring black musician and, Ellington's son declared, served "notice that the black man would no longer stay passive while these things prevailed. We were not turning the other cheek anymore, he was saying. If we got slapped, the next time around the slap would be returned in good measure."[56]

Duke Ellington, Count Basie, Benny Goodman, Artie Shaw, Teddy Wilson, the boogie-woogie pianists, Billie Holiday, Lena Horne, Fats Waller, Cab Calloway—all operated within the space opened up by the integrated Left's attack on segregation in the music business and in American society.

Among other things, they were involved in creating a more pluralistic common culture. The Communist Party was a prime mover in Harlem and then nationally in the Popular Front period. Independent progressives such as John Hammond, Willard Alexander, and Paul Robeson may not have joined the party, but they were caught up in similar battles against racial injustice. Meanwhile, as *Down Beat,* Hot Clubs, and works of jazz criticism reveal, a strong leftist sentiment supported swing as a harbinger of racial justice and a new, integrated America. These utopian hopes were so strong that many musicians, critics, and fans believed that they could even transform an increasingly corporate music business to accord with their vision of a new American culture.

6

The City of Swing

New York and the Dance Band Business in Black and White

Dance bands have become big business. Big business—to the tune of $110,000,000 a year.
—Gerald R. Scott

Lunceford, Hines, Williams, Hawkins—none of these bands plays for dancing in hotels or on the commercial air. Why?—*Metronome*

In November 1939, at the height of his fame, Artie Shaw broke up his orchestra from the bandstand of New York's Hotel Pennsylvania, the most coveted engagement in the nation. Over the pleas of his lawyer, his business manager, and his band agency, General Artists Corporation, Shaw quit the band business and turned his back on lucrative bookings and recording and radio contracts worth millions. After years of traveling the sticks in broken-down buses, playing tobacco warehouses, roller skating rinks, and dance halls, he finally had hit on the style that propelled him to stardom—swing versions of the great standards of the Broadway stage. When the band's recording of Cole Porter's "Begin the Beguine" unexpectedly turned into a major jukebox hit at the end of 1938, Shaw found himself atop the swing world with a featured role in a Hollywood movie, *Dancing Coed*. By the time he reached New York, the city of his birth and the place where he formed his band, he was dissatisfied with the "irregular hours, no recreation, food on the run, nervous tension." Stepping away from the band world, he declared, "I don't like what I do. I like music, but I don't like the damned music business. The music business stinks."[1]

A constant innovator with an artist's temperament, Shaw made a decision that symbolized the tension between art and commerce in swing and in New York City, the music's national capital. Once his band had achieved mass popularity, he found that the bandleader "must base his success intrinsically and fundamentally on public taste—and there the values are anything but musical." As Shaw made clear in innumerable attacks on the industry, the business of swing was run from New York by booking agencies, radio executives, and hotel chains. Following the dictates of a mass audience, the music business evolved into a highly centralized corporate structure. At the same time, however, the world looked on New York as the artistic center of jazz. The cosmopolitan nature of the city matched the exciting energies of the music. On every side, nightclubs, hotel supper rooms, theaters, and ballrooms afforded contact with live American vernacular music, just as black and white musicians found many places for the exchange of musical ideas. But New York not only offered more prestigious engagements in its music venues than did any other American city; it also acted as the national commercial center for dance bands through its music business corporations and its media of mass communication. Eager to be close to the creative and economic pulse of the nation, Duke Ellington, Count Basie, Louis Armstrong, Benny Goodman, Chick Webb, Tommy Dorsey, Glenn Miller, and scores of others chose to reside there when they were not on the road. Capital of art and of commerce, New York stood at the apex of its national musical influence in the 1930s and 1940s.[2]

As New York became the nation's swing capital, however, tensions—especially racial ones—surfaced. Billie Holiday had toured with Shaw's otherwise all-white band through segregated border state areas during the band's rough early days. At New York's Lincoln Hotel in 1938, however, Shaw was pressured to drop Holiday from the band's national broadcasts by agency, radio, and hotel executives who feared that audiences in the hinterland would be offended by a racially mixed band. The hotel management also discouraged Holiday from entering the hotel through the front door or mixing with the customers. Fed up with these endless problems, she handed in her notice. As this incident suggests, while many places in New York allowed for artistic interactions between blacks and whites, many others harbored prejudices that led to segregation in the band business. Commerce and race, art and business, were intertwined in the city of swing.[3]

Let Me Off Uptown

Swing helped restore New York nightlife and the music business to their former preeminence. We can appreciate some of the city's many swing attractions and institutions by examining the visit by Elliot White and several of his friends to the capital of swing in August 1942. The group from Davidson College in North Carolina visited New York City to "see the bands and hear the music" that they had been listening to on radio, on records, and in occasional live performances. Neither he nor his friends were disappointed. As soon as they checked into their Times Square hotel, they rode up to their rooms in the elevator with members of the Glenn Miller Orchestra who resided in the hotel. After "the usual sights of the city," the group rushed to the Brooklyn Paramount to see the Miller band. The theater was packed, but White and his girlfriend endured the movie to stay for two exciting shows. "The fans, including us, screamed and hollered." Several nights later, White celebrated his twentieth birthday dancing with his girl to Harry James and vocalist Helen Forrest on the rooftop of the Hotel Astor.[4]

The highlight of the trip took place at Kelly's Stables on Fifty-second Street, or "Swing Street," as it was often called. After learning of the club's weekly jam sessions from someone they met at the Commodore Record Shop, a mecca for record collectors and jazz fans, they "decided that it was a must." From the Blue Room of the Hotel Lincoln, where they danced to the Jerry Wald Orchestra, the group walked to Kelly's, a tiny club where a crowd of musicians from area bands played "for their own enjoyment and not for . . . outsiders." Members of Gene Krupa's band dropped in after their job at New Jersey's Meadowbrook Ballroom ended, and after much persuasion, Roy Eldridge stood up to blow. White's party "sat enraptured" until dawn, and as they walked back to the hotel, "we felt that we had experienced a stroke of fortune, not granted to everyone who loved that kind of music." For Elliot White, there was no place like New York to see and hear America's best music, played by its best musicians. Buoyed by swing, New York was again the nightlife and music capital of the nation. Revived by the repeal of Prohibition, clubs were booming all over New York in 1937, "as [had] not been enjoyed hereabouts since the whoopee wild days of the late Twenties."[5]

One place White did not go to hear swing was the East Side, where a wealthy cafe society blossomed in exclusive supper rooms and intimate boîtes and where, noted one observer, "it is understood" that the customers "just come in to look at one another." Music for cafe society tended to melodic elegance suitable for romantic conversation. The society dance bands of Emil Coleman, Leo Reisman, Enrique Madriguera, and Eddy Duchin, which had formed in the late 1920s, continued to dominate the circuit formed by the best hotels from coast to coast. *Metronome,* however, found most of these society orchestras hopeless since they were "supposed to dish out very simple, and almost as boring, dance music with little style." Said Reisman, "At the Waldorf I seldom play swing. Such a procedure would be out of keeping with its suave and sophisticated atmosphere." No wonder business was poor when Benny Goodman played the Waldorf's Empire Room in 1940 to a small but rowdy crowd. He did not attract the swells in sufficient numbers, and he was not invited back. Swing's audience was mass not class, and its popular appeal challenged the cultural authority of class itself.[6]

Elliot White and his friends did not find the general Broadway scene very appealing either. It is not hard to see why. Having lost its upper-class audience to cafe society, a ravaged Broadway created new theater-restaurants to lure a mass audience of moderate spenders, businessmen and their wives, and out-of-town visitors. The new nightclubs offered huge chorus girl revues, elaborate urban spectacles, and nostalgic recreations of Broadway's heyday. With their inexpensive meals, clubs such as the Hollywood Restaurant, the French Casino, and Billy Rose's Casa Mañana had something for everyone, but their taste was decidedly middle-brow. It was the music, however, that played the major role in sending White and his party elsewhere. Theater-restaurants offered nondescript dance bands playing the "businessman's bounce." These bands, noted *Metronome,* "border on the pit type and consequently seldom dispense dance music that can be classified as really good." Thus Broadway clubs had lost their innovative cultural energy.[7]

Although White did not report a trip to Harlem, as a swing fan he was aware that to find the sources of popular music, one had to go uptown. Much of the original New York swing style had come together in Harlem's clubs and ballrooms, and in the area's small jazz clubs future white bandleaders had hung out with black musicians during the early 1930s. As swing attained mass popularity, however, prominent midtown hotels took over the presentation of white swing bands for white audiences. Outside of the occasional downtown dance hall, club, or theater, black bands remained locked out of the most lucrative and prestigious swing venues in the country. As a result, Harlem retained its prominence for black bands eager for New York and national exposure and assumed an even more important role in music and dance, but in a new context of mass communication.[8]

Repeal, the depression, and the riot of 1935 transformed Harlem

The Apollo Theater, Harlem, December 1944, in its heyday. Billie Holiday sings at center stage while Hot Lips Page's Orchestra plays and emcee Bobby Evans enters stage left. Note how close the boxes and balconies are to the stage, as well as the number of whites in attendance. Frank Driggs Collection.

nightlife. Repeal led downtown bars, hotels, and clubs to enter the nightlife business, the depression drove many clubs under, and the riot cut into the white night trade so important in the 1920s and early 1930s. By 1936 the Cotton Club had relocated to Times Square. Although whites still visited Harlem, the best-paying location job for black bands was the Cotton Club, home to Duke Ellington's and Cab Calloway's orchestras. Other black bands scuffled uptown. As Harlem declined as a fashionable pleasure zone, it retained its importance as a black entertainment area. In 1935 the Savoy Ballroom assumed its place as the most prominent swing venue in Harlem. Renovated in a moderne style, the hall entered its most profitable era. The Savoy featured black bands, but because of its monopoly over them, according to bandleader Benny Carter, it paid salaries "maybe a cut above the waiters." But, the Savoy provided a New York showcase for the nation's top black bands, and its radio wire afforded them some of the exposure usually denied them in Manhattan's most prestigious band rooms.[9]

The Savoy was Harlem's top dance spot. Black youths danced up a storm at the Savoy, creating communion on the dance floor with the world's best black bands. Indeed, to gain national prominence with African American audiences, black bands had to prove they could propel Harlem dancers. The major steps of the day were created and elaborated in the Savoy by the nation's best jitterbuggers. It was here that Frank Manning and his friends created the lindy's air steps. The dances quickly circulated through New York and out to the rest of the country. Whitey's Lindy Hoppers and other troupes performed on the stages of movie houses such as Radio Music Hall, at the New York World's Fair, and in several Hollywood films. The Savoy also welcomed whites. "Perhaps no other spot in this great country is so symbolic of the American ideal," said the *Amsterdam News*. "The Savoy is truly a melting pot—a cross section of American life. There, every night in the week, every race and nationality under the sun, the high and the low, meet and color lines melt away under the influence of the rhythms of America's foremost sepia swing bands." For black dancers, however, a sense of contest prevailed. Norma Miller noted that Savoy regulars took pride in their dancing and challenged anyone to do them better. The spirit of exchange and contest also marked the short engagements of white bands and the many battles of bands that the ballroom staged, including the 1937 contest between Goodman and Webb mentioned above, in which the Savoy crowd voted Webb the decided winner.[10]

Black bands desirous of national recognition also could impress Harlem at the Apollo Theater on 125th Street. Like the Savoy, its emergence as a major music spot after 1934 exemplifies the shift from elaborate segregated nightclubs to more egalitarian settings. Despite its white ownership, the Apollo had the aura of a "people's" theater because it was opened to blacks only after protests by activists and ordinary black citizens in 1934. As a consequence, the Apollo attracted a broad segment of Harlem with movies, revues, comedians, and hot bands. The Apollo was "the top," noted Andy Kirk. "You had to play the Apollo, and once you did play it, you had it made." Yet, the theater's prominence grew from its control of Harlem's best talent. The decline of area theaters and cafes made the Apollo the only Harlem spot that offered stage shows along with big bands. Bands had to accept what the owners paid or they were blackballed; they also had to agree to play the Apollo's sister theaters—Washington's Howard, Baltimore's Royal, and Philadelphia's Earle—for less money. As the flagship of a black theater circuit and one of the few location jobs for black bands, the Apollo dominated the African American orchestra world.[11]

Inside the theater, ordinary black people interacted with performers on a regular basis. As Andy Kirk noted, the theater was a "home" to black entertainers, a center of the community, and "a communications center, too." The theater's short stage, low balcony that almost overhung the stage, and stageside boxes brought patrons close to the musicians and encouraged participation. Swing bands were integral to the shows; by the late 1930s they had left the pit to perform onstage in a special band car that moved them nearer the fans. A "triumphant homecoming for the mighty Count," as described in the *Pittsburgh Courier*, suggests the intimate link as fans— among them "musicians from every large band" in town and all the top entertainers—filled every inch of the theater. "Jitterbugs completely stopped the show, by calling for repeated requests from Count and the boys." The popular Amateur Nights furthered the intimacy as singers, dancers, and comedians, accompanied by top bands, competed before raucous but knowledgeable patrons who judged the winners.[12]

The Apollo served the black community, but it influenced all of New York. Swing made the theater part of the city's hip music scene; the *New York World-Telegram* called it "a sort of uptown Met." The Apollo also welcomed white bands led by Charlie Barnet, Bunny Berigan, and Woody Herman, and the audience might be 40–75 percent white at the Amateur Night and Saturday midnight shows. WMCA radio broadcast the Amateur Hour across New York, and twenty-one affiliated stations sent it out to other parts of the country. As master of ceremonies Ralph Cooper noted, radio "made a star of our audience." Thus the Apollo and the Savoy played major roles in the larger New York entertainment world and added to its musical cosmopolitanism.[13]

A variety of small clubs—Minton's, in the Hotel Cecil on 118th Street, Monroe's Uproar House, Dickey Wells's—and several ballrooms enabled black musicians to play for dancing and for each other. Harlem musicians nurtured in uptown sessions made their way to downtown clubs and then into general circulation. White and black players continued to jam uptown as well, nourished on trends that emerged from the heart of black culture, and black music and musicians circulated through New York with surprising rapidity, especially as the jazz scene migrated downtown to Fifty-second Street.

Swing Street

Soon after repeal, small clubs blossomed along Fifty-second Street between Fifth and Sixth Avenues. This narrow strip of neon, music, and crowds played an enormous role in the development of Harlem jazz. These new clubs created an informal nightlife zone that united patrons around a vital musical culture. The clubs also offered musical and social links for black and white musicians, attracted devoted swing fans from around the country, and introduced new musical currents to the big bands. The street's prominence grew out of a confluence of several factors. In the late 1920s Rockefeller Center displaced speakeasies from surrounding side streets to the brownstones along Fifty-second Street. Proximity to Radio City Music Hall made the speakeasies hangouts for studio musicians at NBC who wanted to play jazz, and repeal encouraged these speakeasies to become legitimate clubs serving liquor and providing entertainment. So many clubs began featuring jazz groups that the street came to be called "Swing Street," where fans and musicians gathered to participate in an intensely communal enterprise. As *Variety*'s Abel Green wrote, the clubgoers were "disciples of a new musical cult and seem proud to be privy to the charmed inner-circle," and rather than politics or sports, "all they eat, talk, breathe and think is swing." Too tiny for dancing, the clubs became some of the first jazz listening rooms. Informality ruled as musicians wandered by to sit in with each other while patrons, drinks in hand, moved from one bar to another, soaking up the music.[14]

These small clubs served important functions for New York's musicians. The Onyx, the Famous Door, the Three Deuces, Hickory House, Kelly's Stables, the Downbeat, and Tillie's Chicken Shack initially gave white radio musicians, laboring in nearby studios, a chance to play jazz during the early 1930s when few other outlets existed. As a speakeasy, Joe Helbock's Onyx, "the cradle of swing," served as musicians' hangout, a place to get messages, relax between shows, and learn of jobs. The password, "802," referred to the musicians' local. The clubs kept alive a jazz ethic, giving musicians a place to play "for ourselves," Bud Freeman recalled. For songwriter Johnny Mercer, who arrived in New York in the early 1930s, the Onyx "was pleasure and it was business and it was music." A meeting place in the capital of American popular music, the street attracted "everybody you knew in the entertainment field." As the clubs began to draw the public, musicians from around the country went there to meet and play with their musical idols, establish their credentials, or get a job. Because of the circulation of musicians, nearly every new jazz trend could be heard in these clubs.[15]

Equally important, the street brought the Harlem jazz scene downtown as uptown began to decline. Eager for work, many black musicians—along with many Harlem barbecue joints—migrated downtown. Jazz became less strongly associated with Harlem, but it still carried a vital, earthy aura for white swing fans, for whom the music was never more accessible. Most of the important white and black jazz musicians played in small group settings

Nighttime on Fifty-second Street, 1940s. A swing lover's paradise. Frank Driggs Collection.

at minimal pay, as did singers Billie Holiday, Maxine Sullivan, and Lee Wiley. Musicians dropped in to hear the new sounds and new players, and new ideas mixed fast, creating a common musical vocabulary for players of all stripes. Moreover, between sets and after jobs, black and white musicians found the street a natural place to meet. Milt Hinton, longtime bassist with Cab Calloway, found this the essence of New York. "What impressed me more than anything else," he declared, "was being able to experience the melting-pot aspects of New York. Rubbing elbows with people from every ethnic group imaginable is something my Mississippi ancestors never heard of." Continuing a trend begun in Harlem, black and white jazzmen mixed on- and offstage. "It was a beautiful scene."[16]

Initially it was not quite that beautiful. When the clubs first began operation, they attempted to maintain the color line. Black entertainers, as we shall see, were discouraged from mixing with the white clientele even as the black musicians served as entertainers for those same whites. Beginning in 1938, however, the mixing of the musicians and the interests of the fans soon forced racial barriers to fall in the audience too. During the summer of that year, John Hammond, Willard Alexander, and MCA agreed that in exchange for installing air conditioning, the Famous Door would book Count Basie's orchestra and permit Hammond "to bring black friends into the club." Until that time, "you never saw a black face at the tables or even at the bar of the Door." Black and white musicians, however, sat in with each other, implying a camaraderie, as well as "a rare community of interests between performer and audience that placed communication and expression on the same level as entertainment." The attraction of the street to white and black musicians as well as fervent jazz fans from around the country and the world, however, created the momentum for the integration of audiences. As Alec Wilder noted, the street created a "togetherness," and "warmth and the excitement of musical friendship."[17]

The street's location between the East and West Sides also gave young cafe society members an alternative to the upper-class "see and be seen spots" of the East Side. When sexy trumpeter Louis Prima opened at the Famous Door, for example, he attracted many society women eager for excitement. Similarly, Red Norvo noted, "the debs and college crowd . . . crossing Fifth Avenue to hear us" were those who normally went to the Stork Club. Hence, the social geography of Fifty-second Street formed links among Broadway's popular trends, Harlem's jazz, and Park Avenue society in a central New York location. In these clubs, the children of the elite took on an American democratic identity.[18]

Pennsylvania 6-5000

As the experiences of Artie Shaw and Elliot White attest, although Harlem and Fifty-second Street played crucial roles in the new swing culture, the most commercially important venues in New York were the midtown hotels and theaters that could accommodate large bands. As a staple of a national youth culture, swing increasingly found itself in a web of musical institutions that expanded its audience, but this came at some cost to its utopian racial and democratic potential. At the heart of Swing City lay a tension between the ethos of the jazz clubs and that of radio and the hotels. The new national institutions had to accommodate swing, while swing bands increasingly became commodities. The prominence in the band world assumed by hotels and radio symbolizes the important artistic, commercial, and racial tensions that underlay the swing business as New York's musical culture went national.

Essentially, repeal and swing made midtown hotels a central part of the entertainment business. By reducing business trips and tourist travel, the depression had badly hurt the many commercial-class hotels located near

Pennsylvania and Grand Central Stations. Repeal proved a godsend, and so did swing. *Variety* reported that repeal "spells the renaissance of legitimate hostelries once again and the curfew of the speaks." Spurred by liquor revenues, hotels spent more money on music and entertainment. While elegant East Side hotels sought society patrons, those near Times Square—the Pennsylvania, the New Yorker, the Lincoln, the Commodore, the Edison—pursued the youth market. Initially content to offer melodic bands for middle-aged patrons, hotels jumped on the swing bandwagon to revive a lagging supper trade with college-age youths. The switch engendered opposition. When Goodman opened at the Pennsylvania's Madhattan Room in 1936, the hotel and MCA worried that the hotel's affluent older customers, many of them white southerners, would be driven away by black pianist Teddy Wilson, the band's loudness, and the exuberance of the jitterbugs. "Besides," observed Dwight Chapin, a member of Goodman's staff, "where would be the tips from all these college kids?" Tips did fall off, and glasses were broken, but "business [was] colossal." Goodman stayed fifteen months, and the hotel vigorously pursued younger patrons. As Chapin observed, swing turned once-exclusive hotels into bastions of mass entertainment. "Goodbye butter-and-egg business! Farewell to the halcyon days of patronage by the post-prohibition, mid-depression, affluential few!"[19]

Soon white swing bands competed with sweet outfits for the top bookings in Broadway hotels, and the Pennsylvania's Cafe Rouge became the top band room in the entire nation. When the Glenn Miller band recorded "Pennsylvania 6-5000," the telephone number of the hotel, they honored their long stay at the Cafe Rouge and signaled the relationship between hotels and music. Similarly, as Benny Goodman replaced Vincent Lopez at the hotel, so too did Tommy Dorsey, Artie Shaw, and Miller replace him as public tastes changed. Rather than the expensive clubs that catered to an older, more affluent crowd, the hotels became major centers of swing for affluent and middle-class white youths eager to dance, date, and listen to music in reputable big-city environments that combined the excitement of the nightclub and the space of the ballroom. Radio, moreover, transported a nation of young people to these glamorous settings and succeeded in transforming exclusive rooms into key arenas of dance music for the masses.[20]

Well-known bands proved great advertisements for the hotels. In order to compete with nightclubs, theaters, and ballrooms for big-name bands and audiences, local hotels, according to *Billboard*, spent about $25,000 a month to publicize their attractions in newspapers and magazines. Rather than the quality of their rooms or their service, hotels now went "to town on their supper rooms and both the personality and musical styles of their syncopators." Although the hotel made little profit on the bands, their performances generated enough business for the hotel to pay for food, light, and maintenance. The major advantage of booking big-name bands, however, lay in the prestige of the popular orchestras. As celebrities, bandleaders generated mention of their host hotels in the nationally syndicated gossip columns and nightclub departments of New York's many newspapers. When the Pennsylvania first booked Goodman, for instance, the hotel was featured nationally in *Life* and the *Saturday Evening Post*. As bands became associated with certain hotels, "they publicized the hotels' names throughout the region, paving the way for future Manhattan visitors."[21]

Prominent hotel bookings were also plums for bands. An engagement at a major New York hotel provided national exposure and advertised a band's ascension in the music world. As the Commodore Hotel's director of public relations noted, "hotel advertising today is showmanship minded, so that the names of leaders get ballyhooed in the fanciest layout the Madison Avenue copywriters can devise." To overcome its conservative image, *Billboard* noted, the Commodore's Palm Room advertised widely during 1938 that "Tommy Dorsey 'is breaking all records.'" This type of advertising, magnified by stories in the national press, was more important to the bands than their salaries. Hotel jobs were rarely profitable. One band earned $2,500 a week at the Pennsylvania but had to meet an $8,500 payroll that included costs for band members ($1,750 for all musicians plus $125 for each singer), plus fees for press agents, personal managers, road managers, bookers, arrangers, copying, pictures and press books, union dues and various local taxes, transportation, and sustaining broadcasts.[22]

Bandleaders gladly took hotel jobs at a loss, however, because of the prestige and the exposure. New York hotels gave bands access to network radio wires that sent their name and their music across the country as well as to the surrounding area. The frequency of national network broadcasts from New York hotels enabled a band to create an audience and then exploit it by barnstorming across the country during the late spring and summer months. If an engagement went well, moreover, the band would be booked into related hotels in other American cities, with additional local airtime. Thus, hotel jobs promised increased future revenues. In addition, hotels offered long engagements that allowed relief from traveling for several weeks or months while still building audiences. This was especially true in

Manhattan, where long hotel stays enabled bands to play more lucrative movie houses, appear on radio shows, record in the studios, and try to establish a semblance of normal life.[23]

So advantageous to a bandleader was the financially unrewarding "location" job, Irving Kolodin noted, that efforts were made in the greater New York area to "duplicate the conditions of a hotel job without a hotel." Frank Dailey's Meadowbrook Ballroom, a road house on the New Jersey Turnpike twenty-five miles from Times Square, built its "own permanent, glass-enclosed radio control room." Although the hall could hold seven to eight hundred couples, it was the radio that attracted bandleaders. Twelve times a week, the major networks broadcast the music from the Meadowbrook "to radios across the country," and every Saturday afternoon one of the networks allocated a full hour to the ballroom. With all the advantages of a New York hotel—including access to the recording studios, new material, and "comprehensive air time"—a Meadowbrook booking entailed less lost money because the low overhead permitted Dailey to pay bands more. In addition, when MCA found itself with too few radio outlets in New York for its many bands, the agency urged Fifty-second Street's Famous Door to install a radio wire in order to turn the club into a showcase for its rising bands. Because of its national broadcasting capability, a club with minuscule capacity succeeded in launching the orchestras of Count Basie, Charlie Barnet, and Woody Herman to stardom.[24]

A hotel engagement with a radio wire was essential for promoting a band, but theater bookings filled a band's coffers. In New York, a band could play theaters during the day while also working at a hotel in the evening. Movie palaces hurt by the depression turned to big-name bands to attract a youth audience too young or too poor to attend nightclubs or hotel supper rooms. The Strand, Loew's State, the Riviera, and, in the 1940s, the Capitol, competed with the Broadway Paramount and the Brandt theaters in Brooklyn and the Bronx for young audiences and the bands to attract them. Soon downtown theaters in every major city featured well-known orchestras at nominal prices. Just as matinee idols had done for legitimate theaters at the turn of the century, noted *Newsweek,* nationally known bands were "bringing in a daytime audience."[25]

A band with several New York theater engagements could wipe out three months' worth of deficits accumulated by playing hotels. A popular band could bargain for $9,000 for one week and more than $25,000 for a three-week stay. Because theaters competed for live attractions, band agencies pitted them against one another to raise the salaries of popular bands and ensure other favors, such as a strong movie on the bill. An orchestra with broad appeal, such as Fred Waring's, could command $12,000 a week; Goodman received $10,000, while Ellington, Basie, and Calloway earned about $5,500. Less popular bands earned lesser but still substantial amounts. Because of high demand, agencies engaged in block booking, forcing theaters to take several unknowns in order to get a top name. Although the money was good, playing theaters was a grind. Shows started as early as ten A.M. and ran through the evening, with breaks allowed only when the movie was in progress. Yet theater appearances offered location work for superb fees.[26]

Radio City

New York's rise as the nation's band capital lay in its dominance of radio, recording, and music publishing. Radio was the chief national medium for swing during the depression, and bands depended on it for exposure. With little effort, radio transported listeners to an alternative world of nightclubs, ballrooms, theaters, and hotels in which New York, as the headquarters of the NBC Blue and Red Networks, CBS, and Mutual, retained preeminence. The opening of Rockefeller Center marked New York as the national capital of radio. Designed in 1928 as the Metropolitan Opera's new home, Rockefeller Center was transformed by the depression into Radio City, a temple of modern mass culture. When financial problems forced the opera out of the project, the Radio Corporation of America—the parent company of RKO studios and theaters, RCA Victor phonographs and records, and NBC—took over the central building in the complex. When the center opened in 1932–33, Radio City, its most impressive building, housed the means of mass communication. What had been designed as an elite cultural institution was now a center for mass entertainment, symbolized by murals and sculptures glorifying the power of electronic communications. Radio City also had the nation's best recording and radio studios. In another building lay Radio City Music Hall, the nation's premier movie house, and atop Radio City was the sleek Rainbow Room. *Time-Life* occupied its own set of buildings, and in the complex's many offices were the headquarters of the booking agencies that dominated the band business. Nearby, at Madison Avenue and Fifty-third Street, was CBS, and along Fifty-second Street were the many swing clubs. In the Rockefeller Center area, the music business found its national headquarters.[27]

With an audience that grew from 16 million in 1925 to 60 million in 1930, radio assumed national prominence in music, entertainment, and commerce. As the depression deepened, manufacturers introduced cheaper models, and the average cost of a set fell drastically. The price drop made radios available to most families outside the rural South, where listenership continued to lag. With direct access to the nation's homes, radio proved particularly inviting to advertisers, who, themselves hard hit by the depression, aggressively sponsored a wide variety of programs. The partnership between sponsors, agencies, and networks created a golden age of commercial broadcasting for popular music and entertainment. At the same time, many local stations that had suffered in the depression turned to network affiliation to survive.[28]

As a national medium, radio had the power to promote a band and increase its potential audience and earnings. A commercially sponsored program, for example, gave a band an enormous cushion, sometimes as much as $250,000 a year—but such a show usually followed a group's success. For advertisers, one expenditure bought exposure to a national radio audience. Recognizing youth's economic potential, as we saw above, cigarette, soft drink, and hair oil companies assumed major sponsorship of programs directed toward young people. Commercial sponsorship came at a cost to bands, however. Sponsors insisted on romantic ballads as well as swing to draw the broadest youth market, and they added skits and special guests to broaden the music's appeal. But the agencies and sponsors in turn needed the stars to draw listeners and so had to allow bands the leeway to play swing on the commercial airwaves and craft the music as they saw fit. The major cost, however, according to Artie Shaw, was that sponsors and major networks were only interested in contracting with already well-known orchestras. New bands, which could not attract large enough audiences, and black bands, which might discourage southern white listeners—and hence diminish the value of the airtime—would be vetoed by both the sponsor and the national network.[29]

While commercial radio remained centralized in New York, CBS, NBC, and Mutual presented bands live on sustaining, or non–commercially sponsored, broadcasts from ballrooms, theaters, and hotels around the nation. Remote broadcasts built regional and national audiences. Bands and their agencies fought for these bookings, while local outlets sought radio hookups as a means to attract business. Competition between NBC and the aggressive new CBS also increased the number of remotes. The effect of these remotes was to give bands national exposure and to give listeners in local settings a connection to a national youth culture and a national community. Late-night remotes, as we saw, also gave black bands some limited radio exposure.[30]

As dance music consumed more radio time than any other type of programming, music publishers in and around Radio City looked to dance bands as the salvation of the sheet music business. The publishers, who saw in sales of swing arrangements a chance to recover from the depression, sent representatives to every major big band opening at a New York hotel. A band needed hotel engagements in New York to get the chance to hear numbers and to play and record new show tunes and popular hits. Otherwise, noted Irving Kolodin, "it would be hopelessly handicapped in its struggle toward large earnings." Bands plugged new songs on the air, introduced them to large numbers of young people, induced other bands to play them, and thereby helped improve a song's position on *Your Hit Parade*. As a result, publishers used all sorts of inducements to entice bandleaders to plug their songs, sparking early charges of payola. Yet, while publishers were eager to sell stock orchestrations of hit songs, swing bands were in the driver's seat in the popular music industry. They rejected standardized arrangements and demanded exclusive charts tailored to their particular style. In addition, swing bands had their own arrangers, who recrafted popular hits into personalized statements. It proved expensive for publishers to hire special arrangers, but sheet music firms needed the bands to play their work and had to give them wider creative latitude.[31]

Radio City also housed the national headquarters of the record business. The recording industry only slowly recovered from the depression, and it continued to find itself in competition with radio. Recording became profitable again with cheap record players that used radio speakers, the rising popularity of the jukebox, and Decca Records' lowering the price of records from seventy-five to thirty-five cents. As a result, by 1938 the three major labels—RCA Victor, Columbia, and Decca—showed signs of life. Coincident with the rise of swing, the jukebox allowed listeners to hear the choices nurtured by radio cheaply and at their own discretion. One major hit on the nation's 400,000 jukeboxes (in 1942) would do as much for a dance band as six solid weeks on radio. After repeal, the jukebox jettisoned its prior association with hoodlums, speakeasies, and black "juke" joints, redecorated in streamlined designs that stripped away these lower-class associations and the upper-class image of the phonograph, and entered the mass market as a symbol of progress rather than an accessory to dirt and decadence. "The juke is all-American," proclaimed Barry Ulanov, "as star-spangled as the flag, native as the hot dog."[32]

New York, Chicago, and Los Angeles all had recording studios, but New York offered direct access to the new popular hits and major hotel exposure. When bands came off the road they could squeeze in studio time in order to capitalize on their radio appearances and their live performances. Record companies were dependent on swing bands and musicians to sell records to young people, and the continuing lag in sales heightened the dependence. As a result, there were openings for young impresarios able to spot new trends and recruit new talent. John Hammond is a case in point. He was able to play an important role in the record business as early as 1932, when he secured a contract to record American jazz for British-owned Columbia at a time when the industry was in the doldrums. He recorded Fletcher Henderson, Benny Goodman, Billie Holiday, Teddy Wilson, Bessie Smith, and later Count Basie and others for many popular labels. He also found enough room to experiment with groups of musicians who had never played together, the regular recording of integrated sessions, and the superb chamber groups that featured Billie Holiday, Teddy Wilson, and members of the Count Basie Orchestra.

By the end of the 1930s, the jukebox had strengthened the role of recordings in building a band. As *Down Beat* noted in 1939, "one single record throws a band into a national limelight." Bandleaders wanted to record because "the band will be exploited via a dozen methods, and over hundreds of radio stations in the 'hinterlands'—all of which adds up to publicity which, in many cases, the leader himself couldn't buy in a lifetime on his own." Record companies and song pluggers tried to push bandleaders into recording certain songs, but "there's no formula for this phenomenon," because audiences played a big role in creating hits. Artie Shaw's recording of "Begin the Beguine," for instance, made the band, but it was intended as the "B" side of "Indian Love Call." When the wrong side sold, Shaw claimed, "I was as surprised as anybody else." "Marie," Tommy Dorsey's 1937 hit, had been recorded years earlier. Andy Kirk reached a national audience with "Until the Real Thing Comes Along," but never again had such a popular success. Since hits were hard to predict, companies had to give bandleaders room to record what they thought might sell.[33]

By 1940, "the dance band [was] big business." All together, big bands of every stripe earned $110 million that year through the linkage among popular entertainment, modern communication methods, and mass youth culture. New bands proliferated along routes organized in New York. To streamline this far-flung industry, band agencies, headquartered in Radio City, assumed national importance. The agencies elaborated the methods that Mills Artists had worked out for Duke Ellington in the late 1920s and early 1930s. In place of localized, face-to-face negotiations in which individual bandleaders booked their bands personally, the Mills office acted as an impersonal mediator to work the complex negotiations required to book and promote orchestras involved in nightclubs, records, songwriting and publishing, radio, movies, and national tours. As the depression forced local ballrooms and theaters to fire house bands and turn instead to touring well-known bands capable of attracting large audiences, national band agencies became essential.[34]

In the 1930s, agencies, like the bands they represented, evolved into corporations that operated on a national scale. The largest agency, Music Corporation of America (MCA), formed in Chicago by ex-musicians Jules Stein and Billy Goodheart to book local sweet bands, moved to New York in 1928 and became a Radio City fixture. By promoting a band's name rather than the places that an orchestra played, the agency grew to control two-thirds of the country's prominent white dance orchestras. Three other agencies handled the rest: the William Morris Agency, General Artists Corporation (GAC), and Consolidated Radio Artists (CRA). Smaller firms with less power—Mills, Joe Glaser, and Moe Gale, a shareholder in the Savoy—specialized in black bands and entertainers. The evolution of organized agencies whose sole purpose was handling bands gave the band business greater dependability. Smaller offices, in charge of fewer bands, demanded from 20 to 40 percent of a band's earnings. The big ones, able to spread profits over a larger number of orchestras, usually operated legitimately and asked for 10 percent for their services. Local operators could rely on bookings, and bands could expect national tours and extensive publicity on their behalf.[35]

The agencies' power lay in their control of the top New York and national locations—especially hotels—with radio access. "Every worthwhile location—with a radio wire," Shaw noted, "is tied up by one of the large booking offices, and if your band isn't handled by the office controlling a certain hotel you'll never get into it." Hotels made so little money on bands that they delegated talent booking to agencies that handled popular attractions. For instance, MCA controlled the Hotel Pennsylvania in the early 1930s because the agency owned the rights to sweet bands such as that of Vincent Lopez. In return for Lopez's services, the hotel agreed to book other MCA clients when he was on tour. The success of Benny Goodman, another MCA act, secured the agency's hold over the hotel until 1939. A string of MCA bands led by Bunny Berigan, Bob Crosby, Ben Bernie, Kay Kyser, and Harry James played the room. William Morris, GAC, and CRA controlled other locations. When MCA attempted to promote Goodman from a "commercial" to a "class" category by booking the band into the Waldorf-Astoria, GAC, which represented Artie Shaw and Glenn Miller, gained entree to the hotel. With the hold they had over important New York locations, the agencies were able to sign the top bands and as a result gain the right to book music outlets nationwide.[36]

The agencies symbolized the commercialization of music, but they also helped to promote bands on a scale never before envisioned. A creative booker had to be commercial advisor, press agent, artistic supervisor, and shrewd businessman. Unlike the older, hard-boiled agents with little interest in music, the newer generation were younger men who were enthusiastic about bands and music. Willard Alexander, for example, Goodman and Basie's agent at MCA, had been a musician at the University of Pennsylvania and now devoted himself to promoting the best swing units and talented black artists, a "reflection of the incredible mingling of artistry and commercialism which characterizes the whole industry." Because he believed in their worth, he fought MCA, hotels, and other venues to book these bands regardless of racial considerations. It remained an uphill battle.[37]

Once a band had built an audience through radio broadcasts, jukebox play, and appearances at New York hotels, its agency arranged one-night road tours during the summer months to cash in on the exposure. Although going on the road taxed the stamina of even the hardiest bands, one-nighters at ballrooms, high school and college proms, and resorts proved more lucrative than the grind of a five-to-seven-show, twelve-hour day in a theater. Because of their fixed personnel costs, bands found one-nighters very profitable. To earn the big money, the forces of the music business had to build a band's audience. In 1937, MCA parlayed Goodman's long stays at the Hotel Pennsylvania and the Paramount Theater, commercial and remote radio exposure, and extensive jukebox play into "as long a series of one-nighters as the men [could] endure." In two summer months, the band made $90,000 playing jobs from New York to California.[38]

Of all the swing leaders, none surpassed Glenn Miller in his mastery of the system. In early 1939 his band was scuffling for union scale—$1,050 a week and $400 for a one-nighter. A superb businessman and analyst of the music industry, Miller put his stock in radio. According to his drummer, Moe Purtill, "radio made Glenn Miller. Not records, not movies." His theory was, "we go on the air as much as we can. He was paying for the lines sometimes," to broadcast from all the places the band would be playing. "We'd shove the music down their throats." This drew audiences to their live appearances, where they requested tunes heard on the air. Miller would rank the requests and "make records of the ones the public was responding to." After successful bookings at the Meadowbrook, rich with radio time, and one-nighters around the Northeast, the band recorded "Little Brown Jug," "Moonlight Serenade," "Sunrise Serenade," and "In the Mood," which they played ten times a week on broadcasts from the Glen Island Casino that summer. "We just did about 20 tunes at first, played those same 20 tunes over and over," said Purtill. "Pounded them into you on the broadcasts." By the fall of 1939, GAC had booked them into the Hotel Pennsylvania, which afforded them ample airtime and where they remained until 1942. The agency also secured them a nationally broadcast radio show sponsored by Chesterfield Cigarettes, which publicized the band's offerings three times a week and paid Miller $250,000 a year. Movies such as *Orchestra Wives* and *Sun Valley Serenade*—and the exposure they afforded for tunes like "Chattanooga Choo-Choo"—followed. By 1940, Miller's fee for one-nighters had jumped to $4,680.[39]

Radio had built the band a national following, and Miller cashed in with records and personal appearances. On the road, the orchestra broke all records, drawing 5,400 patrons in Saint Louis and 7,800 in Kansas City. "It's an inspiring sight," Miller recalled," to look down from the balcony on the heads of 7,000 people swaying on a dance floor—especially when you are getting $600 for every thousand of them." The demands of the business, however, put a tremendous strain on everyone. Each week during the winter the band played the Hotel Pennsylvania six nights for four or five hours, with three radio broadcasts, plus rehearsals, and three repeats for the West Coast. They also did five shows daily at the Paramount. "And on top of that," noted Purtill, "we had record dates at 2:00 in the morning." The musicians found it a grind, but "in the end, it was Glenn who wound up in the hospital." So did Goodman, with a ruined back, and Artie Shaw, with a near-fatal blood disease. Shaw quit because he was turning into a businessman, however, not because of the hours. He escaped to Mexico to find time for himself. Leaders needed superb business skills to master the music business and youth and a hearty constitution to survive it. To be sure, most white bands never reached the heights of a Shaw, a Goodman, a Tommy Dorsey, or a Miller orchestra, but their color made them competitive. Black bands were handicapped from the start.[40]

Billie's Blues

For many white musicians and fans, black bands played prominent roles in the big band scene. The camaraderie on Fifty-second Street, the mixed settings of the Savoy and the Apollo, and a shared belief in jazz were part of New York's swing world. On the road, demand for black bands grew. Duke Ellington and Cab Calloway commanded high fees in nightclubs, theaters, and ballrooms, as well as in films, while the Louis Armstrong, Jimmie Lunceford, Count Basie, Chick Webb, and Erskine Hawkins bands toured widely. "Colored attractions are now definitely in demand throughout the entire country," noted Helen Oakley in 1938, "and they have become unmistakable box-office draws." Major agencies opened "colored band departments," overcoming earlier views that the market for black bands "was considered limited" and not "a potential money-making field open and profitable to the big booking firms." Yet except for a few top units, by 1939 mass interest in swing pushed white bands ahead of black orchestras in earning capacity and audience recognition. In 1940, *Down Beat* asked, "Are Colored Bands Doomed as Big Money Makers?"[41]

Swing's move from "sinful" Harlem speakeasies and nightclubs to Broadway hotels reinforced racial divisions in the band business. As Irving Kolodin observed, black bands were "almost never to be encountered in a prominent hotel, and never on a commercial radio program." Occasionally, northern hotels such as Chicago's Sherman or Boston's Ritz-Carlton booked Basie or Ellington, but as *Metronome* observed in 1943, despite standing at the head of his profession, Duke "has played at only one major American hotel in this country in recent years. . . . Just one hotel." New York hotel operators and band agencies feared the reaction of southern white tourists and businesspeople, who made up a large portion of the guests, to black bands or integrated groups. The presence of both men and women in an atmosphere of informal intimacy between the races bespoke a measure of racial equality and challenged the deepest southern—and northern—taboos about race and sex. Having barely survived the depression, hotel managers feared that southern boycotts of their hotels would bring financial ruin. Yet, as Kolodin noted, "It is simply an exaggerated prejudice which no hotel manager has the enterprise to challenge or the courage to disregard." That network radio allowed them to use their musical acts to advertise nationally only made hotels more reluctant to sully their reputations with black bands that connoted illicit sexuality and racial transgression. Denied these prominent bookings, black bands lacked the prestige of the hotel's name and the exposure afforded by radio to build large, stable audiences and boost their asking prices for one-nighters.[42]

Commercial radio also deferred to the white South's racial attitudes. Sponsors feared boycotts of products associated with black bands or performers. Since southern cigarette and soft drink firms sponsored most band shows, advertising agencies had to please southern white executives. Even black guests on a dance band's commercial show risked angry responses from southerners, noted Kolodin, and "one which regularly employs such musicians [could] write off, in advance, any hope of sales appeal in Georgia, Louisiana, and Mississippi." Periodically, black bands found sponsors, but as was the case when Standard Brands presented Louis Armstrong on network radio—from April 9 to June 25, 1937—the shows never lasted for very long. But this policy did not start at the height of swing. According to the *Bridgeport Herald* in 1935, "the reason such great names as Ellington and Calloway haven't profited commercially in radio is because national sponsors steer clear of arousing southern race prejudices." Kept off commercial shows, black bands were also excluded from radio fan magazines. From 1935 to 1946, few mentions of black bandleaders—and none of the stories on their careers and personal lives that helped turn white bandleaders into celebrities—appeared. Thus, black bands missed out on the primary sources of prestige, financial reward, and public acclaim and could not equal the earnings of comparable white bands. Nor could black musicians "hope to attain the degree of public prominence which Gene Krupa enjoyed when he received $500 a week from Benny Goodman."[43]

The experiences of Artie Shaw and Billie Holiday point out how New York hotels and network radio reinforced racial segregation. In 1938 a struggling Shaw featured Holiday with his band after she left the Count Basie orchestra. The band encountered little difficulty in Boston, where she joined the tour, but Shaw and Holiday found the going tough everywhere else. Although all mixed bands met resistance, mixing race and sex challenged deeper taboos. During a harrowing time in Kentucky and Missouri playing first-class hotels and ballrooms, Shaw insisted that Billie "sit on the bandstand like Helen Forrest and Tony Pastor and everyone else," rather than leave her in New York while the rest of the band toured below the Mason-Dixon line, a fairly common practice through the 1940s.[44]

Southern racism might be expected, but, Billie said, she "got the crummiest deal of all" in New York at the Lincoln Hotel's Blue Room, which had a national radio hookup that could make a singer and a band. "This was my big chance to sing on the radio coast-to-coast every night. . . . This was big time." However, things went downhill. Worried about her mingling with guests between shows, the hotel forced her to use a suite between sets. "The next thing I knew, the management wanted me to come in the back door of the hotel." Since the band had waited months for a New York engagement, the musicians were susceptible to the pressure of the hotel, the networks, and GAC, all of whom demanded that Shaw limit her radio time. Eventually, they cut her to one song a night, usually apart from the band. "When they cut me off the air completely, I said to hell with it. I just fired myself."[45]

Not all the difficulty was due to race. Holiday's improvisations, inflections, and phrasings were very advanced for audiences, whose complaints were used by ballroom managers to drive down the price of the still-unknown band. Music publishers, meanwhile, balked at giving the band their best popular material if Holiday was not going to sing it straight. Hoping that things would improve down the road, Shaw hired a white singer, Helen Forrest, to perform most of the popular material.[46]

With such strong opposition from the music business, mixed bands were as much a rarity as black ones in white hotels. When black bands played white hotels, the experience could be degrading. In 1943, Basie led the first black band into the Lincoln Hotel, but the management insisted that they use the service elevator and eat in the kitchen to avoid mixing with the clientele. The Park Central's Cocoanut Grove forced Chick Webb into what Kolodin called a "kind of exhibitionism which had a disastrous effect on the playing of musicians." As Kolodin put it, "there was so much 'Jim Crow' in the air, together with the kind of antics which the public believes to be inseparable from the colored man's expression of his immortal soul, that the musicians were humiliated, the knowing public repelled, and the engagement a failure." Mixing was also the issue at Adrian Rollini's Tap Room in the President Hotel. When Red Allen sat down at Leonard Feather's table for a drink, "an angry-looking representative of the management" declared, "'We don't want you people sitting with the customers.'"[47]

A white southern bandleader explained why so many southern whites objected to black musicians in "white" venues. "White people do not want to mix socially with Negroes. It's not a question of equality. It's a matter of privacy." The issue was sex, he asserted, for there were "many instances of Negro musicians making overtures to white women in the cafes they were playing." In an "atmosphere of drinking, where normal restraints are gone—it's murder." Billie Holiday's experiences, and those of other black performers in New York spots, suggest that the myth of the southern audience was real. Because New York was a national city with hotels drawing a white clientele from the South and elsewhere—and even more because radio stations broadcast nationwide—network executives, hotel managers, and band agencies were extremely reluctant to offend future patrons.[48]

It is also true, however, that the white managers of New York hotels, restaurants, and clubs did not go out of their way to dispel these ideas either, suggesting deep-seated white prejudice in New York too. Even when black bands played downtown white ballrooms, they had to obey a code of racial separation. Garvin Bushell related that when he played at midtown's Arcadia Ballroom, black musicians were forbidden to mix with white patrons, and the same held true at Roseland. "When we'd go in, we had to stay close to the wall and go upstairs to the dressing room. We could never venture out on the floor of the ballroom." Yet, white musicians "would come off the stand and go across the dance floor and sit down in the lounge." Social equality with the audience implied sexual equality. When Holiday first sang at the Famous Door in the mid 1930s, she was forced to sit in the bathroom to avoid mixing with the audience in the tiny club. She broke the rules by drinking at a table with Charlie Barnet and was fired. "After this big scandal which might ruin him on the street [the manager] said he didn't want any Negroes in the place at all," Holiday observed. "You can be up to your boobies in white satin, with gardenias in your hair and no sugar cane for miles, but you can still be working on a plantation."[49]

Locked out of most good location spots and those with the best radio wires, black bands had to rely on hit records to make their names and fortunes. Yet the jukebox market was difficult to enter. Although an increasing number of crossovers—such as Chick Webb and Ella Fitzgerald's "A Tisket a Tasket," Kirk and Pha Terrell's "Until the Real Thing Comes Along," and tunes by Basie, Ellington, and Jimmie Lunceford—occurred, for the most part recordings by black bands appeared only in jukeboxes in black areas. In fact, Decca recruited numerous black bands for the race market, on the assumption that they could only play uninhibited swing. Slotted there, black bands found it hard to record the ballads that might catch a mass white audience. Andy Kirk wanted to record "Until the Real Thing Comes Along," for instance, but Decca's chief objected. "'Andy, what's the matter with you?' Jack Kapp asked. 'You've got something good going for you. Why do you want to do what the white boys are doing?'" As Kirk noted, "I saw his commercial motives. . . . [My band] was for the race market only." After much persuasion, Kirk got his wish, the song became a hit, and the band began to "reach people of all levels. It was our breakthrough from race records." But record companies assumed that black bands would do best to rely on jazz for the restricted market that was theirs. Since white bands had the hotel and radio exposure, record firms and music publishers gave them the songs with widest potential. Moreover, when bands of different races recorded the same tune (such as Basie's and Goodman's "One o'Clock Jump," Webb's and Goodman's "Stompin' at the Savoy," or Erskine Hawkins's and Glenn Miller's "Tuxedo Junction"), segregationist policies favored the white band's version.[50]

As aural media in which the color of the musicians was not visible, records and even radio offered African American bands some exposure. This was not the case with movies, which relied on sight *and* sound and which were, according to one press agent, "the greatest source of publicity ever developed for bandleaders." The bandleader's name and photo appeared in newspaper ads and other forms of publicity all over the country, and blow-ups were displayed in thousands of theaters from coast to coast. Black bands had appeared in several early jazz pictures, such as *Murder at the Vanities* (1934, with Ellington) and the Amos 'n' Andy short *Check and Double Check* (1930), in which the Ellington orchestra played a prominent role. They were rarely given speaking parts, however. With his ability to clown, play, and sing, Louis Armstrong popped up periodically, most notably in *Pennies from Heaven* (1935). For the most part, however, studio personnel worried about showing black faces on the screen in roles equal to whites' or as persons in their own right in material that went "coast-to-coast."[51]

Although few movies did justice to swing, established white bands and bandleaders got the plum roles in *Dancing Coed* (1939), *Orchestra Wives* (1940), *Sun Valley Serenade* (1942), and many other films. If black musicians were members of the white bands, studios preferred that they play the music but had white actors appear onscreen so as not to lose the southern audience. Despite the Goodman Trio's and Quartet's managing to appear together onscreen, as late as 1946 Monogram studios insisted that Al Killian and Paul Webster not appear onscreen with the Charlie Barnet band. When Hollywood did focus on swing, in movies such as *Birth of the Blues, Syncopation,* and *Blues in the Night* (all 1941–42), the films had white musicians learning their art from black players, who then conveniently left the picture. Hollywood did the most to whiten swing when it denied black bands the same publicity buildup it gave to white ones, making it impossible to tie record releases in to the appearance of the picture and eliminating the large infusions of cash necessary to keep a big band afloat.[52]

Although records helped build audiences, they could not compare with radio or the movies in building a band. As a result, black bands had to stay on the road doing endless one-nighters to produce a steady source of income. Except for "maybe one four-week location, and a two-week vacation," Jimmie Lunceford noted in 1942, his schedule consisted of "a couple of hundred one nighters a year" and "fifteen to twenty weeks of theaters." Andy Kirk was rarely idle in 1940, but, asked R. L. Larkin, "how long can Kirk, Mary Lou Williams and the boys continue jumping from 200 to 450 miles every night, night after night, year after year, without air time, without a location job, and without the rest human beings must have"? Leading the band after Chick Webb's death, Larkin added, Ella Fitzgerald was "making sleeper jumps and working in holes-in-the-wall out in the sticks where on more than one occasion the operator . . . failed to pay off." Even perennial favorite Louis Armstrong fared badly in 1940. His band played Los Angeles's Paramount, but the public did not know that his well-dressed men

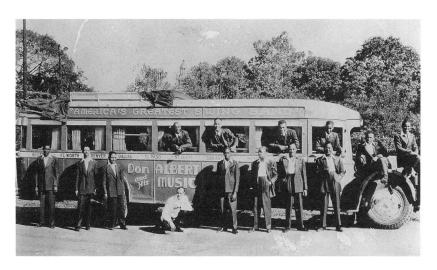

On the bus. The Don Albert Band, Houston, 1938. With so few location jobs available to them, black bands had heavy travel schedules. Frank Driggs Collection.

had "traveled across the western half of the United States in a cold bus, beat and weary," at a salary "about half of what a white musician receives, working under a leader as well known as Armstrong." Under such conditions, Larkin predicted the demise of black bands or a mass exodus of overworked and underpaid black musicians.[53]

Rather than a chance to skim the cream off the band business, the road was a way of life for black bands. Playing the sticks took a special toll since black bands had to put up with so much unreconstructed prejudice, South and North. Well-dressed, professional black northern bands touring the South did not fit the image of racial subordination demanded by the system of segregation. As a result, they encountered what historian Burton Peretti calls highly public theatrical rituals intended to remind them of their racial inferiority. Freedom of movement, decent shelter, and the opportunity to eat and go to the bathroom in privacy and with dignity were denied at every turn. "As long as we were there as servants, we were treated well," noted Kirk of southern dance halls. "On every job the message got to us in one way or another: 'Keep your place. You're here as servants. Please the customers, and everything will be fine.'" As servants, however, black musicians often played separate white and black dances or halls and warehouses where ropes divided blacks from whites.[54]

Off the bandstand, black musicians found constant reminders of their second-class citizenship. Train travel below the Mason-Dixon line meant being herded into cramped, dirty quarters and humiliated by not being allowed into the dining cars. Taking taxis was also a chore. During the war, a white South Carolina cab driver told Dexter Gordon and Leo Parker, "'You niggers get the fuck out of here. I don't ride no niggers in my cab.'" Since white hotels refused to admit black guests, they had to find accommodations in the black sections of town, a practice that built solidarity between black musicians and the community. But as Basie recalled, at times "there were no hotels or even rooming houses," and the band slept on the bus. Since restaurants refused to serve them, "You would hear musicians coming back bitching," guitarist Danny Barker recalled, "saying how they had been insulted, told, 'You can't eat in here.'" Moreover, because of segregated restrooms, black entertainers knew they would be "hitting the bushes on the highways and byways, because the segregation laws did not allow black backsides to sit on the same toilet seats as white backsides. It would be mixing of the races."[55]

Threats of violence stood behind the system. During Ellington's first southern tour, in 1933, the band nearly came to grief. As Barney Bigard noted, "they always had to have four cops stationed at each corner of the place so that the local people wouldn't get any ideas." White members of the audience often used violence to keep black performers "in their place." Liminal artists at the margins of the southern racial system, they came into contact with whites in sexually charged nightlife settings. For many white women, North and South, black musicians assumed the allure of forbidden fruit; in drinking environments the results could be explosive. At a roadhouse in Longview, Texas, for example, a drunken white woman disregarded propriety by offering a drink to Benny Payne, the pianist in Cab Calloway's orchestra. Payne tried to refuse, but the woman got loud, and he was forced to take the drink. As soon as he put down the glass, however, the man with her leaned in close to Payne and, according to bassist Milt Hinton, told him, "'Nigger, you can't be takin' whiskey from my girl.'" Offended by this affront to white womanhood, several white men objected and tore the room apart in their attempts to get at the band. Only a trap door saved the lives of the musicians. Moreover, in the middle of the melee, white men were pushing and pulling, trying to hit Cab. Hinton heard them shout, "'I'll give you two hundred to hit the nigger.'" The mixture of Calloway's fame and allure to women of all races was just enough to ignite the tinderbox.[56]

Presumably stationed at dances to stem such incidents, local policemen used violence to enforce the racial hierarchy. As symbols of white male power, law officers felt empowered to harass black bands, which, playing from the bandstand, were literally above them. In one instance, a white policeman asked that Earl Hines's band play "Honeysuckle Rose" but went to the bathroom while the band played the request. On his return, he asked when the band would play the tune. Informed that they had already played it, the policeman called them liars and "began to use bad language and get very offensive about race." He then ordered the band to leave after intermission. As Hines recalled, southern whites "couldn't understand our being so well dressed, nor the way we carried ourselves." The police also harassed black women, who had the least social power of the entire audience, at dances where both races were present (with a rope between them). Hines recalled that if there was a disturbance, "they used to beat up on the women." At a dance in Texas in the early 1940s, Johnny Otis related, a white cop hit a woman for leaning on the rope. "The men—all of us—had been reduced to dogs. To less than dogs."[57]

After one-nighters in the South and in other rural areas, black musicians longed for New York. Harlem offered a comfortable, exciting, and cosmopolitan home base, while Fifty-second Street served as an entree to a wider urban experience. But New York was also the capital of the dance band industry, an industry that favored whites. Although white musicians and bandleaders were less racially prejudiced than the population at large, they were part of a complex business and, as in the case of Artie Shaw and Billie Holiday, often had to compromise with prevailing racial fears. Yet the music business was not static; it resisted black bands and integrated units, but challenges to the color line and segregated places of entertainment appeared wherever the swing fever was fervent.

It was fervent in New York. By decade's end, the color bar for audiences began to fall on Fifty-second Street, and the nation's first integrated nightclub, Cafe Society, opened in Greenwich Village. It had an enormous impact on the rest of the swing world. In addition, many swing fans demanded to hear black bands and black musicians on a more regular basis. A good part of this demand arose from the professional and dignified deportment of black musicians, as well as from the tremendous creativity and enthusiasm they brought to their playing. It was difficult for white players and white audiences to see blacks as other than equal or even superior swing musicians. At the same time, more swing bands were becoming racially mixed. Although Artie Shaw lost Billie Holiday because of the complicated relation of race to commerce, in the early 1940s, when he rejoined the band business, he worked with Lips Page and attempted to hire Benny Carter. After the war, he toured with trumpeter Roy Eldridge. By 1941, furthermore, Gene Krupa achieved star status leading a band that featured Eldridge performing live and in recorded duets with white singer Anita O'Day. This pairing challenged some of the nation's deepest taboos.

Despite the persistence of racism, swing's growing popularity and its links to the Popular Front atmosphere of the late 1930s forced the music industry to accommodate swing musicians, fans, and impresarios who challenged racial inequality. In a host of integrated jam sessions in Harlem and on Fifty-second Street, in clubs such as the Village Vanguard in Greenwich Village, and in lofts and in concert halls, black and white musicians played together on an equal basis. They also did so in the numerous battles of bands, in which merit, not color, was what mattered. Similarly, mixed recording sessions became a regular part of the music business. As swing musicians recognized their common love of the music and their common professional attitudes, as they socialized on Fifty-second Street or uptown, they came to see that music was good or bad, not white or black. For many musicians, fans, and impresarios, swing was an important weapon in combating the racism of both the music industry and the society. By 1940 swing businessmen, musicians, and young fans had made swing American music, with all the assets and liabilities of American society. When the United States entered the war, the tensions and conflict embodied in the music and the society would come to a head.

PART THREE

Culture Noir, 1942–1954

7

Swing Goes to War

Glenn Miller and the Popular Music of World War II

These boys really play this thing the American way. White bands with colored musicians and arrangers swinging out with America's best, and colored and white band polls being open to all make this ole land really worth fighting for. . . . Yep, Count Basie, Louis Armstrong, Cab Calloway, Johnny Hodges, Benny Goodman, and Tommy Dorsey are all brothers of the downbeat, and that's what makes America—America. . . .—Frank Bolden, *Pittsburgh Courier*

When you're in the position most of us are in, your pent-up emotions run for just one avenue of escape, an avenue leading to the thing you want most of all, your home and all your loved ones and all that they stood, stand, and will stand for. . . .—A G. I. on Glenn Miller's AAF Band.

In September 1942, thirty-eight-year-old Glenn Miller disbanded his successful swing orchestra to enlist in the army. "I, like every patriotic American," he declared, "have an obligation to fulfill. That obligation is to lend as much support as I can to winning the war." Having lived and worked as "a free man," he would use his music to defend "the freedom and the democratic way of life we have that enabled me to make the strides in the right direction." In doing so, Miller embodied a wartime ideal of sacrifice for a nation that allowed individuals to succeed and prosper. Besides lifting morale and encouraging recruitment, he created a model of patriotic duty and a web of connections between military obligation and an American way of life embodied in swing and understood by millions of young people.[1]

His sacrifice was real: in giving up what had become the nation's most lucrative swing band from 1939 to 1942, Miller stood to lose millions. The orchestra had broadcast three nights a week on the prestigious *Chesterfield Hour*, set theater, hotel, and ballroom attendance records, and produced a string of hit recordings. His Army Air Force (AAF) Orchestra, however, soon surpassed its civilian predecessor. Under Captain (and later Major) Miller's command, the AAF Orchestra's forty-two-man marching band, nineteen-piece dance unit, radio show, string ensemble, and small jazz combo aided bond rallies, made Victory Discs for the troops, and entertained soldiers at home and abroad. Miller's disappearance in a small plane over the English Channel on 15 December 1944—his ultimate sacrifice—made him a national icon. His story highlights the powerful role that swing played in World War II and helps explain the effects that the war had on American music and culture.[2]

In going to war, Miller infused the depression's popular music with national purpose. Swing's participation in the conflict signified that the war was being fought to defend popular values nurtured during the depression and imbued with particular ideals of American life. Indeed, the music played by black and white bands was the conflict's "war" music, despite efforts by the Office of War Information and Tin Pan Alley songwriters to produce patriotic songs like those of World War I. Except for "Coming In on a Wing and a Prayer" and "Praise the Lord and Pass the Ammunition," few patriotic songs met the test of popularity. Americans were united by the unprovoked attack on Pearl Harbor and the existence of a clearly defined enemy. In addition, immigrants who were cut off from their country of origin as a result of immigration restrictions in the 1920s now felt allegiance to the United States. It was thus possible to ideologize the war as a defense of a superior American culture.[3]

Furthermore, the United States fought the war with civilian-soldiers who wanted to return to their domestic lives once the job was done. As Miller put it, GIs wanted "as narrow a chasm as possible between martial and civilian life." Radio, film, records, and big band appearances made popular music "a great new factor in the American way of life," as vital for the young "as food and ammunition." A central ingredient in dating, personal freedom, and consumption, big band music also conveyed the virtues of ethnic and racial cosmopolitanism. For millions of young people, swing was firmly associated with the benefits of American life. Hence Miller's desire to streamline military music, lift morale, and symbolize national unity with swing met with conditional acceptance by officials bent on mobilizing society for total war. Yet Miller's version of swing also brought to a head musi-

Captain Glenn Miller, 1942. Glenn Miller Archives, University of Colorado, Boulder.

cal, racial, and sexual tensions that ultimately led to major disaffections from swing.[4]

Swing against Fascism

Miller did not act alone. As part of the attempt to define national objectives and create national unity around familiar symbols of everyday life, popular music was drafted into the conflict on an unprecedented scale. In fact, President Roosevelt declared, music could "inspire a fervor for the spiritual values in our way of life and thus to strengthen democracy against those forces which subjugate and enthrall mankind." Fighting Aryan supremacy, Roosevelt envisioned music helping to "promote tolerance of minority groups in our midst by showing their cultural contributions to our American life." His choice of Benny Goodman as the popular music chair of Russian War Relief acknowledged swing's importance as a symbol of American pluralism. According to Broadway impresario Billy Rose, all of show business had a role to play in the crisis—to "make us love what is good in America and hate what Hitler and the minor thugs around him stand for," such as the Nazi and Japanese suppression of jazz, popular music, and American films created by the "inferior" black and Jewish races.[5]

Wartime films made explicit the links between swing and American values. In *Casablanca* intolerant Nazis close down the fun-loving, democratic world of Rick's Cafe Americain, a haven for drinkers, gamblers, and various refugees, many of them Jews, fleeing the Nazi suppression of their different nations and cultures. The cabaret's major attraction—aside from the suave, leftist expatriate Rick—was Sam, the black pianist, singer, and bandleader. In his rendition of "Shine" he depicted the harmful effects of prejudice, while as the black leader of a white swing band, he also demonstrated American racial pluralism. *Stage Door Canteen* enlisted the bands of Benny Goodman and Count Basie to help Kay Kyser entertain an interracial audience of GI jitterbugs. Moreover, as the multiethnic crew of *Airforce* flew toward Pearl Harbor, they heard Roosevelt's declaration of war followed by Duke Ellington's "It Don't Mean a Thing If It Ain't Got That Swing." In these and many other films, swing embodied an American way of life—democracy, pluralism, and personal freedom—under attack.

As central figures in youth culture, Glenn Miller and other swing musicians helped make the music of the home front a vital part of the war. Ruled nonessential to war production, many musicians enlisted or were drafted and served in military bands. Artie Shaw led a navy swing unit in the South Pacific; Bob Crosby led a marine swing band; and Sam Donahue's navy band toured Europe. In giving up his career for the marines, Claude Thornhill found "something far greater at stake . . . and that is the protection of the democratic way of life." To be sure, not all musicans were so eager. Because of segregation, black players found few spots in service bands and usually served in regular units. Out of shape, Lester Young, for example, was assigned to regular duty and ended up in detention barracks, an experience immortalized in his "D. B. Blues." Musicians of all colors advised each other on how to evade the draft. "I had taken so much soap that my insides must have been nothing but bubbles and suds," recalled Buck Clayton. "I had taken that benzedrine–coca-cola formula until I hadn't been able to sleep for three days." He also was told "to act like I was gay and they wouldn't want me. I couldn't figure out how to do that but I did keep it in mind." Nothing worked, and Clayton served honorably at Camp Kilmer with Sy Oliver, Mercer Ellington, and Jimmy Crawford in one of the few black service bands. Other musicians from the bands of Count Basie, Cab Calloway, John Kirby, and many others went off to war. At home, Goodman, Basie, Calloway, Ellington, Armstrong, and others played USO tours, bond rallies, and concerts at bases and hospitals.[6]

To boost morale, the music industry worked with the government and the army to bring popular music to the troops. Victory Discs brought together musicians, singers, recording and radio executives, the American Federation of Musicians (AFM), and army personnel to record and distribute popular music. Despite an AFM strike against the recording industry, union musicians were allowed to record for the troops. The army also installed phonographs and radios in barracks and service centers so that GIs could hear American music rather than the music of the country in which they were stationed (as occurred in World War I). "Wherever there are American soldiers with juke box and jazz tastes," noted jazz critic Barry Ulanov, "there are V Discs to entertain them." Similarly, the army created the Armed Forces Radio Service, which produced shows such as *Command Performance, Mail Call,* and *Jubilee,* the latter aimed at black troops. Because of the lack of popular music on the BBC prior to D-Day, General Eisenhower ordered the Armed Forces Network (AFN) to "be as much a duplication of American broadcasting at home as it was possible." Not to be outdone, the enemy competed for GI allegiance with the swing-laced radio propaganda of Tokyo Rose and Axis Sally.[7]

Sousa with a Floy Floy

Of all the popular bandleaders, Glenn Miller played an especially important role in the war effort. His achievement lay in taking the safest parts of swing youth culture to war against the Nazis. Miller's military career crowned his civilian accomplishments, in which he had codified swing, polished its jazz elements, and used it to paint an idealized picture of American life. In his person and his art Miller blended swing with more traditional conceptions of national life and made it acceptable to the farthest reaches of American society. Unlike most other white swing bandleaders, Alton Glenn Miller had roots in the "typically American" farms and small towns of the West and the Midwest. Born in Clarinda, Iowa, in 1904, he grew up in Fort Morgan, Colorado, where his itinerant handyman father and prohibitionist mother, head of a WCTU chapter, instilled in him the values of self-control, persistence, hard work, and the need to succeed. He took up the trombone as a youngster and after two years at the University of Colorado turned professional. After discovering jazz in the 1920s, he played with the best white musicians in the Ben Pollack Orchestra. When his career took him east in 1928, he became an enthusiastic New Yorker. A midwesterner who formed his musical identity in New York, Miller fused disparate traditions to create a type of swing that captured national attention in 1939.[8]

Miller made swing all-American by merging the two popular music strains of the 1930s—adventurous swing and romantic, more melodic sweet music—into a powerful amalgam. Once he decided he would never out-swing Goodman, Shaw, or Basie or best Tommy Dorsey on trombone, Miller emphasized his strengths—arranging and organizing the talents of others into a more unified, romantic sound. The result was a synthesis: "sweet swing," a clean-cut version of jive suitable for expansion into the nation's heartland via jukeboxes and radio. Tex Beneke, the band's singer-saxophonist, noted that Miller was successful because the public "liked sweet ballads, reminiscent melodies, sentimental words. He found that it liked new pleasant sounds which did not clash." Miller succeeded by taking the standard swing format—setting brass against reeds over a four-four rhythm section—and using clarinetist Willie Schwartz to play lead melody over the other reeds. This smoothed out the sound, giving a "silvery," romantic context to the swing beat. Uniting adventure and security, Miller took the edge off the hard-charging Goodman style and made it comfortable for the less experienced white dancers. Thus his codification of the major elements of big band performance into a streamlined sweet swing made his musical product appealing to a much wider audience. It was Miller, not Goodman, who set the pattern for white bands after 1939.[9]

Using his superb business skills to master radio and jukebox play just as these media were peaking, Miller was able to achieve popularity in the small towns of the Midwest as well as in the big urban areas. "When we started out three years ago," he declared, "none of the big bands played pretty tunes . . . and the majority of people like to hear pretty tunes. We've tried to hit a happy balance between the two." On another occasion he asserted, "I haven't a great jazz band, and I don't want one. Our band stresses harmony." Legitimate study "finally is enabling me to write arrangements employing unusual, rich harmonies, many never before used in dance bands."

At the same time, he organized his band according to a formula—what music historian and critic Gunther Schuller calls a "sound world"—built on everyone's fitting into his concepion of a tight arrangement. He demanded ensemble perfection rather than "one hot soloist jumping up after another to take hot choruses." One critic noted that "the band solos more than any one individual in it." As a result, though, the band suffered from stiffness. As trombonist Jimmy Priddy put it, "If you're not going to be a little sloppy, you're bound to be stiff. And that band was stiff!" Woody Herman agreed. "He was so intent on making a success, he lost all reasoning about anything else. You know, cleanliness, even the . . . uniforms of the musicians. . . . He was building an erector set. And that's the way it sounded."[10]

Creating a uniform sound required patriarchal authority and discipline. As an extremely image-conscious corporate executive, Miller demanded perfect deportment and perfect notes. Musicians had to have everything— uniforms, socks, neckties, handkerchiefs—"just right," recalled trumpeter Billy May, "or else you'd be fined." This went for the music too. "He would hit on a formula and then he would try to fit everything into it. There was no room for inventiveness. Even the hot choruses were supposed to be the same. [Arranger] Jerry Gray was perfect for the band. He followed the patterns exactly." His insistence on band uniformity and his "sharply disciplined routines bugged many of the musicians." According to singer Chuck Goldstein, Miller "was always the General. Everybody knows what a disciplinarian he was."[11]

Although his commanding style angered some musicians, many players and fans appreciated his authority and his patriarchal air, which later enhanced his stature as an air force officer. His aura of fatherly reassurance was heightened by a modesty and a stoicism that helped him overcome the many problems that plagued traveling bands. He was a confident model of masculinity. Tall, "bespectacled and scholarly looking," he "was a commanding guy, youthful but mature," according to his press agent, Howard Richmond, who found that Miller "looked like security, like all the things I'd never found in a band leader." True, "Mickey Mouse band leaders looked like security. I'm talking about jazz leaders. To me they always looked like they didn't know where they were going to sleep the next night." Seventeen-year-old singer Marion Hutton concurred. As her legal guardian, Miller "was like a father. . . . He represented a source of strength. . . . He fulfilled the image of what a father ought to be." As a leader and organizer Miller brought these same traits to jazz, making it clean-cut and respectable, less a challenge to society than one of its commodities.[12]

Similarly, Miller's hits combined big-city swing with the currents of a more stable and conservative Midwest. Music critic Irving Kolodin noted that Miller's music had "a kind of inland sentiment that differed considerably from the 'big town' aura that pulses in Ellington or Goodman." His best-known swing numbers—"In the Mood," "Tuxedo Junction," and "String of Pearls," for example—reveled in big-city excitement and sophistication. At the same time, the band was known for songs about distinctively American regions and symbols: "Dreamsville, Ohio," the folksy "Little Brown Jug," "[I Got a Gal in] Kalamazoo," and "Boulder Buff." In 1942 "Chattanooga Choo-Choo" became the first song to sell a million records by combining a thrusting train imagery with a "carry me home" theme. In fact, "Chattanooga" was the first popular hit since 1935 that was about yearning for home. "Don't Sit under the Apple Tree" also conjured up a small-town couple hugging in the backyard. In Miller's music, the romantic context and the small-town imagery made freedom seem less open-ended and more the product of typical American places and settings found somewhere in a harmonious past. During the war, GIs could defend those real places, not just some abstract ideal.[13]

Besides merging swing and sweet, Miller consciously sought to build an All-American team that fused the ethnically varied big city and the Protestant heartland. A New Yorker with a midwestern face, glasses, and a folksy tinge to his voice, he recruited clean-cut musicians and singers such as Tex Beneke and Marion Hutton. (Initially he introduced Hutton as Sissy Jones, a name he felt connoted "apple pie, ice cream and hot dogs," and dressed her to emphasize her girl-next-door look.) Yet Miller still conceived of an orchestra as a religiously pluralist vision of an all-American team. The Modernaires, his singing group, included a Jew, a Catholic, a Presbyterian, and a Christian Scientist. He also recruited ethnic musicians—whom he stereotyped. "Italian trumpeters," he said, "seldom play good jazz" but made "great lead men," while "you can't have a good band without at least one Jew." The Miller team, like his "sweet swing," included ethnic minorities, but in an idealized middle-class depiction of the nation.[14]

Black musicians, however, played no visible role in this homogenized assemblage. The band used the energy of black jazz, but unlike the harder-swinging outfits of Goodman, Shaw, Barnet, or even Jimmy Dorsey, employed no black players. Miller did, however, engage the services of black arranger Eddie Durham for some of his uptempo numbers, such as "In the Mood." Miller's racial conservatism probably derived less from prejudice than from his desire to attract the largest possible white audience and his lack of sympathy for rough improvisers and gritty musicians. Including blacks would have disrupted the band's carefully tended image and totally streamlined sound and denied the orchestra bookings at top hotels and ballrooms that were segregated. His personal preferences fit well with army policy, which was to maintain strict segregation in service bands. In this "whitened" version of the all-American team, blacks stayed on the bench while polished black music played a prominent role.[15]

When he enlisted in the armed forces, Miller set out to create a military version of his band for battle against the enemy. Courtesy of Uncle Sam, Miller had at his disposal native Protestant, Italian, and Jewish musicians from all the top white bands. Accordingly, the AAF Orchestra served as the "ethnic platoon" writ large. Under the baton of a reassuring father figure who had sacrificed profit for duty, the band smoothly melded civilian values and military goals in a common cause. Service musicians kept alive civilian standards of personal freedom for men often at odds with military hierarchy. Even as he became an officer, for example, Miller chafed at the higher brass's attempts to control his music, while many of his players struggled against army discipline. In general, though, musicians lived far freer lives than did average GIs. As *Metronome* noted, the Curtis Bay Cats were "the despair of the Coast Guard officers, who had to plead with them to give up their civilian habits of living, to get their hair cut and get up in the morning." After taps they held jam sessions, and on weekends they hit their favorite New York clubs. To reassure a worried military hierarchy that his swing musicians posed little threat to military order and purpose, Miller insisted on the discipline and decorum that had made him a watchword for control before the war.[16]

No longer a questionable part of national life, swing was, in Miller's hands, capable of transforming the rigidly old-fashioned army marching band into a modernized emblem of cosmopolitan American society. In a letter to Brigadier General Charles D. Young, Miller declared that "the interest of our boys lies definitely in modern, popular music, as played by an orchestra such as ours" rather than in their fathers' music, "much of which is still being played by army bands just as it was in World War days." The bandleader added that he wanted to "do something concrete in the way of setting up a plan that would enable our music to reach our servicemen here and abroad with some degree of regularity." A modern army band under his leadership would raise money for the USO and the Army Relief Fund and might put "more spring into the feet of our marching men and a little more joy into their hearts."[17]

Yet his most ambitious plans clashed with those of the army. Relying on his organizing and arranging skills, Miller initially proposed to transform the entire army band structure by creating seventeen-piece dance bands at thirty Army Air Force training fields. When army brass vetoed this grand idea, he instead built a modernized super marching band for the Army Air Force Training Corps. Unveiled at the Yale Bowl during a giant bond rally in July 1943, the forty-man unit electrified the cadets. Instead of the usual twelve marching snare and bass drums, the rhythm derived from just two drummers with complex swing band drum kits and two string bass players, who rode atop two jeeps rolling beside the marching orchestra. When Sousa's "Stars and Stripes Forever" blared out "in jive tempo," charged *Time*, "sober listeners began to wonder what U.S. brass-band music was coming to. Obviously, there was an Afro-Saxon in the woodpile." Other jazz influences surfaced in the swinging marches created out of blues and swing numbers such as "St. Louis Blues," "Blues in the Night," and the "Jersey Bounce." Critic George Simon called this fusion of jazz and military music "the loosest, most swinging marching band we'd ever heard," filled with syncopation. "The horns played with zest and freedom, occasionally bending some notes and anticipating others, the way true jazz musicians do so well."[18]

The army brass were aghast at the idea of transforming the marching band—and by implication the army itself—into a looser, jazzier organization. *Time* noted that "old-time, long-haired U.S. Army bandmasters had the horrors" as the AAFTC Band "suddenly, and disconcertingly, got rhythm." As United States Army Band Master Edwin Franko Goldman told the magazine, "Personally I think it's a disgrace! . . . No one can improve on a Sousa march. . . . My God!" Given the opposition, Miller turned his attention overseas, where his AAF Orchestra raised troop morale from 1944 to 1946. Although military marching units resisted swing, Miller succeeded in injecting it into the war effort. Few military bands could omit swing entirely since young GIs demanded this freer and more vital music.[19]

As long as they did not threaten military discipline, swing bands were permitted to perform a variety of roles. Miller's broadcasts, for example, featured propaganda playlets that dramatized the Four Freedoms and equated American music with free expression and American culture. The orchestra's novelty tunes, for instance, hailed America as a cosmopolitan nation. "There Are Yanks" (1944) praised the unity of diverse Americans, linking Yanks from "the banks of the Wabash" to "Okies, crackers," and "every color and creed / And they talk the only language the Master race can read." Miller's weekly show for the Office of War Information, *The German Wehrmacht Hour,* beamed from England to Germany, also equated a pluralistic nation and its music. The program used a German announcer, Ilse, the vocals of Johnny Desmond, and German dialogue to trumpet the blessings of music and democracy. After the orchestra played "Volga Boatmen" in one episode, for example, Ilse declared that an American could play any music he liked without "barriers . . . whether the music is American, German, Russian, Chinese or Jewish." Miller underlined the point: "America means freedom and there's no expression of freedom quite so sincere as music." Typically, the band would conclude each episode with a swing tune associated with Duke Ellington, Benny Goodman, or Miller himself.[20]

Equally important, the orchestra became the living embodiment of American culture abroad. In England the band endured a grueling schedule to bring American music to GIs a long way from home. They broadcast thirteen times a week over AFN, flew up and down the British Isles for live concerts and special events, and continued to record V-Discs. Committed to providing a variety of American popular music, Miller divided the band into a group that played the *Swing Shift* radio program with Ray McKinley, a seventeen-piece orchestra that played many of Miller's civilian tunes, and Uptown Hall, a seven-piece jazz group led by Mel Powell. In addition, singer Johnny Desmond appeared on the radio program *A Soldier and a Song*, and the string section starred in another radio show, *Strings with Wings*. In its short stay in England the band played seventy-one concerts for 247,500 listeners, often in huge airplane hangars on makeshift stages. Live shows ran to older hits demanded by the soldiers and a series of army-related songs such as "Tail-end Charlie," "Snafu Jump," and "G.I. Jive," which humorously relieved the rigors of war and reminded GIs that they were defending the nation responsible for such personally liberating music. As Miller put it in a letter to George Simon, "We came here to bring a much-needed touch of home to some lads who have been here a couple of years" and were "starved for real, live American music."[21]

At home and abroad, Miller's band helped personalize the war. As early as 1940 his civilian band broadcast from army camps and dedicated songs to various units, a practice the AAF Orchestra continued abroad. On a Chesterfield show in 1940, for example, Marion Hutton sang "Five o'Clock Whistle" to the "boys" in the "New Fighting 69th," originally from "around New York way" but now at Fort McClellan, Alabama. "They were among the first to leave in service for our country." Other shows featured a "top tune of the week" for soldiers at various bases, interspersed with references to home: baseball, Ebbets Field, and other bandleaders. Every week on *I Sustain the Wings* Miller urged families and girlfriends to "keep those V-Mail letters flying to the boys overseas. Mail from home is number one on their hit parade. They're doing the fighting. You do the writing." Enlisted men appreciated the effort. "Your 'Sunset Serenade' is a fine tribute to all of us

Glenn Miller's AAF Orchestra, somewhere in England, performing in an airplane hangar, 1944. Note servicemen sitting atop planes and hanging from the rafters. Glenn Miller Archives, University of Colorado, Boulder.

in the service," said a letter in the Salinas, California, Army Air Base *Observer.* "We all listen to it every Saturday."[22]

Because of its ability to re-create familiar personal ties, Miller's twenty-piece concert unit became "the most popular band among the boys in the service." As a private noted of one concert, "The troops were a cheering mass of swing-hungry GIs. The Joes ate up everything the massive band dished out, most of them in a dream world." But he tired of repetitious "arrangements . . . played and replayed, all in the same precise, spiritless manner" characteristic of Miller's bands "since he first attained commercial success." Miller angrily replied, "We . . . didn't come here to set any new fashions in music or to create any new swing styles." The musicians might want to experiment, but "we play only the old tunes" because the GIs, away from home and out of touch with current hits, "know and appreciate only the tunes that were popular before they left the States." Most GIs agreed. One serviceman wrote to *Metronome* that millions of GIs "want to hear things that remind them of home, that bring back something of those days when we were all happy and free and when we used to be able to put on a Miller record or listen to a Miller broadcast or even hear the band in person." The average guy, he added, looked to music "strictly for its emotional content" and "wants the songs he used to know played as he used to hear them played." Facing death, cut off from family, "your pent-up emotions run for . . . the thing you want most of all, *your home, and all your loved ones and all that they stood, stand and will stand for.*" For "99.4 per cent of all G. I.'s, that's what Miller and his Men and their Music stand for too."[23]

The popularity of Miller's civilian hits reflected the desire of GIs to remain connected to personal memories of an idealized, perfectly ordered, and secure home front that would be waiting for them after the war. Perhaps this explains why GIs created their own swing bands and nightclubs and why at "mission parties" men who used to go to Roseland "now knock[ed] themselves out to the music of GI bands with the English lassies jumping with 'em." Enlisted men wrote *Metronome* of their longing for music. "Circumstances," wrote one soldier, kept him from hearing live bands, "but you have brought them to me through the medium of your magazine." He just wanted to "come back home, pick up my alto," and then "run out and catch a million measures of Barnet, Hodges, Joe Phillips, and Bothwell." For Leonard Pratt, a pilot shot down over Germany and imprisoned for the rest of the war, music evoked even more powerful memories of home. He and his fellow inmates eagerly awaited Red Cross record shipments and begged newly captured officers for news about big bands. Using a piano donated by the Red Cross, he "brought the big band numbers to many who were in the small room or stood outside." Occasionally German guards "would shout through the window 'In De Mood.'" When he finally returned to Iowa, Pratt was eager to dance again to the sounds of his youth. Unable to find any of his old flames, he took his mother dancing to the sounds of the Duke Ellington Orchestra.[24]

I'll Be Seeing You

The look homeward often assumed a nostalgic glow in the face of death and military regimentation. Freedom could only be achieved in a remembered past or a dreamed future. Miller himself gazed backward as his presentiments of death rose and his frustrations with army red tape grew. His radio director recalled, "I don't know of anyone who was as homesick as Glenn." He talked often of his wife and adopted children at home and envisioned for his postwar life a suburban ranch home—Tuxedo Junction, a balsa replica of which he carried with him—where he planned to get away, relax, play golf, and devote time to his family. This preoccupation surfaced increasingly in the sweeter, more romantic songs he played in person and on *I Sustain the Wings*. With lush chords and wafting clarinet leads they established a dreamy memory of romantic togetherness and security back home. "Serenade in Blue" put it well: "When I hear that serenade in blue / I'm somewhere in another world alone with you / Sharing all the joys we used to know / Many moons ago."[25]

At the center of the homeward gaze was the American woman, who embodied the virtues of American civilization and reminded soldiers of a personal obligation to defend her. Pinups, according to historian Robert Westbrook, reminded servicemen of their personal ties to the home front, occasioning emotions of love, lust, and longing. The Miller band acknowledged this in novelties such as "Paper Doll" (1943), a hit for the Mills Brothers, and "Peggy, the Pin-Up Girl" (1944), which chronicles Peggy Jones, a girl "with a chassis that made Lassie come home," whose pictures in *Life* and *Look* were carried into battle "all over the world." The song ends with an obligation: "Pilot to Bombardier / Come on boys, let's drop one here / For Peggy the Pin-up Girl." Armed Forces Radio supplied servicemen with a living pinup in the "fresh-faced blonde," disc jockey GI Jill. After spinning records and reading letters, she whispered "in the sexiest voice imaginable, 'Goooood Niiight,'" followed by sighs all over the Pacific. Black GIs, prevented by white officers from having white pinups, made singer Lena Horne their dream girl and dubbed her "Sgt. Horne" for her commitment to entertaining the troops and to challenging segregation in camp shows.[26]

The band itself evoked memories of the home front and the women who dwelt there. On one AFN broadcast, for example, Miller followed "Flying Home" with "Smoke Gets in Your Eyes." "We'll supply the music," he said. "You supply the girl." An RAF pilot caught the band in a smoky English hangar crowded "to capacity with uniformed boys and girls swaying gently or 'jiving' wildly," the vocalist singing "of love not war." As the band wove its spell, they "were conscious of the music . . . the exhilarating rhythm and of course, the girl in our arms . . . she was Alice Faye, Betty Grable, Rita Hayworth or whoever our 'pin up' of that particular week may have been." Perhaps it was Dinah Shore, on a USO tour with the band, who as a living pinup was the idealized image of the girl left behind. She cemented this image on AFN whenever she sang Cole Porter's "You'd Be So Nice to Come Home To," because it brought GI husband George Montgomery "closer to me."[27]

Ostensibly, women waited and thereby symbolized home front faithfulness. The anguish of parting became the subject of "dialogue songs" between soldiers and the women at home. Miller's version of "Don't Sit under the Apple Tree" (1942), for example, features a GI and his girl urging each other to remain true. As he tells her, "Don't go walking down lover's lane with anyone else but me / 'Til I come marching home," she demands, "Watch the girls on foreign shores / You'll have to report to me." In Ellington's "Don't Get Around Much Anymore," which the AAF Orchestra also played, the singer goes out on dates but finds, "It's so different without you." Loneliness and frustration led to songs such as "No Love, No Nothin' (Until My Baby Comes Home)," or "Saturday Night Is the Loneliest Night in the Week." Separation also produced vows to be true made by women in "I'll Walk Alone" and "I Don't Want to Walk without You," top hits of 1944. Waiting fell hardest on women. Jane Easton wrote her husband that she longed "more than ever to spend my youth with you. I'm tired of being half dead." Under such conditions, love flared intensely, in a race with the relentless march of events. Miller's version of Kurt Weill's "Speak Low" uses surging dynamics to convey building passion defeated by the pressure of time as the vocalist sings, "Our moment is swift / Like ships adrift, we're swept apart, too soon." Such songs conveyed the anguish of separation and suspended personal lives as boys went off to war and girls remained behind.[28]

During the war, musical tastes began to change subtly. According to *Down Beat* columnist and GI Mike Levin, soldiers wanted to do a job and return as quickly as possible to "home, family, friends, and everything else that makes up his private conception of what he left behind." Only in music could GIs express their "own hopes," Levin maintained. "That's why old songs and sentimental ballads as such have seen more interest than was ever thought possible in as desperately a bitter war as this; why war songs and patriotic marches by and large have fallen flat." Listening to "I'm a Little on the Lonely Side," Marjorie Kenney wrote her fiance, "It hits me right where it hurts. Me and a couple of million other lonely gals in this country. It's no wonder swing is on the decline and ballads are in again. It's the mood of the whole country with most of its lovers separated." After Evelyn Marks's high-school beau enlisted in 1943, she heard "I'll Walk Alone" with "tears streaming down my face." At their senior prom there were "a lot of teary-eyed girls. It was really quite an emotional time for all of us." *Down Beat* found that draft-age boys and their girls requested sentimental ballads as the war hit them directly: "They are not only more serious about it than others, but aren't so inclined to escape by means of *Sing, Sing, Sing* with added anvils."[29]

Sweeter bands and singers able to express the pain of separation and the dream of future togetherness increased in popularity, especially with young women, who dominated the audience at home now that young men were away. Harry James's Orchestra, for example, shot to the top in late 1942 with a syrupy trumpet, a string section, and beautiful ballads. Tommy Dorsey, Gene Krupa, and Artie Shaw followed suit, while Count Basie, noted *Variety,* "discarded almost completely the typically-Negro rideout style" to become "an outstanding example of the way swing bands are softening up more and more." A reviewer caught how James expressed the feelings of a seventeen-year-old girl out with a soldier: "Tomorrow he will have gone back to duty and you to the dull, lonely routine of your life without him— waiting, waiting for the day of his return." Helen Forrest helped James's rise in popularity with increasingly romantic songs of loss and parting. "We had the same feeling for a song," she said, and he made her the first singer with arrangements written for her rather than for the band. Her frustrated longing for James meshed with the emotions felt by millions of women. As she put it, her songs "aimed at wives and lovers separated by the war from their men in the service." In songs such as "If That's the Way You Want It Baby," women were portrayed as the ideal of stability and civilization for which the men were fighting. Forrest also conveyed how difficult it was to achieve fulfilling love during the war. In "I Had the Craziest Dream" a nighttime reverie ("There you were in love with me") contrasts with reality ("When I'm awake such a break never happens"). Male singers idealized the "true" woman who waited, as in the Ink Spots' "I'll Get By (As Long as I Have You)" and the Mills Brothers' "Till Then." In the face of death, both sexes sought peace and security in the hope of a reunion that was possible only in dreams.[30]

Under the surface, however, songs of home-front devotion reveal deep anxieties about sexuality that belied the war's master narrative of unity. "Don't Sit under the Apple Tree" and "Everybody Loves My Baby" expressed fears over women's newfound economic and sexual independence at home. In 1943 Frank Sinatra brought these concerns to a head as an idol who made bobby-soxers scream and swoon with sexual fervor. "I looked around at the faces of the girls," said the narrator of Frederick Wakeman's *Shore Leave.* "It was mass hysteria, all right. Those kids were having a mass affair with Sinatra." In a lonely era he gave young, often poor girls a vulnerable, sexy, dark boy-next-door who expressed their desires. Ballads such as "I'll Never Smile Again" or "All or Nothing at All," sung in bel canto style, stretched emotions to the breaking point and made girls think of clinging forever to their partners. "When he looked at you, you melted and screamed and clutched your heart," declared June Canter. "The attraction was definitely sexual." Indeed, at New York's Paramount in 1943, noted Sinatra's friend Nick Sevano, "it was absolute pandemonium . . . they threw panties and their brassieres. They went . . . absolutely nuts." With boys in short

Frank Sinatra, solo at New York's Paramount Theatre, 1944. Women go wild, men get mad, the individual stands out from the group, and big bands begin to crumble. Frank Driggs Collection.

supply, girls were drawn to a pied piper who, unlike the bands, gave vent exclusively to their emotional and sexual yearnings.[31]

Sinatra engendered male jealousy over women's home-front temptations and the commitment of civilians in general to the war effort. Enlisted men were angry at a "4-F slacker" who enticed the women of America while they were away. "I think Frank Sinatra was the most hated man of World War II, much more than Hitler," recalled William Manchester, because "we in the Pacific had seen no women at all for two years, and there were photographs of Sinatra being surrounded by all these enthusiastic girls." Irate at his draft status, sailors pelted his photo outside the Paramount with tomatoes, while one GI yelled from the audience, "Hey, wop, why aren't you in uniform?" The press reported that GIs wanted "to gang up on the guy who had 'stolen' their sweethearts' affections." Narrow-shouldered and frail, moreover, Sinatra's desirability to women challenged wartime images of male toughness and increased men's insecurities. Wakeman's narrator, for example, asks a girl what "Sinatra had that [he] didn't have, besides a voice. . . . 'Oh, you've got shoulders,' she said disgustedly. 'We don't go for shoulders since Frankie came into our lives.'" Her boyfriend underlined the men's anxiety: "Us tall, dark and handsome guys ain't gotta chance, brother." Men worried that all women were susceptible. "It's hysteria, all right, but I can't explain it," muses one of the male characters in the novel. "There's some kind of germ around, I guess. It affects older women too." As one woman told *Time*, "My sister saw him twice and she was afraid to go again because she's engaged." The Sinatra flap demonstrates male fears about women's independence and underscores the fragility of their dreams of home.[32]

In fact, the war whipsawed women with opportunities for greater independence and increased demands for fidelity. Geographic mobility, the loosening of patriarchal and familial authority, and the need for women workers in defense plants and USO troupes opened new vistas and gave married and single women greater control over money and leisure time. As a result, nightspots were jammed with women whom Wakeman depicts as consumed by "war fever," which "brings out the boldness in them, turns the hunted into hunters, encourages the natural hunters—the men." Although they never left with men, for example, Barbara Paris and her college girlfriends in San Francisco went to USO shows and local dances several times a week to meet servicemen. "We now felt we were doing our bit for the war effort to dance, sing, and talk with the military men," but "I suppose much of it was female teen-age gratification that we were attractive to men and could have a marvelous social life in spite of the devastation." Rita Luther got an office job in an ordnance depot miles from her Pennsylvania hometown. A friend of "the swing in-crowd" girls, she danced at juke joints with them or with GIs in town on passes. After high school Louise Holloway did office work at Tinker Air Base in Oklahoma City; the USO bused her to dances at local bases, where she met and married her husband. As sailor and avid dancer Leon Meenach found, with able-bodied men gone, "there were plenty of ladies . . . to jitterbug with" in the nightspots of Chicago, Miami, and Des Moines.[33]

Tensions over women's new freedoms also surfaced as women sought to replace drafted male musicians in swing bands. "Why not let girls play in big name bands?" asked drummer Viola Smith. Women worked with men in offices and factories, "so why not in dance bands?" Citing the ability of so many women musicians, she argued that "there are 'hep girls' who can sit in any jam session and hold their own." Indeed, the war years witnessed an increase in the number of women in male bands as well as in the formation of black and white women's units to cash in on the wartime band shortage. Women also gained more visibility in recording and in the booming club scene. Pianist Beryl Booker's all-woman record, "A Woman's Place

Eddie Durham's Sweethearts of Rhythm, Savoy Ballroom, 1943. During World War II all-girl bands found new opportunities and a lot of old prejudices. Left to right: Eleanor Parker, piano; Mildred Lee Jones, tenor sax; Edith Farthing, bass; Marion Freeman (dark dress), vocals; Selma Lee Stanley, alto sax; Alma Cortez, baritone sax; Ellariz Thompson, alto sax; Edna Williams, trumpet; Jean Starr, trumpet; Helen Scott, tenor sax; Nova Lee McGee, trumpet; Sammy Lee Jett, trombone; Jessie Turner, trombone; Lela Julius, trombone; Eddie Durham, leader, arranger, trombone. Frank Driggs Collection.

Is in the Groove," signaled the shift. As David Stowe points out, however, Smith's argument hit a nerve in the male swing fraternity and revealed the limits of its concept of democracy. With notable exceptions—trumpeter Billie Rogers and vibist Marjorie Hyams with Woody Herman, bassist Lucille Dixon with Earl Hines—bands remained gender-segregated. Despite a shortage of musicians, men were unwilling to let "off the beam fems who think they're good enough to take over from Pee Wee, Muggsy, James and all the great musicians of American music." Older male musicians could "jive better than fanatical housewives."[34]

Men remained the arbiters and creators of the "democratic" art of swing. Decorous string players might play in a recording session, but the International Spirits of Rhythm, Ina Ray Hutton's Melodears, the Prairie View Co-Eds, the Darlings of Harlem, and Eddie Durham's All-Star Girl Orchestra were seen as novelties admired more for their looks than their ability. Male musicians defined jazz as essentially male, and they thought that women lacked the aggression and power needed for swing. *Down Beat* said, "Good jazz is a hard, masculine music with a whip to it. Women like violins, and jazz deals with drums and trumpets." The magazine also noted that women had been deprived of jazz's redlight classrooms, while their "fear of looking unattractive" hindered them from blowing hot. Most damning, desire for marriage and family betrayed a lack of "male" ambition.[35]

Women musicians protested, but they were faced with an unyielding barrier because men saw them as temporary wartime annoyances. They could either be "good girls" or "play like men." The former forced them to emphasize looks over musical ability; the latter used their unexpected musical talent to nullify their sexuality. Even singer Anita O' Day's wish to don a band jacket "just like the guys," rather than a gown, led to sexual innuendo. She wanted audiences to "listen to me, not look at me. I want to be treated like another musician," not a trinket "to decorate the bandstands." Soon, however, rumors circulated "that I preferred ladies to men!" Because they defined women by their physical attributes, men also feared their potential for sexual chaos, especially on the road. Hostility toward "girl" singers, as Stowe points out with regard to the film *Orchestra Wives* (starring Glenn Miller), drew on their ambiguous role in bands—they were neither male musicians nor wives. Sexual jealousy on the part of musicians and band wives threatened to disrupt the otherwise all-male orchestras.[36]

Sexual tensions, however, could be resolved by the emphasis on women's independence as only a temporary phenomenon. Although Helen Forrest pined and Glenn Miller died before returning to Tuxedo Junction, for example, Harry James and Betty Grable achieved a new suburban family dream. When he wed Betty Grable, the war's most popular pinup girl, in 1943, James attained legendary status. Men in and out of uniform sang "I Want a Girl Just Like the Girl That Married Harry James." He exemplified a shift from cosmopolitan New York to more relaxed Los Angeles, and *Variety* noted that he refused "to work more often than absolutely necessary. He prefers lolling in Hollywood." He also preferred Betty to touring. As wartime prosperity made marriage possible for the masses, James and Grable projected togetherness by engaging as a couple in golf games, movies, and ballgames, activities that previously he had enjoyed primarily with bandmates. Grable had been a free-spirited working girl at USO canteens and bond rallies who had saved her sexuality exclusively for her man and subordinated her career to homemaking. As one columnist said, she had the "wholesome domestic habit of putting everything her husband does first." Enlisted men prized her photos because of her all-American blonde looks, which merged

"I Want a Girl Just Like the Girl Who Married Harry James." Betty Grable and Harry James at the height of their wartime popularity, mid-1940s. Frank Driggs Collection.

sexuality and the "model girlfriend, wife and finally mother." In fact, the marriage enhanced the popularity of Grable and James. As one GI wrote to James, "we ought to be mad at you for marrying the sweetheart of our camp. But it couldn't have happened to a nicer guy." When Grable became a mother, GIs sent baby gifts, the Betty Grable Fan Club became the James Family Fan Club, and servicemen wrote to her about their wives and babies. The sexpot career woman became a wife and mother, and the James-Grable marriage exemplified the dream of a suburban home to which a sexually attractive woman confined her energies. It was a dream that appealed to GIs yearning for a world that had not changed and to anxious women concerned that they might have changed too much.[37]

Double V

Although sexual tensions remained an undercurrent in the music world, it was in the area of race that musical tensions reached their height. Miller's orchestra both served the government purpose and fed popular desire for unity between home front and war effort, but it was undeniable that for most listeners his idealized home front was white. As part of the goal of including blacks in a unified, democratic war effort, the orchestra incorporated elements of black swing and even particular songs—doses of Ellington, Basie, Fats Waller, and Lionel Hampton—in its repertoire. Yet Miller's commitment to cultural pluralism, like the government's, remained largely abstract when it came to African Americans. His preference for a clean-cut version of American jive and a sanitized conception of American culture worked with the government's policy of military segregation and its decision not to disturb deeply held racial values in a time of war. As a result, Miller's AAF Orchestra was all-white rather than all-American. By playing black music, however, Miller demonstrated that racial issues were a critical part of national musical identity.[38]

During the war, racial tensions increased in the music world over the meaning of America's "home" values. Black and white radicals—and many swing players and fans—believed that swing carried a vision of democratic community rooted in ethnic and racial pluralism—the concepts that defined the war's purpose at home and abroad. The elevation of swing to national symbol allowed musical leftists and racial activists to link war and music to the fight for social democracy. They mounted benefits for Negro GIs, Russian war relief, and Spanish Civil War veterans, and many top musicians played benefits for Harlem Communist Ben Davis's election campaign. Meanwhile, John Hammond used his *Music and Rhythm* magazine to crusade against segregated music union locals and radio's exclusion of black musicians. As an army entertainment officer, he fought for integrated camp shows and more dignified bookings for black bands. Many players identified more broadly with liberalism and supported Franklin Delano Roosevelt in 1944, playing concerts sponsored by the American Labor Committee. Duke Ellington and Frank Sinatra joined Count Basie and Benny Goodman to campaign for Roosevelt, a supporter of racial and religious tolerance. Indeed, at the height of his popularity, Sinatra drew on his childhood experiences of anti-Italian prejudice to fight anti-Semitism and racial bigotry in personal appearances and in an Oscar-winning song and short film, *The House I Live In*. For many, jazz was the model of a more tolerant national identity. At the war's start, for example, the *Pittsburgh Courier*'s music columnist, Frank Bolden, held up swing's interracialism as what made "this ole land really worth fighting for." He declared that Count Basie, Cab Calloway, Johnny Hodges, Benny Goodman, and Tommy Dorsey "are all brothers of the downbeat, and that's what makes America—America."[39]

While *Down Beat* stories such as "Music Can Destroy Our Racial Bigotry" operated on an ideological level, the conflicts engendered by a segregated society's fighting a white supremacist enemy heightened the elements in swing that were favorable to racial equality. Black and white liberals in entertainment established racially integrated canteens in Hollywood, New York, and Washington, D.C., sponsored by local labor unions, the American Theater Wing, and the CIO, respectively. In defiance of USO and government policy, which decreed separate but equal facilities to avoid racial conflicts, these institutions pursued a policy of integration. Top bands like Goodman's and Basie's entertained for free, and couples could dance together regardless of race. According to Margaret Halsey, manager of New York's Stage Door Canteen, the policy was designed "to close the unseemly gap between our democratic protestations and our actual behavior." She added, "the Canteen considered that a Negro serviceman who was good enough to die for a white girl was good enough to dance with her." She employed black and white hostesses who were instructed to dance with GIs regardless of color. When several board members of Los Angeles's Hollywood Canteen tried to ban mixed dancing, a vigorous fight led by the all-black AFM Local 767 and board members Bette Davis and John Garfield won the day. Although southern whites often protested these practices, black GIs wrote Halsey that the canteens "had given them hope for the first time in their lives." The issue was not white hostesses. "What they liked was being free to choose with whom they would dance." White servicemen also wrote, saying that the canteen operators "were the kind of people they were glad to go overseas and fight for."[40]

Liberals in the music press, many of them Jewish, utilized the discrepancy between America's fighting an anti-Semitic, white supremacist enemy and the country's racial and ethnic realities to make common cause with civil rights groups and the black press in a wider attack on Jim Crow. As he had often done, John Hammond picked up demands by these groups to pressure CBS and NBC radio to integrate their studio orchestras at a time when civilian musicians were increasingly scarce. He also attacked the pervasive segregation of the AFM. *Down Beat* columnist Mike Levin, a Jew emboldened by the battle against Aryan supremacy, picked up the fight, arguing that "musicians have tried doing without Jim Crow and found it worked. There is no excuse for it in the AFM." Indeed, AFM policy was "a downright insult to what we got into khaki for, especially if we're musicians." Under editors Barry Ulanov and Leonard Feather, also liberal Jews, *Metronome* increasingly fought the racial bigotry in radio and in hotels that had denied Duke Ellington and other black musicians recognition and just recompense. At the same time, Ellington's concerts and the music business's growing racial sensitivity won his band its first number one ranking in *Down Beat.* As the *Amsterdam News* noted, "not only is it the first time Duke has thus been given just recognition in his own country, but it's also the first time any Negro band has ever won a nationwide poll in a white publication." The *New York Age* commended *Metronome's* commitment to "the fight for Negro integration in all phases of American life." *Metronome* replied that the fight against discrimination and for recognition "of the rights and achievements of the Negro in music" was an important function of "any self-respecting music magazine."[41]

The black press and African American entertainers did the most to challenge the standard definition of the home front Americans were defending. The *Pittsburgh Courier,* the Brotherhood of Sleeping Car Porters, and the NAACP launched the Double V Campaign for victory abroad and victory at home, and as part of their efforts they focused on how the treatment of black entertainers compared to the goals of the war. When Ellington's orchestra was denied hotel accommodations, the *Courier* said, "It didn't happen in Tokio or Berlin, but right here in the good American city of Moline, Illinois, U.S.A." In condemning Los Angeles ballrooms for excluding black patrons and bands after the Zoot Suit Riot of 1943, the paper charged, "Democracy and race equality are forgotten, apparently, while nine million American men—including hundreds of thousands of American Negroes—are in the service attempting to restore those ideals which Axis leaders would take from America and its people." According to a scathing article in the *Courier,* ballroom owners followed "Uncle Tom and Jim Crow, not democratic ideals."[42]

After a period of hesitation and total exclusion, the USO in late 1943 bowed to demands by black soldiers, the NAACP, and African American entertainers to establish separate troupes to entertain black GIs. While they agreed to serve in these separate units, black performers aided the Double V by objecting to entertaining segregated audiences under humiliating conditions. Vocalist-actress Lena Horne, who had appeared at Cafe Society and sung with Charlie Barnet's band and now starred in all-black movies, played a special role. As the top African American pinup she represented the home for which black soldiers were fighting. As part of that mutual obligation, she refused to "entertain the white soldiers first, then the Negroes—and often under the most degrading conditions for the soldiers and me." She also objected to the army's policy of giving German prisoners of war front-row seats at shows for black soldiers. Similarly, Calloway and Ellington refused to play the Great Lakes Training Station *unless* they could perform for

The all-black U.S. Navy Band, New York, 1943–44. Military bands, like the military in general, practiced racial segregation. Back row, left to right: Kansas Fields, drums; Charles Devonish, trumpet; Clarence Beraton, trumpet; unidentified, trumpet; Roseteele Reese, trumpet; Walter Jenkins, trumpet. Middle row, left to right: Jim McLin, guitar; unidentified, trombone; Nat Allen, trombone. Rhythm Section: Jimmie Jones, bass; Howard Johnson, piano. Front row, left to right: Oyese Bass-Mackay, tuba; Tapley Lewis, baritone sax; Charlie Frazier, tenor sax; Pete Clarke, alto sax and clarinet; Cornelius King, alto sax; Bob McRae, bandleader and singer. Frank Driggs Collection.

the eight thousand black trainees, even if separate from whites. Many other top black bands and musicians also performed in benefits for black soldiers victimized by bigotry.[43]

The discrepancy between defending democracy and perpetuating the racism in American society intensified the efforts of the black press, sympathetic black musicians, and black and white activists to forge a new national identity. The *Courier* gloried in the "Salute to Negro Troops," for instance, attended by blacks and whites—Paul Robeson, Willie Bryant, W. C. Handy, Lucky Millinder, and Eleanor Roosevelt among them—who "lashed out with stinging rebukes against discrimination, prejudice and bigotry in a land that fosters democracy." The American way of life had to be for all, argued the newspaper, "not just a chosen few." It was in this spirit that Ellington launched his Carnegie Hall concerts with "Black, Brown and Beige," which memorialized the military contributions of African Americans to the United States. In "New World a-Comin'" he held out hope for racial equality as the promise of World War II. As the *Amsterdam News* declared, "To accept half a loaf as better than none is silly in the light of what a war is being fought over."[44]

Yet the hope for a new national community was constantly belied by the increase in racial conflicts in the music world. At its simplest, black bands had greater problems getting buses for their tours than did white bands. For their one-nighters in the South, they were forced to ride segregated trains in which they encountered an endless series of racial humiliations. "Riding these Goddamn Jim Crow cars through the South were these dirty cracker conductors, we all sitting in the aisles and all of this bullshit, in a little car that's got eight seats, and here we getting on there with twenty guys and no room," recalled Billy Eckstine of his band's 1944 southern tour. The conductors would say, "'Hey, ain't no more room. You all sleep, stay in the baggage car.'" Black musicians also encountered heightened conflict as southern—and northern—white soldiers and civilians hassled black musicians and entertainers for "race mixing" in the clubs and ballrooms where they played.[45]

The mixture of hope and anger surfaced wherever black bands and entertainers made inroads. The war was a liminal period in which the dramatic movement of military and civilian populations, as well as newfound economic opportunities for blacks and the ideological challenges to racial inequality, undercut the fixed racial standards of many communities. In Los Angeles, for example, an active music scene along Central Avenue, in the heart of the growing African American neighborhood, attracted whites as well as blacks. At the same time, black bands broke into Hollywood clubs for the first time. The Nat King Cole Trio, Benny Carter, and Louis Jordan appeared at the Trocadero, Ellington headlined down the street at Ciro's, and Art Tatum and Coleman Hawkins played The Streets of Paris on Hollywood Boulevard. Meanwhile, Benny Carter employed white musicians in his band and also witnessed the loosening of racial norms in the rise of interracial dancing at Hollywood's Swing Club in 1942 and the influx of black and Mexican youths eager to dance wherever hot bands played.[46]

While Carter saw signs of hope, he also witnessed heightened racial tensions. Competition over jobs and housing, added to differences in cultural mores, sowed the seeds of racial conflict. The music world was the locus of white fears about interracial sex. Los Angeles's Zoot Suit Riot of 1943 grew out of racial and sexual tensions between white sailors and Mexican American youths aggressively displaying themselves, battling for power and rights to women on the street. Each group complained that the other disrespected the young women of their race. That young *pachucos* wove a rebellious subculture around hot music and a clothing style that mocked the restrictions of wartime sacrifice only added to the anger of the sailors, who focused on home-front women whose sexuality would be liberated when the sailors went off to war. The zoot suiters stood for the rapacious, unpatriotic darker males who would then grab their women and overturn the social order. After the riot, tensions increased all over southern California. Ballrooms and clubs that had employed black bands and permitted Mexican and black youths now feared that race-mixing would lead to rioting. They adopted white-only policies.[47]

It was in swing's capital, however, that racial conflict came to a head. During the war, southern and northern white GIs saw New York City's tradition of racial mixing—and the new generation of young black hipsters—as threats to their conception of white supremacy. The hipsters, who dressed in flashy zoots, spoke hip jive, and smoked marijuana, flocked to Harlem's Savoy Ballroom. In what many Harlemites took as a racial insult, however, civilian and military authorities closed the Savoy in June 1943 because white servicemen had contracted venereal diseases from prostitutes working there. "Harlem," observed Malcolm X, "said the real reason was to stop Negroes from dancing with white women." In fact, Walter White, president of the NAACP, protested that the closing occurred because "the management had consistently refused to stop mixed dancing." The black press also fought the closing, charging that "the cult of Southernism" and the fear of "interracial socializing" had ruined a ballroom that had "failed to make social jimcrow a prerequisite for their pattern of entertainment." Justice Cornelius O'Leary, who signed the order, found no evidence of prostitution. Conversely, the black press found even more unpunished prostitution in downtown clubs and halls. As *Newsweek* pointed out, the police had been trying to close the Savoy for a year and a half "on the theory that this would remove a potential source of race trouble." Ironically, Harlemites considered the closing of the ballroom one more insult and a contributing cause of the riot of 1943, which occurred two months later.[48]

The fear of black men cavorting with white women in places of amusement also infected Fifty-second Street as black swing fans—some in zoot suits—and white southern servicemen confronted each other in "the Street's" swing clubs. In a series of articles for the *Amsterdam News* in the summer of 1944, Abe Hill called Fifty-second Street "New York's Real 'Melting Pot,'" where "customers literally check their racial identity along with their hats and coats as they enter." Was this, he wondered, the sign of "a new social order?" Not quite, since groups of white GIs attacked black musicians numerous times that summer. The large brawls led club operators to fear another race riot. For many, Fifty-second Street symbolized the hopes of a new interracial order; for others, this interracialism proved that the war had undermined white supremacy. The issue was interracial sex, especially anger at black men socializing with white women. Not only did white southerners encounter black musicians being lionized, they also ran into the black pimps and addicts attracted by the music. Their preference for white women challenged white supremacy and sexual purity. Some black pimps flaunted their white women, offending not only whites but also black middle-class defenders of the Double V who feared that zoot-suited lowlifes would ruin the scene for all black people. To prevent violence, the police tried to bar all blacks from the White Rose Bar on Sixth Avenue, around the corner from Fifty-second Street. When the club's owners resisted, the police began to harass pimps, prostitutes, and drug dealers of both races. Foreshadowing postwar policy, the authorities attacked drugs to maintain sexual and racial order in the music world. Still, while mixed couples and zoot-suited black men continued to earn abuse from the authorities, mixing—in the audience and onstage—had won the day.[49]

Caught in the upsurge of possibilities for racial equality and in the concomitant reaction, younger black musicians—and a number of white ones—exhibited much greater militance in matters of segregation and race by 1943. Increasingly, they viewed American society as hypocritical. Having ridden segregated trains in the South, fought with white sailors on Fifty-second Street, and heard and read stories of black soldiers who were denied their rights, many young black musicians became convinced that idealized depictions of American life were a sham. In many ways, the war brought black musicians face to face with the American dilemma and engendered in them a fierce determination to defy white supremacy. This militant stance undergirded the bebop revolution, which simmered during the war and then exploded like a bombshell once the conflict came to a close.

Glenn Miller Day

As the realities of war undercut dreams of perfect racial and gender unity on the home front, the epitome of American culture—the swing band—began to lose its energy. Sweet music enjoyed an upsurge, and the highly organized war effort altered swing. In a total war dominated by large-scale bureaucracy and military hierarchy, swing was no longer an outsider to the establishment. Following the Miller orchestra's lead, other bands became more organized, tightly arranged and sentimental, adding string sections for the more romantic songs. There was even less room for individual invention. The result was a subtle taming of the musical and utopian vision of swing. Many of Miller's AAF musicians grew resentful of his demand for military authority and discipline. Other musicians who found the military and the growing regimentation of life stifling turned to more spontaneous traditional jazz for improvisatory freedom. As one observed, "The individuality of a hot musician became a liability when orchestrators, who are the draftsmen for bands of twenty or thirty men," took over. Another group of rebels, the black musicians who were pioneering bebop, challenged the stilted, sweet, and "popular" nature of an increasingly "white" sound. In jazz, fans and creators were on the verge of revolt. Although Glenn Miller and his AAF Orchestra sought to define the American way of life, this vision of the home front was a matter of much contention.[50]

Yet Miller's music lived on, rooted in personal memories of wartime experiences and the collective memory of sacrifice and national unity. Conveying hopes for personal freedom, ethnic assimilation, and security, Miller's band symbolized the American dream of freer lives made possible by American culture. His death, moreover, elevated his personal sacrifice to mythic status. It became a metaphor for the lost lives and interrupted careers of GIs and all those affected by the war, including the many women who, like Mrs. Miller, waited for husbands or boyfriends who never returned. In fact, a year after he disappeared many theaters observed "Glenn Miller Day," the first such tribute ever accorded a bandleader. Swing remained a symbol of victory too. After Miller's death the band performed a concert for forty thousand Allied troops in Nuremberg Stadium on 1 July 1945, marking a victory over Hitler's belief that swing was a decadent example of a "mongrelized" society and making a statement about the personal and musical freedom accorded citizens of a nation devoted to cultural pluralism. At the National Press Club in Washington, moreover, the nation's highest political and military officials saluted Miller. After the opening bars of "Moonlight Serenade," President Truman and Generals Dwight Eisenhower and Hap Arnold led the assembled dignitaries in a standing ovation for a man who "felt an intense obligation to serve his country" and "made the supreme sacrifice."[51]

Critic George Simon declared that for GIs Miller's band was "the greatest gift from home they'd known in all their Army days, a living symbol of what America meant to them, of what they were fighting for." A GI correspondent agreed. Listening to a memorial broadcast of "Moonlight Serenade" in an army recreation center in Britain, Mike Levin "saw men openly crying." The music was "tied up with individual memories, girls, hopes, schools. It [was] a tangible tie to what we [were] fighting to get back to."

But the message was ambiguous. "We haven't forgotten, nor can we ever. You owe these guys when they get back, not so much money or gadgets, but a shot at the way of life that many of them have been dreaming about."[52]

Many soldiers expected a national commitment, through a GI Bill, to their personal enjoyment of life in the future. For soldier boys and the girls they left behind, the attempt to capture and define the American way of life would dominate the late 1940s. But the dream of enjoying the American way of life was illusory. For many it represented the fulfillment of personal dreams and family security away from public life. For young ethnic men and women it meant opportunities to have a place in American life. For many blacks it meant "victory at home" or rejection of American society as racially restrictive. As *Down Beat* asked in reference to continuing racism, "How can we hope for one world in peace, when we fail to check the spread of the same insidious poison within our own vaunted civilization?" These conflicting themes would shape the postwar jazz scene, which became a battle for America's musical soul at the very time the nation embarked on its sentimental journey home.[53]

8

The War in Jazz

These days the music business is just one big headache. Just when everyone is supposed to be relaxing and enjoying life and the pursuit of happiness again, along comes a lot of trouble and everything comes out all screwed up.—*Down Beat*

Yet, within our own ranks, we snarl at each other like a pack of derelict hounds. Isn't it about time we tried to be that big, happy, democratic family we would have the rest of the world believe we are?—Letter to *Down Beat*

In 1946, director Orson Welles emceed an hour-long concert on ABC radio featuring some of the winners of *Esquire*'s annual swing poll. The high point in a series that started in 1943, the "All-American Concert" showcased the orchestras of Duke Ellington and Woody Herman and the Nat King Cole Trio. "Esky" winners also recorded together on Commodore Records and were featured in *Esquire's Jazz Book*. For his part, Welles delivered "a sensitive tribute to jazz" and received an Esky for his radio shows honoring traditional jazz musicians. Swing, traditional jazz, and the most modern jazz—bebop—all found a place at the concert and in the book; so did black and white musicians. The emphasis on jazz's interracial nature was no accident. Created by exiled Belgian jazz critic and antifascist Robert Goffin, jazz critic and racial liberal Leonard Feather, and *Esquire* editor Arnold Gingrich, the poll emerged during World War II as a statement of confidence in America's commitment to musical and racial democracy in a war against Fascism. In an effort to fulfill the conflict's pluralist goals, the poll relied on swing critics and past awardees to choose the winners from a racially open field, while *Esquire's Jazz Book* and the concert raised money for the Navy League and the war loan drive.

This belief in a united jazz world with stable roots in American culture did not long outlast the war. The reaction to *Esquire's* polls shows the fragmentation in swing that occurred soon after the cessation of hostilities. Initial response was positive. The *Amsterdam News* ran a four-column banner: "20 of 26 Winning Musicians in *Esquire* Band Are Negroes." Yet resentment quickly grew. *The Jazz Record,* one of many traditional jazz magazines, attacked the results as a "foul and dismal smirch" on "our reputation as critics" because most white critics voted for black modernists. "If this isn't inverted Jim Crow, what on earth is?" Other revivalists attacked swing and bop as commercial perversions of hot jazz and lambasted the board's preference for the "jump boys" over "Dixieland or New Orleans . . . the music that is real, that is jazz." As lines hardened, modernist Leonard Feather called foes "Moldy Figs" and charged that "just as the fascists tend to divide group against group and distinguish between Negroes, Jews, Italians and 'real Americans,' so do the moldy figs try to categorize New Orleans, Chicago, swing music and 'the real jazz.'" When Eddie Condon took over *Esquire's Jazz Book* in 1947 and used it to promote his white Dixielanders, past poll winners refused to participate, and eighteen of twenty critics resigned. "It was," noted a disappointed Feather, "a melancholy ending to a glorious four-year ride."[1]

Esquire's Jazz Book fell victim to an unprecedented war in jazz that destroyed the harmony among musicians and the faith that swing represented American culture. As swing bands declined in the late 1940s, the music world fragmented into warring cults, each portraying itself as the one true jazz. The partisan rancor between revivalists who sought more collective improvisation in small combos and boppers who sought greater individual freedom in a harmonically and rhythmically complex modern mode made the postwar period the most tumultuous era in American popular music. Usually ignored is that both forms of music arose during World War II, shared a common origin and foe in swing, and wove their own separate fabrics out of the common threads of swing culture. Both rejected swing as commercialized jazz and attempted instead to elaborate new racial and cultural identities. The battle between past and future, modern and traditional, expressed the unraveling of a common tradition and the conflict and anxiety that emerged in the late 1940s.[2]

The King Is Dead

The increasing fragmentation of the postwar music world followed the dramatic decline of swing bands soon after World War II. After a burst of postwar exuberance by big bands, *Metronome* noted in October 1946 that "Goodman and swing are no longer considered monopolistically synonymous by the public." Soon the journal declared, "The King Is Dead," as his and other top swing bands broke up. By December Woody Herman, Harry James, Tommy Dorsey, Ina Ray Hutton, Jack Teagarden, Benny Carter, and Les Brown had lost their bands. They were followed shortly thereafter by Cab Calloway, Charlie Barnet, Ray Bauduc, Boyd Raeburn, and Artie Shaw. Only a year earlier Woody Herman had swept the swing polls and been ranked by *Metronome* "with the half-dozen greatest bands of jazz." In what *Newsweek* called "the biggest depression the band business had ever known," the growing funeral parade of bands sent shock waves through the music world. Gloom descended. "The band business looks like it is finished," observed a booking executive. "It will never again attain the prominence and earning capacity it enjoyed pre-war."[3]

The end of so many top orchestras ran counter to people's hopes for the postwar music scene. With victory near, swing journals had looked forward to a great future. Service bands such as Glenn Miller's had helped export American swing to the world. Wherever American troops had been stationed, interest in a music associated with American democracy and prosperity was high. Fans worldwide besieged American GIs for information about the music and asked them to take part in jam sessions. *Down Beat* found a clear message: "The world has been introduced to Americans and American music as never before. If we proceed fairly and diplomatically, we and everyone else will profit." Things looked good at home too. During the war free-spending GIs and defense workers had pushed bands and amusements to record prosperity. More people than ever before were interested in hot music, and as a result musicians enjoyed high salaries. *Down Beat* predicted that returning GIs would boost the swing market, that service bands would flourish at home, and that 26,000 music industry jobs would employ returning servicemen. "Everyone hoped it would be a bright, new world . . . insofar as music is concerned. We predicted the boys would come home, all of them with a new or renewed interest in music, the musicians with broader visions and fresh ideas, inspired by contact with the culture of other lands."[4]

Pessimism quickly replaced optimism. Bands' fees dropped precipitously from their wartime high, ballrooms closed or ran only on weekends, and swing bands no longer drew, on tour or in the clubs of Harlem and Fifty-second Street. As *Variety* observed, gloom spread because the "band industry didn't immediately begin to fulfill the prophecies of a tremendous boom as soon as the Japs had capitulated." Equally gloomily, *Metronome* held that the downturn doomed the dream of swing as a truly democratic American art form. "Who ever believed that the cessation of hostilities would also mean the close of another great battle, the one waged to make jazz acceptable to everybody?" But now the orchestra world believed, as Charlie Barnet put it, that "the band business is in a slump and getting worse." In swing the conversion from war to peace was fraught with conflict and anxiety. The postwar depression that so many had feared became a reality in the band business; bright hopes turned dark. *Down Beat* concluded, "The war is over, the buggy ride done."[5]

As Americans journeyed home, a number of factors led to swing's sorry fate. The draft had created a demand for scarce musicians at the same time that their touring expenses rose. Despite the doubling and tripling of side-men's salaries, leaders added extra men and even whole sections. They passed these costs—in the form of higher guarantee prices—on to hotels and ballrooms, which easily raised ticket prices during the war's flush times. A wartime federal amusement tax of 20 percent also boosted ticket rates. When price controls came off in 1946, living costs jumped, and returning veterans and their families could no longer afford the price of going out. Promoters of one-nighters, the backbone of the industry, found themselves in a bind. Proven stars such as Benny Goodman still demanded a $4,000 guarantee while drawing only 750 people. As a result, ballroom operators blamed bandleaders for forcing them to raise admission prices too high and in many cases to close. Bandleaders argued that promoters were unreasonable: "We aren't getting enough money to meet our payrolls—and if we don't pay the prices, we can't get sidemen, any sidemen, let alone good ones." Meanwhile, musicians complained that they could not travel for less than $125 a week, given the high costs of room and board. *Down Beat* warned that big bands were too big and urged a cut from fifteen or twenty members to twelve to reduce the price structure of the entire business. This only added to the anxiety. As Buddy Rich noted, "You can't do it—people are too accustomed to big bands on the stand—they'll feel cheated with anything less."[6]

While band outlets continued to dry up, sidemen and new bands glutted the market. Eager to achieve economic and artistic independence, many sidemen started their own bands in 1945, including Johnny Bothwell, Corky Corcoran, Bill Harris, Chubby Jackson, Tommy Pederson, Buddy Rich, Willie Smith, Charlie Ventura, Earl Warren, and Trummy Young. Several service bands, notably those of Sam Donahue and Glenn Miller, remained intact and entered the competition after demobilization, while former GI bandsmen returned to their old jobs. There was now a good deal of confusion. Woody Herman noted that the draft had caused such a high rate of turnover that at least 108 men could reclaim their jobs in his fifteen-man band. According to *Metronome,* ex-servicemen and young musicians congregated in the big cities waiting for new bands to form. Having had their lives disrupted by war, they now expected their just rewards. Oversupply and the scaling back of big bands to smaller combos, however, made work scarce and paychecks "a mere shadow of previous stratospheric levels." Some players went into the radio and movie studios, but for most, a vibrant future seemed unlikely.[7]

Although economics played an important role in the decline of the big band industry, the underlying cause lay in the massive generational change under way in swing's core audience. "They, too, are going through a reconversion period," noted *Variety;* "the finding of jobs and attention to numerous other details of returning to civvies now occupies all their attention." Having been forced to put off starting families during the depression and the war, the older swing generation returned home with little interest in going out. The depression and the war had demanded that they pull together, but once the crises were over, they began to pursue personal dreams and desires. They wanted to resume their lives, start or re-cement families, go to school on the GI Bill, find jobs and places to live. Amid postwar inflation and social disruption, this could be exhilarating, but also fraught with anxiety. "Swing and pessimism don't mix," noted bandleader Ray McKinley, and audiences had much to be pessimistic about. Unemployment and inflation made it hard to do the simple things that GIs had dreamed about; they certainly had little time or money to do these things *and* go dancing. Their youth already cut short, they had to grow up in a hurry. For them, adulthood meant starting and supporting families. In its core audience, thus, the demand for swing fell.[8]

In seeking to "buy this dream," moreover, the war generation sought to realize the lifestyle depicted in wartime popular songs—one that revolved around personal consumption, security, and family, removed from bureaucratic institutions. The bands of Glenn Miller and Harry James had responded to these dreams by becoming larger, more tightly arranged, and much more sentimental during the war. Separated by war, audiences demanded ballads of loneliness and longing at the same time they yearned for depictions of a perfectly ordered world to be achieved afterward. Similarly, singers attained new stature during and after the war as they personalized the hopes and longings launched by the conflict: of waiting, of a perfect domestic existence unchanged by time, of life beginning again for a generation long put on hold. Newly prominent female vocalists represented the girls left behind, new girls to be found, the civilization for which the boys were fighting. Male singers such as Sinatra, who in many cases were married with children, were idolized by young women on the home front. This adulation expressed the desire for romance and family that was denied by the war but would be capable of fulfillment once the emergency was over. Between 1944 and 1947, Helen Forrest and Dick Haymes, both exiles from James's orchestra, enacted this private romantic quest on their radio show and in million-selling records such as "I'm Always Chasing Rainbows," "Oh, What It Seemed to Be," "It Had to Be You," "Buy That Dream," "Long Ago and Far Away," and of course, "Together." When the war ended the depression in 1943, young men and women had begun to marry in record numbers. As they began families they established a trend that continued after the war. In this atmosphere, singers, not big swing bands, dominated the music business as they gave expression to heightened individual dreams.[9]

The strike by the American Federation of Musicians against the record companies between 1942 and 1944 fueled the trend toward vocalists. In an attempt to counter mechanized music's displacement of live musicians in many places of amusement, AFM president James C. Petrillo barred bands from recording. While bands were banned from recording, vocalists—who were not unionized—could do so at will. Until 1942 instrumentalists had controlled the shape and direction of the bands while singers earned less than the average sideman. They had to put up with songs arranged for the players and were allowed to sing the choruses of two songs per set. Like all big band players, they were part of the larger team, and their fortunes rose or fell with those of the group. As a result of the strike, singers left the bands to perform as solo attractions and earn the big money and fame formerly denied them. When Frank Sinatra left Tommy Dorsey's orchestra in 1942, singers began their ascendancy. In 1943 Sinatra stole the show from the Benny Goodman Orchestra at the New York Paramount Theater as bobby-soxers screamed for "the Voice" as they used to do for the band. Whereas Harry James's orchestra remained the top record seller through the first half of 1943 on the strength of his old discs, Sinatra took over by the middle of that year, when his records "couldn't be made fast enough." By the time bands resumed recording in 1944, tastes had changed.[10]

By the end of the war, vocalists were featured on radio programs sponsored by the same cigarette companies that had once supported bands. Radio had played a central role in the entire big band industry, and its abandonment of live orchestras proved ruinous. Having risen out of the Great Depression partly on the back of swing, radio—ever sensitive to audience ratings and advertising rates—now cut back sharply on big bands because of audiences' lack of interest. "We've had bad luck with musical shows," noted the head of CBS's popular music division, "from both the standpoint of ratings and potential sales." In 1945, in fact, the major networks dropped twelve big bands from their regular shows. Hurt by inflation, radio executives replaced big bands with disc jockeys and singers. Not only were they cheaper, but singers now outdrew bands. Advertisers—and the radio stations dependent on them—could not resist. As *Metronome* noted, "When you want popular music at CBS now, you turn to singers and singers alone." By 1947, CBS's top music shows featured only white vocalists such as Frank Sinatra and Dinah Shore or singing bandleaders such as Vaughn Monroe. Networks also dropped sustaining programs such as *Mildred Bailey and Company,* which featured the top swing players regardless of race and a house band that played new symphonic and jazz works, and Raymond Scott's *Jazz Laboratory,* which used a mixed band and featured modern jazz. As *Metronome* lamented, the picture was "a shocking return to 1925 radio, radio at its beginning."[11]

While swing bands declined, sweet bands that played endless strings of romantic ballads remained popular. With the boys home, explained Ray McKinley, "the man-hunt is on afresh on the biggest scale ever," and "it is the girl who decides where to go dancing." Young women wanted "an actual assist from Beneke's violins or Vaughn's hairy-chested vocals." The music was keyed to what men and women seemed most eager to do: marry and create families. As they pursued these private dreams, meanwhile, audiences wanted quiet, soothing sounds, as if loud brass were a jarring intrusion by the public world from which they sought release. They stayed away "in droves from the louder and brassier combinations" but continued to patronize bands that played melody and relegated "most of the screaming riff tunes to the back of their books." Charlie Barnet blamed his band's collapse on "loud brass and race horse tempos," and he and other leaders learned that "we must play tamer music too. . . . I now know we must forget about the few screaming fans who line up against the bandstand and applaud flag-wavers." Arrangements should stress easy dance tempos. "'Tension music' was O.K. during the war. Now we're done with it." Indeed, promoters pleaded for softer music. Whenever Hal McIntyre played college proms in 1948, for example, the bookers "specif[ied] that no loud music [should] be played, only one jump tune to a set." After the jangled nerves of wartime, "the biggest sellers [were] sweet."[12]

As a result of these dramatic changes, the band business plunged into a postwar recession from which swing never recovered. According to music critic Charles Miller, writing in 1947, at one time millions of people "could go to the nearest nightclub or juke box and hear big, powerful dance bands playing real jazz." Bop and Dixieland flourished, but in the absence of a common tradition, players faced economic and musical insecurity. Debates about the nature of real jazz were more than arcane; in the absence of secure careers, the success of one's jazz style was a matter of economic survival. As traditional clarinetist Bob Wilber put it, players went from a "feeling of optimism" to despair. Many attacked the commercialization of music, but it had meant, he noted, that "jazz was finally being accepted as the great American art form" and that swing players were receiving "recognition for doing what they did best." After the war, though, "the music profession changed, turning into a freelance life with everybody competing, everybody scrambling around to put together a living." Acrimony was rife. Forced to break up his band in 1947, Cab Calloway changed from someone who grossed $200,000 a year "to someone who couldn't get a booking." He became angry when he saw white bands being booked into the big rooms when all he could get "was some small hotel rooms and nightclubs." Everyone in the business, *Down Beat* noted, "ha[d] a gripe" against everyone else for causing the slump. A bitter Charlie Barnet blamed boppers, who "didn't want to play with anyone but their fellow cultists," for destroying "the great fellowship that had previously existed among all jazz musicians." Demoralized, Coleman Hawkins and Lester Young turned to drink, Artie Shaw and Benny Goodman to shrinks. "The musicians were so good," observed trumpeter Red Rodney, "yet we were so screwed up. It was a period of being very bugged. Why, I'll never know, but we were."[13]

Looking Backward

As swing lost energy, traditional New Orleans and Chicago jazz reemerged as one reaction to the overly arranged world symbolized by wartime big bands. As Eric Hobsbawm noted, "trad" was "the first large-scale revolt within the framework of popular music against art as mass production."

The traditional revival in full swing. Bunk Johnson and his New Orleans Jazz Band, Stuyvesant Casino, New York, 1945. Left to right: Jim Robinson, trombone; Baby Dodds, drums; Bunk Johnson, trumpet; Lawrence Marrero, banjo; George Lewis, clarinet; Alton Purnell, piano; Slow Drag Pavageau, bass. Frank Driggs Collection.

Starting in the late 1930s, radical critics, collectors, and fans argued that older jazz was the authentic voice of individual freedom, the true expression of democracy. Initially a minor note in the swing surge, the revival formed part of the Popular Front's search for the people's musical culture in the 1930s. For many radical critics, hot jazz—the pure, albeit forgotten, music of a preindustrial southern black culture—was superior to the music of the failed capitalist world, and they sought to challenge arranged swing by resurrecting the authentic jazz styles of New Orleans and Chicago. In addition, depression-era record collectors looked for the pure sounds of traditional jazz, formed clubs, and read discographical newsletters and George Hoefer's "Hot Box" column in *Down Beat*. In the 1930s, revivalists actively promoted the idea of swing as democracy but believed that swing musicians and popular bands had become slaves to New York–style arrangements and commercial success. Most, like John Hammond and the contributors to *Jazzmen*, believed in reconciling the freedom of the past with the modern band and hoped to spur the big bands to greater cultural authenticity.[14]

By 1943, the traditional revival emerged as a real opponent of swing. Emboldened by swing's flagging during the war, a core of critics and traditional fans who had lost faith in swing's ability to embrace true jazz founded small opposition sheets such as New York's *The Record Changer* and *The Jazz Record* and began inundating the established swing press with letters on the superiority of spontaneous jazz. *The Jazz Record,* begun in 1943 by white blues pianist Art Hodes and leftist critic Dale Curran, for example, was part of the Greenwich Village radical scene. Hodes, who edited *The Record* in his Village apartment, drew support from the many radical writers and fans who lived in the area. He described his tastes in populist terms. "My music?" asked Hodes. "It's people's music. It never had a color to distinguish it"; it derived from "the insides of a downtrodden race." Contributors "were to the left of the left." Politically, he noted, "I was a working man . . . and I was going to vote Democrat every time I could." Until the red scare's onset in 1947, he played for Popular Front groups because they accepted his racially mixed bands. Like other small jazz magazines, *The Jazz Record* fought to keep "true" jazz alive, informed readers about where to hear traditional jazz, and helped them locate old discs. The magazine also attacked New York as the epitome of commerce and glorified the Chicago of Hodes's youth, where jazz musicians had played "for kicks," without recognizing any irony in Hodes's New York address. According to this view, New York's commercialization of jazz also had led to the impoverishment of the music's original black creators. Blues and jazz artists such as Montana Taylor, noted contributor Rudi Blesh, "who gave the world the most significant and challenging musical development of this century," were "beaten down into oblivion," yet still fought "against the dollar sign that took the place of the clef sign in music." Interviews resuscitated "true jazz" players for "a new generation—unspoiled by commercial music."[15]

Despite the revival's disdain, swing's creation of a mass jazz audience established the basis for an alternative scene in New York. Fans patronized concerts and clubs, as well as specialized record shops such as Milt Gabler's Commodore Music Shop and Stephen Smith's Hot Record Exchange, and demanded reissues of older records. "By the time this war is won," Hodes declared in the first issue of *The Jazz Record,* "there can be such a great number of jazz lovers and collectors that the recording companies will have to take our desires into consideration." Record companies responded because the AFM recording ban had dried up sources of new material. To fill the vacuum, Decca hired Gabler, who supervised Commodore Records's reissues, to oversee its classic jazz plans. With the majors now on board, New Orleans and Chicago greats were heard once again on record.[16]

The hot music cult's most notable achievement, however, was the resurrection of Bunk Johnson. The impoverished trumpeter from New Orleans's heyday was discovered working in the Louisiana rice fields by Pittsburgh jazz enthusiast William Russell. With the aid of Harry Bridges, president of the International Longshoreman's Union, and Orson Welles (both leftists and traditional jazz fans), critics such as Rudi Blesh and Eugene Williams, and students from the University of California at Berkeley and Stanford University, Johnson came to San Francisco in 1943 to join Papa Mutt Carey, Kid Ory, Wad Whaley, and Bertha Gonsoulin for what *Time* called "the most historic jam session in the annals of jazz." In 1945, Bunk and his New Orleans stalwarts played New York's run-down Stuyvesant Casino, far from "Town Hall or Carnegie Hall trappings." Blesh declared that Bunk's music "speaks ever so quietly something that we need very much to hear amidst the roar of machinery and the clamors of war or armed peace." Blesh hoped that this "full flowering of jazz in its purest form" would rejuvenate even "sophisticated Sugar Hill and Lenox Avenue" with a voice from the "country church" and the "country blues." In fact, the traditional music critic and partisan maintained that Bunk's New York success heralded a new era of freedom. Both white and black listeners would "find their own chains miraculously dropping away in this vibrant air that all may breathe."[17]

"It was the war itself that was the decisive factor in bringing about the recognition for jazz," noted Max Kaminsky, because it enabled musicians dissatisfied with big bands to join the revival. The draft took young musicians, leaving room for older players. The taxation of entertainment and dancing led clubs to hire bands for listening only; concert venues opened up at the same time. Older black New Orleans players such as Bunk, Baby Dodds, Wilbur de Paris, and Sidney Bechet joined black Chicagoans Albert Nicholas and Jimmy Noone, as well as older white Chicagoans such as Hodes, Mezz Mezzrow, and Eddie Condon, to play as the revival hit full steam. Others, such as Bud Freeman, Dave Tough, George Wettling, Kaminsky, and others joined small combos as a revolt against the regimentation of the big units. Kaminsky had enjoyed the small "ad-lib jazz" units in the big bands—Goodman's Trio, Shaw's Gramercy 5, Tommy Dorsey's Clambake 7—that had been "the secret of the big band's success." Pulling the combo out of the big band, these musicians sought creativity and spontaneity in the musical forms of their youth.

Significantly, New York was the center of the revival, as new clubs in the Village and on Fifty-second Street—Nick's, Condon's, Jimmy Ryan's—joined Cafe Society and the Village Vanguard in hosting interracial jams and "jazz" bands for appreciative fans. When a soloist played, Kaminsky noted, "You could *feel* them listening." Thanks to Eddie Condon's Town Hall Concerts, begun in 1942 and broadcast via network and Armed Forces radio, traditional jazz reached wider audiences with its "unadulterated hot music, most of it unrehearsed and improvised," in which "every man is expected to be an accomplished soloist" and an individualist even in dress. Disdaining the flashy uniforms in which most bandleaders delighted, the Town Hall crowd saw the uniform as "a badge of shame," a sign that "the wearer is not a free-lance artist but merely a rule-of-thumb workman."[18]

Younger middle-class white rebels, working-class radicals, and a small coterie of male college students were attracted to the revival by postwar jazz autobiographies glorifying the freewheeling days of the 1920s when the jazz revolt first flowered and young men seemingly had fewer restrictions on their lives. Mezz Mezzrow, Hoagy Carmichael, Eddie Condon, and Wingy Manone elaborated the themes first enunciated in Dorothy Baker's popular novel *Young Man with a Horn*. In these autobiographies, working-class and déclassé white young men, committed to pure black jazz, remain true to their principles or, like Baker's hero Rick Martin, modeled on Bix Beiderbecke, give in to the blandishments of big bands and glamorous women, exchange their ideals for commercial success, and die tragically. The memoirs also venerated Bix as a doomed genius in a corrupt world. The heroic male musicians were outsiders committed to art and free expression. "We were the keepers of the faith, the purists, the cats who stayed with it," declared Mezzrow in his influential memoir. "The others were out to make money, not music." As idealists in revolt against organized musical corruption, traditional fans and players entered the postwar era determined to have their day.[19]

Having built an audience and an ideology throughout the war, the revival peaked in the late 1940s. By 1947, the war in jazz reached a fever pitch. Many former swing musicians returned to hot jazz, most notably Louis Armstrong, who disbanded his big band in 1948 and toured with his New Orleans All-Stars. Yet the bright future anticipated by revivalists was increasingly embattled. New opponents appeared: young black boppers and white progressives, whose music seemed to the traditional jazz fans to be merely outgrowths of commercial swing. In this atmosphere, the revival grew increasingly rigid. This rigidity was encouraged as the red scare dawned, brought on by the collapse of the Popular Front, the growing leftist sectarianism, and the deepening alienation of leftists from modern American political and cultural life. In a parallel to events in the USSR, many Communists criticized modern jazz as bourgeois formalism, the opposite of a people's music. Hardly impartial, modernists such as Leonard Feather charged that "progressive forces" in the United States had grown rigid and reactionary in their musical tastes, a charge echoed by Lionel Trilling. More work needs to be done on the jazz critics who waged this war, but it is clear that many revivalists, most notably Rudi Blesh and Art Hodes, saw all developments after "pure" New Orleans jazz or early Chicago as corruptions. Even Ellington was said to have too much European technique, leading to a "de-Africanization" of jazz. The regulated swing solo, meanwhile, represented "vanity" and "indulgence." Some bands, such as Lu Waters's Yerba Buena band in San Francisco, another traditional stronghold, took up the banjo and tuba of the original New Orleans style. Ultimately, traditional jazz became a cry against the modern world in favor of a pure but static past.[20]

Traditional critics and collectors had elevated jazz's social meaning and its "significance as an art form," noted Kaminsky, but "snuffed the life out of it." He and other white players resented the purist view that New Orleans musicians and practices were sacrosanct. Even Bunk "couldn't understand why the jazz fans wanted him to play all those old New Orleans tunes from 40 years ago!" said Bob Wilber. Young white players had other problems: Fans preferred the original fathers to their aspiring sons. As Kaminsky noted, "A whole school of amateur critics arose to preach a sort of Negro mystique." As with The Jazz Record's response to the Esquire poll, charges of "Crow Jim" soon surfaced. Most disturbing, young black musicians and fans rejected the revivalists' attempts to promote older jazz. Perhaps these internal divisions explain the ferocity with which revivalists attacked bop, which threatened to surpass swing in popularity after the war. For revivalists, bop seemed merely an extension of soulless swing, filled with technical tricks, a selling out of traditional culture. As heirs of the Popular Front and radical New Deal sensibilities, revivalists believed that only an organic folk jazz could act as a cry of protest. This growing dogmatism signaled the Left's inability to affect the modern world or to capture a mass public in the new Cold War atmosphere, while the desire among collectors and fans for the older styles suggested that they had lost faith in the future. Arguing that black music was the opposite of European technique and remained encapsulated in only one form, revivalists held that modern black music was not black enough. No wonder younger boppers spurned them. Cut off from new music, unable to pass down a living tradition to younger white and black musicians, the traditional revival lost touch with a living community of cultural innovation or resistance. The future belonged to the boppers.[21]

Diz and Bird: John Birks "Dizzy" Gillespie (right) and Charlie "Yardbird" Parker (left), Town Hall, New York City, 1945. Modern jazz for a modern world. Note the integrated audience. Frank Driggs Collection.

Things to Come

In 1946 a young veteran of many black swing bands recorded "Things to Come," a tune that presaged a new era in jazz. Like other bebop melodies, it was filled with dissonance and extended solo lines and was played at a frenetic pace. Sounding shockingly new at the war's end, bop had actually "emerged from the war years," observed Dizzy Gillespie, "and it reflected those times in the music. Fast and furious, with the chord changes going this way and that, it might've looked and sounded like bedlam, but it wasn't." As the war and the recording ban ended, a widespread public had the opportunity to hear bebop for the first time. Many older swing players and fans, along with traditionalists, saw it as an attack—a musical and so-cial revolution. Ralph Ellison declared that bop "was itself a texture of frag-ments, repetitive, nervous, not fully formed; its melodic lines underground, secret and taunting; its riffs jeering—Salt Peanuts! Salt Peanuts!" Equally important, Ellison and Gillespie saw bop as part of a new racial assert-iveness, a desire to break from the secondary role of black music and musicians. "Musically," declared Dizzy, we were changing the way that we spoke, to reflect the way that we felt."[22]

Given bebop's role as the major jazz innovation of the 1940s, it was, noted Ellison, "a momentous modulation into a new musical sensibility; in brief, a revolution in culture." It was also an evolution among younger black swing players that emerged during the war years and then spread to other black musicians and to younger white players when the conflict came to a close. As saxophonist Dexter Gordon observed, "It was wartime and people were moving back and forth all over the United States and constantly traveling—armies, war jobs, defense jobs. It was a time of change, and the music was reflecting this. And we were putting our voice into what we thought was about to be the thing." Stimulated by the rise in cultural consciousness among blacks during World War II, bop presaged a racial and generational revolt for the postwar world. On all fronts, the war magnified the awareness among young blacks of their secondary social and economic status in the new national culture symbolized by Glenn Miller's all-white, all-American AAF Orchestra. Fighting a racist foe with a segregated army underlined the hypocrisy of national ideals of unity and stimulated greater African American militancy.[23]

In this context, the new music created by these alienated musicians was more than a technical innovation in form. Rather, it was a protest against the failed expectations embodied in swing, fueled by the new racial and cultural possibilities unleashed by a war against Fascism and Aryan supremacy. Indeed, we miss the full meaning of bop if we do not see it as a profound criticism of the failure of swing's ecstatic promise of a modern America rooted in pluralism and individualism. Two of the major bop figures, John Birks "Dizzy" Gillespie and Charlie "Bird" Parker, for instance, evidenced that criticism even during the war. "I saw a lot of stories about how they wouldn't respect a black U.S. soldier down South," Gillespie said. "He had to go in the 'colored' entrance and everything, and he's out there dying for his country. It was awful." Determined not to serve in a segregated army, he asked his draft board, "In this stage of my life here in the United States whose foot has been in my ass?" He told his board that if given a gun he was "liable to create a case of 'mistaken identity,' of who I might shoot." He was classified medically unfit. So, because of heroin use, was Parker. Lester Young, one of the major influences on young bop tenors, was jailed for drug addiction in a southern army stockade. He realized, noted a friend, "the injustice and inhumanity under which Negroes in the South lived. And not only the South. A feeling of revenge lingered in him for years." While serving in England, bop drummer Kenny Clarke discovered that white MPs had orders to shoot black troops if they crossed the street from their base to mingle with British women. In many ways, then, the war brought black musicians into direct contact with the American Dilemma. Gillespie and the others refused, however, to accept "racism, poverty or economic exploitation, nor would we live out uncreative humdrum lives merely for the sake of survival."[24]

Maturing musically during the war, boppers were caught up in its conflicting racial currents. On one hand, both black and white jazz combos played the same clubs on Fifty-second Street in front of audiences with "very little racist feeling." On the other, "once you left Fifty-second Street," Gillespie recalled, "look out." Gillespie and bassist Oscar Pettiford once had to battle a group of white sailors who attacked them just off the street for talking to a light-skinned African American woman whom the sailors had mistaken for white. "I was standing there with my horn but I used to carry a carpenter knife. Yessir, I was ready for Fifty-second Street." If American society would not accept them, they would defy American society.[25]

As a result, many boppers attacked the music industry for only half-heartedly living up to swing's pluralist ideals. "There was less discrimination in the field of jazz than in any other part of American life," Gillespie noted, but only Goodman "hired black musicians on a permanent basis." It still rankled years later that Jimmy Dorsey would not hire him because he was "too dark." Even as more black and white players worked together in bands, in jam sessions, and on recordings, it was clear that the all-black bands in which they toiled operated at a disadvantage. According to Mary Lou Williams, seeing others continuously get credit for their work left black musicians "disgusted and dried out." The pattern persisted, recalled Gillespie, because the bands "profited from the injustice, because they were insulated from the competition with black bands and musicians." Boppers protested the way race and economics worked in the music business and demanded full credit for creating America's art form.[26]

They also drew inspiration from the radical currents in Harlem and other black communities during the war. Gillespie recalled that Bird was "very much interested in the social order, and we'd have these long conversations about it, and music." In addition, they admired radical Harlem congressman Vito Marcantonio's efforts on behalf of New York's poor. "We liked Marcantonio's ideas because as musicians we weren't paid well at all for what we created." Some musicians joined the Communist Party, but "I never got that involved politically," Dizzy said. "I would picket, if necessary." In fact, Gillespie played Communist dances and carried a party card in the early 1940s "because it was directly associated with my work." The boppers also derived important inspiration from black leftist Paul Robeson, who was "a politically committed artist." As Gillespie declared, "I dug Paul Robeson right away, from the very first words." The same outspokenness characterized bop.[27]

Bop evolved among young black swing musicians in the after-hours jam sessions held during the war in small Harlem clubs such as Minton's Playhouse and Monroe's Uproar House. The same 20 percent entertainment tax that favored traditional players also led club owners to hire more advanced instrumentalists who worked in smaller groups. As the center of black swing, Harlem attracted the many touring bands, while the hardships of wartime travel concentrated musicians in the area. These younger players had been nurtured by the big bands to see themselves as virtuosos capable of solo freedom, musical literacy, and harmonic sophistication. Modern jazz was a self-conscious revolt by such instrumentalists. The music evolved in these clubs as part of an isolated black underground, an "in-group" expression that allowed relatively undisturbed experimentation away from white eyes. Former bandleader Teddy Hill took over Minton's in 1941, and he gave musicians freedom to play what they liked on Monday Celebrity Nights, which featured free soul food suppers and a house band led by Kenny Clarke on drums, Thelonious Monk on piano, Nick Fenton on bass, and Joe Guy on trumpet. With this nucleus, Minton's allowed participants to jam free of show and audience demands and achieve their "self-determined identity" as musicians. The rule that anyone could participate frustrated regulars, who, to discourage amateurs, played in hard keys and at double time. In this laboratory environment, they also explored higher extensions of the chords as the basis for improvisation. To the same end, they broke jam session etiquette by leaving solos unresolved, forcing newcomers to pick up the pieces. The setting encouraged artists to play for one another at the highest level. As Miles Davis noted, the hip young black musicians of the early 1940s were "all trying to get our master's degrees and Ph.D.'s from Minton's University of Bebop."[28]

In this in-group atmosphere, boppers formed a new community of avant-gardists rebelling against musical conventions, racism, and the limitations of an organized and routinized world. Yet they were also filled with hope. They emphasized the improvisatory freedom of the individual soloist, who drew from his own emotions a burst of creative power and meaning. The high value placed on the outsider searching for honest self-expression in a hostile world perhaps explains the importance of Charlie Parker, the innovative alto saxophonist who helped create the new sound. Having first successfully figured out how to improvise in startling new ways on the old standard "Cherokee" in 1939, Parker arrived in New York with the Big Jay McShann Band in 1942 eager to jam with equally advanced players. A child of the Kansas City ghetto, Bird was raised in the southwestern jazz tradition, which was steeped in the blues and which honored the improvisatory freedom of the soloist. He was an outsider from an early age. Instead of sticking with big bands, he took his rejection by the armed forces as his call to the New York underground. Teaming with Gillespie, Clarke, Monk, and others in the clubs, he inspired a musical revolution. Hearing sounds no one had played, he spent a lifetime pursuing them and in the process invented a new chordal improvisatory style.[29]

During the war, Parker lacked a regular home or job, living, McShann writes, "his music twenty-four hours a day. He never played the same way two nights running. His head was full of ideas and melodies. . . . He couldn't wait for the job to start so that he could play solos and get his ideas out." His spontaneity, speed, and inventiveness made him the fountainhead of the new music. He was no organization man. "There is no boundary line to art," he declared. "Music is your own experience, your thoughts, your wisdom. If you don't live it, it won't come out of your horn." The quest for new experience led to enormous indulgence, and he remained a "bad boy" in organized orchestras (as did Gillespie), clashing with leaders over discipline, solos, drugs, and punctuality. A formidable soloist, Bird preferred small combos, in which he spurned written lines to play what he felt, often at terrific speed. "Bebop is convenient only for small combos and ought to be played pretty fast," he said. "In a big orchestra arrangements suppress the spontaneous imagination." Like other boppers, after the war Parker attracted a hip cult of black and white fans who were drawn to what Ellison called a "suffering, psychically wounded, lawbreaking, life affirming hero" fighting to affirm his identity in an oppressively rationalized society.[30]

Yet Parker was not alone. He was merely the most salient hero of the bop world, where artists rebelled against swing in the name of individual creativity, spontaneity, and modernism. In the process, they created a new and complex musical expression that transformed jazz. Swing players had improvised on popular melodies suitable for dancing. Boppers followed Parker in improvising on the chord patterns underlying popular songs and standards, thus transforming elements of the older swing culture with new energy and spirit. The swing standard "Cherokee," for example, became the startlingly different "Ko Ko," while the chords of "How High the Moon" formed the basis for "Ornithology." "Hot House" derived from "What Is

This Thing Called Love?," while "Groovin' High" came from complex chord substitutions on "Whispering." Gershwin's "I Got Rhythm" was used for similar inventions. Whereas swing moved steadily, moreover, bop was often frenetic; it removed familiar signposts, seemed unstable and filled with urgency and restlessness. When musicians changed both the harmony and the beat, a tune became more abstract and less soothing, and it was up to the listener to supply the missing threads in the music. As pianist-composer Mary Lou Williams noted, bop "was like riding around and taking in the scenery rather than having a steady beat going." Bop not only made greater demands on listeners, it also elevated the role of chance and spontaneity in creative life.[31]

Changes in the entire rhythm section of the bop combo underscored the emphasis on the soloist and complex rhythms. Under Kenny Clarke and Max Roach, the drums moved away from the steady 4/4 timekeeping function on bass drum to a greater emphasis on polyrhythm and a subtler beat. While the bass took over the time, the drummer used the cymbal to provide continuous rhythm and placed accents ("bombs") on the drums between the beats. According to Gillespie, "Kenny was modifying the concept of rhythm in jazz, making it a much more fluid thing, and changing the entire role of the drummer, from just a man who kept time for dancers to a true accompanist who provided accents for soloists and constant inspiration to the jazz band as a whole." In this fragmented, jagged world, the other rhythm instruments—guitar bass and piano—either supported the soloist or soloed themselves. This implied a rejection of swing's father-leader and a new sense of equality. "We had to be as sensitive to each other as brothers," declared Gillespie, "in order to express ourselves, completely, maintain our own individuality, yet play as one."[32]

When bop traveled downtown to Fifty-second Street in 1944 it was clear that the social and racial attitudes of the boppers mirrored their musical stance. Gillespie noted that artists were "always in the vanguard of social change, but we didn't go out and make speeches. . . . We played our music and let it go at that. The music proclaimed our identity. It made every statement we wanted to make." At heart bop was "a manifestation of revolt" against the stereotypes of black music as "primitive" and the black performer as an entertainer who had to please whites. As revivalists attacked bop after the war as too intellectual, young black boppers and fans recoiled from Dixieland's definitions of black art and the black musician. On the contrary, these younger musicians maintained that Dixieland was "Uncle Tom" music, "representative of a meeker generation than theirs." As arranger Gil Fuller put it, "modern life is fast and complicated, and modern music should be fast and complicated." Musically and socially, "we're tired of that old New Orleans beat-beat, I-got-the-blues pap."[33]

The boppers directed much of their anger against the great father figures of jazz whom they considered too servile toward whites. When Louis Armstrong attacked bop in 1948, the generational battle flared in the open. "They want to carve everyone because they're so full of malice. . . . So you get all them weird chords which don't mean nothing." In music and self-presentation, boppers rejected much of the black entertainer identity. "We didn't appreciate that about Louis Armstrong," Gillespie said, "and if anybody asked me about a certain public image of him, handkerchief over his head, grinning in the face of white racism, I never hesitated to say I didn't like it. I didn't want the white man to expect me to allow the same things Louis Armstrong did." It was not that Dizzy and Bird were humorless. In fact, some boppers found Gillespie's antics too much. But his humor showed a deep and aggressive racial awareness and a willingness to ridicule white supremacy. At Harvard he thanked an audience member for handing him a chair: "Mighty white of you, old man." Like his playing, Gillespie was a protean force who turned the racial world topsy turvy. Bird used aggressive put-ons, publicly imitating whites with a variety of roles and accents that reversed racial expectations of who was in charge. In this way, he was "the cool, wiggy cat with everything under control," never "at a loss, or disadvantage." Onstage, though, he just planted his feet and blew. In general, boppers minimized entertainment. Miles Davis took this stance the farthest, rejecting even Gillespie's style of hip humor. "I didn't look at myself as an entertainer like Armstrong and Gillespie. I wanted to be accepted as a good musician and that didn't call for no grinning."[34]

In the revolt against traditional racial stereotypes, boppers identified themselves as artists. As Thelonious Monk declared, "we liked Ravel, Stravinsky, Debussy, Prokofiev, Schoenberg." To be considered a serious artist, one had to master Western harmony and theory. Since it was often assumed that black musicians only played from instinct, many boppers developed their technical virtuosity and theoretical skill. Kenny Clarke called the bop era "the most intelligent phase of our music." Many boppers had been to colleges and music schools. Having studied briefly at Juilliard, for example, Miles Davis challenged the common view that studying theory would "make you play like you were white." Instead, he studied scores by the modern composers "to see what was going on in all of music," saying, "ignorance is slavery." Bop's message was, noted Clarke, "Whatever you go into, go into it *intelligently*." As artists, moreover, boppers challenged the definitions of art in America. They were black musicians who used modern harmonics and chord progressions to create art out of the black experience; their innovations remained steeped in the rhythmic and emotional expression of black America. Like older players, the new men grew to musical awareness in the black churches and the black community. Even Monk, the most abstract of the boppers, was rooted in sanctified rhythms and spirituals, while Bird came out of southwestern blues. In building on these traditions to liberate individual expression and emotion, they challenged the notion of what was art and who was qualified to make it. As Clarke recalled, "we never labeled the music. It was just modern music."[35]

In their desire to expand their black identities, boppers also revolutionized the swing canon by looking to non–North American rhythms for inspiration. Gillespie, for one, revitalized jazz by incorporating Afro-Cuban elements and by exploring non-Western sounds, as in the motifs of "Night in Tunisia" and "Congo Blues." His postwar contacts with Cuban drummers and with African students and cultural figures in New York enabled him to see the connections "between Afro-Cuban and African music and discover[ ] the identity of our music with theirs." Trumpeter Mario Bauza, Gillespie's roommate in his Cab Calloway days, broadened his musical scope by impressing on him the importance of Afro-Cuban music, particularly the congas. In 1947, Gillespie hired Chano Pozo, the great Cuban drummer, for his big band and memorialized the Afro-Cuban connection with "Cubana Be," "Cubana Bop," and "Manteca," which was the Cuban expression for "give me some skin." Asked how they communicated, Pozo explained, "Deehee no peek pani, me no peek Angli, bo peek African." As co-composer George Russell said, "Chano's concept came from Africa. . . . we were striving for exactly that kind of world grasp, a kind of universality." Many boppers also experimented with Islam and with Arabic names and rejected American Christianity. Kenny Clarke converted to Islam after leaving the army in 1946 and became Liaquat Ali Salaam, Edmund Gregory became Sahib Shihab, Bill Evans became Usef Lateef, and Art Blakey became Abdullah Buhaina. According to Clarke, Islam "brings people together. . . . But Christians—shit, they don't allow black people in the church even. What kind of religion is that?" Although he did not become a Muslim, Gillespie agreed. "Don't say I'm forsaking Christianity, because Christianity is forsaking me. . . . In Islam there is no color line."[36]

The rejection of mainstream middle-class society found expression in noncomformist personal styles built around elements of northern black working-class male culture. Like the traditional players, boppers rejected uniforms, putting their energy into elaborating a personal style. Monk's and

Gillespie's "wiggy" berets, lip goatees, horn-rimmed glasses and modified zoot suits marked them as unorthodox people with an off-center view of the world: Gillespie was "Dizzy like a fox." Their style became iconic. As *Metronome* put it, "young boppers who had never worn a hat donned the Dizzy cap; young boppers who had never been able to raise a sufficient hirsute covering to prove their age, struggled with chin fuzz in an attempt to convey the Gillespie goatee." The bop costume derived from zoot suits, the hip ghetto dress that embodied defiance of a world that usually belittled lower-class black and Chicano males. Whereas middle-class blacks and whites saw the wearers of zoot suits as clowns or criminals, those who sported them cultivated the fashion as an inversion of their objective role of social outcast. Sunglasses also became hip. Worn at night, they set one above and apart from the square world. This style of defiance, however, was linked to the stance of the intellectual through the oft-copied beret and horn-rimmed glasses. As the first generation of black musicians associated with the popular arts to stylize themselves as bohemian intellectuals, boppers created a new cultural pastiche as a weapon against the squares. Black musicians elevated elements of urban culture into a personal and oppositional stance at the same time they built a critical art out of black life.[37]

Boppers also emphasized other elements of black ghetto culture to assert their personalities against a depersonalized world. With slang, "we didn't have to try," Gillespie noted. "As black people we just naturally spoke that way . . . as we played with musical notes, bending them into new and different meanings that constantly changed, we played with words." Although the slang arose from the jive language associated with swing and even earlier jazz, boppers created new words—*hip* (for *hep*), *crazy, square, dig*. The word *square* defined the black and white middle class as obsessed by work, dominated by a repressed sexual ethic, and racially prejudiced. *Crazy* functioned as a term of approval and implied that that which was good was outside the normal world. To be hip was to realize that the dominant world was insane. But it was drugs that really marked one as a nonconformist in such a world. Drinking and marijuana smoking were not new, of course. Heroin, which spread rapidly after the war, offered long-lasting release from the painful and mundane world of everyday oppression. Aping Bird's habit in order to play as he did, the modernists took to heroin in large numbers, unaware of how addictive it was. Heroin also contributed to the development of the music. As Art Blakey noted, "Although you do not play better with heroin, you do hear better." Added Red Rodney, "heroin allowed you to shut out the honking of the world" and just blow. Given the fierce official reaction to use of the drug in the late 1940s and early 1950s, heroin marked

Dizzy Gillespie's Big Band, recording for RCA Victor, 1947. The most innovative big band of the 1940s. Frank Driggs Collection.

maladjusted world. Despite its splintering into dancing and listening music, swing had succeeded in nurturing a large body of fans who appreciated the music's inherent qualities enough to support both bop and traditional jazz.[40]

At the same time, young people were attracted to the jazz club ambiance created by a multiracial set of male hipsters. In that world, musicians—especially black boppers—offered a way to solidify one's identity. For black hipsters who appeared in the major cities of the nation, the new music, clothing, and drugs were symbols of an improvisational ethic based on pleasure and emotional experience. As black hipsters became a part of the downtown club scene, they brought with them a disdain for the narrow roles offered them in an America that glorified the work ethic, conformity, and adjustment to organized society. Instead, they looked to music for "its sacred, almost mystical quality," its openness to new depths of experience. As one study of black working-class Chicago hipsters observed, a cat might give up all else, but "he never gives up music." Coming of age during this period, LeRoi Jones saw bop as an alternative to his striving Newark middle-

its users as bohemian outsiders as well as members of
cult removed from the professionalism and team unity of

In music and in personal style boppers pioneered a mo
quickly found favor among white musicians and fans afte
lespie noted, "for a generation of Americans and young pe
world, who reached maturity during the 1940s, bebop syn
lion against the old order, an outcry for change in almost e
cially in music. The boppers wanted to impress the world wi
the uniquely modern design of a new generation coming of
tion of the square world and the search for new identities d
of black and white youth to bop. As the music migrated fr
Fifty-second Street in 1944, it quickly revolutionized the mu:
white players and became the embodiment of style for hip y
races. But as Dexter Gordon put it, the bop anthem "Things t
"meant freer personal lives lived in an open racial environ
white musician or fan to feel part of the group, however, requ
ing up to a difficult black aesthetic and abandoning racial p
saxophonist Sonny Rollins noted, Fifty-second Street in the 19
place "in which black and white musicians could interact in a v
to natural bonds of friendship. The audience, or at least a part
cue from this, leading to an unpretentious flow of social interco

The immediate postwar environment witnessed a surge in the
tion of bop. Although most boppers preferred small combos, Gil
ceeded in building a big bop band between 1945 and 1950
"greater recognition of . . . the whole culture of our music" and
more universal appeal." By 1947 he found that larger audience
band played Carnegie Hall, earned Band of the Year honors, and
on RCA Victor. A number of jazz critics and impresarios who had
with swing and were favorable to more modern music—especially l
Feather and Barry Ulanov at *Metronome*—used their influence in the
try to promote both Gillespie's band and bop in general. The initial p
exuberance provided room for experimentation, and Gillespie happil
peted with other leaders of progressive bands such as Woody Herman,
Raeburn, and Stan Kenton. Dizzy was a star, a model for a new inter
young audience. "Everybody was trying to look like me," Gillespie m
"Now, why in hell did they want to do that? They even pretended to l
like me . . . and it was not a racial phenomenon. These were black and w
people alike, by the tens of thousands, willing to stand up and testify
bebop." For a minority of black and white swing fans, bop swung m
intensely than swing and expressed their alienation from a regiment

class black family and to the black street men who had given up. "It was a way into ourselves further," he wrote. For Jones, being "hip" opened up a wider identity, "another mode of being. Another way of living."[41]

Many young white fans and musicians also flocked to music and learned the new idiom. What distinguished the bop era from the swing era was how central black musicians were in the lives of white fans, how jazz clubs became interracial settings, and how the black musicians stood as bohemian alternatives to a narrowing middle-class world. Many young white musicians who played with Woody Herman, Boyd Raeburn, and Stan Kenton came from backgrounds similar to those of the swing musicians. They were working- or lower-middle-class Italians and Jews, but they took black artists as models and developed their own stance of nonconformity. Having grown up during a depression and a war, they were alienated from a wartime society that stressed conformity to national ideals but left little room for male individualism. In 1944–45 bandleader Harry Jerome employed many of the Brooklyn Jewish contingent who went on to white progressive bands. They "never wanted a uniform," recalled Jerome. "It was a rebellion in music really, and they also carried it through in their life-style." Some players—pianist-arranger George Handy, composer Bob Graetinger—had proved unfit for army duty, and they brought their nonconformism into their search for distinctive musical identities. Many of them got hooked on heroin. Young Jewish trumpeter Red Rodney, who played with Bird, linked drugs to alienation. "We were growing up. . . . We wanted something that, I don't know, psychoneurotic is the word . . . and we all had a good case of it."[42]

New clubs emerged to cater to an interracial youth audience attracted to bop. In late 1946, club owner Monte Kay opened the Royal Roost on Broadway because Fifty-second Street clubs were "rough on kids," hustling them for drinks every fifteen minutes. For a ninety-cent admission fee—not a cover charge—young people could sit in a nondrinking bleacher section; during Sunday jam sessions they did not have to buy anything. The "peanut gallery" that made the clubs open to young people, including young women, became the bop club policy across the country. Equally important, the Roost fostered "a complete rapport" between musicians and fans. "I haven't seen such a thing recaptured since," noted fan Gil Sorrentino. Musicians engaged each other in numerous battles, which led to a "lot of bad playing" but also let fans feel that they were "'in' on things." And, he added, "to us, it was bop—it *had* to be good." With the encouragement of the musicians, "we were members of the same cult."[43]

At the heart of the white audience were male hipsters, marginal men comfortable in neither an ethnic nor an American identity. Jazz hustler

Teddy Reig, for example, was born in 1918 to a Jewish insurance salesman who was reduced to running a candy store in the depression. Reig rebelled against his parents' hopes that he become a pharmacist and instead married a black woman and gravitated toward black music, Harlem, and Fifty-second Street. Eligible for the draft, he was left dangling, with no secure future. He lived from day to day. Ethnicity was not enough. "I was scuffling, dreaming, trying to be a Jewish boy who didn't wanna be Jewish." He hit his peak after the war when he recorded his idol, Charlie Parker, and other boppers for Savoy Records. Similarly, saxophonist and future artist Larry Rivers was also drawn to a black experiential ethic. Raised in the Bronx by Jewish parents who wanted him to be a dentist, he rebelled by hanging out on Fifty-second Street, playing bop, scoring heroin, and living by a "hip code." He wanted to be "as black as I could seem."[44]

For younger fans, bop was a sign of generational distinction and the key to new identities opened up by the war. Born in 1929 to a lower-middle-class New York Italian family, Gilbert Sorrentino and his friends reached adolescence as the war ended and found bop at the same time. "We were young, naive, very romantic: above all, we wanted a music of our own, something removed from school dances, the Hit Parade, and 'long hair.'" Miller and James catered to an older set who had gone to war and who danced. The war "absolutely disoriented" Sorrentino's generation, placing them "at a great remove from the 'world' in general." Older boys left for the army and came back eager to marry and start families; the younger boys had to forge their own futures. "The tenuous contact we had with them was gone forever." Swing held no meaning for a generation too young to achieve manhood and social meaning in war. It was Parker's "Ko Ko," however, that became Sorrentino's music. Bop's searching, battling quality let young men express their conflicts with generational, class, and ethnic restraints.[45]

The young bop fans refused to dance. Woody Herman became a hero, because "it was almost impossible to dance to him." Squares and bobby-soxers danced; hipsters preferred intense listening. Snobbery played a role too; the younger men formed themselves into an elite cult disdainful of social acceptance. "To our immense satisfaction," bop cut them off entirely as lovers of "'nigger music.'" The fierce opposition of traditional critics, meanwhile, confirmed their belief that they were an avant-garde. "You had to *know*; if you didn't know, you were on the other side, a square or a fig." Figs were the worst. "The reason that we loathed them more than the squares," recalled Sorrentino, was that "the figs purported to be serious about jazz—and yet wouldn't accept what be-bop was all about, an absolutely new method of playing." Rejecting swing and traditional jazz, bop fans "formed a cult, which perhaps more than any other force in the intellectual life of our time, brought together young people who were tired of the spurious."[46]

The war and its aftermath provided the economic means for working-class rebels to elaborate a youth culture that expressed their alienation from their backgrounds and from their prescribed roles—domesticity for women and workplace success for men. As these formed the road to social stability, young bop fans opted for more open-ended experiences and identities in the music and in the black cats of the night who played it. The ability to express these desires musically and culturally transformed the boppers into idols of white and black youths. LeRoi Jones said, "Diz was my hero." Sorrentino declared, "Dizzy was our king and our god." Fans modeled their fashions on his beret, horn-rims, bop ties, huge-shouldered jackets, pegged pants, and goatee. So popular were these items that in 1946 Symphony Sid sold "bop glasses," while other vendors advertised paste-on goatees. Before bop, glasses had invited taunts of "four-eyes," noted Jones; now they were cool. "What they signified," said Sorrentino, "was a blind reaching out for rapport not only with the musicians who had 'invented' them, but, more significantly, a rapport with a 'world of intellect'" he normally considered "fruity." Bop fans, in other words, took themselves farther outside "by becoming identified with that most contemptible segment of American life, the intelligentsia." Add this to the slang and the dress, and one can understand why Larry Rivers's parents thought he was "wending his way down the road to disgrace."[47]

Bop fans also associated black musicians with sexual adventure. Swing musicians had downplayed their adventures under a veneer of professional respectability designed to appeal to a heterosexual audience. Bop musicians, however, seemed to live vital lives of personal exploration unchecked by societal expectations. Male hipsters who idolized the musicians fit the model of Norman Mailer's "white Negro," who rejected organized society, conformity, and success in favor of living in the present. While overdoing black primitivism, Mailer's projection of the orgasmic onto blacks reflected the desire of a group of postwar white and black urban males for a greater intensity of lived experience than conventional society could provide. In this search, bop and marijuana were "the two most important components of the hipster's life," although it could also embrace the greater ecstasy of heroin. As Chicago bop fan Don Rose noted, the war opened up the world of black jazz and bohemian experience to "kids my age" who could jam with great musicians. "That was a thrill. And the hit from heroin

Woody Herman's Second Herd, Commodore Hotel, New York City, 1948. Along with Stan Kenton, Herman, standing left, led a series of innovative and popular "progressive" white bands. Frank Driggs Collection.

was a stupendous feeling." These new adventurers, a core of whom would become the Beats of the 1950s, were young men in revolt against what Mailer called the "single mate, the solid family and the respectable love life."[48]

Less is known about young women attracted to bop. Although men dominated, there were young women such as Nica (Baroness Konnigswater), Chan Parker (Bird's second wife), and other "hip chicks" who were drawn to this experimental music. Interracial liaisons were not unusual. Dizzy denied that boppers "had a penchant for loose sex and partners racially different from themselves, especially black men who desired white women," but such relationships sometimes did occur. Although critics focused on sex, especially the potential risks to young white women who frequented the clubs, the music also offered women a space to oppose the restrictions on their identity and to promote racial change. Gillespie said that "socially speaking" it was a "concrete effort of progressive thinking black and white males and females to tear down and abolish the ignorance and racial barriers that were stifling the growth of any true culture in modern America."[49]

The attempt to promote new musical, racial, and personal identities, however, foundered on the general collapse of the band business and the nation's growing social conservatism. After 1948, Gillespie's big band, like Woody Herman's and Stan Kenton's, found it rough going. In 1950 Dizzy called it quits. Bop could not build the mass audience enjoyed by swing bands because big bands were no longer economically or culturally feasible, especially black bands playing "music too complex for the average person to coordinate into dancing." As bookings declined after 1948, he was faced with "the old bebop dilemma, whether jazz is primarily a music for dancing or listening." For most blacks, danceable rhythm and blues was preferable to bop. Gillespie thus ran into the same problem faced by the first big bop band. "We didn't have it easy; our music was more or less a concert style of jazz," noted its leader, Billy Eckstine. "People would start to dance, and then they'd turn around and listen. Sometimes our tempos were almost not danceable either." While few bookers would gamble on black orchestras in concert settings, jazz clubs could not support traveling big bands. Except for Norman Granz's Jazz at the Philharmonic traveling concerts, there were few concert venues for bop. "Everybody can blame Woody Herman and Dizzy Gillespie and me for ruining the dance band business," declared Stan Kenton in 1950. "What we wanted to play wasn't dance music, but despite this, agents and promoters insisted on handling us just as they would a dance band." Dance fans came to dance, listeners to listen, and "we'd try to give a little of both and everybody went away unhappy."[50]

Bop was also enmeshed in the musical and cultural battles of the late 1940s. As the last gasp of swing, with its emphasis on American vernacular music, its unleashing of new democratic energies, and its modern techniques, bop also revolted against the softening of swing during the war. Even more, boppers represented the emergence of a new militant urban African America. Some jazz critics supported bop as the emblem of modern African American and American culture. To do so, however, placed them at some remove from former allies. Through the 1940s, partisans of each brand of music fought over the future of jazz. Many swing critics and musicians despised boppers for their cultishness and bebop itself for its lack of a danceable beat. Revivalists, who had close ties to the the Popular Front, attacked bop for selling out. For them, only traditional jazz, untouched by commerce, could act as a critique of modern American society. For modernists, however, a radically transformed commercial music system and modern urban blacks were capable of resistance and of creating a sophisticated avant-garde musical art. Meanwhile, swing's mass audience turned to domestic life, and the band business collapsed. Caught between past and fu-

9

Coda and Conclusion

Red Scares and Head Scares

Let's wake up. The threat to music today is not a red scare. . . . It's a head scare.—*Down Beat*

Over and over during the late 1940s and early 1950s, jazz musicians found their names splayed across the headlines of the daily newspaper, the gossip column, the jazz press: Cops bust Billie Holiday . . . Goes to jail . . . Artie Shaw called before HUAC . . . Frank Sinatra a Red? . . . Aaron Copland a Red? . . . George Gershwin a Red? . . . Charlie Parker committed to Camarillo . . . Thelonious Monk arrested on drug charge . . . Anita O'Day and husband arrested . . . Gene Krupa arrested . . . Stan Getz arrested for narcotics . . . Barney Josephson a Red? . . . Lena Horne a Red? . . . Dope—the shameful U.S. jazz record . . . Who will escape this stigma? . . . The dope leeches . . . Weed out the weeders. If swing represented the rebirth of dreams, the post-war jazz world seemed stuck in a never-ending public nightmare.

In order to understand the public concern with the subversive impact of modern jazz, we need to examine the unraveling of the swing synthesis in bitterness and recrimination during the tension-filled post-war years. By 1947, as swing fragmented into competing factions amid the band industry's decline, all forms of jazz had difficulty attracting a mass audience. The unprecedented internecine warfare in the jazz world led to the decline of common allegiances. Each faction blamed the others for the public's lack of interest, and intense self-doubt and introspection among musicians, critics, and fans replaced the former confidence in swing's ability to achieve wide popularity. Big band modern jazz (bebop) faced the longest odds of reviving the dance band industry, but all forms of jazz were thrown on the defensive, trapped between past and future. Indicative of this loss of momentum is that *Down Beat* mounted a contest in 1949 to find a replacement for the terms "Ragtime, Jazz, Boogie-Woogie, Dixieland, Swing, Be-Bop," which had "lost much of their original significance. . . . We need a new term to describe our music—ALL of our music, regardless of the school to which it belongs."[1]

Lacking even a common terminology, the jazz world proved vulnerable to outside enemies. Criticism of jazz as a racially alien and immoral influence on young men and women had waxed and waned in the music world since World War I. However, the economic and cultural weaknesses of the dance band industry and the splintering of a united front allowed critics to attack on moral and political grounds with a virulence and effectiveness hitherto impossible. Throughout the war, jazz musicians and critics had put aside stylistic and racial differences to make common cause against "Mickey Mouse" bands and attacks by moralists and reactionary politicians determined to paint jazz in the most lurid un-American colors. When Congress had attempted to denigrate boogie-woogie and swing during the war, for instance, black and white musicians and singers had stood together with a concerted argument that every facet of swing represented American culture. After the war, however, that common defense proved impossible against a rising fear that American institutions and values were being weakened from within by subversion at the very moment that the Cold War posed a threat from without.

Like the other arts, the music industry found itself caught up in the anti-Communist attacks on subversive New Deal radicalism in American entertainment. The first inkling of trouble came in 1947 when *Down Beat* announced that a congressional subcommittee planned to subpoena "certain well known musicians and singers" for "being Communists." No evidence of specific hearings on the music business exists, but conservatives turned up many individuals associated with the "swing left" as part of their probe into the arts and entertainment in Hollywood and New York. The FBI, for example, probed pianist and revivalist critic Art Hodes's politics and tapped his phone because, he believed, "the wrong people were coming in to see *Jazz Record*."[2]

Conservative groups also targeted Frank Sinatra. Having experienced ethnic prejudice as a boy, he strongly supported FDR and the New Deal ethic of ethnic and racial pluralism. In January 1946, however, America Firster Gerald L. K. Smith told HUAC that Sinatra was "a Mrs. Roosevelt in pants" who "acts as a front" for Communist organizations. "The minute anyone tries to help the little guy," Sinatra noted, "he's called a Communist." In 1949 the California State Senate Committee on Un-American Activities labeled Sinatra a Fellow Traveler. When Robert Ruark linked this "savior of the country's small fry, by virtue of his lectures on clean living and love-thy-neighbor," to the mob in 1947, the twin sins of crime and Communism badly weakened his audience appeal. In a pattern common during the late 1940s, Artie Shaw was pressured to declare his loyalty to free enterprise and American compromises with equality. In 1948 he was attacked for support-ing various Popular Front groups, and, living under "a haze of rumor," he agreed in 1953 to testify before HUAC. He told the committee that when he returned from the navy in 1945 he was angry at domestic reactionaries and black marketeers and set out to fight for the Fair Employment Practices Commission and other leftist causes as part of his conception of American war ideals. He confessed to being "duped" and pledged to "defend American institutions and American folkways" and never to sign any petitions or pro-test letters ever again. He also swallowed his anger at the anti-Semitism that had scarred his personality and the racism that had marred his attempts to integrate bands. Instead he expressed his gratitude for what the nation had done for him, "a member of a minority." Humiliated by having to repudiate his former beliefs, Shaw exiled himself to Spain.[3]

While a number of musicians got caught up in congressional investiga-tions aimed at Hollywood and New York, Barney Josephson and Cafe Soci-ety found themselves under attack as emblems of New Deal radicalism. Home to integrated jazz and humorous attacks on segregation and the up-per classes, Cafe Society's uptown and downtown branches were pilloried by the entertainment columns. In his appearance before HUAC in 1948, Josephson's brother Leon, who had been involved in an attempt to kill Hit-ler in 1935, told the public—but not the committee—that he was a Com-munist and proud of his anti-Fascism; he was jailed for contempt. When Barney refused to condemn him, tabloid gossip columnists began a smear campaign. Westbrook Pegler, for example, implied that Leon was also a drug addict—"and there is much to be said about his brother Barney." He had welcomed black members of the audience and introduced inflammatory songs such as "Strange Fruit" and "The House I Live In." As a result of the campaign, business declined, Josephson was forced to sell both of his clubs, and by 1950 he was broke. The FBI and Congress also pressured those associated with Cafe Society: John Hammond, Ivan Black (the press agent), Hazel Scott, Teddy Wilson, Zero Mostel, Lena Horne, Jack Gilford, and Josh White. Black, Mostel, and Gilford were blacklisted in movies, radio, and television. In 1951, the Hearst press tried to bar Lena Horne from television too. Along with Josh White and Hazel Scott, she saved herself by pledging her loyalty to the United States and branding friend and former Cafe Society regular Paul Robeson, as well as Henry Wallace, as Communists. In this "hysterical political climate," *Down Beat* advised musicians, "if you're anywhere to the left of Rep. Rankin . . . just keep your views to yourself."[4]

Yet the jazz community already was cutting its ties to the Popular Front. In 1946, when Soviet authorities censored and then jailed Eddie Rozner, their best-known swing bandleader, for playing decadent bourgeois music, Barry Ulanov editorialized in *Metronome* that "dictatorships inevitably get around to censuring, censoring or altogether forbidding jazz," just as Hitler and Japan had done. "Now Russia, logically suspicious of a musical form which is based upon spontaneity of expression, finds jazz offensive." Defending swing as the "peculiarly American" embodiment of freedom, he argued that jazz fans and musicians "should be proud of its low mark in totalitarian countries" and urged that "the large number of Communists and Fellow-travelers in American jazz should do some serious thinking about this latest cultural development in their shabby Utopia-by-the-Volga." Soon after, the swing ideology of jazz as freedom and tolerance was turned outward against the Communist world. In 1947, the State Department and the Voice of America chose Benny Goodman to broadcast America's best dance music to the USSR. After *Metronome*'s editors publicly quarreled with his selections, the State Department invited Ulanov, along with George Simon and the editors of *Down Beat,* to add modern jazz to these broadcasts. Sensitive to orthodox Communist attacks on modern jazz as formalistic, modernists were consistent in their criticism of the USSR's lack of creative freedom. Outside and inside the music world, the Cold War placed pressure on jazz to sever its ties to the Left.[5]

Nevertheless, swing musicians continued to promote pluralism and tolerance at home during the late 1940s. Immediately after the war, black and white musicians performed interracial concerts and benefits to honor the memory of President Roosevelt. During this period Duke Ellington produced "Deep South Suite," his musical criticism of segregation and injustice, followed in 1947 by "Beggar's Holiday," a show of social protest that featured interracial casting. In early 1947, Goodman supported the United Nations because it fulfilled swing's dream of greater freedom for all. "Freedom gets around in this country, and it better," he urged. "It has to start on our own street—in our willingness to give the right guy a job—or let him into our free schools—no matter what his race, creed or nationality. It's either freedom for all of us or freedom for none of us—anywhere in the world." Meanwhile, *Down Beat* and *Metronome* challenged baseball to follow swing's example and integrate the major leagues. Lionel Hampton, moreover, linked swing to a growing national commitment to desegregation. A replacement for an ailing Goodman, Hampton happily joined Lena Horne and a host of white stars in January 1949 to play for the inauguration of Harry S. Truman, the first president to make civil rights a plank in his campaign platform and the president who ordered the desegregation of the armed forces. In the meantime, Shaw and Goodman publicly defied HUAC in 1947 to support the Committee for the First Amendment. After 1948, however, the red scare would make it difficult to move so boldly again on civil rights or to oppose the growing power of the right.[6]

The red scare took its toll, but as *Down Beat* put it, "the real threat to music today is not a red scare . . . it's a head scare." Although all players were affected, the boppers were the primary target of a growing antidrug crusade because their racial, generational, and personal rebellion symbolized the disturbing disruptions that the war had left in its wake. Many who had dreamed of an ordered world of security and domesticity during the war now found that ideal difficult to achieve amid strikes, inflation, and sexual and familial disjunctures. The result was a war on drugs from 1947 to 1954, the cultural equivalent of the red scare in the defense of middle-class values. Fear about the changes brought by war came to a head in the anxiety about juvenile delinquency: absent fathers and working mothers had created independence for teenagers, and they elaborated a youth culture filled with angst and alienation. Bop music, black and white zoot-suited hipsters, and promiscuous "victory girls" hanging out in jazz clubs reinforced unresolved wartime fears about the sexual activity of young women. The concern with social deviance was a way to police the boundaries of convention and squeeze recalcitrant men and women back into the mold of a secure and ordered family life. Moral and political authorities focused on the dangerous "hopped up" bopper in order to contain the spread of decay. Jazz and drugs were the means by which the American character was being weakened. At a time when the nation needed to be united and morally strong to fight the cold war, boppers and the ills they spread signified a threat that the war had unleashed.[7]

Starting in 1943, federal and local authorities attempted to keep drugs and other forms of vice from weakening the war effort by demoralizing soldiers and civilians. In a sensational case that year, the crackdown nabbed

Gene Krupa for possession of marijuana and for contributing to the delin-quency of a minor—the band boy who supplied him with the pot—which was a felony. He served ninety days and lost his band, his livelihood, and his reputation. Shocked by the government's action against a common mu-sician's habit—smoking marijuana—the swing world rallied to his defense. As George Simon charged, "One of the quickest ways to stamp out an evil is to make an example of somebody everybody knows. Everybody knows Gene Krupa and so he was picked on." Soon, federal and local agents clamped down on all prominent jazz venues, especially 52nd Street, Holly-wood, Los Angeles's Central Avenue, and Chicago's Loop and South Side.[8]

The concern with drugs and jazz musicians as causes and symptoms of individual and national demoralization rose dramatically as heroin surfaced and as fears about external and internal threats to the nation intensified. Arrests increased and national attention grew after 1947. Billie Holiday, for example, was arrested for heroin possession in 1949 and tried in U.S. Dis-trict Court in Philadelphia. "It was called 'The United States of America versus Billie Holiday.' And that's just the way it felt," she wrote in her auto-biography. She pleaded guilty and asked to be sent to a hospital to take "the cure," but the judge noted that she was a well-to-do entertainer and sentenced her to a year in jail. As she put it, "People on drugs are sick people. So now we end up with the government chasing sick people like they were criminals, telling doctors they can't help them, prosecuting them because they had some stuff without paying the tax, and sending them to jail." Arrests of musicians for marijuana also rose. In Hollywood, singer Anita O'Day and her husband Carl Hoff were arrested in 1947 by under-cover police for possession of "tea," but this was only part of a larger crack-down. According to Assistant Chief of Police Joseph Reed, officers in Los Angeles set up roadblocks downtown to stop a "crime wave" and raided after-hours jazz clubs "in a new attempt to break up the breeding places of crime." In 1948, Akron police picked up several of Alvino Rey's musicians. Across the nation, George Simon noted, police were anxious to break up "tea parties," especially among prominent entertainers who acted as well-publicized examples of the wages of sin. All the while, the same tabloids and gossip columnists who spread the dirt on the political sins of celebrities fueled the drug furor with tales of secret moral decay in the popular arts. According to Simon, "sensation-mongering columnists" convinced the public "to look down upon musicians."[9]

The attacks on youth culture, music, and narcotics reached a crescendo in January 1951, at the height of the Cold War, when newspapers, civic organizations, police, and federal narcotics officers alarmed New York with the news that the city had "15,000 teen-age dope addicts," a number that had been increasing since the war. The New York Medical Society had offered to help treat the problem as early as 1946, but it took panic over the teenage crime and promiscuity that provided money for drugs to convince Police Commissioner Thomas F. Murphy that a full-scale crackdown was necessary. Councilwoman Bertha Schwartz charged, "Girl addicts become prostitutes. . . . They admit they would kill their own father or mother if the parent 'stands between me and a fix.'" By June, New York and other cities were holding hearings on the teen drug problem, producing lurid stories of "degradation in New York" that crowded General Douglas MacArthur out of the headlines. The public seemed fascinated by teenage confessions. A sixteen-year-old girl said, "I used to get intimate with [my boyfriend] whenever we got high." For money, she "began to have sexual relations with an older man." A nineteen-year-old former model testified that it was easy to buy heroin near the Roseland Ballroom and the Fifty-second Street jazz clubs. Short on solutions, city officials urged greater police vigilance and stiffer penalties. At times, more money for hospitals and treatment was suggested, but the focus was on rooting out the evil cancers that had been spreading since the war and causing teenage sexual and criminal delinquency: drug pushers, jazz musicians, and jazz clubs. When Harry J. Anslinger, head of the Federal Bureau of Narcotics, blamed the heroin supply on Red China, the links between internal moral decay and external threat were solidified.[10]

Thanks to the scandal sheets, claimed Simon, by the early 1950s, "all musicians [were] assumed to smoke marijuana regularly before breakfast and to use heroin for the rest of the day and night." As a result, the jazz press had to admit that "everybody close to this music knows that heroin and related filth has infiltrated the jazz world" and began to insist that the music business "weed out the weeders." Industry concern was bound up with the belief that addicts bore responsibility for the dismal state of the band business. As *Down Beat* argued in 1947, "just at a time when musicians, singly and as an organized group, need to pull some of the hottest public relations they can grab out of the bag" and do "everything we possibly can to bring back the band business," a few "stupid, thrill-seeking nitwits" alienated the public by missing engagements and getting themselves arrested. Their "hop-headed bliss" and lack of a sense of any "basic debt to society" was "lousing up the music world" and turning "whole clubs and bands into cesspools." Fearful of arrests and bad publicity, promoters would not hire bands with "T" users since it was "too dangerous and too much trouble." As a result, *Metronome* and *Down Beat* called for weeding out "the rotten apples in the barrel" to prevent the collapse of the whole industry. Ralph Gleason argued in 1953 that the industry was on the verge of losing all of its young fans because of parental fears. "It is time for the musicians, the jazz fans, and the musicians' union if necessary to clean house" and "see to it that the cancer is contained, that the infection is stopped and a thriving business, that is a way of life, is not penalized" by an irresponsible few. Only then, Simon argued, would bands regain popularity and musicians "once more be accepted as healthy, respected members of society."[11]

The jazz press continued to defend the innocent against overzealous narcotics agents and the tabloids, but they could not resist the pressure to label all drugs as equally dangerous. Nationally syndicated columnists described all musicians as tea addicts, and dailies everywhere blared any jazz-related marijuana arrest, forcing hotels and clubs to fire whole bands to stop adverse publicity. Ulanov cited the LaGuardia Report on Marihuana in support of his belief that "marihuana does not produce the wild dope fiend of popular imagination," nor was it "the debilitating factor in their lives that its most violent detractors have made it." Yet, he argued, "insofar as it provides escape from reality it is serious, it is bad and it must be removed from the musical picture." Despite the position of the music magazines, federal narcotics chief Harry Anslinger told a Senate crime hearing in 1951 that *Down Beat* was leading the young to drugs. In this climate, rational discussion and humane treatment gave way to punitive measures.[12]

Having become enemies of national strength and morals, jazz musicians—especially boppers—were often treated the same as Communists. Undercover agents infiltrated their circles to find and arrest drug users and peddlers, browbeat musicians into informing on each other to save themselves, and busted many clubs and dance halls where addicted musicians were suspected of working and scoring. New York's cabaret card, which required fingerprints and a clean record, worked to keep convicted musicians from playing in the city's clubs and hence spreading their vices to the innocent. As a result, Billie Holiday, Charlie Parker, Thelonious Monk, Miles Davis, Red Rodney, and many others lost their livelihoods in the clubs of the capital of jazz in the early 1950s. Other convicted addicts, such as John Simmons, Gerry Mulligan, Chet Baker, Ike Quebec, Lou Fromm, Art Blakey, and Stan Getz were marked for continuous surveillance and harassment. This situation also led to the growth of an underground economy in which those who lost their cards found their only outlets in after-hours spots playing for substandard wages. They suffered degradation as artists and were often forced to go through demeaning hearings to prove their rehabilitation.[13]

By the early 1950s, all forms of jazz were labeled as dangerous threats to the American way of life. The reemergence of black jazz was quickly equated with juvenile delinquency and drugs, as well as with challenges to the values of success and domesticity. As symbols of immorality, black and white musicians became pariahs, scrutinized, arrested, and sensationalized as un-American. For the moment, containment worked; the spread of bop was checked, and traditional jazz lost its political content. As a result, popular music in the early 1950s became much more conventional.

In this hostile climate, the dance band world turned nostalgic and backward-looking. Once the promoters of new music, the music industry now attempted to resurrect the great dance bands of the past to restore the reputation of the industry and bring back audiences and job opportunities. During the early 1950s, *Down Beat* repeatedly tried to revive dance bands and social dancing on the theory that after the war, "the bands lost contact with the dancers." The major record companies released albums by the swing bands of the 1930s, ballrooms sponsored dance contests, and the music press tried to educate musicians on the proper dance beat and the dictates of professional decorum: Musicians should dress well and exhibit enthusiasm to prove they were not disdainful of the public. In addition, bands should copy the moderate tempos and clean-cut sound of Glenn Miller and even the beat of Guy Lombardo. Although many Miller "ghost" bands followed this advice, the campaign went on for at least three years with no visible increase in audience. Stan Kenton declared that the music industry turned to the "safe bet" of the Miller style because it had become "obsessed with fear—the fear of insecurity" and of the loss of money. "But," he asked, "how long can the Miller ghost last?" In promoting middle-of-the road bands, the industry acceded to the containment of modern musical, racial, and cultural hopes. Moreover, jazz critics, once crusaders, increasingly turned away from debating the music's public and political relevance to dissect its formal qualities. Musicians became more isolated from the audience, using a stance of cool remove, without confidence that they could capture a mass audience or transform American life. Jazz musicians, critics, and promoters were forced to give up the dream of jazz as America's popular music. Jazz was alive; the dream was dead.[14]

It had not been very long since optimistic visions of jazz's role in American culture still reigned. What is notable about the swing era is how its creators, promoters, and fans saw it as part of a cultural rebirth. Benny Goodman, for example, saw swing in the 1930s as part of a revival of larger American cultural traditions in the Great Depression. The innovations he helped promote were a vital dance music and a contribution to jazz, but they were much more. The improvisation that lay at the heart of the music, he said, was "the expression of an individual kind of free speech in music." Our "music ha[d] grown out of our brand of government," and if swing died, "it [would] die over the body of American freedom." It is not that musicians were politicians or that they had political platforms. But, as this language suggests, their music carried a message of hope for personal freedom as well as cultural regeneration. Certainly, as they entered the concert hall on a regular basis, swing bands and the dance band industry could hope that a true American music rooted in democratic culture had triumphed over European and hierarchical cultural forms.[15]

Swing brought jazz to the center of American music and culture. As Paul Whiteman's mission of refinement gave way to the limpid Guy Lombardo style in the early 1930s, space opened for white and black musicians to accelerate the pace of exchange and appropriation on a regular basis. The depression wounded young men and women, weakened conceptions of individual potency and power, and dethroned the remaining hierarchical conceptions of American culture. Under these pressures, the modern swing band, rooted in the achievements of black jazz bandleaders and arrangers, became the dominant paradigm in popular music during the 1930s and 1940s. Part of the populist thrust of the era, this musical culture was less firmly rooted in the past than in new pluralist visions of American life. Swing was more racially and ethnically mixed than any other arena of American life. With New York once more music's vital cultural and business capital, swing held out a more utopian and cosmopolitan vision of swinging the American Dream. Although black bands continued to operate at a disadvantage, they also had the opportunity to aspire to national acclaim for the first time. They kept alive the Harlem Renaissance dreams of urban freedom during the dark days of the depression and added to this ferment a populist music from Kansas City that expressed the aspirations of ordinary black youth. This cultural pride interacted with the rebirth of leftist political forces in music and in American society to promote the advancement of African Americans as full-fledged Americans.

Swing's appeal to a nation of youth turned it into a mass culture. Most accounts have missed how powerful young people became in the music market of the 1930s and why such "commercial forms" appealed to them. Looking back from the vantage of the postwar decline, Mike Levin noted that the "unified taste of the kids and the musicians was enough to swing large groups of the general public which normally wouldn't be interested in these bands." Because of mass interest in bands, black and white jazz musicians could dream of national acceptance and stable careers as popular idols, surpassing movie stars in the eyes of youth. As pianist-arranger Ralph Burns put it, "It was a fantasy world for us, because people thought differently about bands then, probably the way they think about rock groups now. . . . If you were a jazz musician playing with Woody Herman, you were almost like a movie star."[16]

Swing bands offered young people powerful visions of personal freedom and generational solidarity, defined a mass youth style around music, dance, and fashion, and conveyed hopeful visions of the future. By combining and undergirding wounded male individualism with the encompassing support and security of the large group, these bands also created powerful models for young people eager to keep alive the personal and moral experimentations of the previous decade. While bands served as all-male families, the ritualized relationship of male band and female singer emphasized that women would help support male creativity. Playing a subordinate public role, the singers also offered young women models for how to adjust as romantic objects and working women in a man's world. In personal terms, swing dancing promoted the committed couple who improvised in a much more egalitarian way in the private realm. Swing was a public, democratic art that helped ease the gender and social tensions of the era.

As swing went to war, it did so with a divided legacy. As a relatively pluralist mode of expression, swing became a symbol of American culture in a war against against Fascism and racial supremacy. For many black musicians and racial liberals, Hitler's defeat would also challenge segregation and second-class citizenship at home. While the war enabled black bands—and the African American population—to make substantial strides, it also increased racial and cultural tensions that undermined those advances. The war heightened and then exhausted swing as it brought the central tensions of the 1930s to a head. As swing became enmeshed in national purpose, it became more bureaucratic and sentimental. Although Glenn Miller supported pluralism, his orchestra was a whitened and corporate vision. In this, swing was part of a public culture that lionized the crowd and the group— on the stage and in the audience. During the war the popularity of sentimental ballads and singers expressed powerful individual demands for personal fulfillment and the security of ordered domesticity removed from the public sphere. This vision ultimately clashed with the demand by younger black—and some white—musicians that public life reflect the national ideal of a pluralistic and equalitarian society.

Young black jazz musicians nurtured on the tension between the utopian hopes of swing and the racial and commercial realities for black bands created a powerful critique of American life and music in the 1940s. Many of the most fervent swing fans followed the musicians into bop. They were drawn by the new style's intense musical vision and alienated from "whitened" big bands. Even more, however, it was a younger generation of black and white fans who supported bebop. This generation was born in the depression and came of age during the war, and as a result of the drop in marriage and fertility rates in the early 1930s formed the smallest generation cohort of the twentieth century. This generation was also one of the most alienated. The depression and the war had shown them that the world was not ordered; it was out of joint. Bebop expressed their reality: chance and spontaneity ruled a universe devoid of fixed guideposts. They would have to search for identity in an overly organized and bureaucratized world. Holding to an older racial and musical vision, traditional jazz musicians and leftist music supporters revolted against the homogenization of swing and of the music business. But they turned to an older form of collective improvisation and a paternalistic conception of the African American performer. At the same time, much of the older swing audience turned to fulfilling wartime swing dreams; they still loved swing, but they had neither the time nor the money to go dancing or even buy records. Washing machines, not record players, were first on their agendas. Swing bands and the dance band industry collapsed, and jazz bands split off from dance orchestras. Listeners and dancers also split, cults developed, and the jazz world broke down into musical, generational, and racial factions.

Working in a declining band industry, promoting modern sounds and bohemian values, the boppers met with a storm of protest. Music expressed the fierce divisions in American culture as those who sought to re-create an ordered home front clashed with modern jazz musicians over the nature of music, new forms of personal freedom, racial assertiveness, and generational alienation. Given that modern jazz seemed to symbolize the disturbances unleashed by the war, it is no surprise that the mass audience was content to keep retreating toward private domestic fulfillment. The Cold War put the final nail in the coffin. At the same time that anti-Communists railed against subversive threats to the American "home front," police and civic authorities cracked down on drug use among jazz musicians as a way to contain the cancer of personal decay and alienation. Between 1947 and 1954, jazz returned to its culturally subversive outsider status; the big band industry never recovered. The hope of swinging the dream that coincided with the New Deal's attempts to create a more democratic society and culture came crashing down in bitterness and recrimination as entertainment institutions, the public, and the musicians went their separate ways.

Although the great public moment of the big bands faded, jazz remained very much alive. Bebop had established itself as the fountain of all modern jazz and as a key part of a new, more assertive African American identity. Despite tremendous obstacles, the new music continued to exert enormous influence throughout the early 1950s. When ballrooms no longer proved inviting to modern big bands, jazz clubs and lounges modeled on the listening rooms along Fifty-second Street and in the Royal Roost and Birdland spread across the country. In most jazz clubs outside the South, noted Leonard Feather, black patrons made up anywhere from 25 to 50 percent of the customers, and combos were made up of musicians of any race who chose to play together. On a smaller scale, jazz as the democratic art form continued, aided still by swing-era promoters such as Norman Granz, whose Jazz at the Philharmonic programs transported large numbers of musicians from city to city and demanded that auditoriums and halls be integrated wherever they played. Although audiences were smaller, they followed the music passionately and saw their interest in modern jazz as a declaration of personal independence from the tyranny of middle-class values that were now buttoning down America. As the hipster visual artists, poets, and novelists who came of age with modern jazz matured and took on the Beat mantle, they created works of art that drew on the spontaneity, movement, and experimentation of bop. The Beats also adopted the bop search for new identities removed from fixed social institutions and defined roles. For blacks and whites, jazz still carried powerful impulses and attractions as well as a critique of American life as uptight and racially rigid. Having lost their mass audience, jazzmen were freer to develop some of their best music in the mid- to late 1950s, once the cold war—cultural as well as political—abated. By this time, however, mass popularity had fallen to rock and roll, another mixture of black and white music blasting across the crazy landscape of American culture.[17]

Notes

PREFACE

1. "Sixty Years," *M*, October 1943, 11.

2. Gunther Schuller, *The Swing Era* (New York, 1989), for example, is a masterful musicological study that emphasizes the overwhelmingly commercial nature of the music. For Eric Hobsbawm, see his article "Some Like It Hot," *The New York Review of Books*, 13 April 1989, 33.

3. Lizabeth Cohen, *Making a New Deal* (Cambridge, U.K., 1990). An important literature has grown on the culture of New York since Lewis Erenberg, *Steppin' Out: New York Nightlife and the Transformation of American Culture, 1890–1930* (Westport, Conn., 1981). See William R. Taylor, ed., *Inventing Times Square: Commerce and Culture at the Crossroads of the World* (New York, 1991); Taylor, *In Pursuit of Gotham* (New York, 1992); and most recently, Ann Douglas, *Terrible Honesty: Mongrel Manhattan in the 1920s* (New York, 1995).

4. Max Horkheimer and Theodor Adorno, *Dialectic of Enlightenment,* trans. John Cumming (1944; reprint, New York, 1987), focus on the power of the culture industry. Cohen, *Making a New Deal,* and Lawrence Levine, "The Folklore of Industrial Society: Popular Culture and Its Audiences," in Levine, *The Unpredictable Past* (New York, 1993), 291–319, emphasize audience creativity but divorce it from the content of mass culture.

5. See John Gennari, "Rhythmic Integration," in Gennari, *Critiquing Jazz: The Politics of Race and Culture in American Jazz Discourse* (University of Chicago Press, forthcoming).

6. LeRoi Jones, *Blues People* (New York, 1963).

7. David Stowe, *Swing Changes* (Cambridge, Mass., 1994). My analysis suggests that the concept of whiteness, while valuable in many ways, has to be seen as permeable and open to debate. For a discussion of the concept, see Alexander Saxton, *The Rise and Fall of the White Republic* (New York, 1990); David R. Roediger, *Wages of Whiteness* (New York, 1991), and his essays, *Towards the Abolition of Whiteness* (New York,

1994); Eric Lott, *Love and Theft: Blackface Minstrelsy and the American Working Class* (New York, 1993). David Nasaw, *Going Out* (New York, 1993) applies the concept to twentieth-century amusements.

8. Jones, *Blues People*, 142–65; Albert Murray, *Stompin' the Blues* (New York, 1982); Ralph Ellison, *Shadow and Act* (New York, 1966), and *Going to the Territory* (New York, 1987).

9. Elaine Tyler May, *Homeward Bound: American Families in the Cold War Era* (New York, 1988).

10. Schuller, *The Swing Era*, is the best musicological account of the period; Ira Gitler, *Swing to Bop* (New York, 1985), is an oral account of the emergence of boppers from the big bands. Both stay close to the jazz world, as do the many wonderful accounts of individual bandleaders and musicians quoted in the text. *The new jazz history*, which focuses on context and uses primary documents, is an expression I apply to the work of William H. Kenney, *Chicago Jazz* (New York, 1993); Burton Peretti, *The Creation of Jazz* (Urbana, Ill., 1992); Stowe, *Swing Changes;* Kathy Ogren, *The Jazz Revolution* (New York, 1989); Thomas J. Hennessey, *From Jazz to Swing: African-Americans and Their Music, 1890–1935* (Detroit, 1994); and Gennari, *Critiquing Jazz.* Much of this work derives from Jones, *Blues People;* Lawrence Levine, *Black Culture and Black Consciousness: Afro-American Folk Thought from Slavery to Freedom* (New York, 1977); and Neil Leonard, *Jazz and the White Americans* (Chicago, 1961), which still has not received its due.

11. The hegemonic approach is advanced best in T. Jackson Lears, "The Concept of Cultural Hegemony: Problems and Possibilities," *American Historical Review* (1985):567–93. For the dialogical approach, see Mikhail M. Bakhtin, *The Dialogic Imagination: Four Essays* (Austin, 1981), and the wonderful essays of George Lipsitz, *Time Passages: Collective Memory and American Popular Culture* (Minneapolis, 1990). Janice Radway, *Reading the Romance: Women, Patriarchy and Popular Literature* (Chapel Hill, 1984) shows the value of reader-response methodology in a contemporary cultural form. To get at past forms, however, I relied on the letters.

12. On the era as a popular moment, see Warren Susman, "The Culture of the Thirties" and "Culture and Commitment," in his *Culture as History* (New York, 1984), 150–210; Lawrence Levine, "American Culture and the Great Depression" and "Hollywood's Washington: Film Images of National Politics during the Great Depression," in his *The Unpredictable Past* (New York, 1993), 206–55. For the split between advanced intellectuals and conservative popular culture, see Richard Pells, *Radical Visions, American Dreams* (New York, 1973). On the conservative nature of popular myths, see Charles Hearn, *The American Dream in the Great Depression* (Westport, Conn., 1981). For movies, see Andrew Bergman, *We're in the Money* (New York, 1972); Robert Sklar, *Media-Made America* (New York, 1976), 175–214. For different views of popular culture, see Lary May, "Making the American Way," *Prospects* 12 (1987):89–123; Robert S. McElvaine, *The Great Depression in America, 1929–1941* (New York, 1984), 196–223; Cohen, *Making a New Deal;* Robert Sklar, *City Boys* (Princeton, 1992). Alan Lawson, "The Cultural Legacy of the New Deal," in *Fifty Years Later: The New*

Deal Evaluated, ed. Harvard Sitkoff (New York, 1985), 155–86, shows many of the New Deal's effects on culture. David Stowe's *Swing Changes,* in an argument closest to my own, holds that in the broadest sense swing represented the cultural expression of the New Deal in music.

CHAPTER ONE: JUST ONE MORE CHANCE

1. On the radio show, see *V,* 18 December 1934, 41; Benny Goodman interview, COHP, 1085–86. On the tour, see *KOS,* 198–201; James Lincoln Collier, *Benny Goodman and the Swing Era* (New York, 1989), 158–67; Ross Firestone, *Swing, Swing, Swing: The Life and Times of Benny Goodman* (New York, 1993), 141–51; Stacy is quoted in Whitney Balliett, "Back from Valhalla," *New Yorker,* 18 August 1975, 32; "most humiliating" is quoted in Benny Goodman with Richard Gehman, "That Old Gang of Mine," *Collier's,* 20 January 1956, 28.

2. Berigan is quoted in an interview with James Maher in Collier, *Benny Goodman,* 165; Goodman is quoted in Firestone, *Swing, Swing, Swing,* 148, 149; "a roar" is quoted in *V,* as in Henry Anton Steig, "Alligator's Idol," *New Yorker,* 17 April 1937, 31. See also *KOS,* 198.

3. On Chicago and New York, see Collier, *Benny Goodman,* 170–971; "Times Square" is quoted in *Saturday Evening Post,* May 1938, 22; *BB,* 6 March 1937, is quoted in Collier, *Benny Goodman,* 187.

4. Willard Alexander, interview, COHP, 1106.

5. For the rise of popular culture in the twentieth century, see Lewis A. Erenberg, *Steppin' Out: New York Nightlife and the Transformation of American Culture, 1890–1930* (Westport, Conn., 1981; reprint, Chicago, 1984); Lary May, *Screening Out the Past: The Birth of Mass Culture and the Motion Picture Industry* (Chicago, 1983); Kathy Peiss, *Cheap Amusements* (Philadelphia, 1986); John Kasson, *Amusing the Million* (New York, 1980); Warren Susman, "'Personality' and the Making of Twentieth Century Culture," in *New Directions in American Intellectual History,* ed. John Higham and Paul Conkin (Baltimore, 1979), 212–26; David Nasaw, *Going Out: The Rise and Fall of Public Amusements* (New York, 1993). Paula Fass, *The Damned and the Beautiful* (New York, 1978), analyzes college youth culture in the 1920s. For a brilliant analysis of "mongrel Manhattan," see Ann Douglas, *Terrible Honesty: Mongrel Manhattan in the 1920s* (New York, 1995).

6. For the general development of black culture and jazz, see LeRoi Jones, *Blues People* (New York, 1963); Lawrence Levine, *Black Culture, Black Consciousness* (New York, 1977); Burton Peretti, *The Creation of Jazz* (Chicago and Urbana, 1992); William Kenney, *Chicago Jazz* (New York, 1993); Thomas Hennessey, *From Jazz to Swing: African-American Musicians and Their Music, 1890–1935* (Detroit, 1994).

7. Douglas, *Terrible Honesty,* 73–107, 303–433, emphasizes that jazz was a crucial part of the Harlem Renaissance. The best book on Chicago jazz is Kenney, *Chicago Jazz.*

8. Gunther Schuller, *Early Jazz* (New York, 1968), 244–45, 256–57; Hennessey, *From Jazz to Swing,* 219–38, 252–55; Samuel Charters and Leonard Kunstadt, *Jazz in*

New York (New York, 1962), 165–83; Hsio Wen Shih, "The Spread of Jazz and the Big Bands," in *Jazz,* ed. Nat Hentoff and Albert McCarthy (New York, 1959), 173–84.

9. Kenney, *Chicago Jazz,* 58–60 (on Armstrong); Schuller, *Early Jazz,* 256–70; Hennessey, *From Jazz to Swing,* 87–95.

10. Schuller, *Early Jazz,* 339–40.; for Ellington's appeal, see Ted Fox, *Showtime at the Apollo* (New York, 1983), 83; for Ellington's biography, see James Lincoln Collier, *Duke Ellington* (New York, 1987); John Edward Hasse, *Beyond Category* (New York, 1993).

11. Quotes are from Collier, *Duke Ellington,* 94–95. Hugues Panassié, *Hot Jazz: The Guide to Swing Music* (New York, 1936), 161–92, remains a superb source on Ellington's style of composition. Houston Baker, Jr., discusses challenges to white cultural dominance in "Modernism and the Harlem Renaissance," *American Quarterly* 39 (spring 1987):84–97. For more on Ellington's style, see Nat Shapiro and Nat Hentoff, *Hear Me Talkin' to Ya* (New York, 1955), 231; Ralph Ellison, "Homage to Duke on His Birthday," in *Going to the Territory* (New York, 1987), 219–21; Burton Peretti, *The Creation of Jazz* (Champaign-Urbana, Ill., 1992), 117–19.

12. The white Chicagoans are discussed sensitively in Neil Leonard, *Jazz and the White Americans* (Chicago, 1961), 55–68; Peretti, *The Creation of Jazz,* 76–99; and Kenney, *Chicago Jazz,* 87–116.

13. John Philip Sousa, *Marching Along* (Boston, 1941), 357–58; "asphalt jungle" is discussed in MacDonald Moore, *Yankee Blues: Musical Culture and American Identity* (Bloomington, Ill., 1985), 73–108. Kathy Ogren, *The Jazz Revolution* (New York, 1989), sees the opposition to jazz as based on the fear of urban modernism and the breaking of sexual, racial, and ethnic boundaries.

14. On Whiteman and symphonic or sweet jazz, see Leonard, *Jazz and the White Americans,* 73–89; Albert McCarthy, *The Dance Band Era: The Dancing Era from Ragtime to Swing, 1910–1950* (Radnor, Pa., 1971), 19–72; Thomas A. DeLong, *Pops: Paul Whiteman, King of Jazz* (Piscataway, N.J., 1983), 64–65; Henry Anton Steig, "Profiles (Benny Goodman)," *New Yorker,* 17 April 1937, 31; Paul Whiteman and Mary McBride, *Jazz* (New York, 1926); Russel B. Nye, "A Word about Whiteman," *Popular Music and Society* 1 (summer 1972):231–41.

15. DeLong, *Pops,* 149–58.

16. I. A. Hirschmann, "The Musician and the Depression," *Nation,* 15 November 1933, 565.

17. On entertainment's decline, see *V,* 29 December 1931, 3; Stanley Walker, *The Night Club Era* (New York, 1933), 201–3. For Times Square, see Brooks McNamara, "Reconstructing Broadway: The Times Square Entertainment District at the End of the 1930s," in Taylor, *Inventing Times Square,* 178–82. On dance halls, see *V,* 12 November 1930, 1, 31; Warren Vache, Sr., *Crazy Fingers: Claude Hopkins' Life in Jazz* (Washington, D.C., 1992), 33–34. Carol Martin, "Dance Marathons," *The Drama Review* 31 (spring 1987):48–63, is the best analysis of the subject.

18. On nightclub decline, see *V,* 7 January 1931, 9; 13 December 1932, 38; 7

February 1933, 57. On East Side speakeasies, see *V,* 9 January 1934, 1, 51. On Harlem, see David Levering Lewis, *When Harlem Was in Vogue* (New York, 1981), 241–42; *V,* 22 January 1935, 1, 60. On national trends, see *V,* 13 December 1932, 46. On Kansas City, see Nathan W. Pearson, Jr., *Goin' to Kansas City* (Urbana, Ill,. 1987), 83–106.

19. On sheet music, see David Ewen, *All the Years of American Popular Music* (Englewood Cliffs, N.J., 1977), 408; Russell Sanjek, *American Popular Music and Its Business* (New York, 1988), 3:47–56; Hazel Meyer, *The Gold in Tin Pan Alley* (Philadelphia, 1958), 71–72. On the slump in record sales, see "Phonograph Records," *Fortune Magazine,* 20 (September 1939): 72. John Hammond with Irving Townsend, *John Hammond On Record* (New York, 1977), 210–19, summarizes Columbia's history. On record players, see *V,* 31 December 1930, 48; Dane Yorke, "The Rise and Fall of the Phonograph," *The American Mercury* 27 (September 1932):1–12.

20. On race records, see Bob Landrum, "This Phonograph Year," *V,* 31 December 1930; Ronald Foreman, Jr., "Jazz and Race Records, 1920–32," (Ph.D. diss., University of Illinois, 1969), 172–204. On shift in music styles, see Landrum, "1931's Shellacked Pancake Leaders," *V,* 29 December 1931, 41; Sanjek, *American Popular Music and Its Business,* 3:117–46. "Last throes" in Ben Bodec, "Boom on Wax in 1938," *V,* 4 January 1939, 165.

21. Mezz Mezzrow and Bernard Wolfe, *Really the Blues,* 152–241 (New York, 1946); Max Kaminsky with V. E. Hughes, *My Life in Jazz* (New York, 1963), 67, 55–56.

22. Artie Shaw, *The Trouble with Cinderella* (New York, 1952), 232–36 for commercial bands, 236–38 for radio.

23. Some musicians were forced to move from band to band. See Arthur Rollini, *Thirty Years with the Big Bands* (Urbana, Ill., 1987), 23–33. On radio experiences, see Kaminsky, *My Life in Jazz,* 63–64; Shaw, *The Trouble with Cinderella,* 256–60; and *KOS,* 117–22. On Goodman's mental state, see Collier, *Benny Goodman,* 90–91.

24. Statistics on all youth are from Josephine Strode, "Swinging the Depression," *Survey* 75 (April 1939):108–10. Statistics on New York high school youth are from Nettie McGill and Nathalie Matthews, *The Youth of New York City* (New York, 1940), 26, 44–45, 153. For the rise in high school attendance, see John Modell, *Into Their Own* (Berkeley, 1989), 122.

25. Modell, *Into Their Own,* 126–32; Robert S. Lynd and Helen Merrell Lynd, *Middletown in Transition* (New York, 1965), 149–51.

26. Ronald Cohen, *When the Old Left Was Young* (New York, 1993), 15–21. For student presidential election straw vote, see the Columbia *Spectator,* 28 October 1932, 1. Hoover won everywhere outside the South.

27. For Dutch dating and informal parties, see Elston D. Herron, "Campus Inactivities," *Daily Illini,* 2 December 1931, 2; 5 February 1932, 4. On needy students, see *Daily Illini,* 9 December 1931, 1, 2; 3 January 1932, 1. For criticism of fraternities at Columbia, see the Columbia *Spectator,* 10 January 1932, 2.

28. "We realize" is from Maxine Davis, *The Lost Generation: A Portrait of American Youth Today* (New York, 1936), 74. This is the theme of Warren Susman, "Culture and

Commitment," in his *Culture as History* (New York, 1985), 184–210; and Lawrence Levine, "American Culture in the Great Depression," *The Yale Review* 74 (winter 1985), reprinted in his *The Unpredictable Past* (New York, 1993), 206–30.

29. Kaminsky, *My Life in Jazz,* 56. On movies, see Howard Mandelbaum and Eric Meyers, *Screen Deco* (New York, 1985), 13–32, 101–4. Robert A. Caro, *The Power Broker, Robert Moses and the Fall of New York* (New York, 1974), 338–39, 397–401, 506–7, explores one particular upper-class nightclub and its fate.

30. Charlie Barnet with Stanley Dance, *Those Swinging Years* (Baton Rouge, 1984), 61. For material on Duchin, see unidentified clipping in Duchin file, LPA. For Reisman, see Paul Charosh, "The Leo Reisman Story," *Record Research,* April 1964, 3–12.

31. Guy Lombardo with Jack Altschul, *Auld Acquaintance* (Garden City, 1975), 102, 27, 43, 59–62, 94 for radio's role, 161–64 for the band's influence. On the music, see McCarthy, *The Dance Band Era,* 64–74. See also Victor R. Greene, "Friendly Entertainers: Dance Bandleaders and Singers in the Great Depression, 1929–1935," *Prospects* 20 (1995):181–207.

32. Lambert quoted in Gilbert Seldes, "The People and the Arts," *Scribner's Magazine,* 101 (May 1937), 65. Henry Pleasants, *The Great American Popular Singers* (New York, 1974), 16–61, is the best study of the subject and contains the quotes on Jolson and the crooners. On Sophie Tucker, see Erenberg, *Steppin' Out,* 176–205. Tucker disliked radio's censorship. "I couldn't even say 'hell' or 'damn,' and nothing, honey, is more expressive than the way I say 'hell' or 'damn.'" *NYT,* 10 February 1966, 1, 31.

33. For the effects of technology and the depression on singers, see H. F. Mooney, "Popular Music since the 1920s: The Significance of Shifting Taste," *American Quarterly* 20 (spring 1968):67–85, and "Songs, Singers and Society," *American Quarterly* 6 (fall 1954): 221–32. For Vallee quotes, see Rudy Vallee with Gil McKean, *My Time Is Your Time* (New York, 1962), 82; Vallee, *Vagabond Dreams* (New York 1930), 90–92, 258, 262; "Mr. Vallee Looks at the Nation; Tour Over . . . ," newspaper clipping, 13 September [1932], New York City, in Rudy Vallee Scrapbooks, Larry Kiner Collection, Redmond, Washington, is quoted in Greene, "Friendly Entertainers," 194.

34. Crosby, *Call Me Lucky,* 146–49.

35. Hoagy Carmichael, *The Stardust Road* (New York, 1946), 180. Dixie Lee Crosby, as told to Marva Peterson, "My Husband, Bing," *Movieland,* February 1948, 47, 84, in Bing Crosby file, MPAS; Crosby, *Call Me Lucky,* 45–46.

36. On nostalgia, Spaeth, *The Facts of Life in Popular Song,* 51–59. Norman Charles, "Social Values in American Popular Song," (Ph.D. diss., University of Pennsylvania, 1958), 78–85, notes that the early 1930s were the high point for songs of reassurance and philosophical questioning. For songs of the depression, see David Ewen, *All the Years of American Popular Music* (Englewood Cliffs, N.J., 1977), 410.

37. Timothy Scheuer, "Goddesses and Golddiggers: Images of Women in Popular Music of the 1930s," *Journal of Popular Culture* 24 (September 1990):30–31.

38. Anita O'Day with George Eells, *High Times, Hard Times* (New York, 1982), 42–43; see also Maxwell Gilbert, *Helen Morgan: Her Life and Legend* (New York, 1974); Hamilton Darby Perry, *Libby Holman: Body and Soul* (Boston, 1983).

39. Scheuer, "Goddesses and Golddiggers," 32–33. For similarity to movie heroines of the same period, see Marilyn Campbell, "RKO's Fallen Women, 1930–33," *Velvet Light Trap* 10 (fall 1973):13–16; Elizabeth Kendall, *The Runaway Bride: Hollywood Romantic Comedy of the 1930s* (New York, 1990), 1–21.

40. Milt Hinton and David G. Berger, *Bass Line* (Philadelphia, 1988), 53. For breakup of bands, see Hennessey, *From Jazz to Swing,* 147–48, 151–52; Zilner Randolph, JOHP, 88–91. See also Peretti, *The Creation of Jazz,* 164–71.

41. Hammond, *On Record,* 120, 89; Bob Landry, "1931's Shellacked Pancake Leaders," *V,* 29 December 1931, 41; Foreman, Jr., "Jazz and Race Records," 172–204; Sanjek, *American Popular Music and Its Business,* 3:71–73. On Ellington's record releases and radio generally, see Hasse, *Beyond Category,* 150, 166.

42. Hennessey, *From Jazz to Swing,* 122–34.

43. Ibid.; Walter C. Allen, *Hendersonia: The Music of Fletcher Henderson and His Musicians* (Highland Park, N.J., 1973), 273–303.

44. Hennessey, *From Jazz to Swing,* 140–46.

45. On the new swing style, see ibid., 136–38; Schuller, *Early Jazz,* 271–79.

46. Collier, *Duke Ellington,* 131–54, describes this period in Ellington's life and music. See Barry Ulanov, *Duke Ellington* (New York, 1946), 113–29, for Ellington's European trip in 1933. For a discussion of the music of the period, see Hasse, *Beyond Category,* 188–92.

47. On repeal, see David F. Kyvig, *Repealing National Prohibition* (Chicago, 1979). For FDR's pronouncements on repeal, see Samuel Rosenman, ed., *The Public Papers of Franklin Delano Roosevelt* (New York, 1938–50), 1:318–23, 399–404, 684–92. For Will Rogers, see Lawrence Levine, "American Culture in the Great Depression," *The Yale Review* 74 (winter 1985):210.

48. "Roosevelt Inauguration Changes Political Lineup of Industry," *BB,* 11 March 1933, 1, 53; "All Locals to Aid Repeal by States at AFM Request," *BB,* 11 March 1933, 1, 5.

49. Billy Rose in *V,* 26 June 1934, 48, 59. On New York nightclub revival, see *V,* 11 December 1934, 47. "More niteries" in Abel Green, "Nighteries on Road Back," *V,* 6 January 1937, 195. See also H. I. Brock, "Now Our Nightlife Glows Again," *NYT,* 11 February 1934, sec. 6, 10, 19; Erenberg, "From New York to Middletown: Repeal and the Legitimization of Nightlife in the Great Depression," *American Quarterly* 38 (winter 1986):765–66.

50. John Hurley, "Ballrooms' Cafe Style," *V,* 21 April 1937, 49. For Henderson's decline, see Allen, *Hendersonia,* 273–316.

CHAPTER TWO: THE CROWD GOES WILD

1. "Free public truckin'" from *Chicago Daily Times,* 24 August 1938, 3, which also notes the presence of Earl Hines's band and tap dancer Bill "Bojangles" Robinson playing for black and white dancers. *CD,* 27 August 1938, 9, featured a picture of one of the black bands and a group of black dancers. "Deafening groan" and "barrel-

house" from Paul Wittenmyer, "Jitterbugs Wreck Chicago Stadium," *M*, October 1938, 16.

2. *Chicago Daily Times*, 24 August 1938, 3; Gene Morgan, *Chicago Daily News*, 24 August 1938, 1.

3. "Jitterbug ecstasy" from *M*, October 1938, 16; "world's largest crowd" from *Chicago Daily News*, 24 August 1938, 3. For psychologists' reactions see *Chicago Daily Tribune*, 26 August 1938, 17, and *Chicago Daily Times*, 25 August 1938, 19.

4. Paul E. Wittenmyer, "Jitterbugs Wreck Chicago Stadium," *M*, October 1938, 16. Ralph Gleason quoted in *The Swing Era, 1941–42: Swing as a Way of Life*, ed. George D. Daniels (New York, Time-Life Records), 6. For a similar view, see John Gennari, *Critiquing Jazz: The Politics of Race and Culture in American Jazz Discourse, 1935–1995*, (University of Chicago Press, forthcoming), chap. 2.

5. Sexual boldness discussed in Gama Gilbert, "Higher Soars the Swing Fever," *NYT*, 14 August 1938, 14; Kreisler quoted in J. Fred MacDonald, "'Hot Jazz,' the Jitterbug, and Misunderstanding: The Generation Gap in Swing 1935–1945," *Popular Music and Society* 2 (fall 1972):47–49. For "jungle discords," see James H. S. Moynahan, "Ragtime to Swing," *Saturday Evening Post*, 13 February 1937, 15. Archbishop of Dubuque quoted in *NYT*, 26 October 1938.

6. *Chicago Daily Tribune*, 24 August 1938, 1, 10. On the Los Angeles riot, see *M*, April 1940, 10, and Stowe, *Swing Changes*, 31; "musical Hitlerism" from *NYT*, 2 November 1938. This criticism is akin to Theodor Adorno's view of swing and the jitterbug as the emotionally bereft product of mass industrial culture and the modern culture industry. See T. W. Adorno, "Perennial Fashion—Jazz," in *Critical Theory and Society: A Reader*, ed. Stephen Eric Bronner and Douglas MacKay Kellner (New York, 1989), 205–6. Adorno is discussed in Gennari, *Critiquing Jazz*, 76–78.

7. William Allan White quoted in *Time*, 20 May 1940, 41. David Stowe, in *Swing Changes*, 26–27, develops the new cultural relativism. Recollections by swing fans are culled from about three hundred letters sent to me, the most revealing of which are cited in this and other chapters. For parents courting each other to the Charleston, shag, and fox-trot, Tom McNulty, letter to author, 2 August 1994, 1. For "wild and strange" music and behavior, Orin Stambaugh, letter to author, 14 July 1994, 2.

8. Irving Kolodin, "What about Swing?" *The Parents Magazine*, August 1939, 18; "horses and buggies" from "Jitterbugs—We're Not What You Think," *Radio Mirror*, February 1939, 12; Cecelia Ager, "Swing Dancing," *V*, 6 January 1937, 188; "swing is the voice of youth," Lillian Breslau, letter to editor, *NYT*, 26 February 1939, 51.

9. Kolodin, "What about Swing?" 18; Gama Gilbert, "Swing It," *NYT Magazine*, 16 January 1938, 21; "music of the cities" and Mischa Elman in MacDonald, "Hot Jazz," 50. For a more recent analysis of this belief, see Alice Goldfarb Marquis, *Hopes and Ashes: The Birth of Modern Times, 1929–1939* (New York, 1986), 3.

10. Larry Clinton, "Swing Grows Up, A Prophecy," *Good Housekeeping*, October 1938, 13, 92; "Goodman a la King," *Playboy*, February 1958, 61; Holman Harvey, "It's Swing!" *Delineator* November 1936, 10. On Hot Clubs, see Oro, "United We Stand—Hot," *BB*, 26 December 1936, 42–43.

11. Columbia *Spectator* and UCLA's *Bruin* both followed swing in about 1935; the *Daily Illini* printed swing stories and ads for swing bands only in March 1939. See also H. M. Cooper, "Swing Tops; But Weakening," *BB,* 16 April 1938, 11; "College Rhythm," *V,* various issues, 1936–38. For the University of Missouri, see George J. Schulte, Jr., *V,* 4 January 1939, 164.

12. Pence James, *Chicago Daily News,* 24 April 1943, n.p., notes the popularity of swing among Chicago high-school students. Jack McNulty, letter to author, 22 July 1994, 1; Stambaugh, letter to author, 1. For high-school attendance, see John Modell, "Dating Becomes the Way of American Youth," in Leslie Page Moch and Gary D. Stark, *Essays on the Family and Historical Change* (College Station, Tex., 1983), 91–126; Modell, *Into One's Own: From Youth to Adulthood in the United States, 1920–1975* (Berkeley, 1989), 122–26; Susan Ware, *Holding Their Own: American Women in the 1930s* (Boston, 1982), 56.

13. Sidney Curran, letter to author, 20 June 1994, 3; Jack McNulty, letter to author, 17 August 1994, 1; Ted Karamanski, interview with author, 15 June 1990; Jean Lukhard, letter to author, 16 November 1994, 1; Louise Strayer, letter to author, 13 July 1994, 1.

14. Nettie Pauline McGill and Ellen Nathalie Matthews, *The Youth of New York City* (New York, 1940), 260–66; Malcolm X with Alex Haley, *The Autobiography of Malcolm X* (New York, 1963), 34–35; Gloria Vargas, letter to author, 8 September 1994, 1; ibid., 21 October 1994, 12.

15. On one-nighters, see Joe Bookman, "One-Night Tour," *Collier's,* 1 November 1941, 22; "marble halls" quoted in Alvin Levin, "Swing Glories in Its Humble Origins," *The Musician,* April 1939, 6, 68.

16. See Gennari, "Rhythmic Integration," in "Critiquing Jazz."

17. Elliot White, letter to author, 21 July 1994, 3; Sidney Curran, letter to author, 30 June 1994, 1. Philip K. Eberly, *Music in the Air: America's Changing Tastes in Popular Music, 1920–1980* (New York, 1982), 84–99, 114–24, is excellent on radio and swing. Roland Marchand, *Advertising the American Dream* (Berkeley, 1985), 285–333, discusses "hard sell" advertising on radio.

18. John Wilson, "The Great Big Bands" (booklet, Reader's Digest), n.p. Carl Smaida, letter to author, 4 January 1995, 2; Howard Becker, interview with author, 20 January 1984. The Essex House is described in Eberly, *Music in the Air,* 70–72.

19. Roy Porter with David Keller, *There and Back* (Baton Rouge, 1991), 25–27. See also Dave Dexter, Jr., *Jazz Cavalcade* (New York, 1946), 165–71.

20. George Simon, *The Big Bands,* 4th ed. (New York, 1981), 55, for DJs. Elliott Grennard, "Jamming the Jam," *NM,* 9 September 1941, 26–27.

21. Leonard Pratt, letter to author, 11 July 1994, 1; Lukhard, letter to author, 2. Parent's quote in Pence James, "Swing Is Here to Stay; Poll Puts It 'Solid,'" *Chicago Daily News,* 19 April 1943, 1; Elliot White, letter to author, 21 July 1994, 3; Leonard Pratt, letter to author, 22 October 1994, 1–2; Sara B. Vann, letter to author, 7 November 1994, 1; Louise Strayer, letter to author, 29 October 1994, 2.

22. Curran, letter to author; White, letter to author, 3; June Canter, letter to au-

thor, 24 October 1994, 3. A similar sentiment is in Rita Luther, letter to author, 9 July 1994, 1; Lukhard, letter to author, 2. In his letter dated 26 July 1994, Ed MacLeod described listening to his favorite bands every morning in Boston on WHDH's 920 Club.

23. Orin Stambaugh, letter to author, 26 December 1994; Louise Strayer, letter to author, 13 July 1994, 2; Ann M. Medaris, letter to author, 24 January 1995, 1; Chuck Arnold, letter to author, 11 August 1994, 2; Luther, letter to author; White, letter to author, 21 July 1994, 2; Jack McNulty, letter to author, 22 July 1994; Geoffrey Mark Fidelman, *First Lady of Song: Ella Fitzgerald for the Record* (New York, 1996), 18–25.

24. Irving Kolodin, "The Dance Band Business," *Harper's Magazine*, 76–77; "In Person Policy of New Paramount Shows Public Trend," *M*, March 1936, 16; *New York Enquirer*, 29 November 1948, n.p., in BG; Harry Kalchein, "The Trend in Stage Shows," *BB*, 10 April 1937, 35; Woody Herman and Stuart Troup, *The Woodchopper's Ball: The Autobiography of Woody Herman* (New York, 1990), 36; Johnny Otis, *Upside Your Head!* (Hanover and London, 1993), 120. See Daniels, *The Swing Era*, 17, for a fan recollection. *BB*, 25 June 1938, 4 discusses how movie houses ran low-grade pictures with top-rated bands and made large profits.

25. On contests, see "Mid West Ballrooms Ban Jitterbugs," *M*, December 1938, 29; *V*, 22 March 1939, 1; Ralph Cooper with Steve Dougherty, *Amateur Night at the Apollo* (New York, 1990), 70–80. On the theme of audience participation through contests on radio, see J. Fred MacDonald, *Don't Touch That Dial* (Chicago, 1979), 47–49.

26. Goodman is quoted in Ross Firestone, *Swing, Swing, Swing: The Life and Times of Benny Goodman* (New York, 1993), 200. *The New Yorker*, 17 April 1937, 31, and James Dugan, "The King of Swing Holds Court," *DW*, 31 January 1938, 9, describe the Paramount engagement. For "Carnival," "Goodman-Goofy,"see *Los Angeles Times*, 21 March 1937, n.p., BG. "Goodmaniacs" and "theater history" are quoted in *San Francisco Chronicle*, 22 March 1937, n.p., BG.

27. McGarrity is quoted in Esther Kitzes, "Benny Recalls Riot," unidentified Pittsburgh newspaper, 1956, in BG. Charles Travelbee, letter to author, 2 August 1994, 2; Leonard Pratt, letter to author, 11 July 1994, 2; Leon Meenach, letter to author, 30 November 1944, 4; "effervescent" in *V*, 1 November 1939, 1; and Travelers Aid incident, unidentified newspaper clipping, n.d. (ca. 1937), BG.

28. *Cleveland Plain Dealer*, 7 December 1939, n.p., and 10 January 1942, n.p., in John Flower, *Moonlight Serenade: A Bio-Discography of the Glenn Miller Civilian Band* (New Rochelle, 1972), 106–7, 404. For Rochester, see A. J. Warner, "Goodman Welcomed by Crowd," Rochester, New York *Union*, 18 November 1940, BG.

29. Don Congdon, "Let's Dance," in his *The Thirties* (New York, 1962), 356; John Hurley, "Ballrooms' Cafe Style," *V*, 21 April 1937, 49.

30. Cooper, *Amateur Night at the Apollo*, 52–53. The Arcadia manager is quoted in "Making a Ballroom a Social and Financial Success," *M*, January 1936, 42.

31. Charles Hayden, letter to author, 27 July 1994, 1. For *Metronome's* surprise, see "White Big Bands in Harlem," *M*, January 1940, 10.

32. R. L. Larkin, "Are White Bands Stealing Ideas from the Negro?" *DB,* 15 December 1940, 5; Ruth Shapiro, telephone interview with author, August 1994; Elliot White, letter to author, 21 July 1994, 3, 5. Andy Kirk recounts playing many white ballrooms and country clubs. Kirk as told to Amy Lee, *Twenty Years on Wheels* (Ann Arbor, 1989), 74–100.

33. *New York Times,* quoted in Marshall and Jean Stearns, *Jazz Dance* (New York, 1962), 331; letter to author (identity deleted), 21 September 1994, 2; "Mad 'Suzy-Q' Is Harlem's New Gift to Swing," Bangor Maine *News,* 27 March 1937 and Holdenville, Oklahoma *Tribune,* 28 March 1937, BG.

34. Snowden is quoted in Stearns and Stearns, *Jazz Dance,* 315–25.

35. Stearn and Stearns are quoted in their *Jazz Dance,* 329 Ernie Smith is quoted Stearns and Stearns, 329–30, and in "New Worlds, New Forms," *Dancing,* episode 5, PBS television series; "The Lindy Hop," *Life,* 23 August 1943, 95. Wendler is quoted in Stearns and Stearns, 328–29.

36. Wendler's "sophisticated mask" is quoted in Stearns and Stearns, 329; Cecelia Ager, "Swing Dancing," *V,* 6 January 1937, 188; Mike Levin, "Be Not Bitter with the Jitter," *DB,* 15 December 1944, 1, 15.

37. Levin, "When Johnny Comes Marching Home," *DB,* 15 December 1944, 15; Ager, "Swing Dancing," 188, for "care less than nothing . . . trance."

38. Dean Collins, quoted in Dean Stewart, "Remembering Swing Dancing," *Los Angeles Times,* 5 August 1984; letter to author from a woman in the Bronx (identity deleted), 21 September 1994, 1–2; John Martin, "From Minuet to Jitterbug," *NYT,* 7 November 1943, 16; Leonard Pratt, letter to author, 22 October 1994, 2.

39. Susie Tucker, letter to author, 21 July 1994, 2; Chummy MacGregor, "Moonlight Serenade Revisited" (typescript, 1966), 162, GM; Leonard Pratt, letter to author, 22 October 1994, 2.

40. On the new style of singing, see Henry Pleasants, *The Great American Popular Singers* (New York, 1974), 127–40, 159–64. See also Helen Forrest with Bill Libby, *I Had the Craziest Dream* (New York, 1982), and Anita O'Day with George Eells, *High Times, Hard Times* (New York, 1982).

41. Ward, quoted in Firestone, *Swing, Swing, Swing,* 197; Gloria Sadowski, quoted in the Chicago *Daily News,* 23 April 1943, n.p.; Leonard Pratt, letter to author, 22 October 1994, 2.

42. For swing clothes, see James L. Collier, *Benny Goodman and the Swing Era* (New York, 1989), 191; Malcolm X, *Autobiography,* 51–58. For one zoot "inventor," see David Grimes, "Zoot Sweet," *Chicago Tribune,* 28 September 1988, sec. 7, 17–19.

43. Collier, *Benny Goodman,* 192–93; Harold Fox, quoted in Grimes, "Zoot Sweet," *Chicago Tribune,* 28 September 1988, 17. See also Richard Williams, "Basic Swing-lish, or How to Know What the Younger Generation Is Talking About," *House Beautiful,* February 1944, 27, 94–95; Cab Calloway, *Hepster's Dictionary* (New York, 1936); Benny Goodman, "Jam Session," *Pictorial Review,* May 1938, 15, 59.

44. Hep Cat, "To Hell with the Jitter-Bugs," *DB,* October 1938, 1, as cited in Firestone, *Swing, Swing, Swing,* 476; Goodman as told to Ted Shane, "Now Take the Jitter-

bug," *Collier's*, 25 February 1939, 11 (the story is probably apocryphal); E. J. Kahn, Jr., "Young Man with a Viola," *The New Yorker*, 29 July 1939, 19.

45. "Hep musicians," in *BB*, 2 July 1938, 11; Jack McNulty, letter to author, 22 July 1994, 2; Charles Hayden, letter to author, 27 July 1994, 1.

46. Forrest, *I Had the Craziest Dream*, 68. For "autograph hounds" see Bernice O'Kane, "It's a Fact," Watertown, Mass. *Tribune*, 7 May 1937, n.p., BG. "Ella Fitzgerald Mobbed by Crowd," *DB*, 15 July 1940, 1; Jesse E. Lehman and Louie McMillan, "Chords and Discords," *DB*, 15 September 1940, 10–11.

47. Torme, *It Wasn't All Velvet*, 50–51; Goodman, "Now Take the Jitterbug," Collier's, 25 February 1939, 12.

48. George Frazier, "Stupid Critics Misjudge 3,000 Ickies' Action," *DB*, June 1938, 4; Dick Jacobs, "They're Turning Swing into a Caricature," *M*, October 1938, 67; Artie Shaw, *The Trouble with Cinderella* (New York, 1952), 350–51, "shrieking," 344.

49. One of Them, "Jitterbugs—We're Not What You Think," *Radio Mirror*, February 1939, 60; Alice Goldfarb Marquis, *Hopes and Ashes* (New York, 1986), 3; William Glackin, telephone interview with author, July 1994; Nat Hentoff, in "Where Swing Came From," *The Swing Era 1938–1939* (companion book to Time-Life Records, I, 1970), 32; "Ellington Refutes Cry That Swing Started Sex Crimes!" *DB*, December 1937, 2, reprinted in Mark Tucker, ed., *The Duke Ellington Reader* (New York, 1993), 128–29; For Teddy Hill's audience see Otis Ferguson, "Breakfast Dance in Harlem," in *The Otis Ferguson Reader*, ed. Dorothy Chamberlain and Robert Wilson (Highland Park, Ill., 1982). For a larger discussion of fans' listening to swing, see Scott Deveraux, "The Emergence of the Jazz Concert, 1935–1945," *American Music* 7 (spring 1989): 6–29.

50. Edward Pessen, "The Kingdom of Swing: New York City in the Late 1930s," *New York History* (July 1989), 279–82, for Goodman's battles; Count Basie, *Good Morning Blues* (New York, 1952), 207–10, describes his bouts.

51. See *M*, June 1937, for the Webb-Goodman battle. For Basie-Goodman, see George Avakian, "'Barrelhouse Benny' Drops Decision to 'Kansas City Killer," *Tempo*, July 1938, 4–5.

52. See Gennari, *Critiquing Jazz*, 69; Dave Dexter, Jr., *Jazz Cavalcade* (New York, 1946), 114–26; Ron Welburn, "Jazz Magazines of the 1930s: An Overview of Their Provocative Journalism," *American Music* 5 (fall 1987):255–70. The Becker quote is from interview with author, 20 January 1984; Elliot White, letter to author, 20 December 1994, 5.

53. Barbara Wright, "Squawks," *M*, April 1943, 6; P. Biagini, "We're Not Righteous," *M*, January 1943, 4; comments on Freeman are quoted in "Impressions in Wax," *M*, July 1937, 24.

54. For KFAC, see "Goodman-Goofy," *Los Angeles Times*, 21 March 1937, n.p.; for WNEW, *Radio Daily*, 29 March 1937, n.p.; *Radio Guide*, 3 April 1937, "Vote for Radio's Star of Stars Now," n.p., all BG.

55. Welburn, "Jazz Magazines," 261. For "your votes," see Frank E. Bolden, "Orchestra Whirl," *PC*, 22 November 1941, 20. See *CD*'s first poll, 20 December 1940, 20.

56. James is quoted in *Chicago Daily News*, 24 April 1943, n.p.; Albert Murray,

Stomping the Blues (New York, 1982), 182–83; Leonard Pratt, letter to author, 22 October 1994, 2; Elliot White, letter to author, 20 December 1994, 5; Charles Hayden, letter to author, 27 July 1994, 1; Miller Tucker, letter to author, 31 October 1994, 3; Orin Stambaugh, letter to author, 14 July 1994, 1.

57. Frank Mathias, *G.I. Jive: An Army Bandsman in World War II* (Lexington, 1982), 3–4; Leonard Pratt, letter to author, July 1994, 1; Torme, *It Wasn't All Velvet*, 17–19; Goodman, "Jam Session," 15. For more on amateur bands, see Pence James, "Make It Hot, Maestro! School Bands Swing It," *Chicago Daily News*, 21 April 1943, 1; Stevenson Swanson, "The House the Hettlers Built," *Chicago Tribune*, 13 December 1984, sec. 5, at 3.

58. For more on concerts and festivals, see Carl Cons, "Society and Musicians Sit Spellbound by Brilliance of Goodman's Band," *DB*, December 1935–January 1936, 1; *NYT*, 13 June 1938, 15, and 30 May 1938, 13; "All Day Swing Carnival Draws 25,000," *M*, July 1938, 9.

CHAPTER THREE: SWING IS HERE

1. W. W. Nash, quoted in Whitney Balliett, "S.R.O.," The *New Yorker*, 26 December 1977, 39; George Simon, "Benny and Cats Make Carnegie Debut Real Howling Success," *M*, February 1938, 15, 18, 44; Irving Kolodin, "Notes on the Program: Benny Goodman and His Orchestra," January 1938, quoted in Ross Firestone, *Swing, Swing, Swing: The Life and Times of Benny Goodman* (New York, 1993), 209. For other descriptions of the concert, see James Lincoln Collier, *Benny Goodman and the Swing Era* (New York, 1989), 214–29; Firestone, *Swing, Swing, Swing*, 207–17. For "short hair," see *M*, February 1938, 44. Scott Devaux, "The Emergence of the Jazz Concert, 1935–1945," *American Music* 7 (spring 1989): 6–29, discusses jazz concerts.

2. For "cold feet," James and nerves, see Firestone, *Swing, Swing, Swing*, 209–11; for "whore," *Wall Street Journal*, 7 January 1988, as cited in Collier, *Benny Goodman*, 215; for "emitted" and "cheered," see Simon, "Benny and Cats," 15, 18, 44.

3. For "blasted" and "New York," see *M*, February 1938, 18; For the trio, quartet, and "Bei Mir Bist Du Schon," see Firestone, *Swing, Swing, Swing*, 213–14.

4. For "misprints in Esquire" and "responding," see *DB*, February 1938, 1; for "new dance," see *M*, February 1938, 44.

5. For descriptions of the concert and "short hair" see Simon, "Benny and Cats," 15, 18, 44; for the Savoy battle, see Buck Clayton assisted by Nancy Miller Elliott, *Buck Clayton's Jazz World* (New York, 1987), 109; "jammed into" is quoted in "Basie's Band Conquers Chick's," *M*, February 1938, 15; Count Basie as told to Albert Murray, *Good Morning Blues: The Autobiography of Count Basie* (New York, 1985), 207–10.

6. Albert McCarthy, *The Dance Band Era: The Dancing Era from Ragtime to Swing, 1910–1950* (Radnor, Pa., 1971), 122; and Steig, "Profiles (Goodman)," 33–34 note how Goodman's success at the Palomar Ballroom came as a surprise to MCA.

7. For "weak sister," see Goodman, "Is Swing Dead?" *M&R*, August 1941, 10; for "Mickey Mouse," see George Simon, "Dance Band Review (Sammy Kaye)," *M*, No-

vember 1938, 24–25; for "daintily around," see George Simon, "Review of Shep Fields," *M*, June 1936, 16. Sammy Kaye responded to *Metronome*'s anti–sweet band bias, "Sammy Kaye Tells Us Off!" *M*, May 1947, 18, 43. For "sock," see Edward Stein, "The Brown Bomber of Jazz," *M*, May 1936, 26.

8. Benny Goodman, "Is Swing Dead?" *M&R*, August 1941, 40. John Kouwenhoven, *Made in America* (New York, 1962), 197–224 is the classic statement that jazz is the democratic art.

9. See *KOS*, 19, for the quotation, 15–25 on musical apprenticeship. David Goodman's socialism comes from Ida Winsberg, Goodman's sister, interview with the author, 30 May 1990. Collier, *Benny Goodman*, 6–12 describes their poverty; see 13–18 for his musical apprenticeship. On "kicks," see *KOS*, 32.

10. Goodman is quoted in *KOS*, 210–17. For a discussion of Jews and blacks, see Hasia Diner, *In the Almost Promised Land: American Jews and Blacks, 1915–1935* (Baltimore, 1995), especially 68–69, 105–15.

11. Collier, *Benny Goodman*, 21–27; "play free" and "barrelhoused," *KOS*, 29–45; Firestone, *Swing, Swing, Swing*, 17–35. For the effect of segregation on white jazz musicians, see William H. Kenney, *Chicago Jazz* (New York, 1993), 85–86, 87–116 and ch. 1 of this book. See John Chilton, *Stomp Off, Let's Go* (London, 1983), 11–12 for the Lawson quote and Pollack's early years. Collier, *Benny Goodman*, 45–59 discusses the conflicts in the band. See also McCarthy, *The Dance Band Era*, 25–27.

12. *KOS*, 119–22; Collier, *Benny Goodman*, 90–91. For more on his unhappiness, see Annemarie Ewing, "Benny Goodman's Amazing Life, Rebel's Road to Glory," *Radio Mirror*, 10 May 1938, 10–11, 63.

13. *KOS*, 122–23, 127; John Hammond, "King of Swing," *The Crisis*, April 1937, 110, discusses Goodman and race. For "burning desire," see Goodman interview, COHP, 1085; for "only interested in jazz," see Benny Goodman and Richard Gehman, "That Old Gang of Mine," *Collier's*, 20 January 1956, 27.

14. *KOS*, 161, 256–70 credits Henderson's arrangements for the band's success, as does Hammond, "King of Swing," 110, from whence the quote; for "stranglehold," see John Hammond with Irving Townsend, *John Hammond on Record* (New York, 1981), 142. Recently, James Collier, *Benny Goodman*, 133–35, has emphasized arranger Spud Murphy's contributions to the early Goodman band. He may have written a number of arrangements, but it was always Henderson that Goodman credited with setting the band's style. John Hammond, "Landmark in White Jazz Circles," *MM*, 28 May 1935, 5.

15. Morroe Berger, Edward Berger, and James Patrick, *Benny Carter: A Life in American Music* (Metuchen, N.J., 1982), 45–46.

16. Benny Goodman, "Jam Session," *Pictorial Review*, May 1938, 15. Kolodin's remarks are in *KOS*, 171; for Busse, see H. Allen Smith, "Tommy Dorsey Is Rated Best Trombone," *New York World Telegram*, 16 September 1938, 25, in BG. Ward is quoted in Leonard Feather, "Helen Ward Comes Back," *M*, March 1943, 12.

17. "Inspired freedom," in Carl Cons, "What Is Swing?" *DB*, April 1936, 2; the description is from John S. Wilson, "Gene Krupa Obit.," *NYT*, 17 October 1974, 50,

cited in Firestone, *Swing, Swing, Swing,* 121. On drums, see Krupa, "Drummer's Dope," *M,* May 1938, 36, and "Krupa's Band," *M,* May 1938, 37 for "tom toms." On Baby Dodds, see "Gene Krupa on Drummers," *M,* October 1943, 33. For more on Krupa's drumming, see Bruce Crowther, *Gene Krupa* (New York, 1987), 67–71. Dave Tough, who played drums for Goodman, Artie Shaw, and Tommy Dorsey, learned from black drummers in Chicago. See Barbara Hodgkins, "that's RICH!" *M,* October 1946, 19 for Buddy Rich.

18. Andre Hodeir, *Jazz: Its Evolution and Essence* (New York, 1956), 195–217, analyzes the new styles of black jazz that emerged in the late 1920s and early 1930s, and especially the changes in the rhythm section. Collier, *Benny Goodman,* 152–53 analyzes the rhythm section; for "the rhythm section" see Collier's interview with Jimmy Maxwell, Collier, *Benny Goodman,* 152. See Benny Goodman, "What Swing Really Does to People," *Liberty Magazine,* 14 May 1938, 6, BG file, IJS, for "to know."

19. For "sustained," see Goodman, "That Old Gang of Mine," 31.

20. See *KOS,* 237 for "the most important element . . . "; "the song not the thing, . . ." Irving Townsend, liner notes, "Benny Goodman: All-Time Greatest Hits," Columbia Records KG 31547. For baseball, see Goodman, "What Swing Really Does," 6.

21. Benny Goodman, "'The Public Is Sick of Stick-Wavers!'" *M&R,* April 1942, 15. For Kaye, see Simon, "Dance Band Reviews," *M,* November 1938, 24–25.

22. See Dorothy Chamberlain and Robert Wilson, eds., *The Otis Ferguson Reader* (Highland Park, Ill., 1982), 74–80, for group spirit; *KOS,* 172–73 for solos, 238 for consistency; Steig, "Profiles (Goodman)," 31 for barrel house; Collier, *Benny Goodman,* 151–52 on rehearsals. Leonard, *Jazz and the White Americans,* 123 discusses the importance of ensemble playing.

23. For "collective improvisation" and "tight band quality," see *KOS,* 173; "the feeling" and "each man who plays" are quoted in Chamberlain and Wilson, *Otis Ferguson Reader,* 79. Steig, "Profiles (Goodman)," 32. Max Kaminsky with V. E. Hughes, *My Life in Jazz* (New York 1963), 99. See also Carl Cons, "What Is Swing?" *DB,* April 1936, 2.

24. *KOS,* 100 notes the "hot clique." "Players took over," in Irving Kolodin, "What about Swing?" *Parents Magazine,* August 1939, 18. Goodman, "'The Public Is Sick of Stick-Wavers!'" 15. Krupa is cited in John Wilson, "Benny Goodman Gave Much to Dance Business," *DB,* approx. December 1951, n.p., BG.

25. See John S. Wilson, "Benny Goodman, King of Swing," *NYT,* 14 June 1986, 30 for the Alexander quotations and "college professor"; see Steig, "Profiles (Goodman)," 32 for "not a personality lad"; for "Prince Charming," see P. A. James, "He Plays Hot!" (unidentified, 1935 or 1936), BG; Shaw, *The Trouble with Cinderella,* 203–4; "Hi-Ho" is quoted in Michel Mok, "A Band Leader Thinks," *New York Post,* 26 September 1939, n.p., AS file, LPA. For Shaw on integrity, see John McDonough, "Artie Shaw's Big Band Obsession," *DB,* February 1986, 28.

26. John Hammond, "Musicians Desert Gin and Weed to Swing Again," *DB,* July 1936, 1.

27. "Honest-to-goodness" is quoted in Emanuel Eisenberg, "Up Beat on Broadway," *New York World-Telegram*, 3 April 1937, 2, in BG; Ellington is quoted in Duke Ellington, "Duke Says Swing Is Stagnant," *DB*, February 1939, 17. Chummy MacGregor, "Moonlight Serenade Revisited" (typescript, 1966), 244, in GM. For "dedicated," see Goodman, "That Old Gang of Mine," 31. "Dignity" and "don't swing" are quoted in Steig, "Profiles (Goodman)," 34, 31–32; John Wilson, "Benny Goodman Gave Much to Dance Business," *DB*, approx. December 1951, n.p., BG.

28. For Goodman's leadership, see Eisenberg, "Up Beat on Broadway," 2, BG; James, "He Plays Hot!," BG; for Shaw's leadership, see Mok, "A Band Leader Thinks," LPA; Lionel Hampton, *Hamp*, 62; see *KOS*, 239 on drugs and alcohol. Also see Leonard, *Jazz and the White Americans*, 129–32 for the return to traditional standards.

29. See Kolodin, "The Dance Band Business," *Harper's Magazine*, 183, June 1941, 81, for "real sturdy stuff" and a list of the leaders of sweet bands who came out of colleges, including Ozzie Nelson (Rutgers), Sammy Kaye (Ohio University), Hal Kemp (North Carolina) and Kay Kyser (North Carolina).

30. Shaw, *The Trouble with Cinderella*, 33–38, notes his disaffection from his Jewish roots and Protestant anti-Semitism. For Barnet and "Basin Street," see Les Zimmerman, "The Mad Mab," *M*, November 1943, 16–17; Charlie Barnet with Stanley Dance, *Those Swinging Years*, 1–13 on his background; Sinatra is quoted in George Simon, *The Big Bands*, 4th ed. (New York, 1981), xiii. In the 1940s Sinatra supported FDR and spoke out against racism and anti-Semitism as un-American. See Tony Scaduto, *Frank Sinatra* (London, 1976), 34–35, 41, 43, 66–67. O'Connell appears with a crucifix in the film *The Fleet's In* (1944), with the Jimmy Dorsey band, and in *M&R*, October 1941, 24–25.

31. Hampton, *Hamp*, 63–65; "not a crusader" is quoted in Charles Gruenberg, "The Other Benny Goodman Story," *New York Post*, 11 March 1956, n.p., BG; Teddy Wilson, JOHP, reel 2, 44; reel 3, 5–6.

32. For "real swing bands," see Steig, "Profiles (Goodman)," 38; for "admiration and allegiance," see *New York World-Telegram*, 3 April 1937, 2; for "completely democratic," see "Goodman a la King," *Playboy*, February 1958, 61; for "classics," see Douglas Gilbert, "Goodman, Standing Where Toscanini Stands," *New York World-Telegram*, 11 January 1938; for Teddy Wilson, JOHP, reel 3, 5–6. See also Lionel Hampton, "Tell Me What's on My Mind!" *M*, March 1938, 16.

33. Helen Ward is quoted in Firestone, *Swing, Swing, Swing*, 129; Helen Forrest, *I Had the Craziest Dream*, 50–54. See also Anita O'Day with George Eells, *High Times, Hard Times* (New York, 1982); Peggy Lee, *Miss Peggy Lee* (New York, 1989); Geoffrey Mark Fidelman, *First Lady of Song: Ella Fitzgerald for the Record* (New York, 1996); Robert O'Meally, *Lady Day: The Many Faces of Billie Holiday* (New York, 1991). I have relied on the brilliant work of Sherrie Tucker, "Working the Swing Shift: Women Musicians During World War II," *Labor's Heritage* (summer 1996), 46–66; and Margaret McFadden, "America's Boyfriend Who Can't Get a Date," *Journal of American History* (June 1993), 125–31.

34. Will Friedwald, *Jazz Singing* (New York, 1990), 23–49, discusses the origins of jazz singing; for swing singers, see 91–153. My view of singers owes much to Eliza-

beth Kendall, *The Runaway Bride, Hollywood Romantic Comedy of the 1930s* (New York, 1990).

35. Louise Strayer, letter to author, 29 October 1994, 1–2. On Wright, see "Swing Stuff," Utica, New York, *Observer Dispatch,* 30 May 1937, 11.

36. Frances Tilton, "My Daughters Sing Swing," *Radio and Television Mirror,* September 1939, 33, 51, 53, 55; Judy Starr, "I Sing While You Dance," *Radio Mirror,* November 1938, 12–14, 71–72.

37. Helen O'Connell, "I Sing of Romance," *Radio and TV Mirror,* July 1941, 10–11, 50–51; for "quiet dignity," see "Why Vocalists Go Over Big," *M&R,* October 1941, 25.

38. Goodman, "What Swing Really Does," 6.

39. *Camel Caravan,* 31 August 1937, in MacDonald Archives of Popular Culture, Chicago, Illinois.

40. John Okada, *No-No Boy* (1957; reprint, Seattle and London, 1988), 204–5, 209.

41. Hashimoto is quoted in Ted Shen, "Crossing cultures," *Chicago Tribune,* 27 October 1996, 10; Vernon Jarrett is quoted in Studs Terkel, *American Dreams: Lost and Found* (New York, 1980), 87.

42. For "intelligentsia, see Goodman, "That Old Gang of Mine," 31. On jazz as "freedom" and as "American," see H.E.S., *International Musician,* n.p., BG; for "sort of freedom," see Howard Taubman, "Swing and Mozart Too," *NYT Magazine,* 29 December 1940, 15.

43. Otis Ferguson, "The Spirit of Jazz," *The New Republic,* 30 December 1936, reprinted in Chamberlain and Wilson, *Otis Ferguson Reader,* 68–73, emphasis mine.

44. For Rhythm Club concert, see Carl Cons, "Society and Musicians Sit Spellbound by Brilliance of Goodman Band," *DB,* December 1935–January 1936, 1. Other jazz concerts are listed in Devaux, "Emergence of the Jazz Concert."

45. All quotations are from Firestone, *Swing, Swing, Swing,* 245–52.

CHAPTER FOUR: NEWS FROM THE GREAT WIDE WORLD

1. Clayton is quoted in Buck Clayton assisted by Nancy Miller Elliott, *Buck Clayton's Jazz World* (New York, 1987), 109; "Basie's Band Conquers Chick's" and related articles, *M,* February 1938, 15, 29; for other press reports, see Count Basie as told to Albert Murray, *Good Morning Blues: The Autobiography of Count Basie* (New York, 1985), 207–10.

2. For southwestern swing, see LeRoi Jones, *Blues People* (New York, 1963), 182–84; Stephan Palmie, "Jazz Culture in the Thirties: Kansas City Here I Come!" *jazz forschung/jazz research* 16 (1984):43–85; David Stowe, "Jazz in the West," *Western Historical Quarterly* 23 (February 1992):53–73; Ross Russell, *Jazz Style in Kansas City and the Southwest* (Berkeley, Calif., 1971); Stanley Dance, *The World of Count Basie* (New York, 1980), 3–5.

3. Albert Murray, *Stomping the Blues* (New York, 1982), and Ralph Ellison, *Shadow and Act* (New York, 1966), see swing music and musicians as deeply embedded in

African American culture. Isadora Smith, "Duke Ellington Rated 'Joe Louis of Music,'" *PC,* 7 July 1938, 20.

4. The quotation is from Ted Fox, *Showtime at the Apollo* (New York, 1983), 83. For details of Ellington's life, see Edward Ellington Kennedy, *Music Is My Mistress* (New York, 1976); James Lincoln Collier, *Duke Ellington* (New York, 1987); and John Edward Hasse, *Beyond Category* (New York, 1993).

5. On the riot, see Cheryl Lynn Greenberg, *Or Does It Explode?* (New York, 1991).

6. Clayton is quoted in Nathan W. Pearson, Jr., *Goin' to Kansas City* (Urbana, 1987), 146; on Hammond's interest in Basie, see John Hammond with Irving Townsend, *John Hammond on Record* (New York, 1977), 164–80; see 132–39 for his views on Ellington. Helen Oakley is quoted in Freddie Green, JOHP, 106. See also E. J. Hobsbawm, "'Playing for Ourselves,'" *New York Review of Books,* 16 January 1986, 3–4.

7. Hammond, *On Record,* 170–71.

8. Hammond, *On Record,* 178; Basie, *Good Morning Blues,* 196–97, 217–18.

9. Murray, *Stomping the Blues,* 3–6.

10. George Lipsitz, "Against the Wind: Dialogic Aspects of Rock and Roll," in Lipsitz, *Time Passages* (Minneapolis, 1990), 109–13. The themes that Lipsitz finds in rhythm and blues go farther back. They are best articulated by Basie, but they found expression in different ways in Ellington too. For similar themes, see Hobsbawm, "Playing for Ourselves," 3.

11. Ellison, "Homage to Duke Ellington," in *Going to the Territory* (New York, 1987), 219–21; Ellington is quoted in Barry Ulanov, *Duke Ellington* (New York, 1946), 142. Houston Baker, Jr., "Modernism and the Harlem Renaissance," *American Quarterly* 39 (spring 1987):84–97, has shaped my views of Ellington's music.

12. Ellison, "Homage to Duke Ellington," 219–21.

13. For details of Basie's life, see Basie, *Good Morning Blues,* 85–155.

14. Gene Ramey is quoted in Dance, *The World of Count Basie,* 268; Clayton, *Buck Clayton's Jazz World,* 103. For "no account," see Eddie Durham, JOHP, 69, and Basie, *Good Morning Blues,* 147.

15. His early life is discussed in Basie, *Good Morning Blues,* 24–48; his various Harlem and burlesque experiences are found at 49–106. For background on Kansas City, see Palmie, "Jazz Culture in the Thirties," 54–56; Russell, *Jazz Style,* 1–10.

16. On jam sessions, see Palmie, "Jazz Culture in the Thirties," 59–64; Russell, *Jazz Style,* 6–30; Pearson, *Goin' to Kansas City,* 83–106, 117–19; Basie is quoted in Pearson, 108.

17. Edison is quoted in Dance, *The World of Count Basie,* 103. Hobsbawm, "'Playing for Ourselves,'" 4, discusses the rhythm section. See also Schuller, *The Swing Era,* 226–30. Jones is quoted in Dance, *The World of Count Basie,* 52–53 and his JOHP interview, 55. Wells, is quoted in Dance, *The World of Count Basie,* 93.

18. Wells is quoted in Dance, *The World of Count Basie,* 87; see Murray, *Stomping the Blues,* 164 for "good time."

19. See Palmie, "Jazz Culture in the Thirties," 69, on riffs. Clayton is quoted in

Pearson, *Goin' to Kansas City,* 116–17. For the Basie quote, see *Good Morning Blues,* 161–62.

20. Basie, *Good Morning Blues,* 194–96.

21. See Robert O'Meally, *Lady Day: The Many Faces of Billie Holiday* (New York, 1991), 121–26 for her Basie experience and for the Edison quotes.

22. Basie, *Good Morning Blues,* 5; Jones is quoted in Palmie, "Jazz Culture in the Thirties," 71.

23. Schuller, *The Swing Era,* 222–25, discusses Basie and the blues. Jimmy Rushing, cited in Dance, *The World of Count Basie,* 20, notes that Basie had to learn the blues. The blues songs are listed in Jo Jones, JOHP, 71–74. "Social interpreter" is quoted in Dan Burley, "Basie Plunking Way to Top at Famous Door," *AN,* 29 October 1938, 20.

24. Ellison, "Remembering Jimmy," in *Shadow and Act,* 235–29.

25. Basie, *Good Morning Blues,* 151–52; "Ride On" is at 257. Gene Ramey is quoted in Pearson, *Goin' to Kansas City,* 115–16.

26. Hobsbawm, "'Playing for Ourselves,'" 3.

27. Ellington, *Music Is My Mistress,* 441; Basie, *Good Morning Blues,* 57.

28. Murray, *Stomping the Blues,* 124; Basie, *Good Morning Blues,* 240.

29. Jarrett is quoted in Terkel, *American Dreams,* 83–88.

30. Jarrett is quoted in ibid., 81–83.

31. Murray, *Stomping the Blues,* 118–25.

32. Lipsitz, "Against the Wind," 109–13. See also Hobsbawm, "'Playing for Ourselves,'" 3.

33. Malcolm X with Alex Haley, *The Autobiography of Malcolm X* (New York, 1963), 49–50.

34. Basie, *Good Morning Blues,* 201–2; Malcolm X, *Autobiography,* 50, 56–57, 64.

35. Malcolm X's descriptions, *Autobiography,* 51 (emphasis mine). James is quoted in Marshall Stearns and Jean Stearns, *Jazz Dance* (New York, 1962), 325; Dicky Wells, *The Night People* (Washington, D.C., 1991), 38–39, discusses dancer-musician interaction. See also Katrina Hazzard-Gordon, *Jookin': The Rise of Social Dance Formations in African-American Culture* (Philadelphia, 1990).

36. Malcolm X, *Autobiography,* 70–71, 50.

37. Ellison, "Homage to Duke Ellington on His Birthday," 220.

38. Horace Silver, *Jazzletter,* April 1990, 4; Hinton is quoted in Milt Hinton and David Berger, *Bass Line* (Philadelphia, 1988), 74–78, 109–10, 122; *PC,* 31 January 1942, 21; Gillespie is quoted in *NYT,* 1 May 1984, A1, B4.

39. Hinton is quoted in Ira Gitler, *Swing to Bop* (New York, 1985), 11.

40. Ellison, "Homage to Duke Ellington," 221, 219, 218; Isadora Smith, "Duke Ellington Rated 'Joe Louis of Music,'" *PC,* 16 July 1938, 20; Burley, "Basie Plunking Way to Top," 20; see "Big Apple," *PC,* 11 June 1938, 15, for "excluded."

41. Smith, "Joe Louis of Music," 20.

42. Billy Rowe, "Basie Tops," *PC,* 31 January 1942, 21.

43. "Basie at Lincoln Hotel," *PC,* 11 September 1943, 21; for "free man," see "How Count Basie paid $25,000 for His Own Contract," *CD,* 24 March 1945, 17; "Municipal Auditorium Fracas," *AN,* 30 June 1945, 1; Gould, a white entertainment columnist, is quoted in Isadora Smith, "Count Basie's Opening," *PC,* 30 July 1938, 21.

44. See Smith, "Count Basie's Opening," 21, for Gould; Stokowski is quoted in *PC,* 12 December 1936, 7. For the superiority of black musicians, see Billy Rowe, "Swing More Popular Than Ever," *PC,* 29 January 1938, 20; Major Robinson, "Set Arrangements for Millers, Shaws," *CD,* 15 February 1941, 20; Billy Rowe, "Famous French Critic's Book Says Colored Musicians Tops," *PC,* 23 January 1943, 21.

45. Lawrence Levine, *Black Culture and Black Consciousness* (New York, 1977), 433–40; Mercer Ellington with Stanley Dance, *Duke Ellington in Person: An Intimate Memoir* (New York, 1979), 79.

46. Lena Horne and Richard Schickel, *Lena* (Garden City, 1965), 75; Hinton is quoted in Gitler, *Swing to Bop,* 14; Dizzy Gillespie with Al Fraser, *To Be, or not . . . to Bop* (Garden City, 1979), 288–89.

47. Basie, *Good Morning Blues,* 250–51. The lyrics are reprinted in Chris Mead, *Champion: Joe Louis* (New York, 1985), 203.

CHAPTER FIVE: SWING LEFT

1. Howard Taubman, "Negro Music Given at Carnegie Hall," *NYT,* 24 December 1938, reprinted in *The Black Perspective in Music* 2 (1974): 207–8; John Hammond, *John Hammond on Record* (New York, 1977), 199, for the second concert, 231–32; "close alliance" is quoted in John Sebastian, "From Spirituals to Swing," *NM,* 3 January 1939, 28; James Dugan and John Hammond, "The Music Nobody Knows," reprinted in *The Black Perspective in Music* 2 (1974):197–207. See also John Hammond, "'From Spirituals to Swing,'" *NYT,* 18 December 1938, sec. 9, at 10.

2. See Dugan and Hammond, "The Music Nobody Knows," program notes to From Spirituals to Swing, 197–207.

3. For the quote on Bessie Smith, see John Hammond, "Did Bessie Smith Bleed to Death While Waiting for Medical Aid?," *DB,* November 1937, 3. Dugan and Hammond, "The Music Nobody Knows," 197–207.

4. For "Number One," see Irving Kolodin, "Number One Swing Man," *Harper's Magazine,* September 1939, 431; Warren Susman, "Culture and Commitment," in Susman, *Culture as History* (New York, 1985), 184–210; "political and cultural milieu" is quoted in E. J. Hobsbawm, "Some Like It Hot," *The New York Review of Books,* 13 April 1989, 33, has influenced my views of Hammond. For a positive reevaluation of the idea of a "people's culture," see Alan Lawson, "The Cultural Legacy of the New Deal," in *Fifty Years Later: The New Deal Evaluated,* ed. Harvard Sitkoff (New York: 1985), 155–86. On this generation of critics, see John Gennari, *Critiquing Jazz: The Politics of Race and Culture in American Jazz Discourse, 1935–1995* (University of Chicago Press, forthcoming), especially chap. 2.

5. See Hammond, *On Record,* 10–20 for his family background, 13 for "both fasci-

nating," 28 for sharing "her religious fervor." The best discussion of women and Christian Science is Donald B. Meyer, *The Positive Thinkers* (Garden City, 1965).

6. See Hammond, *On Record*, 38–51 for influences; 67 for "discrimination"; 48 for "changed young man"; 66–67 for "did not revolt." See John McDonough, "John Hammond: Rebel with a Cause," *Jazz Times*, January 1987, 16 for "journalism."

7. See McDonough, "Rebel with a Cause," 16, for "an authentic." Donald Meyer, *Sex and Power* (Middletown, Conn., 1987), 360, notes that the popularity of jazz helped raise questions about racial segregation.

8. Hammond, *On Record*, 35.

9. McDonough, "Rebel with a Cause," 16; Hammond, *On Record*, 156–58. For his views of the Communist Party, see Hammond interview, COHP, 20.

10. Hammond, *On Record*, 89–93.

11. See McDonough, "Rebel with a Cause," 16, on the legend and for "sounds of social change." See Irving Kolodin, "Number One Swing Man," 431 for "'Johnny.'" See Otis Ferguson's critical portrait, "John Hammond," *Society Rag* (September 1938), reprinted in Dorothy Chamberlain and Robert Wilson, eds., *The Otis Ferguson Reader* (Highland Park, Ill., 1982), 97–103, which damns Hammond for his harmful, opinionated reviews of jazz musicians. James Lincoln Collier, *Benny Goodman and the Swing Era* (New York, 1989), 100–1 criticizes his paternalism.

12. Hammond, *On Record*, 91, 187–90, 189 for "hottest"; see Hammond, "Jim-Crow Blues," *NM*, 13 December 1938, 27 for "systematic policy."

13. McDonough, "Rebel with a Cause," 18.

14. Hammond, *On Record*, 148, 165–80. Count Basie as told to Albert Murray, *Good Morning Blues: The Autobiography of Count Basie* (New York, 1985), 166.

15. Kolodin, "Number One Swing Man," 435.

16. Hammond, "I thought," is quoted in Charles Gruenberg, "The Other Benny Goodman Story," *New York Post*, 11 March 1956, n.p., in BG. Hammond, *On Record*, 158–59.

17. See Lionel Hampton, *Hamp* (New York, 1989), 63, for "pioneering effort," 65 for "selling music"; see *Zit's*, 1 May 1937, n.p., BG, for "we had it understood."

18. For "crusader," see Gruenberg, "The Other Benny Goodman Story," *New York Post*, 11 March 1956, n.p.; James Dugan, "The Stars Aid Spain," *DW Sunday Magazine*, 27 March 1938, 8; see *DW*, 6 May 1938, 7 for attacks on Goodman. For the Congress of the American Youth for Democracy dance, see *DW*, 30 March 1938, 7. *DW*, 2 December 1943, 5 notes his playing for Ben Davis and Judge Rivers; for "does not share," see Wilson's FBI file, 100—341221, 5; on the FBI, see the report from San Antonio, Texas, 16 March 1942, in Paul Robeson's main FBI file (number is blurred, but probably 100—123042), cited in Martin Bauml Duberman, *Paul Robeson* (New York, 1988), 654–55 n. 51.

19. Teddy Wilson, "Who Said the South Was Race-Conscious about Musicians?" *M&R*, April 1941, 34.

20. For praise of Goodman, see Martin Mack, "Blow at Jim Crow," *NM*, 5 August 1941, 30; for "best American tradition," see Peter Somerset, *DW*, 17 July 1941, 7; for

"champion," see Charles Glenn, "Artie Shaw Rebuffs Jim Crow Band Agency," *DW,* 21 September 1941, 7; "he would undergo" is quoted in Billy Rowe, "Contest Takes on True American Aspect," *PC,* 20 December 1941, 21. For other comments, see *PC,* 28 November 1936, 6; Billy Rowe, "Rowe's Notebook," *PC,* 7 February 1942, 19.

21. Mark Naison, *Communists in Harlem during the Depression* (Urbana, Ill., 1983), 36, 71–72. The Scottsboro Defense Ball featured a "Battle of Swing Music" at the Savoy with stars of the Isham Jones, Duke Ellington, and Chick Webb bands. See *DW,* 15 February 1936, 3.

22. "Shame of jazz" is quoted in Mike Gold, "What a World," *DW,* 29 August 1933, 6. See also Gold's columns of 6 September 1933, 6; 20 September 1933, 6.

23. Dale Curran is quoted in Michael Gold, *DW,* 20 September 1933, 6. Charles Edward Smith, "Class Content of Jazz Music," *DW,* 21 October 1933, 7.

24. Naison, *Communists in Harlem,* 127–28; see 171 for "romantic aura," 186 for "particularly musicians."

25. Naison, *Communists in Harlem,* 193–94, discusses artists and intellectuals in the Popular Front, and Streater is quoted at 197; for Wilson's appearance at the Disabled Veterans benefit, see *DW,* 22 September 1939, 8; for Claude Hopkins, see *DW,* 3 October 1939, 7.

26. For the Davis benefit, see *DW,* 23 October 1943, 7; for Roberts's remarks, see *DW,* 29 October 1943, 5; on the Goodman quartet, see *DW,* 2 December 1943, 5; for Wilson at the twenty-fifth anniversary, see *NM,* 19 September 1944, 31; see the ad in *DW,* 27 October 1937, 8 for "Celebrity Night" at the Savoy Ballroom in support of the Abraham Lincoln Brigade.

27. "Some persons," Dugan are quoted in *DW,* 8 May 1940, 7.

28. For samples of benefits and dances, see *DW,* 27 October 1937, 8; 16 December 1938, 4. For the Savoy, see *DW,* 20 October 1937, 5. For Swing America and "kids . . . kicking out," see *DW,* 3 May 1939, 7. See also ads for swing balls, *DW,* 10 December 1937, 8.

29. Dave Farrell, "As 'Fats' Waller Would Have Wanted It," *DW,* 4 April 1944, 5. For radical youth in the depression, see Robert Cohen, *When the Old Left Was Young* (New York, 1993).

30. Curran is quoted in Mike Gold column, *DW,* 12 January 1939, 7; "Negro musicians" is quoted in *DW,* 12 September 1937, as cited in Naison, *Communists in Harlem,* 211; James Dugan, *Young Communist League Review* 4 (July 1939):3.

31. See Naison, *Communists in Harlem,* 218 for cultural distinctiveness; "stream of the peoples" is quoted in Martin McCall, "Negro and White Jazz Bands," *DW,* 16 July 1938, 7; Hammond, "There Are No Better Musicians—But They Can't Find Jobs," *DW,* 26 May 1942, 7.

32. On jazz criticism and magazines, see Ronald G. Welburn, "American Jazz Criticism, 1914–1940" (Ph.D. diss., New York University, 1983), 54–62, 79–100; Welburn, "Jazz Magazines of the 1930s: An Overview of Their Provocative Journalism," *American Music* 5 (fall 1987):255–70. John Gennari, "Jazz Criticism: Its Development and Ideologies," *Black American Literature Forum* 25 (fall 1991):449–523 provides an excel-

lent overview. See David Stowe, *Swing Changes* (Cambridge, Mass., 1994), 73–80 for a superb treatment of *Down Beat*.

33. Stearns is cited in Oro, "United We Stand—Hot," *BB*, 26 December 1936, 42–43. See also "Rhythm Clubs Hit Stride—Now 7 in U.S.," *DB*, October 1935, 3.

34. Schaap is quoted in Gennari, *Critiquing Jazz*, 64, and in Welburn, "American Jazz Criticism," 269. George Frazier, "Stupid Critics Misjudge 3,000 Ickies' Action," *DB*, June 1938, 4.

35. Editorial, "Fine Sportsmanship," *DB*, May 1936, 2; for "talent suffering," "we still believe," and "subscribe to," see "Negro Press Runs Temperature," *DB*, October 1936, 2; Editorial, "Not German, Not Jew . . . but AMERICANS ALL!" *DB*, October 1938, 10.

36. Frank Marshall Davis, "No Secret—Best White Bands Copy Negroes," *DB*, June 1938, 5. I was alerted to Davis's importance by Gennari, *Critiquing Jazz*.

37. Editorial, "Negro and White Band Folds," *DB*, December 1937, 12.

38. "Mixed band" is quoted in "Can a Negro Play His Best in a White Band?" *DB*, 3; John Hammond, "Predicted Race Riot Fades as Dallas Applauds Quartet!" *DB*, October 1937, 1, 4.

39. "Should Negro Musicians Play in White Bands?" *DB*, 15 October 1939, 1, 10. "Benny Should Be Congratulated for His Courage," *DB*, 10, 23.

40. Lomax is quoted in Jon Pareles, "A Life Giving Voice to the Voiceless," *NYT*, 7 March 1989, C15. For discussion of the Lomaxes, see Joe Klein, *Woody Guthrie: A Life* (New York, 1980), 143–50; and Benjamin Filene, "'Our Singing Country': John and Alan Lomax, Leadbelly, and the Construction of an American Past," *American Quarterly* 43 (December 1991):602–24.

41. Francis Newton, *The Jazz Scene* (London, 1959), 232; "life and art" is quoted in Neil Leonard, *Jazz: Myth and Religion* (New York, 1987), 146. On collectors, see Gennari, *Critiquing Jazz*.

42. For quotations, see Frederic Ramsey, Jr., and Charles Edward Smith, *Jazzmen* (New York, 1939), xi–xiii, 62–63; Leonard, *Jazz: Myth and Religion*, 132–33, discusses the book.

43. Charles Edward Smith, "Swing," *New Republic*, 16 February 1938, 39–41. For jazz as a derivative of class and culture as opposed to being racially inherent, see Gennari, *Critiquing Jazz*, 66.

44. Otis Ferguson, "John Hammond," *Society Rag*, September 1938, reprinted in Chamberlain and Wilson, *Otis Ferguson Reader*, 96–103.

45. John Hammond, "The Tragedy of Duke Ellington, the 'Black Prince of Jazz,'" *DB*, November 1935, 1, reprinted in *The Duke Ellington Reader*, ed. Mark Tucker (New York, 1993), 118–20. See also Hammond, *On Record*, 136–39.

46. Duke Ellington, "Duke Says Swing Is Stagnant," *DB*, February 1939, 2, 16–17; "Situation between the Critics and Musicians Is Laughable—Duke Ellington," *DB*, April 1939, 4, 9; "Duke Concludes Criticism of the Critics," *DB*, May 1939, 14; "Duke Becomes a Critic," *DB*, July 1939, 8, 35. All are reprinted in Tucker, *Duke Ellington Reader*, 132–40.

47. See Hammond, *On Record*, 206–7 for "the concert." For background on Jo-

sephson and the club, see Whitney Balliet, "Profiles of Max Gordon and Barney Josephson," *New Yorker,* 9 October 1971, 50–92; Helen Lawrenson, "Black and White and Red All Over," *New York,* 21 August 1978, 36–43; Peter J. Silvester, *A Left Hand Like God: A History of Boogie-Woogie Piano* (New York, 1989), 127–60.

48. Josephson, interview with author, September 1971.

49. Ibid.

50. Ibid. The ad is reproduced in Silvester, *A Left Hand,* facing 151.

51. Josephson, interview with author, September 1971.

52. Billie Holiday and Bernard Dufty, *Lady Sings the Blues* (New York, 1956), 82. Hammond always believed that "Strange Fruit" ruined Holiday's style by forcing her natural spontaneity and buoyancy into false and mordant directions.

53. Basie, *Good Morning Blues,* 250–51.

54. Hammond, "The Tragedy of Duke Ellington," 1, 6, attacked "Reminiscing in Tempo" for being too much like Debussy and Delius and the Duke himself for ignoring his own exploitation and the struggles of his people. "Our music . . ." is from Ellington, "Duke Says Swing Is Stagnant," 2, 16–17.

55. Mercer Ellington with Stanley Dance, *Duke Ellington in Person: An Intimate Memoir* (New York, 1979), 181. Edward Ellington Kennedy, *Music Is My Mistress* (New York, 1976), 239.

56. "Take Uncle Tom" is quoted in Duke Ellington, *Music Is My Mistress,* 175–76; the other quotations are from Mercer Ellington, *Duke Ellington in Person,* 182. These remarks are also based on the revival of *Jump for Joy* by the Pegasus Players, Truman College, Chicago, 19 October 1991. The production's director, Jonathan Wilson, gave me program notes and interviews.

CHAPTER SIX: THE CITY OF SWING

1. Artie Shaw with Bob Maxwell, "Music Is a Business," *The Saturday Evening Post,* 2 December 1939, 14; Michel Mok, "A Band Leader Thinks," *New York Post,* 26 September 1939, n.p., Shaw file, LPA. For all his unhappiness, however, Shaw could not stay away. By 1940 he was back leading another successful band.

2. Artie Shaw, *The Trouble with Cinderella* (New York, 1951), 326; Shaw, "Music Is a Business," 14.

3. Billie Holiday and Bernard Dufty, *Lady Sings the Blues* (New York, 1956), 79–81.

4. Elliot White, letter to author, 21 July 1994, 5–6.

5. Ibid.; "as [had] not been enjoyed" is quoted in Bosley Crowther, "Hi-De-Ho! The Night Clubs Turn 'Em Away," *NYT Magazine,* 21 March 1937, 14. See also Abel Green, "Nighteries on Road Back," *V,* 6 January 1937, 195; H. I. Brock, "How Our Nightlife Glows Again," *NYT,* 11 February 1934, sec. 6, at 10, 19.

6. "Look at . . . another" is quoted in Douglas Gilbert, "Present 'Cafe Society' Double Elbow Benders," *New York World-Telegram,* 22 November 1937, n.p. On cafe society entertainment see Douglas Gilbert, "The Cafe Crowd Favors Some of Its Severest Critics as Its Star Entertainers," *New York World-Telegram,* 26 November 1937, n.p.,

Cafe Society vertical file, *New York Herald* morgue, New York University. For "dish out," see George Simon, "Review of Shep Fields," *M,* June 1936, 16. Leo Reisman, "Why I Won't Play Swing," *Liberty Magazine,* 15, 28 May 1938, n.p., swing vertical file, IJS.

7. For the quotation see George Simon, "Review of Charles Dornberger, Paradise Restaurant," *M,* June 1936, 16. See also Green, "Nighteries on Road Back," 195; *V,* 12 December 1933, 1; Jack Foster, *New York World-Telegram,* 28 December 1937, n.p., International Casino scrapbooks, LPA; Brock, "How Our Nightlife Glows," 10, 19; Jack Foster, "Neon Nights," *The Oklahoma News,* 6 January 1938, n.p., International Casino scrapbooks, LPA. For nightclub audiences, see Lori Witt, "Resurrecting the Cocoanut Grove: A Study of Night Club Patrons and Changing Perceptions" (M.A. essay, History Department, Loyola University, 1987).

8. Edward Pessen, "The Kingdom of Swing: New York City in the Late 1930s," *New York History* (July 1989):291–95, discusses Harlem nightlife.

9. Carter is quoted in Morroe Berger, Edward Berger, and James Patrick, *Benny Carter: A Life in Music* (Metuchen, N.J., 1982), 188.

10. *AN,* April 1939, 20; Miller is cited in *Dancing,* PBS television series, episode 5. Unfortunately, Norma Miller with Evette Jensen, *Swingin' at the Savoy: The Memoir of a Jazz Dancer* (Philadelphia, 1996), came out too late to be included here.

11. Kirk is quoted in Ted Fox, *Showtime at the Apollo* (New York, 1983), 67; on monopoly, see 29–30, 53–55.

12. Kirk, "communications center," is quoted in ibid., 67; for physical layout see 124; for band presentation, 80–81. *PC* is quoted in Count Basie as told to Albert Murray, *Good Morning Blues: The Autobiography of Count Basie* (New York, 1985), 238–39. On Amateur Night see Ralph Cooper with Steve Dougherty, *Amateur Night at the Apollo* (New York, 1990), 70–80.

13. *New York World-Telegram,* January 1937, quoted in Fox, *Showtime at the Apollo,* 67; Cooper, *Amateur Night at the Apollo,* 110.

14. The authority is Arnold Shaw, *52nd St.: The Street of Jazz* (New York, 1977). Abel Green, *V,* "Swing It!" 1 January 1936, 188.

15. See Shaw, *52nd St.,* 52–74, for Helbock and the Onyx; Freeman is quoted at 62; Mercer is quoted at 78–80.

16. Milt Hinton and David Berger, *Bass Line* (Philadelphia, 1988), 82. On the decline of Harlem see *V,* 22 January 1935, 1, 60. On Harlem's move downtown, see Shaw, *52nd Street,* x–xi; Wilder Hobson, "Fifty-Second Street," in Frederic Ramsey, Jr., and Charles Edward Smith, *Jazzmen* (New York, 1939), 249–53. Pessen, "The Kingdom of Swing," 296–99 analyzes the role of Fifty-second Street in the 1930s. Some of the musicians who played the street were Teddy Wilson, Art Tatum, Cozy Cole, Chu Berry, Stuff Smith, Count Basie, John Kirby, the Spirits of Rhythm, Red McKenzie and Mike Farley, Jack Teagarden, Joe Marsala, Bunny Berigan, Red Norvo, Joe Sullivan, Louis Prima, and Joe Bushkin.

17. Hammond is quoted in Shaw, *52nd St.,* 20–21; see xi–xii for sitting in; Wilder is quoted at xii.

18. Norvo is quoted in ibid., 119.

19. "Repeal Spells . . . ," *V*, 12 December 1933, 1; see also *BB*, 16 December 1933, 11, for the hotel renaissance. Irving Kolodin, "The Dance Band Business: A Study in Black and White," *Harper's*, June 1941, 74, notes the revival of the supper trade. Dwight Chapin, "New Band," *Concerto*, December 1949, 13, in BG.

20. Chapin, "New Band," 14, notes that three radio networks broadcast Benny Goodman from the Madhattan Room in one evening. On radio, see Gerald R. Scott, "The Dance Band Is Big Business," LPA.

21. "They publicized" is quoted in "Bands Get Hotel Build-up," *BB*, 15 January 1938, 14, an excellent discussion of how hotels advertised bands. See also Kolodin, "Dance Band Business," 74.

22. The Commodore's public relations director is quoted in "Bands Get Hotel Build-up," 14; for expenses see Kolodin, "Dance Band Business," 75.

23. For hotels and radio, see "Bands Get Hotel Build-up," 14; LeRoy Ostransky, *Jazz City: The Impact of Our Cities on the Development of Jazz* (Englewood Cliffs, N.J., 1978), 226; Kolodin, "Dance Band Business," 75–76; Philip K. Eberly, *Music in the Air: America's Changing Tastes in Popular Music, 1920–1980* (New York, 1982), 70–73; Leo Walker, *The Wonderful Era of the Great Dance Bands* (Berkeley, 1964), 189–90.

24. Kolodin, "Dance Band Business," 76.

25. Ibid., 76–77; "In Person Policy of NY Paramount Shows Public Trend," *M*, March 1936, 16; "Battle of Bands," *Newsweek*, 10 May 1943, 67. For more on stage band presentations, see *New York Enquirer*, 29 November 1948, n.p., BG; Harry Kalcheim, "The Trend in Stage Shows," *BB*, 10 April 1937, 35.

26. Kolodin, "Dance Band Business," 75–76; "Band Salaries Terrific," *BB*, 21 January 1939, 19.

27. Walter Karp, *The Center: A History and Guide to Rockefeller Center* (New York, 1982), 11–27.

28. See Jeffrey Meikle, *Twentieth Century Limited* (Philadelphia, 1979), 97–98, and Daniel Czitrom, *Media and the American Mind: From Morse to McLuhan* (Chapel Hill, N.C., 1982), 76–80, for sponsorship of radio programs.

29. Shaw, "Music Is a Business," 67. Roland Marchand, *Advertising the American Dream* (Berkeley, 1985), 285–333, discusses "hard sell" ads. Eberly, *Music in the Air*, 84–99, 114–24, is good on radio, and 61 provides the figures.

30. Annemarie Ewing, "Celluloid Fife Gets Hot on 1 1/2 Hour Swing Broadcast," *DB*, July 1937, 8.

31. Kolodin, "Dance Band Business," 74. See generally Paul Lazarsfeld and Frank Stanton, eds., *Radio Research, 1942–1943* (New York, 1944), 335–52; Hazel Meyer, *The Gold in Tin Pan Alley* (Philadelphia, 1958), 72–75. For early payola, see George Simon, *The Big Bands*, 4th ed. (New York, 1981), 59–61. For black bands on radio, see "Ella Fitzgerald 'Stuck' in Elevator," *DB*, October 1937, 2;

32. Barry Ulanov, "The Jukes Take Over Swing," *The American Mercury*, October 1940, 172. For the boost that the jukebox gave to records, see Ben Bodec, "Boom on Wax in 1938," *V*, 4 January 1939, 165. See J. Krivine, *Juke Box Saturday Night* (London, 1977), 20–23, 70–73 on its upgraded image.

33. Danny Baxter, "One Record Can Push a Band into 'Big Money,'" *DB*, August 1939, 4; Artie Shaw, *The Trouble with Cinderella*, 333–34.

34. Scott, "Dance Band Is Big Business."

35. For agencies, see Kolodin, "Dance Band Business," 73–74; Walker, *Wonderful Era of the Great Dance Bands*, 232–39.

36. Shaw, "Music Is a Business," 66. For agencies and hotels, see Kolodin, "Dance Band Business," 75–77; Simon, *The Big Bands*, 46–49. See also "CRA Celebrates 2nd Anni," *BB*, 25 June 1938, 13; "$100,000,000 Band Czar," *V*, 16 August 1939, 1, 35.

37. Kolodin, "Dance Band Business," 72–73.

38. Ibid., 78. See also John Desmond, "Making Catnip for the Hepcats," *NYT Magazine*, 20 June 1943, 17.

39. Maurice Purtill is quoted in "'Nostalgia Is a Very Dirty Word,'" in Chip Deffaa, *Swing Legacy* (Metuchen, N.J., 1989), 121. For salaries and one-nighter fees, see Kolodin, "Dance Band Business," 78. Desmond, "Making Catnip," 17.

40. Kolodin, "Dance Band Business," 78. Purtill is quoted in Deffaa, *Swing Legacy*, 123.

41. Helen Oakley, "Black Bands Who Made Over $1,000,000 Arouse Interest of Big Bookers," *DB*, July 1938, 20; R. L Larkin, "Are Colored Bands Doomed as Big Money Makers?" *DB*, 1 December 1940, 2. See also Paul Eduard Miller, "'Money Invested in Swing Music Will Keep It Alive,'" *DB*, 15 April 1940, 6.

42. Kolodin, "Dance Band Business," 79–80; "has played" is quoted in "Why?" *M*, March 1943, 34. See also "Because," *M*, April 1943, 4.

43. Kolodin, "Dance Band Business," 80; *Bridgeport Herald*, 13 January 1935, in DE, as quoted in John Edward Hasse, *Beyond Category* (New York, 1993), 151. I examined issues of the radio fan magazines *Radio Mirror*, *Tune In*, and *Radio Varieties* dating from 1935 to 1946 at MacDonald and Associates, Chicago. As late as 1947, when Ella Fitzgerald was at the height of her career and singers were in demand, she could not land a regular radio show. See Geoffrey Mark Fidelman, *First Lady of Song: Ella Fitzgerald for the Record* (New York, 1996), 52–53.

44. Holiday, *Lady Sings the Blues*, 70–81.

45. Ibid.

46. See liner notes, *Billie Holiday: The Legacy*, Columbia Jazz Masterpieces AAD 47725 (1991), 20–23. In his interview, in JOHP, Teddy Wilson notes that he greatly preferred Ella Fitzgerald to Holiday, who lagged behind the beat too much.

47. Kolodin, "Dance Band Business," 80; Leonard Feather, *The Jazz Years! Earwitness to an Era* (New York, 1987), 115, reports on Rollini's Tap.

48. "Should Negro Musicians Play in White Bands?" *DB*, 15 October 1939, 10.

49. Garvin Bushell as told to Mark Tucker, *Jazz from the Beginning* (Ann Arbor, 1988), 84. Holiday, *Lady Sings the Blues*, 95–96.

50. Andy Kirk as told to Amy Lee, *Twenty Years on Wheels* (Ann Arbor, 1989), 84–87, discusses the problems of black bands recording ballads.

51. David O. Alber, "Motion Pictures Make Magnificent Publicity for Bandleaders," *M*, May 1942, 18.

52. Elliott Grennard, "Jazz as It Isn't," *NM*, 21 July 1942, 27–28; Barry Ulanov, "The Movies," *M*, March 1944, 16; Ulanov, "The Films, Phony and Otherwise," *M*, July 1943, 15; "Movies Fix Merit by Color of Skin!" *DB*, 29 July 1946, 10; Frank E. Bolden, "Orchestra Whirl," *PC*, 13 December 1941, 19, all discuss movies and race. Teddy Wilson interview, JOHP, on problems with "The Big Broadcast of 1937," is quoted in Ross Firestone, *Swing, Swing, Swing: The Life and Times of Benny Goodman* (New York, 1993), 179.

53. Jimmie Lunceford, "Is Airtime Essential?" *M*, October 1942, 9. R. L. Larkin, "Are Colored Bands Doomed as Big Money Makers?" *DB*, 1 December 1940, 2. Kirk, *Twenty Years on Wheels*, 94.

54. Burton Peretti, *The Creation of Jazz* (Champaign-Urbana, Ill., 1992), 178. Kirk, *Twenty Years on Wheels*, 98.

55. Gordon is quoted in Ira Gitler, *Swing to Bop* (New York, 1985), 128–29, 132–33; Basie, *Good Morning Blues*, 58–59; "bushes" is quoted in Danny Barker, *A Life in Jazz* (New York, 1986), ed. Alyn Shipton, 166–67.

56. Barney Bigard, *With Louis and the Duke: The Autobiography of a Jazz Clarinetist*, ed. Barry Martyn (New York, 1986), 69; Cab Calloway, *Minnie the Moocher and Me* (New York, 1976), 140–41; Hinton, *Bass Line*, 132.

57. Stanley Dance, *The World of Earl Hines* (New York, 1977), 81–82; Johnny Otis, *Listen to the Lambs* (New York, 1968), 81. For many more such incidents, see Peretti, *Creation of Jazz*, 177–210.

CHAPTER SEVEN: SWING GOES TO WAR

1. Miller is quoted in Frank Stacy, "Glenn Miller Day Boosts Band Sale," *DB*, 15 May 1945, 14.

2. On his career see George Simon, *Glenn Miller and His Orchestra* (New York, 1974); *Current Biography*, 1942, 597–99. On his music see Gunther Schuller, *The Swing Era* (New York, 1989), 661–77. On the political obligation as personal see Robert B. Westbrook, "'I Want a Girl Just Like the Girl That Married Harry James': American Women and the Problem of Political Obligation in World War II," *American Quarterly* 42 (1990):587–614; John Morton Blum, *V Was for Victory* (New York, 1976). For an early account of his mysterious death, see "Music World Waits Word about Miller," *DB*, 15 January 1945, 1.

3. On the Office of War Information and music see John Costello, *Virtue under Fire* (Boston, 1985), 120–21. For Tin Pan Alley's call for patriotic tunes, see *V*, 5 January 1944, 187; Olin Downes, *NYT*, 23 August, 1942.

4. "Narrow chasm" is quoted in Glenn Miller, "Travel's Tough But the Jazzmen Hit the Road for Army Camps," *DW*, 3 July 1942, 7. Bruce Tyler, *From the Harlem Renaissance to Hollywood: The Struggle for Racial Democracy, 1920–1943* (New York, 1992), discusses jive culture's expansion during the war. On the desire for pluralism and unity see John Higham, "Ethnic Pluralism in Modern American Thought," in Higham, *Send These to Me* (New York, 1975), 196–230.

5. For Roosevelt's views see *NYT*, 19 June 1941, 23, and "May 2–8, National Music Week—Help Spread the Story!" *DB*, 1 May 1943, 10. "Make Us Love" is quoted in Billy Rose, "'Escapology' Not the Answer, Showmen Must Sell Americanism to Everybody," *V*, 7 November 1942, 28. For the Japanese ban on jazz see "Japs Can't Hear Jazz," *DB*, 15 October 1940, 1.

6. "Claude Thornhill in the Pacific," *Tune In*, July 1945, 29. For Young's bitter experience, see Frank Büchmann-Møller, *You Just Fight for Your Life* (New York, 1990), 117–30. On the draft see Buck Clayton, *Buck Clayton's Jazz World* (New York, 1987), 114–15.

7. "Wherever they are" is quoted in Barry Ulanov, "V Discs," *M*, May 1944, 20–21. See also *DB*, 15 March 1944, 3; Paul Gould, "The Armed Forces Networks," *Tune In*, September 1945, 9–11. Eisenhower is quoted in Trent Christman, *Brass Button Broadcasters* (Paducah, Ky., 1992), 39–40. On Tokyo Rose, see Bob Klein, interview with author, March 1992.

8. For "typically American," see "Glenn Miller," *Current Biography*, 1942, 597.

9. Tex Beneke, "Swing Was Never Really King," *M*, February 1947, 20–21.

10. "When we" is quoted in Clarissa Start, "Man of Musical World," *St. Louis Post-Dispatch*, 1 August 1940, n.p., GM; "one hot soloist" is quoted in Dave Dexter Jr., "I Don't Want a Jazz Band," *DB*, 1 February 1940, 8; "the band solos" is quoted in Irving Kolodin, "A Tonefile of Glenn Miller," *Saturday Review*, 1953, 63, Glenn Miller file, IJS; Schuller, *Swing Era*, 671–73; Priddy is quoted in Simon, *Glenn Miller*, 238, 246; Herman is quoted in Chip Deffaa, *Swing Legacy* (Metuchen, N.J., 1989), 354.

11. Billy May is quoted in Simon, *Glenn Miller*, 232, Chuck Goldstein quoted at 245–46. Tommy Mace, in Mort Good, liner notes to *The Complete Glenn Miller*, vol. 3 (1939–40) (RCA–Bluebird Records, 1976), recalled that musicians considered Miller "a boy-scout leader" and noted Glenn's desire to be called "'Skipper' or 'Captain' or something like that. And that was before the war. Discipline was terrible in that outfit. Rough."

12. Richmond is quoted in Simon, *Glenn Miller*, 135, Hutton is quoted at 139.

13. Kolodin, "Tonefile," 63. "Choo Choo Chugs to Million Mark," *M*, February 1942, 11. Herb Caen, "Miller AAF Band Carries on for GI's," *DB*, 15 May 1945, 1, 3 notes the prevalence of civilian material. Norman Charles, "Social Values in American Popular Song" (Ph.D. diss., University of Pennsylvania, 1958), 77–78, notes the homeward direction in songs of the 1940s.

14. Simon, *Glenn Miller*, 184.

15. Ibid.

16. On the ethnic platoon, see Richard Slotkin, *Gunfighter Nation* (New York, 1992), 318–26, and Lary May, "Making the American Consensus: The Narrative of Conversion and Subversion in World War II Films," in *The War in American Culture*, ed. Lewis Erenberg and Susan Hirsch (Chicago, 1996), 71–102. "Curtis Bay Cats Overseas," *M*, September 1944, 23. Comedian Larry Storch, who served in a band unit, confirmed this, interview with author, 1982.

17. Miller letter, 12 August 1942, in Simon, *Glenn Miller*, 311–12.

18. Miller's plans are discussed in Mike Levin, "Miller to Build 30 TTC Bands," *DB*, 1 February 1943, 1; Simon, *Glenn Miller*, 324, 311–12 (for Simon's reaction, see 337–38, 349–52). "Jive tempo" is quoted in "Sousa with a Floy Floy," *Time*, 6 September 1943, 48–49.

19. "Old time," Goldman are quoted in "Sousa with a Floy Floy," 48–49. For more on the controversy, see "Letters," *Time*, 27 September 1943, 4.

20. For broadcasts, see Edward Polic, *Glenn Miller Army Air Force Band: Sustineo Alas/I Sustain the Wings* (Metuchen, N.J., 1989), 1:51, 2:1027. Examples of the *Wehrmacht Hour* are in GM.

21. Simon, *Glenn Miller*, 334, 361–71; the Miller letter to Simon is quoted in ibid., 361.

22. On broadcasts, and especially the Chesterfield show of 1940, see Polic, *Glenn Miller Army Air Force Band*, 1:3, 2:714. The V Mail is quoted in Judy Barrett Litoff and David C. Smith, *Since You Went Away: World War II Letters from American Women on the Home Front* (Lawrence, Kans., 1995), 126. *Salinas Army Air Base Observer*, 7 March 1942, 1, GM.

23. The private was Pfc. David B. Bittan, "Miller over There," *M*, September 1944, 26–27; Miller to Simon, 25 September 1944, in Simon, *Glenn Miller*, 384–87; "Miller a Killer," *M*, 15 November 1944, 15 (emphasis in original).

24. See Harry Jaeger, "Buzz Bombs and Boogie Woogie," *M*, May 1945, 11 for parties. Roy W. Stephens, letter to *M*, September 1945, 4; Leonard Pratt, letter to author, July 1994, 2–3, and letter to author, 22 October 1994, 4–5. For clubs in North Africa, see *Depot Dope*, 29 September 1945, 1, kindly shown to me by Caryl Kelly.

25. Simon, *Glenn Miller*, 375–76; for a replica of Tuxedo Junction see ibid., 377.

26. Westbrook, "I Want a Girl," 587–614. For GI Jill see Christman, *Brass Button Broadcasters*, 23, 29. For Horne, see Tyler, *From Harlem to Hollywood*, 179–81.

27. The RAF pilot is quoted in Costello, *Virtue under Fire*, 130–31; Dinah Shore is quoted in "My Ten Favorite Songs," *Tune In*, July 1944, 9.

28. The oppression of waiting is conveyed by the letters of Robert and Jane Easton, *Love and War* (Norman, Okla., 1991), 20, 215.

29. Mike Levin, "Since You Went Away," *DB*, 1 November 1944, 1; Marjorie Kenney to Richard S. Haselton, 27 November 1944, in Litoff and Smith, *Since You Went Away*, 107; Evelyn Marks, letter to author, 12 July 1994, 7. "Dancers Prefer Swing, Draft Age Groups Excluded," *DB*, 1 June 1942, 3.

30. James's style is discussed in *Song Hits*, July 1942, cited in Richard Lingeman, *Don't You Know There's a War On?* (New York, 1970), 285. Count Basie is discussed in Bernie Woods, "Changing Band Styles," *V*, 5 January 1944, 189. Dorothy Anscomb, "Trumpet in the Stars," *Band Leader*, n.d., 62, Harry James file, IJS, describes the girl. Helen Forrest with Bill Libby, *I Had the Craziest Dream* (New York, 1982), 128–37.

31. "I looked around" is quoted in Frederick Wakeman, *Shore Leave* (New York, 1944), 181–82. See David Ewen, *All the Years of American Popular Music*, (Englewood Cliffs, N.J., 1977), 430–65, on wartime ballads and singers. On Sinatra see Gene Lees,

"The Sinatra Effect," in *Singers & the Song* (New York, 1987), 101–15. Dana Polan, *Power and Paranoia* (New York, 1986), 124–27, explores the sexual tensions surrounding Sinatra and informs my remarks. I wish to thank George Lipsitz for calling this to my attention. June Canter, letter to author, 4 July 1994, 2. Nick Sevano is quoted in Kitty Kelley, *His Way* (New York, 1986), 80.

32. William Manchester is quoted in Kelley, *His Way,* 91, "Hey, wop," at 83; For "to gang up" see "Camp Visit," *Tune In,* December 1944, 15. Other responses to Sinatra are quoted in Wakeman, *Shore Leave,* 181–85; "my sister" is quoted in "That Old Sweet Song," *Time,* 5 July 1943, as cited in Polan, *Power and Paranoia,* 125. Enlisted men also called civilian musicians draft dodgers. See Nita Barnet, "Soldier Sneers Spoil Visits to Service Camps," *DB,* 1 January 1944, 17.

33. Polan, *Power and Paranoia,* 132 discusses the difficulties of this time for women; Wakeman, *Shore Leave,* 29; Barbara Paris, letter to author, 12 November 1994, 1–3; Rita Luther, letter to author, 9 July 1994, 1; Mrs. L. Hayster (Louise Holloway), letter to author, 20 September 1994, 4; Leon Meenach, letter to author, 30 November 1994, 4. For a discussion of wartime concerns about female sexuality, see Francis E. Merrill, *Social Problems on the Home Front* (New York, 1948).

34. Viola Smith, "Give Girl Musicians a Break!" *DB,* 1 February 1942, 8. Shelly Placksin, *American Women in Jazz* (New York, 1982), 127–220 is excellent on women musicians during the war. David Stowe, *Swing Changes* (Cambridge, Mass., 1994), 168–74 is very insightful. "Off the beam fems" is quoted in a letter from R. Toney, *DB,* 1 May 1942, 10.

35. For opposition to women musicians, see Marvin Freedman, *DB,* 23 April 1947, cited in Placksin, *American Women in Jazz,* 128; Ted Toll, "The Gal Yippers Have No Place in Our Jazz Bands," *DB,* 15 October 1939, 18, is quoted in ibid., 87, as is "Why Women Musicians Are Inferior," *DB,* February 1938, 88. For a fascinating account that unfortunately appeared too late to treat of further, see Sherrie Tucker, "Working the Swing Shift," *Labor's Heritage* (summer 1996):46–66.

36. For earlier protests, see Leona May Smith, "Is There a Career for Women Musicians?" *M,* January 1938, 1; Gypsie Cooper, "Can Women Swing?" *M,* September 1936, 30. Anita O'Day with George Eells, *High Times, Hard Times* (New York, 1982), 91–92.

37. On Grable see Westbrook, "I Want a Girl," 587–614; Elaine May, "Rosie the Riveter Gets Married," in Erenberg and Hirsch, *The War in American Culture,* 139–40. Jane Gaines, "The Popular Icon as Commodity and Sign: The Circulation of Betty Grable, 1941–45" (Ph.D. diss., Northwestern University, 1982), is the source for "model wife" (51); "we ought to be mad" (291); fan clubs (293); and "domestic habit" (297). On James and "lolling," see Bernie Woods, "Band Biz Now Minus a 'Hot' Personality," *V,* 5 January 1944, 186.

38. Although no race liberal, Miller had hired African American arrangers (such as Eddie Durham) and a light-skinned drummer who could pass for white and had supported the integration of all music locals. He also urged both Durham and drum-

mer Jo Jones to enlist in the Army Air Force. His intentions are unclear. That there were already exceptional black musicians in service suggests that he was not interested in bucking Jim Crow.

39. "Noted Musicians Do Russian Relief Show," *DW,* 17 April, 1943, 7; Edith Anderson, "Music Builds the Spirit of a Fighting People," *DW,* 23 April 1942, 7; "Ace Jazzmen Produce 'Night of the Blues,'" *DW,* 21 May 1942, 7; "Theatre Music World Honor [*sic*] Thomas 'Fats' Waller," *DW,* 28 March 1944, 5; "Election Night Jamboree," *DW,* 7 November 1944, 15. See "John Hammond Says," *Music and Rhythm,* 22 June 1942, 33; "Must There Be Segregation in the Union?" *Music and Rhythm,* July 1942, 21; "Radio to Hire First Negroes in Studios," *Music and Rhythm,* July 1942, 48. Frank Bolden, "The Orchestra World," *PC,* 14 February 1942, 19. On Sinatra, see "Act of the Year," *M,* January 1946, 28; "Sinatra Continues Racial Speeches," *DB,* 15 November 1945, 1.

40. Editorial, "Music Can Destroy Racial Bigotry," *DB,* 15 September 1945, 10; Margaret Halsey, *Color Blind: A White Woman Looks at the Negro* (New York, 1946), 11–13, 31, 33–34. For USO policy, see *AN,* 22 May 1943, 14. On canteens, see "Canteen Heads Have Row over Mixed Dancing," *DB,* 15 April 1943, 1, 5; Carl Van Vechten, "An Ode to the Stage Door Canteen," *Theatre Arts,* April 1943, 229–31. For more in-depth discussion of the canteens and the USO, see Tyler, *From Harlem to Hollywood,* 137–70.

41. Hammond, *On Record,* 238–41, discusses his battle with the radio networks. Mike Levin, "Jim Crow," *DB,* 1 October 1944, 1, 12; Mike Levin, "Still Jim Crow," *DB,* 15 October, 1944, 1, 12; Editors, "Why?" *M,* March 1943, 5; for the *New York Age* quotation, see Editors, "Bouquets," *M,* July 1943, 5. See *AN,* 23 January 1943, 16 for the poll results and Ellington Week. *Metronome* adopted a more militant racial stance during the war.

42. "It Happened to the Duke," *PC,* 18 April 1942, 21. On LA halls, see "Colored Band Bookings Barred in Los Angeles' Big Danceries," *PC,* 13 November 1943, 19. On the black press's militance and the entertainment industry's role in the war, see "'Hurricane' Target for Welter of Criticism," *PC,* 12 June 1943, 21; "To Help Woodward," *PC,* 17 August 1946, 18. On Double V, see *PC,* 14 March 1942, 20.

43. On the USO, see Ramona Lowe, *AN,* 22 May 1943, 14; *PC,* 4 December 1943, 19; Horne is quoted in Lena Horne and Richard Schickel, *Lena* (Garden City, 1965), 173–75.

44. "Salute to Negro Troops," *PC,* 24 January 1942, 21. For "half a loaf" see "Billie Holiday and the 'St. Louis Incident,'" *AN,* 23 December 1944, 9.

45. Eckstine is quoted in Ira Gitler, *Swing to Bop* (New York, 1985), 128–29. For the difficulties with bus travel, see *AN,* 5 September 1944, 15.

46. Ronald D. Cohen, "Music Goes to War: California, 1940–1945," in *Everyman's War in the Golden State: California during World War II* (in press), 10–15, discusses racial tensions in Los Angeles. On Carter, see Morroe Berger, Edward Berger, and James Patrick, *Benny Carter: A Life in Music* (Metuchen, N.J., 1982), 210–29.

47. See Berger, Berger, and Patrick, *Benny Carter,* 227–229 on racial tensions. See

also Edward Escobar, "Zoot Suiters and Cops," in Erenberg and Hirsch, *The War in American Culture*, 284–309. For tensions after the riot see "LA Niteries Facing Race Problem," *DB*, 1 March 1943, 6; "Coast Ops Nix on Colored Bands," *DB*, 1 October 1943, 6; "Only Superiority of Consequence Is One of Intellect," *DB*, 1 October 1943, 10. Gloria Vargas, letter to author, 8 September 1994, 1–2 discusses the Palladium's ban on Mexican American males. For restrictions on black bands, see "Coast Ops Nix on Colored Bands," *DB*, 1 October 1943, 6, and "San Diego OK's 'Jim Crow' Rule," *DB*, 15 October 1944, 5.

48. Malcolm X with Alex Haley, *The Autobiography of Malcolm X* (New York, 1963), 113; *AN*, 1 May 1943, 1; White is quoted in Dominic J. Capeci, Jr., "Walter F. White and the Savoy Ballroom Controversy of 1943," *Afro-Americans in New York Life and History* (July 1981):16, 22; Bruce Tyler, "Black Jive and White Repression," *Journal of Ethnic Studies* 16 (1989):31–66, shows the extreme reactions to the zoot suit; Joe Bostic, "What's Behind Savoy Closing?" *People's Voice*, 1 May 1943, 1, exemplifies the black press; *Newsweek* is quoted in Tyler, "Black Jive," 54. For black zoot suiters see Robin D. G. Kelley, "The Riddle of the Zoot: Malcolm Little and Black Cultural Politics during World War II," in *Malcolm X: In Our Own Image*, ed. Joe Wood (New York, 1992), 155–82; George Lipsitz, *Rainbow at Midnight: Class and Culture in the Cold War* (Champaign, Ill., 1994), 83–86.

49. Abe Hill, "52nd Street: New York's Real 'Melting Pot,'" *AN*, 15 July 1944, 1, 12. "Police 'Warn' 52nd Street Riot May Come from Mixing," *AN*, 22 July 1944, 1, 11.

50. For musicians' opposition, see Simon, *Glenn Miller*, 339; "the individuality of a hot musician" is quoted in Rogers E. M. Whitaker, "Eddie Condon," *New Yorker*, 28 April 1945, 30.

51. Simon, *Glenn Miller*, 427–30.

52. George Simon, "Review of Glenn Miller Orchestra," *M*, March 1946, 14. Mike Levin, "When Johnny Comes Marching Home," *DB* 15 June 1945, 1, 4.

53. See "Only Superiority of Consequence," 10 for "How can we hope . . ."

CHAPTER EIGHT: THE WAR IN JAZZ

1. For the fate of *Esquire's* jazz poll, for the quotations of revivalists, and for "melancholy ride," see Leonard Feather, *The Jazz Years* (New York, 1987), 81–89. "Moldy figs" and "fascists" are quoted in Leonard Feather, "On Musical Fascism," *M*, September 1945, 16.

2. Neil Leonard, *Jazz: Myth and Religion* (New York, 1987), posits that cults define jazz. My point is that sectarian splits predominated in the late 1940s.

3. "Bands Busting up Big," *M*, January 1947, 58; "Strike down the Band," *Newsweek*, 30 December 1946; the executive is quoted in Bernie Woods, "Band Biz Despite Gloomy Prophecies Can Jockey into Boff Postwar B.O.," *V*, 9 January 1946, 247.

4. "The world . . . introduced," is quoted in *DB*, 1 October 1944, 1; music industry jobs are discussed in *DB*, November 1944, 2; "everyone hoped" is quoted in "More They Change More They're Same," *DB*, 25 March 1946, 12.

5. Woods, "Band Biz," 247; see Barry Ulanov, "Obituary in Rhythm," *M,* February 1947, 4, for "who ever believed"; for "The war is over," see Mike Levin, "Music Biz Just Ain't Nowhere!" *DB,* 12 November 1946, 1, 4–5. Barnet is quoted in Bill Gottlieb, "Big Payrolls, Loud Brass Must Go," *DB,* 12 August 1946, 1.

6. "We aren't getting," Buddy Rich are quoted in Levin, "Music Biz Just Ain't Nowhere!," 1, 4–5.

7. Frank Stacy, "War's End to Crowd Biz," *DB,* 1 September 1945, 1, discusses the surplus of musicians. For "mere shadow," see Simon, "Slow Speed Ahead," *M,* February 1946, 8.

8. Woods, "Band Biz," 247; McKinley, "'Ooh, What You Said, Tex!" *M,* March 1947, 19, 39–40.

9. Helen Forrest with Bill Libby, *I Had the Craziest Dream* (New York, 1982), 154–61. For statistics, see Beth L. Bailey, *From Front Porch to Back Seat* (Baltimore, 1988), 41–42.

10. George Simon, *The Big Bands,* 4th ed. (New York, 1981), 31–32, discusses the recording strike; "could not be made" is quoted in "Bands Miss Recordings," *V,* 5 January 1944, 190.

11. "We've had bad luck" is quoted in Barbara Hodgkins, "Jazz on CBS," *M,* June 1947, 18, 42; for "shocking return," see "A Mess at CBS," *M,* May 1945, 6; Mildred Bailey is discussed in "Radio Again Snubs the Righteous Jazz," *DB,* 1 February 1945, 10; For more on radio's problems, see *V,* 3 January 1945, 133; George Rosen, "Don't Look Now . . . But Your Radio's Static," *V,* 8 January 1947, 107.

12. McKinley, "Ooh, What You Said!," 40–41; for "in droves," see "Straighten up and Fly Right," *DB,* 2 December 1946, 10; Barnet is quoted in Gottlieb, "Big Payrolls, Loud Brass Must Go," 1, 12; McIntyre is quoted in *DB,* 6 October 1948, 2.

13. Charles Miller, "Twilight of the Dance Band," *New Republic,* 17 March 1947, 40; Bob Wilber, *Music Was Not Enough* (New York, 1988), 149–51; Calloway is quoted in his *Minnie the Moocher and Me* (New York, 1976), 185–206; Levin, "Music Business Just Ain't Nowhere!," 1, 4–5; Charlie Barnet with Stanley Dance, *Those Swinging Years* (Baton Rouge, 1984), 143; Red Rodney is quoted in Ira Gitler, *Swing to Bop* (New York, 1985), 236.

14. For "first large-scale revolt," see Francis Newton [Eric Hobsbawm], *The Jazz Scene* (New York, 1960), 87; LeRoi Jones, *Blues People,* (New York, 1963), 202–7, treats the revival as a white middle-class reaction to bop but ignores its earlier anti-swing roots. Rudi Blesh's *Shining Trumpets* (New York, 1946), 323–24, notes that *Jazzmen's* flaw was its attempt to reconcile jazz and swing.

15. For Hodes, "My Music," see *The Jazz Sheet,* March–April 1969, reprinted in *Selections from the Gutter: Jazz Portraits from* "The Jazz Record," ed. Art Hodes and Chadwick Hansen (Berkeley, 1979), inside cover. "To left" and "working man" are quoted in Hodes, "Introducing . . . *The Jazz Record, 1943,"* in ibid., 3–4. For the Village scene see Hodes, JOHP, reel 1, 37; reel 2, 11–15, 20–27. Rudi Blesh, interview with Montana Taylor, in Hodes and Hansen, *Selections from the Gutter,* 47–50. See also Rudi Blesh, "Set My People Free," *The Jazz Record,* November 1945, 10.

16. "By the time this war" is quoted in Hodes, "Introducing . . . *The Jazz Record,*" in *Selections from the Gutter,* 3–4. For record collectors, see Gilbert Millstein, "For Kicks," pt. 2, *The New Yorker,* 16 March 1946, 36; Leonard, *Jazz: Myth and Religion,* 148–50.

17. "The most historic" is quoted in "Bunk Johnson Rides Again," *Time,* 24 May 1943, 63–64; "Town Hall" is quoted in Beth McHenry, "Hot Trumpet," *DW,* 30 December 1945, 5; Rudi Blesh is quoted in Blesh, "Set My People Free," *The Jazz Record,* November 1945, 9–11. For more on Johnson, see Rudi Blesh, "'Bunk' Comes East," *New York Herald Tribune,* 18 March 1945, sec. 4, at 5.

18. Max Kaminsky with V. E. Hughes, *My Life in Jazz* (New York, 1963), 99–105, 108–110, 112, 117, 127. See also Bud Freeman, JOHP, reel 1, 50–51; James Lincoln Collier, *The Making of Jazz* (New York, 1986), 281–82; Mike Levin, "Jazz and the Village Lose a Colorful Figure," *DB,* 29 July 1946, 2; John S. Wilson, "Jimmy Ryan's," *NYT,* 24 September 1976, n.p., Jazz Club file, IJS. "Everyman" is quoted in Rogers M. Whitaker, "Profiles (Eddie Condon)," *New Yorker,* 5 May 1945, 40. In 1938 Kaminsky joined Condon, Freeman, Dave Tough, Pee Wee Russell, Dave Bowman, and several others to form the Summa Cum Laude Band, but it failed because long-term bookings, which only appeared with the war, were slow.

19. Mezz Mezzrow and Bernard Wolfe, *Really the Blues* (New York, 1946), 120–22. See Dorothy Baker, *Young Man with a Horn* (New York, 1938).

20. Leonard Feather, "Progressives Called Musical Reactionaries," *People's Voice,* 7 June 1947, as discussed in Murray Chase, "New and Old Jazz," *DW,* 20 June 1947, 11; Lionel Trilling, "The Repressive Impulse," *Partisan Review* 15 (June 1948):720. Ernest Borneman, "The Jazz Cult, II: War among the Critics," *Harper's,* March 1947, 161, discusses the battle among patisans of each style. On the growing musical rigidity of the Left, see Robbie Lieberman, *My Song Is My Weapon* (Urbana, Ill., 1989), 74–114; S. Frederick Starr, *Red & Hot* (New York, 1985), 218–23.

21. Kaminsky, *My Life in Jazz,* 169–70; Wilber, *Music Was Not Enough,* 50–51.

22. Dizzy Gillespie with Al Fraser, *To Be, or Not . . . to Bop* (Garden City, 1979), 201, 141; Ralph Ellison, "The Golden Age, Time Past," in *Shadow and Act* (New York, 1966), 201. The best analyses of bop are Jones, *Blues People,* 175–207; Ben Sidran, *Black Talk* (New York, 1981), 78–115; and Newton, *The Jazz Scene,* 88–90, 113–18, 214–22.

23. Ellison is quoted in "Golden Age, Time Past," in *Shadow and Act,* 200; Gordon is quoted in Gitler, *Swing to Bop,* 311.

24. See Gillespie, *To Be,* 119–20, for his physical, 287 for the racism quote; for Young's army problems, see Frank Büchmann-Møller, *You Just Fight for Your Life* (New York, 1990), 117–30; Kenny Clarke, JOHP, sides 5–8, 85–88.

25. Gillespie, *To Be,* 210.

26. See ibid., 157, for discrimination; Williams is quoted in ibid., 149–50; Gillespie is quoted in ibid., 157–58. Kenny Clarke expressed similar ideas in Ursula Broschke Davis, *Paris without Regret* (Iowa City, 1986), 47.

27. See Gillespie, *To Be,* 287–88 on Robeson and Marcantonio. Gillespie actually

joined the party, probably to play Camp Unity and various Communist benefits. See Gillespie, *To Be*, 80; Leonard Feather, "Dizzy Is Crazy Like a Fox," *M*, July 1944, 16.

28. "Self-determined" is quoted in Ellison, "Golden Age, Times Past," in *Shadow and Act*, 198–210; Kenny Clarke, JOHP, sides 1–4, 101–4; Gillespie, *To Be*, 134–51. Leonard Feather, "'Be-bop??!!'" *M*, April 1947, 21, 44, discusses Teddy Hill's role at Minton's. Miles Davis with Quincy Troupe, *Miles* (New York, 1989), 60–61.

29. Ross Russell, *Bird Lives!* (New York, 1980), 32–129.

30. McShann, *Jazz Research* 3 (November 1960):8; for "no boundary line" and "bebop is convenient," see Russell, *Bird Lives!* 292–93; Ellison, "On Bird-Watching, and Jazz," *Shadow and Act*, 218–27. Dennis McNally, *Desolate Angel* (New York, 1979), notes the similarities among Parker, Jack Kerouac, Allen Ginsberg, and Jackson Pollock.

31. George Simon, "Bop's Dixie to Monk," *M*, April 1948, 20, 34–35; Marshall Stearns, *The Story of Jazz* (New York, 1958), 155–67; Leonard Feather, "How High the Tune," *M*, September 1947, 20, 46. Williams is quoted in Gillespie, 151.

32. "Kenny was modifying" is quoted in Gillespie, *To Be*, 98–100, "sensitive," 134; for the change in drums, see Jones, *Blues People*, 193; Stearns, *Story of Jazz*, 166–67; Clarke, JOHP, sides 1–4, 92; Leonard Feather, "Facts about Max," *M*, November 1948, 26–27.

33. "Always in the vanguard" is quoted in Gillespie, *To Be*, 291; Fuller is quoted in Richard O. Boyer, "Profiles (Bop)," *The New Yorker*, 3 July 1948, 30–31.

34. For Armstrong's position, see "'Bop Will Kill Business Unless It Kills Itself First'—Louis Armstrong," *DB*, 7 April 1948, 2–3; George Simon, "Bebop's the Easy Way Out, Claims Louis," *M*, February 1948, 14–15. See also Marshall W. Stearns, "Re-bop, Bebop, and Bop," *Harper's* , April 1950, 93; "Lombardo Grooves Louis!" *M*, September 1949, 18. Gillespie, *To Be*, 295–96; Miles Davis, *Miles*, 83. Bird's humor is discussed in Russell, *Bird Lives!* 119–21.

35. Monk is quoted in Boyer, "Profiles," *The New Yorker*, 3 July 1948, 30–31. Clarke is quoted in Gillespie, *To Be*, 141–42; Miles Davis, *Miles*, 60–61.

36. Gillespie, *To Be*, 289–93, 115–16, 318–19; Russell, *Bird Lives!*, 324. For Islam, see Boyer, "Profiles," *The New Yorker*, 31–32. Clarke is quoted in Ursula Davis, *Paris without Regret*, 62–63.

37. Jones, *Blues People*, 190–91; Gillespie, *To Be*, 278–80; "Band of the Year, Dizzy Gillespie," *M*, January 1948, 17–18; Lipsitz, *Rainbow at Midnight*, 25–28; Robin D. G. Kelley, "The Riddle of the Zoot: Malcolm Little and Black Cultural Politics during World War II," in *Malcolm X: In Our Own Image*, ed. Joe Wood (New York, 1992), 155–82.

38. On language, see Gillespie, *To Be*, 280–81; Sidran, *Black Talk*, 110–11; Lipsitz, *Rainbow at Midnight*, 188–89. On drugs, see Gillespie, *To Be*, 283–87; Miles Davis, *Miles*, 122–23; Leonard Feather, "Yardbird Flies Home," *M*, August 1947, 14, 43–44. Blakey is quoted in Sidran, *Black Talk*, 113; Rodney is quoted in Gitler, *Swing to Bop*, 283.

39. Gillespie, *To Be*, 342; Gordon is quoted in Gitler, *Swing to Bop*, 311, Rollins in ibid. at 304.

40. Gillespie, *To Be*, 342.

41. "Sacred" is quoted in Harold Finestone, "Cats, Kicks and Color," *Social Problems* 5 (summer 1957):3–13; LeRoi Jones, *The Autobiography of LeRoi Jones/Amiri Baraka* (New York, 1984), 58, 60–62.

42. Jerome is quoted in Gitler, *Swing to Bop*, 276; Rodney is quoted in ibid., 236.

43. Monte Kay is quoted in Arnold Shaw, *52nd Street: The Street of Jazz* (New York, 1977), 272; Gil Sorrentino, "Remembrance of Bop in New York," in *Things in the Driver's Seat: Readings in Popular Culture*, ed. Harry Russell Huebel (Chicago, 1972), 131–32.

44. Reig is quoted in Gillespie, *To Be*, 298. See Teddy Reig with Edward Berger, *Reminiscing in Tempo: The Life and Times of a Jazz Hustler* (Metuchen, N.J., 1990), 1–22. Rivers is quoted in Larry Rivers with Arnold Weinstein, *What Did I Do?* (New York, 1992), 39–40.

45. Sorrentino, "Remembrance of Bop in New York," 125–26.

46. Ibid., 127–28.

47. Barbara Ehrenreich, *Hearts of Men: American Dreams and the Flight from Commitment* (Garden City, 1983), and Elaine May, *Homeward Bound: American Families in the Cold War* (New York, 1988), explore facets of the themes of domesticity and success after the war. Gillespie, *To Be*, 279; Jones, *Blues People*, 187; Sorrentino, 128–29; Rivers, *What Did I Do?*, 137–38.

48. Norman Mailer, "The White Negro," *Dissent* 4 (summer 1957), is quoted in *The Sixties Papers*, ed. Judith Albert and Stewart Albert (New York, 1984), 95–97; "two most important" is quoted in Miles Templar, "The Hipster," *Partisan Review* 15 (August 1948):1053–55; Rose is quoted in Dennis L. Breo, "Confessions of a Political Gadfly," *The Chicago Tribune Magazine*, 13 December 1987, 20–21.

49. Gillespie, *To Be*, 285–86, 281–82.

50. Mike Levin, "Thirty Years of Dancing in U.S.," *DB*, 19 May 1950, 1, 20; Eckstine is quoted in Gillespie, *To Be*, 190; Stan Kenton, "Sure, I Helped to Wreck the Dance Biz," *DB*, 19 May 1950, 1, 26.

51. For "we snarl," see A. Konova, "Cut the Screaming," *DB*, 9 September 1949, 10. For the critical battle, see Ernest Borneman, "The Jazz Cult, I," *Harper's*, February 1947, 147; Barry Ulanov, "Moldy Figs vs. Moderns!" *M*, November 1947, 15, 23.

CHAPTER NINE: CODA AND CONCLUSION

1. Advertisement, *DB*, 15 July 1949, 5. For the winner, see "'Crewcut' Contest's $1,000 Word," *DB*, 4 November 1949, 1.

2. "Don't Fire 'Till You See Reds of Their Eyes," *DB*, 22 October 1947, 12; Art Hodes, JOHP, reel 2, 25–28.

3. On Sinatra see Kitty Kelley, *His Way* (New York, 1987), 119–20; "Mrs. Roosevelt," "the minute," and Ruark comment are quoted in ibid., 134; John Rockewell,

Sinatra (New York, 1984), 92–102 discusses charges of mafia involvement. For Shaw, see House Committee on Un-American Activities, "Communist Activities in the New York Area," 4 May 1953, 1178–94. The idea of a conversion experience is suggested by David W. Noble, "The Reconstruction of Progress: Charles Beard, Richard Hofstadter, and Postwar Historical Thought," in *Recasting America*, ed. Lary May (Chicago, 1989), 61–75; Lary May, "Making the American Consensus: The Narrative of Conversion and Subversion in World War II Films," in *The War in American Culture*, ed. Lewis Erenberg and Susan Hirsch (Chicago, 1996), 71–102.

4. Josephson's recollection of Pegler's attack on him is quoted in Whitney Balliett, "Profiles," *New Yorker*, 9 October 1971, 90, 92; John Hammond with Irving Townsend, *John Hammond On Record* (New York, 1977), 309–12; on Gilford and Mostel, see Kate Mostel and Madeline Gilford, *170 Years of Show Business*, (New York, 1978), 111–21; Editorial, "Advice to the Players," DB, 16 November 1951, 10.

5. For an excellent discussion of Soviet jazz policy, see S. Frederick Starr, *Red & Hot* (New York, 1985), 204–34. Quotations are from Barry Ulanov, "The Editors Speak," *M*, October 1946, 4; Ulanov, "The Square Bear," *M*, April 1948, 15 also criticized Soviet music policy. For the debates over Voice of America, see "A Good Man Is Hard to Find," *M*, June 1946, 6; Benny Goodman, "Benny Goodman Complains," *M*, August 1947, 16, with responses by Ulanov and Simon at 16–17; "Soviet Solution," *M*, September 1947, 9.

6. For "Deep South Suite," see Duke Ellington, *Music Is My Mistress* (New York, 1976), 184–85. Goodman is quoted in the *Elizabethon (Tenn.) Star*, 28 January 1947, n.p., BG. For Hampton and Truman, see Lionel Hampton, *Hamp* (New York, 1989), 93. Challenge to HUAC is in *DW*, 23 October 1947, n.p., BG.

7. Editors, "Threat to Music Is Head Not Red!" *DB*, 17 December 1947, 10. James Gilbert, *A Cycle of Outrage: America's Reaction to the Juvenile Delinquent in the 1950s* (New York, 1986), 24–41, 63–78, details the rising fears of youth delinquency. Elaine Tyler May, *Homeward Bound: American Families in the Cold War* (New York, 1988), makes similar arguments about the fears about women's sexuality.

8. Bruce Crowther, *Gene Krupa: His Life and Times* (New York, 1987), 89–94. See also "Gene in NY," *M*, September 1943, 7, 24; *M*, August 1943, 24; George Simon, "Simon Says," *M*, July 1943, 6, 26. On the growing clampdown, "No Rye for FBI: They'll Take Tea," *M*, August 1945, 7.

9. Billie Holiday with William Dufty, *Lady Sings the Blues*, (New York, 1956), 124—30; L. A. "crime wave" is cited in "Southern (California) Comfort," *M*, May 1947, 8; George Simon, "They Are Innocent until Proven Guilty!" *M*, February 1943, 34; George Simon, "Weed Out the Weeders," *M*, October 1948, 50.

10. "Girl addicts" is quoted in "New York Wakes up to Find 15,000 Teen-Age Dope Addicts," *Newsweek*, 29 January 1951, 23–24; "Degradation in New York," *Newsweek*, 25 June 1951, 19–20; for Anslinger's charges, see "An Ever-Growing Problem," *Newsweek*, 11 June, 1951, 26–27.

11. George Simon, "Marijuana for Breakfast," *M*, August 1951, 34; Editors, "Threat to Music Is Head Not Red!" 10; for "cesspools," see Ulanov, "Narcotics," *M*, September

1951, 34; Simon, "Weed Out the Weeders," 50; for "T" users and "once more be accepted," see George Simon, "More about My Middle Initial," *M,* October 1951, 34; for "rotten apples" see "Dope Menace Keeps Growing," *DB,* 17 November 1950, 10; Ralph Gleason, "Critic Demands Junking of Weakling Jazzmen," *DB,* 2 December 1953, 2.

12. George Simon, "Musicians' Damaged Reputations," *M,* September 1949, 42; Barry Ulanov, "The Real Villains," *M,* March 1949, 42; "marihuana . . . dope fiend" is quoted in Ulanov, "Musicians Are Not Dope Fiends," *M,* August 1947, 12. Editors, "A Position Is Re-emphasized," *DB,* 24 August 1951, 10 contains the Anslinger charges.

13. "Philly Cop Goes Bebop to Snare Tootler Addicts," *BB,* n.d., n.p., bebop file, IJS. For New York's cabaret laws, see Paul Chevigny, *Gigs, Jazz and the Cabaret Laws in New York City,* (New York, 1991), 57–61.

14. On the attempts to revive the dance bands, see "Why the Slump in Dance Biz?" *DB,* 30 December 1949, 1, 10; "This Is the Issue We Yelled About," *DB,* 19 May 1950, 14, 16, 18, 23; "lost contact" is quoted in Mike Levin, "Thirty Years of Dancing in U.S.," *DB,* 19 May 1950, 1, 10; "Anybody Agree?" *DB,* 8 February 1952, 10; Jack Tracy, "'Down Beat' Inaugurates Huge Dance Campaign," *DB,* 14 January 1953, 1, 13. Kenton's views are in Stan Kenton, "Sure I Helped to Wreck the Dance Band Business," *DB,* 19 May 1950, 1, 26.

15. Benny Goodman, "Is Swing Dead? Was Swing Ever Alive?" *M&R,* August 1941, 10.

16. Mike Levin, "Notes between Notes," *DB,* 7 October 1949, 19; Ralph Burns is quoted in Woody Herman and Stuart Troup, *The Wood Chopper's Ball: The Autobiography of Woody Herman* (New York, 1990), 45.

17. On the spread of jazz lounges, see Leonard Feather, "Birdlandish Bistros Boom," *DB,* 18 June 1952, 1, 19.

Index

Page references to illustrations appear in italics.

ABC radio, programs on, 211
Abraham Lincoln Brigade, 133–34, 145, 147
Adorno, Theodor, 262n. 6
Aeolian Hall concert, 65, 67
AFM. *See* American Federation of Musicians (AFM)
AFN (Armed Forces Network), 185, 191, 194
African American bands: and armed forces, 185, 204–6; attacks on, 115–16, 176, 207–8, 226; attitudes toward, 124–25; audience for, 42–43; benefits played by, 115; bookings for, 167, 202; clothing and behavior of, 113–19; dance audience for, 48–49, 110–12; in depression, 24–29; and polls, 62–63; popularity of, 7–8; on radio, 42–44; role of, xv, 73–77, 81–83, 95, 251–52; and segregation, 27, 169–78, 206–8, 226; sponsors for, 170–71; standard setups for, 8–9; venues for, 93, 153–56, 250. *See also* African American music
African American music: attitudes toward, 10–11, 37, 130–36; changes in, 95, 97; characteristics of, 6–10; as democratizing force, 133–36; influence by, 10–11, 72–77, 81–83, 101, 116–19, 139–41, 189, 226; and jazz revival, 223; on jukeboxes, 45; and leftist politics, 120–21, 136–44; role of, 99–101; roots of, 102–3, 105–7, 109,

120–22. *See also* African American bands; bebop; jazz; swing; *names of specific performers*
African Americans: as bandleaders, 95; bop's significance for, 239–40; as dancers, 49–50; dreams of, 109–10; fashions of, 55–56; folk traditions of, 102–3, 105–7, 109; heightened consciousness of, 225; heroes/heroines for, 99, 113–19; and language, 108–9; and leftist ideology, 133; migration by, 6–7, 14, 95, 110; stereotypes of, 229–31; unemployment of, 15, 24–25; and World War II home front, xvi, 201–8; youth culture of, 40–41. *See also* African American bands; African American music
Afro-Cuban music, 231
Ager, Cecelia, 38, 51
"Ain't It the Truth," 108–9
Airforce (film), 184
Albert, Don, 116, *175*
alcohol, use of, 20, 102, 111–12, 232
Alexander, Willard: as booking agent, 4, 127, 168; on Goodman, 79; influence by, 97–98, 145, 158–59; on swing bands, 5
"All-American Concert" (radio program), 211–12
Allen, Henry "Red," 172
Allen, Jap, 25
Allen, Lewis, 146–47

Allen, Moses, *28*
Allen, Nat, *205*
"All or Nothing at All," 196
All-Star Girl Orchestra (group), 199
Amateur Nights (at Apollo Theater), 156
American Federation of Musicians (AFM):
and New Deal reform, 30; pay scale of,
25–26, 98; segregation in, 203; strike by,
216–17, 220; and unemployment, 12–13,
25; World War II efforts of, 185
American Labor Committee, 202
American League for Peace and Democracy,
Hunt's Point Branch, 134
American Music Festival, 134
American Newspaper Guild, 125
American Record, 126. *See also* Columbia
Records
American Theater Wing, 203
American Youth for Democracy (AYD), 119,
129, 134–35
Ammons, Albert, 120–21, 126
Amos 'n' Andy, 174
Amsterdam News (newspaper), 62, 136,
207–8
amusement tax, 214, 221, 227
Anderson, Ivie, 29, 85
Andrews Sisters, 67
"And the Angels Sing," 90
Anslinger, Harry J., 247, 248
Apollo Theater: audiences at, 97, 102; bene-
fits at, 115; performances at, 48, *96*, 98,
154, 155; radio feed from, 43; reputation
of, 112, 155–56
Arabic names, 231
Arcadia Ballroom, 48, 172–73
Arlen, Harold, 11
armed forces: as audience, 186–87, 190–93,
192, 209–10; benefits for blacks in, 202;
segregation in, 184–85, 189, 202–6,
225–26. *See also* Army Air Force (AAF)
Orchestra
Armed Forces Network (AFN), 185, 191, 194
Armed Forces Radio Service, 185, 194, 222
Armstrong, Henry, 95, 114
Armstrong, Louis, *9*; background of, 6; in
band contests, 60; on bebop, 230; in
films, 174; influence by, 8, 10, 14, 135;

and jazz revival, 222; performances by,
66, 174–75, 185; popularity of, 169–70; recordings by, 43; as soloist, 7–8, 29; sponsor for, 171
Army Air Force (AAF) Orchestra, *192;* jazz influence on, 190; music by, 194–95, 202;
musicians in, 189; postwar situation of,
215; restructuring of, 189–90; rigidity of,
209; role of, 182, 190–93
Army Air Force Training Corps, 190
Army Relief Fund, 189
Arnheim, Gus, 20–21
Arnold, Gen. Hap, 209
Arnstein, Nicky, 23
art: vs. commercialism, 151; definitions of,
230–31; democratization of, 59–64; exhibited in nightclub, 145–46. *See also* African
American music; music
Art Kassel Midway Gardens Orchestra, 72
Ashcraft, "Squirrel," 128, 137
Asian Americans, swing's appeal to, 89–90
Associated Booking Corporation, 98
audience: attitudes and expectations of, 10–
11, 77, 155, 171–72; and band contests,
60; for bebop, 233–38; changes in, 160,
195–96, 216–18; characteristics of, 68,
70–71, 89; criticism of, 38; gender of,
83–84; GIs as, 186–87, 190–93, *192*,
209–10; heroes/heroines for, 79, 99,
115–19; integration of, 37, 158–59, 177–
78, *224*, 233–34; as listeners vs. dancers,
91, 239; mob/riot behavior of, 35–37,
46–47; musicians' interaction with, 57–
60, 155–56, 158–59, 172–73, 235; myth
of southern, 170–72; polls of, 62–63, 115,
117, 204, 211–12; for radio, 14, 44,
163–64; role of, xiii–xiv, xvii, 61–62; segregation of, 116; waning interest of, 241–
42. *See also* dance; youth culture; *names of
specific performance venues*
Austin High Gang, 72
autographs, 58
automobiles, with radios, 44
"Avalon," 67
Axis Sally, 185
AYD (American Youth for Democracy), 119,
129, 134–35

Bailey, Mildred, 68, 85, 125, 127, 217

Bailey, William C. "Buster," 72

Baker, Chet, 248

Baker, Dorothy, 222

ballrooms: closure of, 207; decline of, 214; democratization of, 48–54; in depression, 13; integration of, 155; and Prohibition repeal, 31; radio feeds from, 43, 98, 154, 156, 162, 168; segregation in, 49, 172–73, 204, 206–7; transformation of behavior in, 56–57

bandleaders: African Americans as, 95; army enlistment by, 181–83; characteristics of, 78–83, 103–4; in films, 173–74; as idols for audience, 79, 115–19; marriages of, 200–201; pressures on, 150–51, 166, 169, 214; prestige of, 161–62; as representatives of urban culture, 113. *See also names of specific bandleaders*

Band of the Year (award), 233

bands: and audience polls, 62–63, 115, 117, 204, 211–12; benefits played by, 115, 120–22, 131–32, 202, 212; brass section in, 76, 104; competition among, 7–8; components of, 75–78, 85, 103–4, 250–51; concert status of, 46; contests for, 60, *61*, 63–64, 68–69, 94–95; cosmopolitan character of, 81–82; costs of, 161; in depression, 24–29, 99–100, 108–9, 118–19; earnings for, 161–63, 164, 166–69, 213–14; egalitarianism needed in, 229; evaluation of, 61–62; gender in, xiii, 71, 83–88, 198–200, *199*, 251; individuals in, 77; influence by, 40–41; integration of, xiv–xv, 4, 71, 73, 82–83, 91, 128–30, 138–40, 143, 171–73, 177–78, 206, 226; leisure time of, 84–85; local vs. national, 26–28; postwar situation of, 213–18; prestige of, 161–62; resurrection of dance, 249; rhythm section in, 75–76, 103–4; segregation of, 10–11, 74–75; setups for, *100, 101*; style of, 7, 80–81. *See also* African American bands; bandleaders; musicians; singers; soloists; sweet bands

Barbiroli, Jack, 68

Barker, Danny, 176

Barnet, Charlie: and autographs, 58; background of, 81; in band contests, 60; as bandleader, 78; band lost by, 213, 217–18; benefits played by, 134; in films, 174; integration by, 82, 130; performances by, 18, 48, 156; popularity of, 162; role of, 5; on swing's decline, 214

Barron, Blue, 19

Bartók, Béla, 92

baseball, and integration, 245

Basie, William "Count," *106, 123;* background of, 101–2, 107–8, 115; in band contests, 60, *61,* 68, 94–95; as bandleader, 78–79, 103; benefits played by, 115, 121, 133, 135, 147, 202–3; bookings for, 168, 172; earnings of, 163; in films, 184; improvisation by, 104–5; influences on, 102–3, 117–18, *118;* on jukeboxes, 98; performances by, 46, 66, 116, 156, 159, 185, 279–80n. 16; popularity of, xv, 49, 93, 111–12, 112–15, 162, 169–70, 195–96; on radio, 43, 97–99; recordings by, 45, 98–99, 126–27, 166, 173; role of, 5, 202; and segregation, 172, 176; singers for, 95, 102, 105–8; songs of, 46, 66; status of, 95, 99; style of, 95, 97–108, 114, 118–19, 127; support for, 82, 127; on trains, 109–10

"Basie Boogie," 109

Bass-Mackay, Oyese, *205*

Bauduc, Ray, 213

Bauza, Mario, 231

BBC radio, music on, 185

Beat Generation, origins of, 238, 253

bebop: and antidrug crusade, 245–46; as art, 230–31; attacks on, 223, 239; attitudes toward, 248; background of, xii, xv, 208–9, 252–53; and band business collapse, 239–40; characteristics of, xvi, 224–25, 227–28, 235; and improvisation, 212–13, 227–29; political implications of, 229–31, 233; popularity of, 233, 253; and racial tensions, 225–26; and sexuality, 237–38; structure of, 228–29; style of, 231–37

Bechet, Sidney, 26, 221

Becker, Howard, 42, 61

Beckman, Francis J. L., 37

"Beggar's Holiday," 244

Curran, Dale, 132, 135, 220
Curran, Sidney, 39, 42, 44
Curtis Bay Cats (group), 189

"D. B. Blues," 184
Dailey, Frank, 162
Daily Worker (newspaper), 132, 134–36
dance: audience participation in, 56, *57*, 68; contests in, 40, 46, 48, 155; and juke-boxes, 44–45; as musical improvisation, 51–53; origins of, 40, 155; and race, 40, 48–50; and radios, 44; rejection of, 236–37; as release, 88–90; revival of, 249; revolution in, 50–51; as ritual, 97, 110–12; and social class, 50–51; spread of, 53; at Swing Jamboree, 35–36. *See also* jit-terbug (dance); lindy hop
dance halls: democratization of, 48–54; in depression, 13; entrance fees for, 48; and Prohibition repeal, 31; segregation in, 49; transformation of behavior in, 56–57
Dance Time (radio program), 62
Dancing Coed (movie), 150, 174
"Dancing in the Dark," 23
Darlings of Harlem (group), 199
"Darn That Dream," 53
Darrell, R. D., 136
dating: in depression, 16–17, 22–23; and juke-boxes, 44–45; postwar interests in, 217–18; and radios, 44
Davidson College (North Carolina), 44
Davis, Ben, 129, 133, 147, 202
Davis, Bette, 203
Davis, Frank Marshall, 139
Davis, Miles, 227, 230, 248
"Day Break Express," 109
Daye, Irene, 54
Debs, Eugene, 129
Decca Records: black bands recorded by, 173; exploitive contracts by, 98, 126; hits by, 45; and jazz revival, 220; origins of, 14; performers sought by, 98; revival of, 165
"Deep Purple," 23
Dehn, Adolf, 145
democracy: band as examplar for, 67, 88; black music as force for, 133–36; concert as symbol of, 122; jazz as expression of,

81–82, 101, 133–36, 219; vs. racism, 205–10; swing as expression of, 38, 59–64, 69–71, 81–83, 89–92, 98, 202. *See also* democratization; pluralism
Democratic Party, Prohibition repealed by, 30
democratization: of art, 59–64; commitment to, 122, 124–25; of culture, 36–37, 59–64, 89–90, 122, 124–25, 131–33; of music con-noisseurship, 59–64; of performance ven-ues, xiii, 41–54, 97; radio's and record-ings' roles in, 41–44, 63–64
de Paris, Wilbur, 221
Desmond, Johnny, 190–91
Devonish, Charles, *205*
Dexter, Dave, Jr., 60–61, *123*, 126
"The Dirty Dozen," 107
Disabled Veterans Fund, 133
disc jockeys, emergence of, 43
Dixielanders (group), 212
Dixieland (music), 67, 229–30. *See also* tradi-tional jazz
Dixon, Lucille, 199
Dodds, Warren "Baby," 76, *219*, 221
Donahue, Sam, 184, 215
"Don't Be That Way," 66, 111
"Don't Get Around Much Anymore," 195
"Don't Sit under the Apple Tree," 188, 194–96
Dorsey, Jimmy: background of, 81; as band-leader, 78, 226; influences on, 10; integra-tion by, 82, 130, 140; performances by, 31, 36; role of, 5; singers for, 81–82
Dorsey, Tommy: background of, 81; as band-leader, 78–80; band lost by, 213; influ-ences on, 10; performances by, 31, 160–61; popularity of, 195–96; recordings by, 166; role of, 5, 202; small groups of, 221; songs by, 54; sponsor for, 42; and youth culture, 47
Double V Campaign, 204–5, 208
Douglas, Ann, xiii, 7
Dowling, Eddie, 30
Downbeat (club), 157
Down Beat (periodical): on antidrug crusade, 247–48; on audience, 58; on Basie, 127; and dance band revival, 249; description of, 60–61, 90–91, 136–37; on integration,

Down Beat (periodical) (*continued*)
137–40, 202–3, 245; on jazz, 219; polls/
contest by, 62, 204, 242; on red scare,
242, 245; staff of, 136; on swing, 213–14,
218; and Voice of America broadcasts,
244; on women and jazz, 200; on World
War II music, 195
Downes, Olin, 92
"Down for the Double," 108
draft: and drugs, 225; evasion of, 185, 197;
postwar effects of, 215, 221
"Dreamsville, Ohio," 188
drugs: and bebop, 232–33, 235–38; crusade
against, 245–48, 252; police attacks on,
208. *See also* marijuana
Duchin, Eddie, 18, 68, 153
Dugan, James, 121–22, 134, 135
Duncan, Gregor, 145
Durham, Eddie, 188, 199, *199,* 286n. 38
Dylan, Bob, 126

Eagle (newspaper), 136
Earle Theater (Philadelphia), 155
Earl "Fatha" Hines Band. *See* Hines, Earl
"Fatha"
Eastman Theater (Rochester), 47
Easton, Jane, 195
"East St. Louis Toodle-oo," 101
Eberle, Ray, 53
Eckstine, Billy, 206, 239
Edison, Harry "Sweets," 103, 105
Edison Hotel, 160
education: in depression, 16, 30, 39; of musi-
cians, 81; on swing music, 63–64
Eisenhower, Gen. Dwight D., 185, 209
Eldridge, Roy, 44, 77, 130, 152, 177
Elgar, Charles, 24
Eliscu, Joe, 147
Elitch Gardens ballroom, 4
Ellington, Edward Kennedy "Duke," *100;* and
audiences, 59, 110–11; background of, 6,
8, 101; as bandleader, 78, 80, 103; bene-
fits played by, 115, 131, 133, 135, 147,
185, 202, 276n. 21; bookings for, 166–67,
170; compositions/arrangements by, 9–
10, 29, 66, 78, 101, 110, 195, 244; criti-

cism of, 143–44, 223; earnings of, 163; European techniques claimed by, xii, 10,
101; in films, 174; musical by, 101, 118,
147–48; performances by, 66, 91, 101,
113–14, 116, 147–49, 185, 205–6; popularity of, 26–27, 115, 169, 203–4; on radio,
26, 43, 211; recordings by, 26, 43, 173,
184; role of, 5, 68; and segregation, 101,
116, 176, 204–5; singer for, 85; status of,
96–97, 113; style of, 19, 95, 99, 104, 118;
on trains, 109; and youth culture, 47
Ellington, Mercer, 117, 147–48, 185
Ellison, Ralph: on bandleaders, 114; on bebop, 224–25; on black swing bands, xv,
95, 112; on blues, 101, 107; on Ellington,
94, 113; on Parker, 228
Elman, Harry Finkelman "Ziggy," 56, 67, 76,
90
Elman, Mischa, 38
entertainment industry: amusement tax on,
214, 221, 227; centralization of, 27–28;
collapse of, 13–14; live vs. radio, 19–20,
31; New Deal supported by, 30–31; revival of, 70–71; segregation in, 116; in
World War II, 184. *See also* dance halls;
hotels; jukeboxes; music industry; nightclubs; radio; recordings
equal opportunity vs. integration, 139–40,
147
Esquire (periodical), 211–12
Esquire's Jazz Book, 211–12
Essex House Hotel, 42
Ethiopia, benefits for, 133
ethnicity: in AAF Orchestra, 189; and allegiance, 182; and bebop, 235–36; and popular culture, 6; and popularity, 81–82;
stereotypes of, 188
Etting, Ruth, 23–24, *25*
Europe, James Reese, 101
Evans, Bill, 231
Evans, Bobby, *154*
Evans, Herschel, 105
"Everybody Loves My Baby," 196

Fadiman, Clifton, 90
Fair Employment Practices Commission, 243

Hammond, Alice, 124

Hammond, John, *123;* as army entertainment officer, 202; background of, 122–24; on Basie, 97–98; on blues records, 26; and Cafe Society, 144–46; concerts/benefits organized by, 120–21, 131–32, 134, 144; ideology of, 119, 121–25, 128–29, 136, 137, 202, 219; on improvisation, 77–78; influence by, 73–74, 117, 126–28, 158–59, 203; jazz's influence on, 56, 79, 124–25; Louis tribute by, 117–18, 147; as music critic, 61, 136–44; political connections of, 124–25, 130–32, 134; and red scare, 244; on swing, 91; as talent scout, 125–28, 166; threats against, 143

Hampton, Lionel, *84;* and Goodman's band, 80, 82, 117; and integration, 43, 128–29, 139, 245; performances by, 58, 66–67, 91, 128; protest by, 115–16; recordings by, 126; role of, 5, 68; status of, 77, 82

Handy, George, 235

Handy, W. C., 131, 205

"Happy Go Lucky Local," 109

Harlem: as center of swing, 50, 112–13, 153, 227; decline of, 157; in depression, 13; development of, 7; pay scale in, 25–26; racial tensions in, 207–8; riots in, 26, 29, 97, 207; transformation of, 153–54. *See also* Apollo Theater; Cotton Club; Savoy Ballroom

Harlem Musical Committee to Aid Spain, 129, 133

Harlem Renaissance, and black music, 7–10, 96, 101, 250

Harris, Bill, 215

Hashimoto, Steve, 90

Hawkins, Coleman, *9,* 27, 29, 77, 206, 218

Hawkins, Erskine, 43, 49, 169–70, 173

Hayden, Charles, 57, 63

Haymes, Dick, 216

Hays, Will, 30

Heidt, Horace, 42

Heigh Ho Club, 19

Helbock, Joe, 157

Henderson, Fletcher "Smack," *9, 84;* arrangements by, 3–4, 29, 31, 66, 71, 73–75, 82, 127; background of, 6; as bandleader, 78;

benefits played by, 131; bookings for, 27; and integration, 82, 130, 140; performances by, 8, 128; popularity of, 26; recordings by, 126, 166; role of, 5, 96; style of, 95, 104

Hennessey, Thomas J., 26

Hentoff, Nat, 59

"Here's to Broadway" (show), 30–31

Herman, Woody, *238;* band lost by, 213, 239; competition for, 233; on integration, 140; on Miller's band, 187; performances by, 156; popularity of, 162; on radio, 211; role of, 5; sponsor for, 42; style of, 236; women musicians hired by, 199; on youth culture, 45

heroin: crusade against, 246–48; use of, 232–33, 235–38, 246–47

Hickory House (club), 157

Hill, Abe, 207–8

Hill, Teddy, 59–60, 112, 227

Hines, Earl "Fatha," 36, 43, *123,* 130, 177, 199

Hinton, Milt, 113–14, 117, 158, 176

hip, definition of, 232

hipsters, description of, 235–38

Hitler, Adolph, 144, 146, 184

Hit Parade (radio program), 44, 165

Hobsbawm, Eric, xii, 108, 122, 218–19. *See also* Newton, Francis

Hodes, Art, 10, 135, 220–21, 223, 242

Hodges, Johnny, 66, 202

Hoefer, George, 219

Hoff, Carl, 246

Holder, T., 25

Holiday, Billie (Eleanora Fagan), *154;* and antidrug crusade, 246, 248; benefits played by, 135; bookings for, 171–73; discovery of, 125; and integration, 130, 146, 151; performances by, 43, 54, 95, 116, 145–47, 158; racism's impact on, 171–72; recordings by, 73, 126–27, 166; style of, 86, 105, 108

Holloway, Louise, 198

Hollywood Canteen, 203

Hollywood Hotel (movie), 64

Hollywood Restaurant, 153

Holman, Libby, 23

Jones, Isham, 276n. 21
Jones, Jimmie, *205*
Jones, Jo, 103, 105–7, *106*, 286n. 38
Jones, LeRoi (Amiri Baraka), xiv–xv, 234–35, 237
Jones, Mildred Lee, *199*
Jones, Peggy, 194
Jordan, Louis, 206
Josephson, Barney, 144–47, 243
Josephson, Leon, 144–45, 243
Jubilee (radio program), 185
Juilliard School, 230
jukeboxes: education through, 63; hits on, 150, 166; revamped, 165; role of, 41–42, 44–45, 165–66, 168; and segregation, 173
Julius, Lela, *199*
Jump for Joy (musical), 101, 118, 147–48
"Jumpin' at the Woodside," 109
jumps, folk references in, 109
Jurgens, Dick, 18–19
"Just a Gigolo," 22
"Just One More Chance," 3, 22
juvenile delinquency, fears of, 245, 249

Kaminsky, Max: background of, 14–15, 72; band of, 289n. 18; on crooners, 17; on jazz revival, 221–23; on swing style, 78
Kansas City: discrimination in, 115–16; jazz scene in, 95, 97, 102–8, 228; performance venues in, 13, 97–98, 104, 115–16
Kapp, Dave, 98
Kapp, Jack, 173
Karamanski, Ted, 39–40
Kassel, Art, 19, 72
Kattar, Al, 45
Kay, Monte, 235–36
Kaye, Sammy, 19, 69, 77, 270n. 29
Kehelah Jacob Synagogue, 71
Kelly's Stables (club), 152, 157
Kemp, Hal, 42, 86, 270n. 29
Kenney, Marjorie, 195
Kenton, Stan, 233, *238*, 239, 249
Keppard, Freddie, 135
KFAC radio (Los Angeles), 62
killer-dillers: definition of, 46; demands for, 58
Killian, Al, *106*, 174

King, Cornelius, *205*
King, Wayne, 17
"King Joe," 117–18, 147. *See also* Louis, Joe
King of Jazz (movie), 11–12, 20
"King Porter Stomp," 74
Kirby, John, 279–80n. 16
Kirk, Andy: as bandleader, 79, 102; on performance venues, 155–56, 175, 265n. 32; recordings by, 166, 173; role of, 5; schedule of, 174
"Ko Ko," 111, 228, 236
Kolodin, Irving: on Hammond, 125–26; on hotel bookings, 162, 165, 170, 172; on jazz musicians, 81; on Miller's band, 188; on swing, 75; on youth audience, 38
Kouwenhoven, John, 268n. 8
Kreisler, Fritz, 37
Krueger, Art, 18–19
Krupa, Gene, *67*, *83*; and antidrug crusade, 246; and autographs, 58; earnings of, 171; in film, 64; on Goodman, 78; influence on, 127; integration by, 82, 130, 177–78; performances by, 43, 66, 68, 128, 152; popularity of, 195–96; recordings by, 127; role of, 5; status of, 77, 82; style of, 54, 75–76
Ku Klux Klan, and Ellington's musical, 148
Kuller, Sid, 148
Kyle, Aldredo, 134
Kyser, Kay, 62, 167, 184, 270n. 29

labor supporters, 125
labor unions: benefits for, 145; segregation in, 202. *See also* American Federation of Musicians (AFM); Congress of Industrial Organizations (CIO)
Ladies Garment Workers Union, 145
Ladnier, Tommy, 26
Lakeside Ballroom (Denver), 58
Lambert, Constance, 19
language. *See* jive; slang
Lanin, Sam, 7
Larchmont Casino, 60
Larkin, R. L., 49, 174–75
Lateef, Usef, 231
Lawrenson, Helen, 144–45
Lawson, Yank, 73

Marrero, Lawrence, *219*
marriage: in depression, 16–17, 22–23; post-war emphasis on, 215–18
Marsala, Joe, 139, 279–80n. 16
Martin, Freddy, 19
Marvin, Johnny, 14
Marx, Chico, 58
masculinity: for band members, 83–85; and bop generation, 236–38; deflation of, 22, 69; model of, 187; renewed vitality for, 69–71, 79
Mathias, Frank, 63–64
Maxwell, Jimmy, 76
May, Billy, 187
Mayan Theater, 148
Mayer, Louis B., 30
MCA. *See* Music Corporation of America (MCA)
McCall, Martin, 136
McDonough, John, 65, 124–26
McGarrity, Lou, 47
McGee, Nova Lee, *199*
McIntyre, Hal, 218
McKenzie, Red, 279–80n. 16
McKinley, Ray, 191, 215, 217
McLin, Jim, *205*
McNulty, Jack, 39, 45, 57
McPartland, Jimmy, 10
McRae, Bob, *205*
McShann, Big Jay, 228
Meadowbrook Ballroom, *131*, 152, 162, 168
"Mean to Me," 24
Meenach, Leonard, 47, 198
"Meet the People" (revue), 147
Melodears (group), 199
Melody Maker (British periodical), 136
"Memories of You," 53
Mercer, Johnny, 157
Merman, Ethel, 23
Metronome (periodical): on antidrug crusade, 247–48; on band contests, 60; on bebop, 232; on censorship, 244; description of, xi, 61–62, 90–91, 136–37; on integration, 245; polls by, 62; on postwar music, 215, 217; on segregation, 203–4; on society orches-tras, 153; soldiers' letters to, 192–93; on

Swing Jamboree, 36; on swing's decline, 213–14; on white bands in Harlem, 48; on youth participation, 45
Metropolitan Opera, 163
Mexican Americans: fashions of, 55, 207; nightclubs attended by, 206; swing's in-fluence on, 40, 90
Mezzrow, Milton "Mezz," 10, 14, 72, 221–22
microphone, impact of, 19
middle class: and dance steps, 50–51; in de-pression, 16–17; popular culture sought by, 6–7; rejection of, 231–32, 234–35. *See also* youth culture
Mildred Bailey and Company (radio program), 217
Miller, Charles, 218
Miller, Glenn: arrangements by/for, 186–88; background of, 10, 81, 169, 186; as band-leader, 78–80; bookings for, 167; business astuteness of, 168–69, 186; death of, 182, 200, 209; earnings for, 169; in films, 169, 200; performances by, 47–48, 91, 152, 160; popularity of, 193, 208–10, 213; racial conservatism of, 188–89, 202; on radio, 40, 42, 44; recordings by, 160, 168–69, 173; role of, 5, 92, 251; small groups of, 188; style of, 39, 51, 185–94, 202, 215–16, 249; in World War II, 181–86, *183*, 189–95, *192*; and youth culture, 47
Miller, Norma, 155
Millinder, Lucky, 130, 134, 205
Mills, Irving, 11, 27–28
Mills Artists, 166–67. *See also* Mills, Irving
Mills Blue Rhythm Band, 26–27
Mills Brothers, 131, 194, 196
Minor, Dan, *106*
Minton's Playhouse (club), 227
Mitchell, George, 25
Modell, John, 16
Modernaires (group), 188
moldy figs, definition of, 236–37
Monk, Thelonious, 227, 230–32, 248
Monogram studios, 174
Monroe, Vaughn, 217
Monroe's Uproar House (club), 156, 227
Montgomery, George, 194

"Mood Indigo," 29
"Moonlight Serenade," 168, 209
Moore, Monette, 125
Morgan, Helen, 23–24
Morton, Ferdinand "Jelly Roll," 141
Mostel, Zero, 145, 244
Moten, Bennie, 102
movie houses: bookings at, 162–63; closure of, 13; role of, 41–42; segregation in, 116; swing bands staged in, 45–47. *See also* films
Moynahan, James, 37
Mozart Clarinet Quintet, 92
Mulligan, Gerry, 248
Mundy, Jimmy, 67, 74, 82, 127
Municipal Auditorium (Kansas City), 116
Murder at the Vanities (movie), 174
Murphy, Spud, 74
Murphy, Thomas F., 247
Murray, Albert, xv, 63, 99, 109, 110
Murray, Kel, 3
music: vs. commercialism, 151; democratization of connoisseurship of, 59–64; "hot" vs. sweet, 3–4, 11–12, 27, 132; as propaganda, 148, 190–91; about segregation, 147–48. *See also* bebop; blues; boogie woogie; jazz; popular music; swing
"musical Hitlerism," 37
Music and Rhythm (periodical), 126, 202
Music Corporation of America (MCA): Basie's relation with, 116, 127; and Goodman's tour, 4, 69; Hammond's influence on, 97–98; influence by, 158–59, 162; and integration, 160, 168; power of, 167
music critics: changing focus of, 249; differences among, 142, 242; and jazz revival, 222–23; and leftist ideology, 136–44; role of, xiv, 61–62; on swing, 37–38
musicians: alternative businesses for, 26; as artists, 230; audience interaction with, 57–60, 155–56, 158–59, 172–73, 235; as bandleaders, 78–83; gender of, xiii, 71, 83–88, 198–200; heroes of, 117–18; and jazz revival, 221–22; media on, 241–42; postwar abundance of, 215; and red scare, 242–43; terms for, 56; unemployment of,

12–14, 24–25; in World War II, 184–85, 198–200. *See also* bandleaders; *names of specific musicians*
music industry: and antidrug crusade, 245–48; challenges to, 126, 226; collapse of, 239–40; and dance band revival, 249; decline of, 14, 74, 213–18, 252; divisions in, 212–13; expansion of, 38–39; headquarters of, 163–69; influence on, 126–28; Left's link to, 122; and red scare, 242; rejection of, 150–51; revival of, 70–71; segregation in, 26, 74, 82, 116, 126, 129–30, 146–47, 169–78; World War II efforts of, 185. *See also* booking agencies; commercialism
music publications: on antidrug crusade, 247–48; on band contests, 95; on dance music, 165; decline of, 14, 74; description of, 60–63, 90–91; and female singers, 86, 172; jazz covered in, 136–37, 220, 222; and polls, 62–63, 212; and segregation, 171, 203–4; and social change, 126; on swing's popularity, 90–91. See also *Down Beat* (periodical); *Metronome* (periodical); music critics
Musso, Vido, 81, 140
Mutual radio, 163

NAACP (National Association for the Advancement of Colored People), 125, 204, 207
Naison, Mark, 133
Nash, W. W., 65
National Association for the Advancement of Colored People (NAACP), 125, 204, 207
National Biscuit Company, 42
National Press Club, 209
National Youth Administration, 30
Nation (periodical), 136
Nat King Cole Trio, 206, 211
Navy League, 212
Nazis, films about, 184
NBC radio: competition for, 164; integration at, 203; performers dropped by, 69; performers hired by, 15, 19; preeminence of, 163; programs on, 3–4, 31, 42–43

Nelson, Ozzie, 19, 270n. 29
"Never Had Less, Never Felt Better," 54
New Century Committee, 35–36
New Deal programs: impact of, 29–31, 92–93; nightclubs in, 145; renewal through, 70–71; support for, 243; swing as expression of, 252, 256–57n. 12
"New Deal Rhythm" (film), 30
New Jersey, performance venues in, *131*, 152, 162, 168
New Masses (periodical): benefits sponsored by, 120–22, 134; Hammond's exposés in, 126; staff of, 136; on swing's importance, 121
New Orleans, band forms in, 7
New Orleans All-Stars (group), 222
New Orleans Jazz Band, *219*
New Republic (periodical), 136, 142
newspapers, polls by, 62–63, 115, 117
Newton, Francis, 141. *See also* Hobsbawm, Eric
Newton, Frankie, 145
"New World a-Comin'," 205–6
New York: antidrug crusade in, 247, 248; as base for touring bands, 26–28; as capital of swing, 4–5, 95, 97–99, 112–13, 151, 158; commercialism in, 151, 220; jazz revival centered in, 221–23; migration to, 6, 10, 14; as music business capital, 163; racial prejudice in, 172–73, 207–8; segregation in, 74; Social Register in, 124; "Swing Street" in, 152, 156–59, *158*, 207–8, 233; unemployment and depression in, 12–15. *See also* Harlem; *names of specific performance venues*
New York City License Bureau, 13
New Yorker Hotel, 160
New Yorker (periodical), 90
New York Medical Society, 247
Nica (Baroness Konnigswater), 238
Nick's (club), 221
Nicolas, Albert, 221
nightclubs: antidrug raids on, 247; art exhibited in, 145–46; audience in, 157–59; and bebop development, 227; bop club policy for, 235–36; changes in, 253; democratization of, 48; in depression, 13–14; vs. hotels, 159–60; integration of, 144–47, 157–59, 177–78, 206–7; jazz relegated to, 11; jazz revival in, 221–23; and Prohibition repeal, 30–31; and radio, 43, 98, 159–60, 162; role of, 156–59; segregation in, 207–8; and women singers, 23–24; in World War II, 198
"Night in Tunisia," 231
"9:20 Special," 109
"Nobody Knows (But My Baby and Me)," 108
"No Love, No Nothin' (Until My Baby Comes Home)," 195
Noone, Jimmy, 72, 221
Norris, Al, *28*
Norvo, Red (Kenneth Norville), 68, 126–27, 139, 159, 279–80n. 16
Nuremberg Stadium, swing concert in, 209

Oakley, Helen, 98, 128, 137, 170
O'Connell, Helen, 81–82, 86–88
O'Day, Anita, 23, 86, 178, 200, 246
Office of War Information, 182, 190–91
"Oh, What It Seemed to Be," 216
Okada, John, 89
Okeh (record company), 26
Old Gold Cigarettes, 12, 42
"Old Spinning Wheel," 22
O'Leary, Cornelius, 207
Oliver, Joe "King," 6, 24, 142
Oliver, Melvin James "Sy," 185
O'Malley, Pat, 89
"One Hour with You," 108
"One O'Clock Jump," 46, 66, 104–5, 109, 173
Onyx (club), 157
Orchestra Wives (movie), 169, 174, 200
Original Dixieland Jazz Band, 67
"Ornithology," 228
Orpheum Theater (Omaha), 46
Ory, Edward "Kid," 221
Otis, Don, 62
Otis, Johnny, 177

Page, Oran "Hot Lips," 98, 130, *154*
Page, Walter, 66, 103, *106*
Palace Theater (Fort Wayne, Ind.), 47
Palomar Ballroom, 3–4

Quebec, Ike, 248

race: and bebop development, 225–26; and
  booking agencies, 27–28, 97–98, 170;
  conflicts over, 5, 206–8; of dancers,
  48–50; and jazz beginnings, 72; and leftist politics, 136–44; and popular culture,
  6; and World War II home front, xvi, 116,
  129, 201–8. *See also* African Americans;
  whites
race records, 8, 14, 26
racism: and black band music, 29; challenge
  to, 124–25; vs. democracy, 205–10; effects
  of, 115–16, 171–73. *See also* integration;
  segregation
radio: audience for, 14, 44, 163–64; ballroom
  broadcasts via, 43, 98, 154, 156, 162, 168;
  censorship by, 260n. 32; commercial vs.
  noncommercial broadcasts on, 164; as democratizing, 41–43, 63–64; in depression,
  15, 163–64; disc jockeys on, 43; education through, 63–64; hotel broadcasts via,
  160–62, 167, 170–71, 280n. 20; influence
  by, 27–28, 40, 170, 174–75; integration
  of, 203; investment in, 168; New York
  as capital of, 163; and nightclubs, 43,
  98, 159–60, 162; propaganda on, 148,
  190–91; rigidity of, 15, 73, 164; role of,
  42, 160, 163–65, 168–69, 222; segregation
  in, 3–4, 26, 42, 74, 116, 121, 170–71, 202;
  sponsors of, 12, 26, 42, 129, 164, 169–71,
  217; sweet bands and singers on, 18–21;
  vocalists on, 217. *See also* ABC radio; BBC
  radio; CBS radio; NBC radio; recordings
Radio City, 163–69
Radio City Music Hall, 46, 155, 157, 163
Radio Corporation of America (RCA), 163. *See
  also* RCA Victor
Radio Guide (periodical), poll by, 62
Raeburn, Boyd, 213, 233
Rainbow Room (club), 163
Raleigh Cigarettes, 42
Ramey, Gene, 102, 108
Ramsey, Edward, 141
Ramsey, Frederic, Jr., 141–42
Randolph, Zilner, 25
Raymond Scott Quintet, 43–44

RCA Victor: and black performers, 26, 233,
  234; origins of, 14; performers for, 28; revival of, 165. *See also* Radio Corporation
  of America (RCA)
The Record Changer (periodical), 220
record companies: and dance band revival,
  249; decline of, 14–15, 74; headquarters
  of, 165; influence on, 126; revival of,
  165–66; strike against, 216–17, 220. *See
  also names of specific companies*
recordings: changing tastes in, 217; as democratizing, 41–44, 63–64; evaluation of,
  61–62; influence by, 27–28, 173; and integration, 126–28; prices for, 165; reissues
  of, 141, 220; segregation in, 173–74; for
  troops, 185; of women musicians, 198–
  99. *See also* jukeboxes
"Red Bank Boogie," 109
Red Cross, recordings sent by, 193
Redman, Don, 5, 8, *9,* 95
red scare: and individual musicians, 241–45;
  jazz revival affected by, 222–23; night-
  clubs affected by, 145
Reed, Joseph, 246
Reese, Roseteele, *205*
Refergaiz, Anton, 145
Reichman, Joe, 38–39
Reig, Teddy, 236
Reisman, Leo, 15, 18, 153
Reno Club (Kansas City), 97–98, 104
restaurants, jukeboxes in, 45
Rey, Alvino, 246
"Rhapsody in Blue," 68
rhythm and blues, 105, 108, 239
Rhythm Boys (group), 20–21
Rhythm Club, 91
rhythm section, role of, 75–76, 103–4
Rich, Buddy, 76, 214–15
Richmond, Howard, 187
"Ride On," 107–8
"Ridin' High," 76
riffs: Basie's use of, 104–5, 108; in bebop,
  224; and dance music, 111; origins of,
  107
Ritz-Carlton Hotel (Boston), 129, 170
Riverdale Boys Foundation, 115
Rivers, Larry, 236–37

Riviera Theater, 162
Roach, Max, 229
"The Road Is Open" (film), 30
Roberts, Charles Luceyth "Luckey," 133
Robeson, Paul: benefit performed by, 205; in-
    fluence by, 117; and Louis tribute, 117,
    118, 147; nightclub attended by, 146; poli-
    tics of, 133, 227; and red scare, 244
Robinson, Bill "Bojangles," 114, 261–62n. 1
Robinson, Earl, 134
Robinson, Jim, *219*
Rockefeller Center, 157, 163. *See also* Radio
    City Music Hall
Rockland Palace, 125, 131–32
Rodney, Red, 218, 232–33, 235, 248
Rogers, Billie, 199
Rollini, Adrian, 172
Rollins, Theodore Walter "Sonny," 233
Roosevelt, Eleanor, 146, 205
Roosevelt, Franklin D., 16, 31, 70, 184, 202,
    244. *See also* New Deal programs
Rose, Billy, 30–31, 153, 184
Rose, Don, 237–38
"Rose in the Bud," 107
Roseland Ballroom (New York), 7–8, 26, 98,
    111
Roseland Orchestra, *9*
Roseland State Ballroom (Boston), 111–13
Rowe, Billy, 136
Royal Canadians (group), 18. *See also* Lom-
    bardo, Guy
Royal Roost (club), 235, 253
Royal Theater (Baltimore), 155
Rozner, Eddie, 244
Ruark, Robert, 243
Rushing, Jimmy: background of, 107–8; bene-
    fits played by, 135; recordings by, 147;
    style of, 102, 106–8, 110
Russell, Charles Ellsworth "Pee Wee,"
    289n. 18
Russell, George, 231
Russell, William, 221
Russian War Relief, 184, 202
Ryan, Jimmy, 221

Sadowski, Gloria, 55
"St. Louis Blues," 190

Salaam, Liaquat Ali (Kenny Clarke), 225–27,
    229, 230–31
"Salute to Negro Troops" (show), 205
Sampson, Edgar, 66, 74, 127
Samuels, William, 25
sanding, meaning of, 108
Saturday Evening Post (periodical), 161
Saturday Night in Harlem (radio program), 43
"Saturday Night Is the Loneliest Night in the
    Week," 195
Sauter, Eddie, 92
Savoy Ballroom: all-girl band at, *199;* audi-
    ences at, 48, 59–60, 111, 117, 207; band
    contests at, 60, *61,* 68–69, 94–95; benefits
    at, 134, 276n. 21; closure of, 207; as dem-
    ocratic, 97; integration of, 155; lindy hop-
    pers at, *49;* performances at, 98; radio
    feeds from, 43, 45; reputation of, 26, 46,
    112, 154–55; role of, 50; salaries at, 154
Savoy Records, 236
Savoy Sultans (group), 134. *See also* Webb,
    William Henry "Chick"
Schaap, Walter, 137–38
Scheuer, Timothy, 23–24
Schmeling, Max, 117
Schoepp, Franz, 71–72
Schuller, Gunther, 187, 255n. 2
Schwartz, Bertha, 246
Schwartz, Willie, 186
Scott, Gerald R., 150
Scott, Hazel, 244
Scott, Helen, *199*
Scott, Raymond, 43–44, 217
Scottsboro Defense Ball, 276n. 21
Scottsboro trial, 125, 131–33, 147
Secunda, Sholem, 67
segregation: in armed forces, 184–85, 189,
    202–6, 225–26; of audience, 116; in ball-
    rooms, 49, 172–73, 204, 206–7; of bands,
    10–11, 74–75; and black bands, 27, 169–
    78, 206–8, 226; challenge to, 123–24, 147,
    177–78, 203–5, 244–45, 251–52; in dance
    halls, 49; effects of, 115–16, 151, 175–76;
    enforcement of, 170–73, 176–77; in ho-
    tels, 151, 170–71; and jukeboxes, 173; in
    medical facilities, 121; in movie houses,
    116; music about, 147–48; and music

194–95; dream touted in, 215–16; publicity for, 165. *See also* love songs; *names of specific songs*

"Sophisticated Lady," 29

Sorrentino, Gilbert, 235–37

Sousa, John Philip, 10, 190

Soviet Union, jazz in, 244

Spain, leftist support for, 125, 129, 133–34, 146, 202

Spanish Children's Relief Fund, 134

speakeasies. *See* nightclubs

"Speak Low," 195

Speckled Red, 107

Spectator (Columbia University paper), 38

Spirits of Rhythm (group), 279–80n. 16

Spirituals to Swing concerts, 120–22

Spitalny, Phil, 19

sports world, black heroes in, 114, 117–18

Springsteen, Bruce, 126

square, definition of, 232

Stacy, Jess, 4, 10, 68, 127

Stage Door Canteen (club), 203

Stage Door Canteen (film), 184

Stambaugh, Orin, 39, 45, 63

Standard Brands, 171

Stanley, Selma Lee, *199*

Stanley Theater (Pittsburgh), 47

"Stardust," 53

Starr, Jean, *199*

Starr, Judy, 86

"Stars and Stripes Forever," 190

Stars for Spain (benefit), 129

Stearns, Marshall, 136–40

Stein, Jules, 167

Stewart, Sammy, 24

Stewart, Slam, 56

Stokowski, Leopold, 116

"Stompin' at the Savoy," 111, 173

"Stormy Weather," 29

Stover, Sadie, 45

Stowe, David, xv, 199

Strand Theater, 162

"Strange Fruit," 146–47, 243

Strayer, Louise, 40, 45, 86

Strayhorn, Billy, 111

Streator, George, 133

The Streets of Paris (club), 206

"String of Pearls," 188

Strings with Wings (radio program), 191

student movement: expansion of, 134; and jazz's popularity, 130–31

Stuyvesant Casino, *219*, 221

Sullivan, Joe, 121, 130, 279–80n. 16

Sullivan, Maxine, 41, 158

Summa Cum Laude Band, 289n. 18

"Sunrise Serenade," 168

"The Suntanned Tenth of the Nation," 148

Sun Valley Serenade (movie), 169, 174

"Super Chief," 109

Susman, Warren, 122

sweet bands: audience for, 46; bookings for, 167; evaluation of, 62; vs. "hot," 3–4, 11–12, 27, 132; popularity of, 17–24, 195–96, 208, 217–18; revolt against, 69–70, 79; and social class, 132; swing merged with, 186–88

"Sweet Eloise," 58

Sweethearts of Rhythm (group), *199*

Sweet's Ballroom, 4

swing: as American form, 59–64, 66, 68–71, 75, 88, 91–92, 121, 135, 181, 201–2, 242; approach to, xi–xiii, xvii; attitudes toward, 37–39, 69, 82, 116–17, 142, 249–50; challenge to, 219–23; characteristics of, 38, 47–48, 59–64, 81–82, 144–49, 169, 186–88, 235; decline of, xvi, 212–18, 239–40, 241–42; definition of, xiv–xv, 142; in depression, 24–29, 99–100, 108–9, 118–19; as expression of democracy, 38, 59–64, 69–71, 81–83, 89–92, 98, 202; failures of, 225–26; films on, 174; GIs' demand for, 190; and integration, xiv–xvi, 129–30, 202–8; Left's link to, 132–36, 144; legacy of, 234; meanings of, 39–41; Miller's codification of, 185–93, 208; political implications of, 121–22, 132–36, 144, 182, 202, 249–53; popularity of, 88–93; postwar fragmentation of, 212–13; structure of, 29, 75–78; in World War II, xvi, 92–93, 182–84, 190–92, 208–10, 213–14, 251–52; youth's interest in, 88–90

"Swing! Brother, Swing," 105

Swing Club (Hollywood), 206

Swing Shift (radio program), 191

Symphonic Jazz Orchestra, *12*
Symphony Sid, 237
Syncopation (movie), 174
Szigeti, Joseph, 92

"Tail-end Charlie," 191
"'Taint What You Do (But the Way That Ya
    Do It)," 53
"Take Me Back Baby," 107
"Take the 'A' Train," 109, 111
Tap Room, 172
Tate, Erskine, 24
Tate, George Holmes "Buddy," *106*
Tatum, Art, 26, 206, 279–80n. 16
Taylor, Montana, 220
Teagarden, Weldon Leo "Jack," 44, 213, 279–
    80n. 16
technology: impact of, 19–20; and youth cul-
    ture, 41–42
temperance. *See* Prohibition
"Ten Cents a Dance," 24
Terrell, Pha, 173
Theatre Arts Committee, 121, 134
"There Are Such Things," 54
"There Are Yanks," 190
"These Foolish Things," 53
"They Can't Take That Away from Me," 105
"Things to Come," 224, 233
Thomas, Joe, *28*
Thompson, Ellariz, *199*
Thornhill, Claude, 184
Three Deuces (club), 157
Tillie's Chicken Shack, 157
"Till Then," 196
Tilton, Martha, 54, 67, 86, 142–43
Time-Life (periodical), 163
Times Square, in Great Depression, 13
Tinker Air Base (Oklahoma City), 198
Tin Pan Alley: influence by, 73–74; rejection
    of, 122; and World War II, 182
"A Tisket a Tasket," 41, 45, 86, 173
"Together," 216
Tokyo Rose, 185
Tompkins, Eddie, *28*
torch singers: characteristics of, 17, 19,
    23–24; lives of, 23–24, *25*
Torme, Mel, 58, 64

Tough, Dave, 10, 76, 221, 289n. 18
Town Hall Concerts, 222, *224*
Trade Union Service, 126
traditional jazz, 212–13, 218–23, 237, 239–
    40, 249
trains: as metaphor, 109–10; segregation on,
    114, 175–76, 206
transportation, segregation in, 114, 175–76,
    206
Travelbee, Charles, 47
Travelers' Aid incident, 47
Trent, Alphonso, 25
Trilling, Lionel, 223
Trocadero, 206
Truman, Harry S., 209, 245
Tucker, Miller, 63
Tucker, Sophie, 11, 19
Tucker, Susie, 53
turkey trot (dance), 51
Turner, Jessie, *199*
Turner, Joseph Vernon "Big Joe," 120–21
"Tuxedo Junction," 173, 188

UHCA (United Hot Clubs of America), 137
Ulanov, Barry: on antidrug crusade, 248; on
    censorship, 244; as editor, 137; influence
    by, 233; and integration, 203; on juke-
    boxes, 165; on soldiers and music,
    185
"Undecided," 45, 111
Underground Railroad, 110
Union Theological Seminary, 123–24
United Electrical and Radio Workers' Union,
    126
United Hot Clubs of America (UHCA), 137
United Nations, support for, 244
U.S. Congress, House Un-American Activities
    Committee (HUAC), 242–45
U.S. Navy Band, *205*
U.S. State Department, and dance music, 244
University of Illinois, 16–17
University of Missouri, 39
"Until the Real Thing Comes Along," 166,
    173
"Up a Lazy River," 22
Uptown Hall (group), 191
urban culture: attitudes toward, xv–xvi, 6,

10–11; bands as representatives of, 95, 112–19; dispersal of, 41–42; renewal of, 70–71

Urban Room (Congress Hotel), 4

USO, shows of, 189, 198, 203, 204–5

USSR, jazz in, 244

Vallee, Rudy, 17, 19–20, 22

values: challenges to, 17; cultural relativism in, 37–38; racial tension over, 202; swing's connections to American, 183–85. *See also* culture

Vanity Fair (periodical), 136

Vann, Sara, 44

Van Vechten, Carl, 136

Vargas, Gloria, 40

Variety (periodical), 39, 214–15

vaudeville, disappearance of, 13

Ventura, Charlie, 215

Victory Discs (V-Discs), 182, 185, 191

Village Vanguard (club), 178, 221

vocalists. *See* singers

Voice of America, broadcasts by, 244

"Volga Boatmen," 191

WABC radio (New York), 43–44

Wakeman, Frederick, 196, 197–98

Wald, Jerry, 152

Waldorf-Astoria Hotel, 167

Wallace, Henry, 244

Waller, Thomas "Fats": background of, 6; benefits played by, 131, 133; on radio, 26, 44; student of, 102; tribute to, 135

Ward, Helen, 55, 75, 87, *87*

Waring, Fred, 17, 163

war loans, money for, 212

Warner, Harry, 30

Warner Brothers studios, 30

Warren, Earl, *106*, 215

Washington, Jack, *106*

Waters, Ethel, 29, 114, 131

Waters, Lu, 223

Webb, William Henry "Chick," *96;* and audiences, 41, 49, 111; in band contests, 60, *61*, 68, 94–95, 155; as bandleader, 78–79, 103; benefits played by, 134, 276n. 21; popularity of, 169–70; recordings by, 45,

173; role of, 5; and segregation, 172; singer for, 95; style of, 95, 104; support for, 82

Weber, Joseph, 30

Webster, Ben, 110–11

Webster, Paul, *28*, 174

Weill, Kurt, 195

Weitman, Bob, 45

Welles, Orson, 148, 211, 221

Wells, Dicky, 94, 104, *106*, 156

Wendler, George, 51

West, Mae, 23

Westbrook, Robert, 194

Wettling, George, 221

Whaley, Wad, 221

"What Is This Thing Called Love," 228–29

"When the Sun Goes Down," 106

"Where the Blue of the Night," *21*, 22

"Whispering," 229

White, E. B., 90

White, Elliot: on black bands, 49; on music education, 63; on music publications, 61; on New York, 152–53; on radio, 42, 44

White, Gonzelle, 102

White, Josh, 244

White, Walter, 207

White, William Allan, 37

Whiteman, Paul, *12;* benefits played by, 131–32; and black music, xii, 67–68; competition for, 7; depression's effect on, 11–12, 18; performances by, 65–68; singer for, 85; sponsor for, 42; style of, 11, 75, 78, 250; trio of, 20–21

whiteness, concept of, 255–56n. 7

White Rose Bar, 208

whites: attitudes toward jazz, 10–11; as dancers, 49–50; migration of, 10, 14; unemployment of, 15–16; youth culture of, 37–40

Whitey's Lindy Hoppers, 155

"Why Don't You Do Right?" 85

Wilber, Bob, 218, 223

Wilcox, Ed, *28*

Wilder, Alec, 159

Wildroot Cream Oil, 42

Wiley, Lee, 158

William Morris Agency, 167

Williams, Cootie, 9, 66, 77, 128, *131*
Williams, Edna, *199*
Williams, Eugene, 221
Williams, Fess, 25
Williams, Mary Lou, 174, 226, 229
Wills, Bob, 90
Wilson, Gerald, *28*
Wilson, John, 42
Wilson, Jonathan, 278n. 56
Wilson, Teddy, *83;* as bandleader, 79; benefits
    played by, 133–34; and Goodman's band,
    4–5, 43, 66–67, 83, 117; and integration,
    4–5, 43, 66–67, 129–30, 138–40; perfor-
    mances by, 128, 160, 279–80n. 16; re-
    cordings by, 73, 126–27, 166; and red
    scare, 244; status of, 77, 82
WMCA radio (New York), 156
WNEW radio (New York), 43, 62
"A Woman's Place Is in the Groove," 198–99
women: attitudes toward, 86–87, 200; and be-
    bop, 238; fashions for, 55; fears expressed
    by, 23–24; as girl singers, 85–88; as musi-
    cians, 198–201; police harassment of,
    177; and racial tensions, 206–7; roles for,
    86; and World War II home front, 194–
    201, 206–7, 216. *See also* singers; torch
    singers
Wooding, Sam, 25
Woody Herman's Second Herd (group), *238*
Workers' School, 134
working class: and black music, 100, 142;
    and dance steps, 50–51; jazz's role for,
    108; personal styles developed from, 231–
    33, 235; unemployment of, 15–16. *See
    also* youth culture
Works Progress Administration, 25, 141,
    145
World's Fair (1939), *57,* 155
World War I, patriotic songs in, 182
World War II: changing musical tastes in,
    195; Double V Campaign in, 204–5, 208;
    draft in, 185, 197, 215, 221, 225; effects
    of, 92–93, 148, 244–45; jazz defended in,
    242; nostalgia during, 193–201, 209–10,

215–16; personalizing of, 191–93; politi-
    cal implications of, 110, 205–8, 212, 225;
    polls during, 211–12; racial tensions in,
    xvi, 116, 129, 201–8; sexual tensions in,
    193–201; swing's role in, xvi, 92–93, 182–
    84, 190–92, 208–10, 213–14, 251–52;
    V-discs in, 182, 185, 191; youth culture
    in, 185–93. *See also* armed forces; Army
    Air Force (AAF) Orchestra
"Wrap Your Troubles in Dreams," 22
Wright, Barbara, 62
Wright, Edythe, 86
Wright, Richard, 117, *118,* 147

Yale Bowl, 190
Yerba Buena band, 223
"You'd Be So Nice to Come Home To," 194
Young, Brig. Gen. Charles D., 189
Young, Lester, 66, 77, 105, 184, 218, 225
Young, Trummy, *28,* 53, 215
Young Communist League, 134
"You're a Lucky Guy," 54
Your Hit Parade (radio program), 44, 165
youth culture: and antidrug crusade, 246–48;
    attitudes toward, 37–38, 46; bands' influ-
    ence on, 40–41, 79; and bebop, 233–37;
    characterization of, 35–39, 85; commer-
    cialism influenced by, 41–47, 71, 164;
    creolization of, 56; and dance halls,
    48–56; in depression, 15–17, 89; fears of
    juvenile delinquency in, 245, 249; and
    female singers, 85–86; frustrations of,
    17–18; musical venues for, 41–47, 160;
    and New Deal programs, 29–31; role mod-
    els for, xv, 79, 94; roles rejected by, 237;
    and social class, 39–40, 237; swing's popu-
    larity in, 4–5, 38–40, 88–90, 251; in
    World War II, 185–93

Ziegfeld, Florenz, 13
Zoot Suit Riot (1943), 204, 206
zoot suits: boppers' use of, 232; characteriza-
    tion of, 40, 111; link to riot, 204, 206; for
    males, 55–56